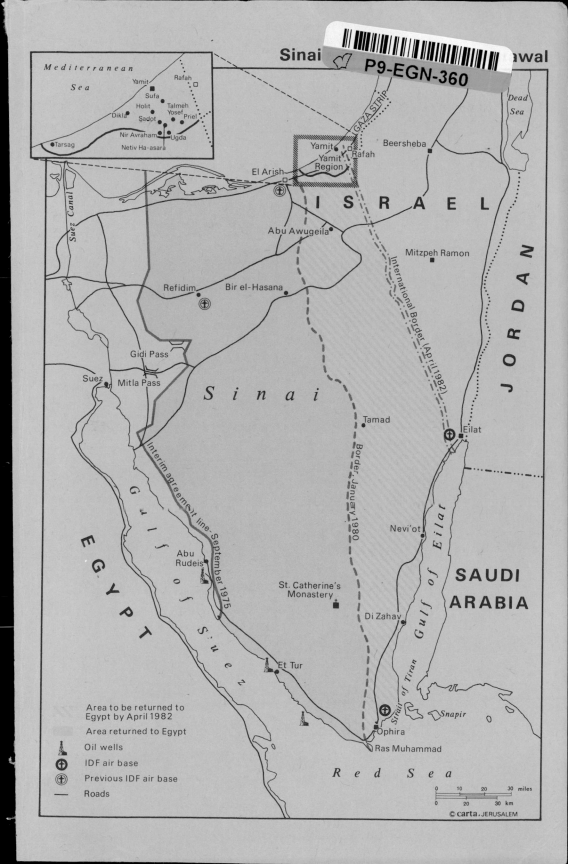

THE BATTLE FOR PEACE

THE
BATTLE
FOR
PEACE

EZER WEIZMAN

BANTAM BOOKS
TORONTO · NEW YORK · LONDON

The author advises the reader that all statements made
in first person and in direct quotation are, to the best of
his recollection, factual and true. The author assumes
full and sole responsibility for all such statements.

THE BATTLE FOR PEACE
A Bantam Book / March 1981

All rights reserved.
Copyright © 1981 by Ezer Weizman

Book designed by Renée Gelman
Special photographic montage effects by
Dave Passalacqua
Photos courtesy of Contact Stock Images

ISBN 0-553-05002-8

Library of Congress Catalog Card Number: 80-71057

Published simultaneously in the United States and Canada

Bantam Books are published by Bantam Books, Inc. Its trade-
mark, consisting of the words "Bantam Books" and the por-
trayal of a bantam, is Registered in U.S. Patent and Trademark
Office and in other countries. Marca Registrada. Bantam
Books, Inc., 666 Fifth Avenue, New York, New York 10103.

PRINTED IN THE UNITED STATES OF AMERICA

0 9 8 7 6 5 4 3 2 1

To my son Sha'ul,
who fought and bears the scars of battle—
To my son-in-law Dubi, who is still fighting—
To my grandson Yiftach; may he never
have to go to war.

CONTENTS

INTRODUCTION

Peace is more than piles of papers, files, and documents. Behind the complex wording of the clauses and subclauses of international legalities are human beings, from either side of the border. It is the human aspect of peace I wish to present here. The book will not be a detailed account of the whole process. Rather, it will be my own private story, a description of events as I saw them, from my personal viewpoint, and a record of my contribution to the historic process that culminated in the peace treaty between Israel and Egypt. The conversations and debates that made up sixteen months of negotiations have been reconstructed from careful notes taken at the time.

This book was written with the help of many friends—in Israel and Egypt as well as in the United States. These friends include politicians and soldiers, government officials and diplomats, jurists and ordinary citizens—the unknown soldiers in the army of peace. For their sake and for the sake of future generations, the efforts were well worthwhile. However, it is incumbent upon me to offer thanks, above all, to Eitan Haber, who labored mightily in assembling this manuscript; I am also deeply grateful to General Avraham Tamir, to Peretz Kidron, and to Nessa Rapoport for their assistance.

THE BATTLE FOR PEACE

EIGHTY-NINE MINUTES
TO EGYPT

There didn't seem to be anything out of the ordinary about the morning of December 20, 1977. Like any other morning, it was still early when my driver came to pick me up from my Ramat Hasharon home. But that day, for once, he did not head for my office at the Defense Ministry in Tel Aviv's Hakirya government complex; instead, he turned off into an orange grove bordering the highway to Ben-Gurion Airport. As the car halted, I jumped out and hurriedly took my seat in the commercial van waiting in the shade of the trees. A security services van had been put at my disposal, and its windows were blacked out by curtains.

As soon as the switch was made, both vehicles drove out of the orange grove. While my driver took the car on to the Defense Ministry, the van sped toward the airport. When we got there, I looked around: as far as I could see, no one paid us any attention. Total secrecy had been maintained.

My expression that December morning must have given away the tension I felt. I could not hide my excitement, nor did I even try. The members of my household—my wife Re'uma and my son Sha'ul—had detected it almost immediately as I paced around the room in my impatience, as did the handful of Defense Ministry and army personnel who were to accompany me on my journey. I kept glancing at my watch; time seemed to creep along at a snail's pace.

That morning, I had awakened swiftly, as usual. Long years of military service have left me with the habit of awakening instantaneously, without any mechanical help—whether alarm clock or telephone. Like a transistor radio that comes to life as soon as it is flicked on, I have gotten used to saving the time I might waste in a drowsy haze. At whatever hour of day or night that I am called, whether by family, friends, or military officials, it takes no more than a few seconds for me to switch on the correct wavelength.

And so that day, as always, I was awake immediately. But it took me far longer than usual to prepare myself for my journey. A few weeks before, on the way to Jerusalem, my car had overturned; I had broken a leg and several ribs in the accident. Now, this morning, waves of agony swept over me as I readjusted the wide elastic bandages swaddling my left leg, which was still tormenting me. My ribs had not yet healed, and I cursed furiously under my breath: on this day of all days, one of the finest moments in my life and a tide mark in my public career, I was setting out on a mission of historic importance—and here I was, battered and tattered.

The physical pain heightened my restlessness. I would have spared no effort to postpone my mission so that I could devote all my energies to its success, but that was no longer feasible. Timing was vital: historic opportunities must not be allowed to slip away. As in a battle, you do not want to miss the crucial event; in my life I have seen pilots and combat officers push and press to take part in what they sense will be a turning point in a conflict.

In Israel and Egypt—indeed, the whole world over—tens of millions of people were still euphoric over the recent train of events. Only a few weeks had elapsed since that electrifying moment at Ben-Gurion Airport when Egyptian President Anwar Sadat first appeared at the head of the gangway leading down from his plane. This generation has seen incredible events: man reached the moon, and Sadat reached Jerusalem! His visit in November 1977 was, perhaps, the most important event of its kind in modern history— and masses of people were still stunned by the sights and sounds they had witnessed: the president of an enemy country, who had not acknowledged Israel's right to exist, saluting our national anthem and addressing our government! The excitement swept everyone in its path.

My mission had its inception in that visit. I was to learn that President Sadat and Israeli Prime Minister Menachem Begin— seeking to step up the momentum—had agreed that I, Israel's minister of defense, and my counterpart, the Egyptian minister of war, should meet as soon as possible. The aim was to lay the foundation for future relations between the two armies and, above all, to forestall any possible misreading of events, political or military, that might lead to violent clashes or even war while the situation was just beginning to change. In view of the suspicion and hostility that had marked the relationship between the two countries—and their armed forces—for some thirty years, the idea was apt and sensible. Any nonessential troop movements in the Suez Canal zone or in the Sinai peninsula could give rise to misinterpretation. Since the 1973 Yom Kippur War, neither army was leaving anything to chance; one false move and the whole peace process might be stifled at birth.

The earliest phases of Sadat's visit—the analysis of his unprecedented offer to address the Knesset and the decisions on invitations and arrangements—had not involved the Defense Ministry, so that when Prime Minister Begin called me one day from his office at the Knesset in Jerusalem to tell me I was to meet with the Egyptian minister of war, I was surprised and gratified. His call came over an open line, but from that moment all preparations for my coming visit to Egypt were conducted in secret. With no other means of communication available between the two countries, contacts were made through the U.S. embassies in Tel Aviv and Cairo.

During their talks in November, Begin and Sadat had agreed that I should leave for Egypt at the earliest possible opportunity. However, my injury had forced me, very reluctantly, to put off the meeting several times. No other course was open to me. If there was one thing I wanted to avoid, it was the dismal sight of an Israeli defense minister hobbling painfully on crutches to his first encounter with Egyptian officials and officers. That was out! I'd go to Egypt when I could walk on my own two feet—and not a day earlier!

I was in great pain, which I found hard to bear. But I had made life equally miserable for the doctors at Tel Hashomer hospital. "A plaster cast on a broken leg has to stay on for six weeks," they'd told me. "That's what it says in the books."

"In that case," I yelled, "get a new book!" I urged them to work miracles, telling them to defy medical history and speed up the rebonding of the fractures in my leg and ribs. They had not the faintest idea why I was in such a hurry.

After endless pleading on my part, the doctors gave in and promised they'd take off the cast within four weeks. With that assurance, I issued the instructions to my aides at the Defense Ministry and to my friends at the U.S. embassy in Tel Aviv to fix a date for my visit to Egypt. Coded cables had flashed back and forth between Cairo and Tel Aviv until the technical arrangements had been settled. I attended to every detail—the flight route, the method of communicating with home, appropriate dress; I even ordered a security guard to get a haircut! There could be no hitches during the first visit by an Israeli minister to Egypt.

A few days before my departure, the first Israeli delegation had left for Egypt, consisting of Dr. Eliahu Ben-Elissar, director general of the prime minister's office, Dr. Meir Rosenne, then legal adviser of the Foreign Ministry, and General Avraham (Abrasha) Tamir. Israeli viewers had watched their arrival in Cairo, staring at their television screens in amazement and delight.

Right from the outset I was told that along with my talks with the Egyptian minister of war I would also get a chance to meet with President Sadat. As I prepared to leave, I racked my brains over what to say to him and how to put it. In addition, I wondered what presents I should bring the Egyptian president and his minister of war. If my gifts were too expensive, I would be suspected of trying to make a grandiose impression. If my presents were too overtly Israeli or military in character, they might mar the atmosphere by dredging up the past, reminding the Egyptians of wars they would rather forget.

I sought advice from my wife, Re'uma, and from friends, though not all of them were told I would be presenting the gifts in person. After much consultation, I made my choice: I would bring the president a large, handsome clock. The idea was prompted by an inscription I had hit upon: "To President Sadat, the leader who moved the clock forward." Two of my friends set out on a mission to the stores of Tel Aviv in search of a suitable timepiece. I did not rest content with this present; remembering that the Egyptian president is a pipe smoker, I called up my friend Motti Hod, who had succeeded me as commander of the air force and now served as El Al's director general. Motti was in Paris, and I asked him to buy a pipe of top quality; a Dunhill was promptly dispatched from the French capital. Still steeped in youthful fantasies about Indian peace pipes, I had it inscribed with the dedication: "May you always smoke this pipe peacefully." My present to the Egyptian minister of war was a Galil assault rifle, manufactured by the Israeli military industry. The inscription on the butt said: "May you never have to use it."

Since the topics likely to come up for discussion in Egypt called for the participation of experts, I decided to take Generals Shlomo Gazit and Herzl Shapir with me. As the heads of, respectively, military intelligence and the Southern Command, these two men were directly concerned with communications between the armies of Israel and Egypt; they were also charged with providing the correct interpretation of Egyptian troop movements and of any possible hidden intent on their part.

Right from the start, we were faced with the problem of how to get to Egypt. The Egyptians proposed that we come by civilian airliner, on an ordinary commercial flight from Europe. I refused. Was the Israeli defense minister to pay his first visit to Egypt on a false passport? No way! Security experts also rejected the suggestion outright: terrorists might hijack the aircraft, taking Israel's defense minister captive. What a trophy I would make! The idea of disguising me was dropped out of hand. "The way *you* look?" said the security experts. "Out of the question!" And undignified, to my mind.

What was to be done? Someone proposed that we fly across the Gulf of Suez in a helicopter, by night; alternatively, that we go to the Abu Rudeis area, on the eastern shore of the Gulf of Suez, where we would be picked up. But that, too, was ruled out. Finally, we decided to make use of the good services of the United States of America.

Accordingly, when we got to Ben-Gurion Airport that morning, we made for a remote runway where a U.S. Air Force DC-9 was awaiting us, having arrived the previous day from Frankfurt. The American air crew had no idea why they had been summoned in such haste to come to Israel or why they were to fly on to Egypt.

Our car nudged the gangway; after a farewell handshake from my deputy, Mordechai (Mottke) Tzippori, and from the chief of staff, Mordechai (Motta) Gur, we jumped out and flung ourselves into the DC-9. In the few seconds that elapsed as I made my way from the van to the plane, I took a deep breath of the smell I have loved these many years: the blend of aviation fuel, oil, and airplane tires. Only those who have spent most of their lives in and around aircraft understand that heady aroma.

We took off.

In the course of my life, I have taken off hundreds of times—it may run into the thousands. I have taken off on combat missions and on commercial flights. But never before have I felt as I did when the wheels of that DC-9 left the runway tarmac. Tempered only by the pain in my leg, my excitement was enormous.

It brought back the memory of a very different flight to meet Egyptians nearly thirty years earlier, during the 1948 War of Independence when I was one of Israel's select little band of combat pilots, Israeli and foreign. Only a few weeks old, Israel was fighting for her survival as the armies of Egypt, Jordan, Syria, Lebanon, and Iraq lunged forward to destroy her. On Saturday, May 29, 1948, just two weeks after the state was proclaimed, it seemed on the brink of collapse—perhaps even annihilation. The Egyptian army was almost at the outskirts of Tel Aviv, its vanguard having halted about twenty miles south of the city where Israeli sappers had demolished a bridge.

The situation was desperate. There was almost no effective Israeli force separating the Egyptian column from Tel Aviv. If the Egyptians managed to repair the bridge, there would be no one to stop them from marching right to the city's center, putting an end to the state of Israel.

At the time, we had four Messerschmitt 109s, supplied by the Communists of Czechoslovakia, who were the first ones to recognize the state of Israel. Delivered dismantled in crates, the planes were reassembled at the Tel Nof air base. On orders from the higher authorities, we had until now refrained from taking the planes into action, hoping to keep their existence a secret so as to surprise the enemy forces at a time and place of our choice. But there was little choice left that sunny Saturday at the end of May 1948 as the Egyptians closed in on Tel Aviv. The decision was taken: the Messerschmitts would attack the Egyptian column in an attempt to delay it—even temporarily. The order was issued in spite of the fact that the planes had not been checked or tested; they had never so much as taken off since being reassembled.

Our agitation was enormous. We looked over the maps, selecting our route and picking out our bombing runs. Then we set off at dusk: four planes, four pilots. It was a very short distance from Tel Nof to the battlefield near the Ashdod bridge. No sooner had we taken off than we were swooping down on the Egyptian column.

Antiaircraft fire pursued me as I dived toward my target. Hurtling downward, I was astounded and even somewhat frightened as I caught a glimpse of the Egyptian force, whose size exceeded all my expectations: thousands of soldiers and hundreds of military vehicles lined the highway to Tel Aviv.

I dropped two bombs and began the steep climb. With the antiaircraft fire still at my back, I dived once more, heading toward the row of armored vehicles. As I dropped more bombs, I saw Egyptian soldiers fleeing in all directions.

When I pulled out of my dive, I caught a glimpse of my "number two," Eddie Cohen, a volunteer from South Africa. As I watched, Eddie's plane plunged downward, dipping lower and lower until it crashed. Eddie's first mission for the Israeli air force was also his last.

Our attack had been successful; it did delay the Egyptian column. The blow we had inflicted was a heavy one, according to the notions then current. However, our triumph was mingled with despondency. The mission had ended with the loss of a fellow pilot as well as one-quarter of the air force's combat planes. One of my first military encounters with the Egyptians brought the sorrow of bereavement at the death of a close friend along with the exhilaration of victory. Subsequent confrontations were to have the same blend of exultation and sadness.

And now here I was flying to an encounter with the Egyptians again—under such different circumstances. The DC-9 was climbing rapidly. The American air crew had identified me, and I proceeded to introduce my companions: Generals Gazit and Shapir; my military secretary, Colonel Ilan Tehila; and bodyguards provided by the security services. The crew was soon infected by our excitement. With the purpose of their mysterious mission revealed, they felt themselves part of history in the making, and they reacted like true Americans: while the steward unearthed a bottle of wine for breakfast, his companions whipped out cameras to record the event and illustrate the tales they would tell their grandchildren.

The plane headed for the international air corridor near Cyprus: it was still not possible to fly the short route from Tel Aviv to Cairo directly, across the Sinai desert.

As we neared the Egyptian shore, everyone pressed against the windows, flattening their noses on the glass. There was plenty to see. I found myself looking below through soldier's eyes. I'm sure my companions did the same. In the course of almost thirty years, I had "observed" Egypt by way of aerial photographs, intelligence maps, agents' reports, penetration routes for photographic reconnaissance missions—not to mention the operational plans still lying in the drawers at General Headquarters (GHQ). Now, on this bright wintry morning, everything unfolding below us was promptly translated in our minds into reports, maps, and photographs. I took a careful look at each topographical feature: in my eyes, Egypt remained a military target.

I glanced at the head of military intelligence, Shlomo Gazit. Like me, he was pressed to the window, drinking everything in as though he were afraid of missing a single grain of desert sand or one drop of blue Nile water. It goes without saying that there were some beautiful scenes: the yellow desert, the green delta, the languid flow of the Nile. But we turned our eyes away from these sights, rejecting them in favor of the army camps and missile batteries.

Gazit and I traded information: that's the Bilbas airfield—the Egyptian air force's training base. And over there—Inshas, an airfield frequently bombed by the Israeli air force. And that's Helwan!

In 1963, we had sent a pair of planes to Helwan on one of our first and most daring photographic missions to Egypt, from which they had brought back the first pictures of a surface-to-air missile battery. Helwan was also the place where missiles were manufactured; in addition, it housed large munitions factories.

The American air crew understood nothing of what we were saying, but I noticed their smiles: they must have guessed.

At 10:30 A.M. we caught sight of the pyramids, looking just as they did in the aerial photographs we had exhibited publicly after the Six-Day War of 1967 in an attempt to embarrass the Egyptians by showing their defenselessness.

Our excitement grew. None of us could sit still. My heartbeat speeded up faster and faster as I attempted to digest this impossible scene: Israel's defense minister in an American plane flying at low altitude over the Egyptian pyramids. Unbelievable.

I was no stranger to Egypt. My first acquaintance with the land of the Nile had been in the mid-1940s, when 775869 Pilot Ezer Weizman of the British Royal Air Force (RAF) sought to make his modest contribution to the war against the German foe. During my service in Egypt, I was very active in getting around the country, paying numerous visits to Alexandria and Port Said. Once, en route from Cairo to Alexandria, I caught my first glimpse of the Giza pyramids—a sight not of this world, I thought. At that time, I still believed—as many others did after me—that these mighty structures, erected centuries ago at the dawn of history, were the handiwork of the Children of Israel, and I racked my brains trying to grasp how our forebears had succeeded in completing such a project. Much later, I learned that I had been in error, but at that moment I was moved to the depths of my heart—one of the few occasions when any vista so moved me. I am not usually affected by panoramas or by the splendors of the past. My love is reserved for people—human beings.

My posting in Egypt had not made me like the country, but I had developed a great affection for its people, finding them courteous and friendly; they possessed a fine sense of humor and appeared resigned to their fate—the Egyptian laborers who live on the land along the Nile had a difficult time of it. Had thirty years of hostility and war wrought changes in their easygoing nature? I wondered.

The pilot of the DC-9 requested permission to land at Cairo International Airport.

Through my military career in the RAF, I had come to know Cairo inside out. I had not liked the city during the daytime; it was a blazing furnace. Along with millions of its citizens, I'd spent the daylight hours seeking refuge from the heat. But my nights were devoted to getting intimately acquainted with the Egyptian capital. In the forties, it was a riotous and lively metropolis. I had no reason to look back on those distant times with any regret.

While serving in Cairo, I had made my home with relatives. A maternal great-uncle of mine had settled in Egypt at the beginning of the century, founding a family. One of his three sons, a Cairo bank manager, had a house in the Zamalak quarter, facing the sports club in 26 El Gazira Street, and this became my home away from home. It was a splendid mansion, affluent and hospitable. However, the succession of wars between Egypt and Israel ultimately forced my relative to leave Cairo and settle in Switzerland. I wondered what had happened to the house that had once welcomed me.

The DC-9 lost altitude. Down below, Cairo—half veiled from sight by the desert haze—looked very large and dreary. But I was captivated by the minarets projecting toward us in their peerless oriental beauty. Very close to Cairo International, where we were to land, my eyes picked out another airfield: Cairo West. Photographs of it, taken from every conceivable angle, are to be found to this day in the defense minister's office in Tel Aviv. I knew everything the airfield contained—and every item it lacked. I knew how swiftly it could be converted into a heap of rubble. I even remembered the names of the pilots who had swooped down on it during the fateful morning hours of June 5, 1967, when the outcome of the Six-Day War was decided by the pounding we inflicted on the Arab air forces, particularly Egypt's.

A moment before we touched down, I looked one last time toward the airfield, where I caught a glimpse of the lineup of Egyptian military aircraft: Soviet-built Antonovs alongside U.S.-manufactured Hercules. Here and there I picked out the tips of missiles, pointed upward, in wait for their prey; until now, their targets had been Israeli combat planes.

Try as I may, I cannot for the life of me recall what I said or thought as our plane's wheels touched the runway. But I do remember the strange feeling I had as it taxied along. We were entering an enemy country, yet from a distance we could make out dozens of red-capped Egyptian soldiers fanned out in a wide protective cordon, a mark of deference to us.

Peering out the window, I noticed a Saudi Airlines plane taking on passengers. Nearby, a Kuwait Airlines aircraft was warming up its engines. A Bahraini airliner was about to depart. The flight to Damascus had taken off two minutes earlier.

Bizarre. All represented countries that had joined forces against us.

Ever since my birth in 1924, I have lived in the shadow of our relationship with the Arabs. I passed the early part of my life alongside them. My childhood home was in Haifa, a mixed city. Unlike Tel Aviv and Jerusalem, where Jews and Arabs lived markedly separate lives, Haifa was not a clearly divided city. My father—Yehiel—conducted neighborly and business relations with Arabs in mutual consideration and understanding. For a time, he even had Arab business partners. Arab friends and acquaintances came and went in our home. My father made frequent trips to Arab villages, and I often accompanied him from one village to another. My childish eyes studied the Arab villagers and their way of life; even then I was aware of the significant differences between the two peoples. Still, at that time, the frontiers were open; Arab-Jewish hatreds had yet to explode into war. We often drove to Beirut or Damascus for a weekend without any fear.

But there were other times, too. My uncle Dunya was shot dead by Arab rioters while driving down a Haifa street. When I was a child, there were many occasions when my mother warned me not to go downtown: "They're killing Jews," she would say. She usually issued her warnings on Fridays, when the Arabs were leaving their mosques after the preachers had whipped them into a frenzy. On those days, we stayed at home.

And yet my family eagerly sought ways of coexisting with our Arab neighbors. My father had come to Haifa from a small town in eastern Europe, but he was quick to adapt to this new atmosphere, with its exotic aromas and the clicking of amber prayer beads. His brother, my uncle Chaim Weizmann, headed our political struggle to become a nation and was later chosen as the state of Israel's first president. He was a man of the world, moderate and universalist in outlook. Abhorring violence, he always advocated talking and negotiating with the Arabs rather than reverting to the language of the battlefield. My mother's family had its roots deep in the soil of the land of Israel—*Eretz Yisrael;* she herself spoke fluent Arabic and did her best to teach it to my sister and me.

On that morning in May of 1948, when I heard the reports of the Arab armies pouring in to destroy the state of Israel, I was astounded. As for the Egyptians, I simply couldn't grasp what had gotten into them. What interest could they have in the conflict in Palestine? I believed they had made a tragic error in permitting themselves to be drawn into a war that had nothing to do with them. At the time, I had no way of predicting what a bitter price they would pay for that mistake. With the passing of time, the Egyptians found themselves ever deeper in the quagmire of the Arab-Israeli conflict, with its psychological and emotional misery. Eighty to a hundred thousand killed, a million refugees from the Suez Canal area after the Six-Day War, and all the loss of honor that repeated defeat brings. My own personal destiny cast me in an active role in the succession of bloody showdowns. During the 1948 war, I served as a young fighter pilot. In the Sinai campaign of 1956, I commanded an air force base. I was commander of the Israeli air force for eight years between the wars of 1956 and 1967. During the Six-Day War, which inflicted such a crushing defeat on Egypt, I headed the General Staff Section at our General Head-quarters—Israel Defense Forces (IDF), and was actively involved in our air force's triumph over the Arab air forces. In the 1973 Yom Kippur War, I was adviser to the chief of staff.

In my own family, my son Sha'ul served in the Israeli army and was wounded by Egyptian forces. My daughter Michal was in the air force and is married to a combat pilot. No one in Israel has not experienced the tragic effects of the ongoing conflict—in death or crippling of relatives and friends.

The eighty-nine-minute flight from Ben-Gurion Airport to Cairo bridged a thirty-year chasm of hostility, embracing five wars, thousands of dead, tens of thousands of wounded. It was a short flight on a long, long road. In the event of another war erupting, it would be my duty as the minister responsible for Israel's defense to wreak vengeance upon the Arab armies. I had spent the past thirty years making—and implementing—decisions that had proved highly painful to the Egyptians. And there they were, a few yards away, preparing to offer me a respectful welcome.

The blond American major commanding the plane wished me luck. I needed it! Looking out of the pilot's cabin, I identified the man waiting to greet me: Mohammed el-Gamasy, Egypt's minister of war. I recognized him from his photographs, which had been prominently featured in the press and on television after the Yom Kippur War. He was tall and slim and somber of expression. He was standing alone—very much alone.

My heart thumped. My injured leg throbbed painfully, and the bandages wrapped around it impeded my movement. Clutching my walking stick, I walked slowly down the gangway.

A few days before my departure for Egypt, I had asked our military intelligence, considered among the best in the world, for its file on General Gamasy so that I could get to know my future colleague. I wanted to know everything possible about him, right down to the tiniest detail. The reports collated in the intelligence file produced a portrait of a gifted man, well educated and very withdrawn; he was also described as a fiercely proud nationalist, fervent in his country's cause. In none of his photographs could I recall the faintest trace of a smile on his face. Overall, the reports sketched a man whose character was the direct opposite of my own. Where I was exuberant, he was introverted and reserved. During the cease-fire talks at Kilometer 101 between Suez and Cairo, where the Israeli army had stopped in its advance in the Yom Kippur War, Gamasy had held long conversations with our generals Aharon Yariv and Israel Tal: however, I did not ask them for their impressions, as I wished to keep the shutters of secrecy clamped down tight over my mission.

Now, as I faced Gamasy, I was apprehensive. With his daunting reputation as a fiery patriot and his reserved temperament, how on earth was I to get into a conversation with him? My excitement over the occasion did nothing to quell the increasing pain in my leg.

Gamasy shook hands with me, inquiring about my flight, and went on to greet my companions. As I'd feared, the atmosphere was cool.

"Thank you for your letter," Gamasy said. "And thank you for your get-well wishes to my wife." In an attempt to thaw out the chill, Egypt's minister of war referred to one of the first messages I'd sent him from Tel Aviv, when I'd wished his wife a speedy recovery from the severe kidney disorder she had suffered.

"I've heard a lot about you from our president," he said, going on to mention a rumor that had made the rounds during Sadat's visit to Jerusalem: "Do you know, when I heard about your accident, I thought for a moment that it was a trick to evade a meeting with President Sadat. I know I was wrong to think so." Sadat himself had said to Begin at the time: "We thought that Weizman was a warmonger."

"Before we start our talks," Gamasy continued, "the president wants to see you."

I was surprised by the timing, not having expected the meeting with Sadat to take place so promptly. My military secretary, Ilan Tehila, hastily produced the box of presents. Taking our leave of Herzl Shapir and Shlomo Gazit, we headed toward the helicopter waiting nearby. There we were greeted with a friendly handshake from the pilot, Colonel Munir.

"Welcome on board!" he said warmly, and we set off.

The helicopter, used to ferry VIPs, was luxuriously furnished in beige upholstery. Inside near the door was a glass cabinet containing a copy of the Koran; above it was the inscription *Bismillah*— "In the name of God the Merciful."

I had already learned how deeply rooted religious belief is in the Egyptian army—just as it is among the general population. I now proceeded to read out the Arabic inscription. Gamasy smiled. I decided to draw him into conversation by remarking that the Arabic *Bismillah* has its equivalent in the Hebrew *B'shem elohim*, to which he nodded politely.

The flight to the presidential mansion in Ismailia lasted some forty minutes. Along the way, I was sorely tempted to peep out of the windows for a glimpse of points of interest on the ground. I knew from my intelligence reports that we were flying over tanks, aircraft, and missiles. But seated as I was opposite my Egyptian counterpart, I could not afford to give in to the temptation without looking too inquisitive and forced myself to rest content with an occasional rapid glance.

There is nothing like seeing things with your own eyes. I knew which Egyptian units were stationed in the sandy expanse stretching from Cairo to Ismailia, but I was surprised by the number of soldiers I saw. The whole area was dotted with military camps, missile bases, military vehicles, and thousands of troops. I did not see any civilian installations. As I quickly looked over the broad shoulders of my bodyguard, Amos, the reconnaissance photographs and intelligence reports suddenly acquired a new dimension: before my eyes, the Egyptian Fourth Army was taking on the bone and flesh of tank emplacements and gun positions.

We landed at Ismailia. A black Mercedes drove us through the streets of the city toward the president's home.

My memories of Ismailia were quite different from what I was seeing now. The city I recalled was full of smoke and rubble, observed at a distance of two hundred yards, from the other side of the Suez Canal. During the Israeli-Egyptian War of Attrition that raged in the late sixties, we had showed no mercy for Ismailia. We'd bombarded the city incessantly, devastating it from the air as well as with land-based artillery. The aerial photographs of Ismailia that reached my desk then showed its western portions resembling the cities of Germany at the end of World War II. Ismailia had been pulverized and destroyed; not a single house was left standing in its eastern quarters. During one of our bombardments of the city, an Israeli shell had killed the Egyptian commander in chief—a severe blow to the Egyptian army's morale, which was already at a low point.

But the Ismailia of this morning in 1977 was totally changed. After its reconstruction, the city looked vibrant and full of life, with nothing to recall the pounding it had endured.

President Sadat's residence lay alongside the Suez Canal. The gate was locked, and the bored sentry on duty showed no eagerness to open it. The driver of our Mercedes hooted once and then again, but the soldier still dawdled.

Gamasy lost his temper. Hauling down the window, he cried angrily: "Open the gate! I'm Gamasy!"

The soldier leaped up and ran to open the gate. I grinned to myself. The tone was only too familiar: it sounded just like home, and all of us laughed.

As we entered the presidential residence, I glanced toward the eastern side of the Suez Canal. There was no doubt about it: on the opposite bank, I saw the shattered ruins of an Israeli fortress—a painful reminder of the Yom Kippur War. I remembered a visit I had paid there while the War of Attrition was at its height; in the course of my tour, I had run into a heavy Egyptian artillery bombardment.

The Suez Canal brought other, equally bitter memories. It was in one of those fortresses that my son Sha'ul had served during the War of Attrition. When Sha'ul was born, I told Re'uma that I had only one wish: that he would not have to go off to war, as we had. My hope was in vain. Sha'ul enlisted in 1969. He trained as a paratrooper and proved to be a good soldier. When he donned his uniform, I asked Re'uma the same question I was asking myself and others: "Where did we go wrong? Why do our sons have to go to war?" And I failed to find an answer.

Sha'ul was in the thick of the fighting, and I worried about him.

When I left the army, I asked a favor of Herzl Shapir, the new head of GHQ's staff section: "Whenever there's a bombardment on the fortress where Sha'ul is stationed, notify me. I've got to know."

In June of 1970, Sha'ul was wounded—hit by a single round from an Egyptian sniper. Then Chief of Staff Chaim Bar-Lev telephoned while I was lunching at a Jerusalem restaurant. During the few seconds it took me to race to the phone, I reassured myself that Sha'ul had not been killed. If he were dead, the news would not have been conveyed by telephone; as I knew from sad experience, IDF tradition would have required me to be notified personally. Several times during Sha'ul's period of service, I found myself starting up from a nightmare in which officer friends were standing motionless at the gateway to my home, not daring to enter because they lacked the courage to tell me the news. Indeed, there had been occasions when I, too, found myself incapable of entering a home—of a superior or of one of my subordinates— where it was my duty to tell the family of the calamity that had befallen them.

Sha'ul was wounded. Ever since that day, my family has lived in the shadow of his injury and the physical and emotional infirmities it brought upon him. Long after it happened, American television reporter Mike Wallace asked Sha'ul if he hated the man who had shot him through the head.

"Definitely not!" my son replied. "I can hate someone I have seen with my own eyes, who fired at me from a distance of a meter or two. How can I hate someone I don't even know?"

Sha'ul's response pleased me very much. I hope that I am equally incapable of hatred. It may sound strange, but I have never harbored any resentment toward those Arabs who have inflicted injury upon the state of Israel or even on my own family. Admittedly, I have long felt scorn and contempt for certain Arab leaders who embroil their citizens in costly and hopeless wars. But, on the whole, I have always respected the Arab people—unlike too many Israelis who invariably regard them as foes.

That glimpse of the demolished Israeli fortification and the haunting memory of Sha'ul's injury followed me as I struggled painfully out of the car.

In a chair placed on the green lawn, wearing a blue safari suit and smoking his pipe, sat President Sadat. The screech of our car's brakes had made him turn toward us.

My leg was giving me even more pain. I gripped my walking stick.

"Ya Ezra!" the Egyptian president roared. Sadat had originally mistaken my name for the more prevalent Ezra, a common name among Egyptian Jews. "Are you still walking on that stick of yours?"

I gritted my teeth. This was too damned much! The idea of an Israeli defense minister limping to meet the Egyptian president was not at all to my liking.

Halting, I twirled the walking stick around my head. With an agonizing heave, I flung it far across the lawn, speeding it on its way with a resounding Arabic curse: *"Yahrab beto!"* "Damn the stick!"

There was a shocked silence. The driver and the Egyptian body-guards were wide-eyed. Ilan and Amos looked stunned. Gamasy seemed rather alarmed.

The silence lasted a second or two. Then President Sadat burst into a roaring laugh that promptly spread to all the others.

2

LONG NIGHTS IN WARD 12

As an Israeli born and bred and as a military man who has spent many years observing Arab-Israeli relations through a gun sight, I had no reason to feel any particular affection for the Egyptian president—the leader of our largest and most dangerous enemy. Standing before me here in Ismailia, laughing unrestrainedly, was the man who had caught Israel by surprise in the Yom Kippur War, which took the lives of thousands of young Israelis—including some of my best friends. There are long winter nights I spend cursing the Egyptian sniper whose accurate aim at my son's head brought the ravages of war into our home, forcing all of us to grapple with the consequences every day, every hour.

In anticipation of meeting the Egyptian president, I had used the brief time at my disposal to do my homework, trying to get to know the man who heads a nation of over forty million. As I studied intelligence reports, I saw that the long years of war and enmity had left their mark upon me, as on many other Israelis, in the way we perceived Egypt's leader. I had never previously shown any great interest in Sadat, regarding him as more or less the stereotype of a totalitarian Arab ruler. He failed to set my imagination on fire. Reports that he had been pro-German and an admirer of Hitler did not add to his stature in my eyes.

When Sadat rose to power after the death of Nasser, we were inclined to dismiss him with scorn. We did him an injustice in comparing him—unfavorably—with his illustrious predecessor.

Nasser always came across as the monarch of a great Arab empire; his mistakes were on a grand scale, as befitted a man of his stature. In comparison with him, Sadat resembled a Saul who set out to look for his asses and chanced to find a kingdom.

From the very first, it was hard to take him seriously. His faulty English, his oft-repeated vows to regain Sinai, "using force to restore that which was taken by force," his bombastic proclamations about the impending showdown with Israel—all these reinforced our negative view. Sadat appeared to be unsophisticated, undemocratic, a fanatical Muslim nationalist who could be toppled by the slightest shove. The dark mark at the center of his forehead symbolized my feelings, recalling films I had seen in my youth about mystical beings from distant planets. Indeed, Sadat, like his land, seemed to belong to some remote, fantastic world.

My error—in which I was not alone—became apparent at the midday hours of October 6, 1973. But by then it was too late. The Yom Kippur War highlighted Sadat's undisputable gifts as a statesman and strategist. Having shown wisdom in his conduct of the military campaign, he exhibited great ability in reaping its fruits; despite the fact that we had crossed the canal and had a strong foothold on its western side, when the fighting ended, Egypt held extensive areas on the eastern side of the Suez Canal zone. Sadat's success on the political front was even greater, in alerting the world to the dangers of a political stalemate with no diplomatic initiatives and therefore no solution to the ongoing instability of the Middle East.

Throughout the Yom Kippur War, I'd felt deep concern about him, and my anxiety grew when the war ended. Exploiting his success, Sadat seized the initiative. He laid siege to the sympathies of Washington, having assessed that he had no chance of overcoming Israel—especially while she continued to be supported by the United States. Sadat always surprised me by his habit of playing with open cards. He announced that he would cross the Suez Canal—sacrificing a million soldiers if necessary—and publicly proclaimed his intention of driving a wedge between Israel and the United States. He did both. In the 1973 war, he crossed the Suez; and in driving out the Russians from Egypt he brought the West closer to him, necessarily diluting its loyalty to us. His campaign was successful, costing us our position as the cosseted godchild of the Western world. Our political situation went from bad to worse.

In the fall of 1977, I began to feel that we were misreading the political map of the Middle East by being insufficiently alert to developments. Repeatedly, I was told by visitors, both media correspondents and diplomats, who had earlier been to Cairo and met Sadat, that he had given up the path of war. They spoke of far-reaching changes in the land of the Nile. For example, we had treated the disengagement agreements after the Yom Kippur War as an intermission between wars. We had not taken sufficient notice of what they signified: Egypt's willingness to separate her forces from Israel's and create a buffer zone; her willingness to bring in the United States through Kissinger rather than the UN. If you kick out the Russians and bring in the Americans, you're not preparing for war.

Needless to say, none of my visitors went so far as to argue that Sadat was interested in genuine peace. That would have been overstating matters. But they did raise questions in my mind, and the interrogation marks made me uneasy.

Would we turn unseeing eyes on the harbingers of peace—just as the Israeli army had failed in 1973 to mark the signs of impending war?

How could I keep my hand on the pulse of events in Cairo? The answer was provided by our military intelligence. Even before I took up the post of defense minister in June of 1977, the intelligence branch had launched an investigation. For over a year, our intelligence experts, working with Orientalists, scholars, and foreign intelligence services, had thoroughly scrutinized the situation to determine whether or not Egypt had undergone a fundamental turnabout. In September, the report was placed on my desk. It was a disappointment: there was no shift of mood in Egypt's ruling circles—in any event, no change far-reaching enough to induce them to come to terms with the existence of Israel. Any modifications were, at most, semantic.

My own personal conclusion was even more gloomy: my generation would have to go on sending its sons to war—and who could predict what would befall our grandchildren? In 1948, when I strafed the Egyptian column outside Tel Aviv, I thought that confrontation would see the whole matter settled once and for all. In another couple of months, we'd be living in peace and quiet. But, all too quickly, when we had scarcely bound the wounds of 1948, the second round was looming on the horizon. And the relaxation of tension following the 1956 Sinai campaign did not last overlong. After the 1967 Six-Day War, I, like many Israelis, believed that this was it! The whole thing was over. The Arabs would never get back on their feet. Two or three months later, I realized my mistake. At their nadir, at the bottommost depths of their humiliation, the

Arabs proclaimed their intention of attacking again. On October 6, 1973, at midday, it transpired that this was no hollow vow.

In the fall of 1977, war clouds again obscured the blue skies of the Middle East.

The Israeli army was conducting a large-scale exercise in the Sinai peninsula. The desert leaped to life as hundreds of tanks thundered across its sandy expanses and planes shattered the silence of the barren wasteland.

They also set the alarm bells ringing in the Egyptian army headquarters. War Minister Gamasy and members of his staff were summoned in all urgency to their GHQ command post. Although I was unaware of it at the time, I know now that the Egyptians viewed our training exercise with suspicion, fearing it was camouflage for a preemptive strike. Apprehensive, they rushed large forces toward the Suez Canal.

This promptly set off warning bells on our side. Something was afoot on the Egyptian front. My predecessor in the defense minister's office had warned me: as Shimon Peres was shaking my hand the day he'd taken his leave in June, he said that there was likely to be an outbreak of hostility in October or November.

I left nothing to chance. Additional units reinforced our garrisons in Sinai. The tension climbed steeply. The situation could have led to war—for no better reason than that no one, on either side, was prepared to take any risk. Had there been a telephone link between us, it would have been easy to dispel the misunderstandings and settle the whole affair. But who so much as dreamed of a telephone link at that time? To us, Egypt was farther than the moon.

The same goes for its president. Sadat is inscrutable, an enigma whose words and actions are hard to predict—as we have learned to our bitter cost. Like a seasoned card player, he is in the habit of remaining poker-faced until he slaps his suits down on the table with a triumphant flourish. Quite often, he uncovers his cards in the course of his tiresomely lengthy speeches to the People's Assembly in Cairo. I've always felt sorry for the members of the assembly, who are saddled with the heroic duty of submitting to these hours-long onslaughts.

One of Sadat's speeches was scheduled for November 9, 1977. As was their custom, the Egyptian media predicted that it would be an important one. Never greatly impressed by the Egyptian president's orations, I took even less notice of the degree of importance trumpeted about by these forecasts. Should he say anything of significance, I knew I could count on hearing about it from the experts of our military intelligence, who display an understandable interest in Sadat's speeches. The Hatzav unit, whose task was to keep track of the press and radio in Arab countries, was placed on alert. Part of the unit's routine then was to report on the main points of such a speech—sometimes managing to complete its summary before the orator had even concluded his words. In recent years, this practice has been abandoned because the radio stations' reports are even faster. I've heard that some of Hatzav's experts used to amuse themselves by predicting the contents of such a speech before its delivery, and the text they prepared ahead of time often turned out to be right on target.

On that day in 1977, while our intelligence experts made their preparations for Sadat's speech, I was busy with other matters. That morning, before seven, I was in my Defense Ministry office in Tel Aviv, glued to the intercom and the telephone. A few moments later, bombs were already raining down on terrorist bases in southern Lebanon. The pilots reported good hits.

The previous day, terrorists had fired Katyusha rockets at the town of Nahariya, killing one woman. The papers reported that she was a survivor of the Holocaust.

Like other native Israelis, or Sabras, I did not personally experience the Holocaust, nor was I closely involved. But—again like most of my generation—I live in its shadow. There is no avoiding it in Israel. The more we try to repress it, the more it springs up out of the depths of our unconscious.

I found myself contemplating the fate of that woman. She had been rescued from the very jaws of purgatory—only to find her death in Nahariya. On hearing the first volley of Katyushas, she had run outside to call her two children to the shelter—and was killed on the spot, before their eyes. That scene would probably haunt them for the rest of their lives.

A defense minister is supposed to make his assessments and reach his decisions by coldly rational thinking. As a rule, there is no room for sentiment. It is his duty to take into account a whole range of considerations: Is a military strike necessary? What will happen in consequence? What will the UN say?

But a defense minister is only flesh and blood. His judgment cannot be totally divorced from his personality, his feelings—perhaps even his philosophy.

During my period as commander of the air force, I had frequently advised the political echelons to employ our airplanes against enemy targets; and then, when my counsel had been adopted, I'd proceeded to send our pilots on their way. As in all democracies, the elected government is in full control of the military forces, and the air force commander reports to the defense minister. But now the final responsibility was mine, and I found myself torn. There were considerations that made me reluctant to use the air force. The Likud government had a hawkish image, which I had no desire to stress further. There was also a substantive consideration: any action on our part was likely to provoke the terrorists into exacting vengeance upon our northern settlements. Such a response from the terrorists was bound to entail a further strike on our part. This exchange would lead to a deterioration of security in a densely populated area. I had to bear in mind that our pilots are no supermen. It needed nothing more than one bomb falling off target to deliver yet another blow to Israel's tattered image in world opinion. It's hard to cope with television clips of Lebanese children scrabbling in the rubble, searching for their parents—the terrible and sometimes unavoidable result of war.

However, in my mind, I saw that woman from Nahariya. There had been no bloodshed in Sinai for more than three years. But in the north, a citizen of Israel could still be mowed down in daily life. There could be no mercy for the terrorists. With the approval of Prime Minister Begin, I gave instructions for the planes to take off on their mission.

That night, I was exhausted. Flopping down on my bed, I fell asleep. No one bothered to brief me on Sadat's speech because it contained nothing new. Sadat made scant reference, little more than a few words, to the deadlocked Geneva conference, where—as in the past—Israel and Egypt were talking only through a third party.

However, near the end of his oration, the Egyptian president expressed a bizarre wish: he desired, he said, to address the members of the Knesset in Jerusalem, with the aim of saving human lives.

The following morning, the speech was reported briefly by press and radio. Sadat's strange remark about coming to the Knesset in Jerusalem received little serious attention. I awaited the full text of the speech, due in from Hatzav; my military aide, Ilan, would have picked out its more important sections, underlining them with colored pencils.

My first response to Sadat's speech was characteristic of the effect of thirty years of enmity and war: I didn't believe a word of it! I thought his statement about coming to Jerusalem was no more than meaningless lip service, and I utterly mistrusted it.

But the evening papers brought a surprise. The headlines high-lighted Sadat's proposal and reported alongside it the response of Prime Minister Begin, who had taken up the gauntlet. I still re-garded the matter as insignificant. It didn't seem serious. *What do you think you're up to?* I demanded of an imaginary Sadat. *One fine morning, after thirty years of hostility, you wake up and decide to come to Jerusalem?*

It wasn't as if we had not wanted to negotiate in the past. We always had; it was the fault of the Arabs that there was war rather than peace between us. In 1936, Britain's Peel Commission to in-vestigate the problems in Palestine recommended that the area be partitioned. We agreed; the Arabs didn't. In 1947, the UN decision was to create a Jewish state and an Arab state. We agreed and were attacked by seven Arab countries. Never was our right to exist acknowledged in any way—despite the fact that we'd been on this land for half a century by 1948, with a Jewish presence here throughout thousands of years before that and despite a world decision after the Holocaust that the creation of a Jewish state was necessary.

It is no wonder that it was difficult for us to imagine that the situation with Egypt would change. This was not the close of a normal war, with emissaries offering peace. It was an ongoing, fundamental, deeply rooted conflict in which one nation had al-ways threatened to completely annihilate another nation—not to occupy the land and impose its government, as happens in war-fare, but to utterly destroy the inhabitants of that country. We Israelis grew up in the knowledge that if we lose the battle, we lose everything. We lived in a world that regarded Israel as a passing episode and among neighbors whose stated purpose was to wipe us off the earth. I have no doubt that had Sadat's offer to come to Jerusalem arisen in the days of the Labor prime ministers of the past—Levi Eshkol, Golda Meir, or Yitzhak Rabin—it would have been rejected scornfully and out of hand. After thirty years of trying to communicate with the Arabs, the conclusion of the Labor party leaders had been: "There's no one to talk to."

The irony was that the first offer had come and met with a response under Begin's leadership. After the total hegemony of the Labor party for decades, Begin's Herut party had finally won its first election as part of the Likud alliance. Begin's reputation was that of a superhawk, a right-wing extremist, and Herut was perceived as a party of war. As it turned out, it was only because Begin was such a blatantly self-declared hawk that he could get away with taking chances. But that was later.

To those about me when I first read of Sadat's proposed visit, I said a few words of praise for Begin, who had managed to dismiss the whole thing with some noncommittal phrases to which no one was bound, while lobbing the ball back into the Egyptian court. Nevertheless, I tried to visualize an imaginary meeting between Begin and Sadat. It made me laugh. Fantasizing about our prime minister's bestowing a courtly kiss on the hand of the Egyptian president's wife, I fired off a number of wisecracks on the subject.

Two days later, I was doing my best to get my listeners to erase them from their memory. What had previously seemed the height of fantasy now became a living reality.

Right up to the last moment, I refused to believe that it would really happen before my eyes. But the assessments of our intelligence branch finally convinced me that the Egyptian president genuinely intended to come to Jerusalem. "He's like a hurdler who bypasses all the obstacles, heading straight for the finish line," said Shlomo Gazit during one of our first discussions. His sporting simile caught my fancy.

The eyes of the whole world focused on our corner of the arena. It seemed as if history had momentarily paused in its stride. All the same, Israel's cabinet did not devote a single moment's consideration to what would happen—and, perhaps, change—the moment our archenemy set foot on Israeli soil. I assumed that Prime Minister Begin and Foreign Minister Moshe Dayan were devoting a lot of thought to the matter—but the other ministers did nothing. I made a number of calls to the prime minister's office in Jerusalem, proposing a discussion in the cabinet—or, at the very least, in the ministerial defense committee—in preparation for the visit and its possible consequences. I got no response. I therefore did my utmost to get the defense establishment deployed effectively and asked Shlomo Gazit to evaluate the situation.

General Gazit is a gifted man, devoted and intelligent; he is very prudent—certainly more than the previous intelligence chiefs, who were responsible for landing Israel in such a difficult quandary in the Yom Kippur War. After that war, the stricken intelligence branch underwent extensive personal and organizational changes, but some of the staff had yet to get over the trauma of being blamed for failing to sound the alert. Gazit had put the intelligence branch back on its feet.

His assessments were always worded carefully and sensibly—and, for all that, I took them with a grain of salt, always keeping in mind that most of Israel's intelligence chiefs had concluded their careers by dismissal or premature retirement. It was not possible to correctly predict the unknown all the time. Gazit believed that Sadat indeed intended to come to Jerusalem. In his view, our prime minister was left with no other choice but to extend an invitation; otherwise, our international position would become even more difficult, and no one would ever take us seriously when we complained that "there's no one to talk to." Gazit predicted that when Sadat faced the Knesset he would present his most far-reaching demands, similar to those that Israel had rejected more than once—full withdrawal to pre-1967 borders and a Palestinian state. Gazit sketched an uninviting picture of a well-laid trap.

On November 14, when our preparations for Sadat's visit were at their height, the thunderbolt landed. The *Yediot Acharonot* daily newspaper carried an interview with chief of staff Lt. General Motta Gur. Normally, any press interview with the chief of staff must be okayed by the defense minister, but Motta had requested no such approval. Reading the interview, I refused to believe my eyes. Gur had used strong terms in discussing the coming visit, including specific hints about the Egyptian president's deceptive intentions. "We know that the Egyptian army is in the midst of preparations for launching a war against Israel toward 1978," Gur said, "irrespective of Sadat's declared willingness to come to Jerusalem."

I was absolutely outraged. How dare he say such a thing in an interview—without requesting my approval, without so much as telling me his views beforehand? How dare he let his private misgivings jeopardize even the possibility of peace? And was I as defense minister supposed to learn the opinions of the chief of staff from the newspapers?

The media seized on the interview eagerly and gave it extensive coverage in all the papers, on radio, and on TV. The storm grew shriller by the minute. The prime minister called me, ministers phoned, Knesset members submitted questions. I was furious with Motta Gur, and he was nowhere in the vicinity. A day or two earlier, he had left for a visit abroad. The interview was published in his absence.

I instructed the Israeli ambassador to locate Gur and send him back to Israel immediately. I was afraid the Egyptian president would seize on the interview to call off his scheduled visit to Jerusalem—that is, assuming he indeed intended to go through with it.

Our ambassador managed to locate Motta. But I had no time for discussion with him; the uproar was too great. We might find ourselves being blamed for missing a historic opportunity on account of one badly timed and unauthorized interview. After consulting the prime minister, I decided to take an unprecedented step: I would reprimand the chief of staff publicly, in the Knesset, without even awaiting his explanations.

Motta Gur was Israel's tenth chief of staff. When I took up my duties as defense minister, in June 1977, he had already been at his post for three and a half years and was on the verge of completing his term of office. At the time, I foresaw difficulties of communication between us: he was experienced at his job, and I was new at mine. I hoped we would find the right way of working together, but I knew it wouldn't be easy.

Personally, I had a liking for Motta Gur. I have always adopted an attitude of indulgence toward that outspokenness of his that often gives the impression of overconfidence. Gur is a good soldier, and he's got good sense. He had taken over an army still smarting from the wounds of Yom Kippur and done a great job of binding up those wounds, using his own methods. He tried to put a stop to the arguments and bickering over who was at fault and why. Although there were times I felt it was whitewashing, there is no doubt that his policy put the Israeli Defense Forces back on their feet. I could not help admiring him for his role as healer.

Shimon Peres, my predecessor in the Defense Ministry, had given Motta a relatively free hand. Peres has never served in the army proper. He did serve in the civilian defense establishment as director general of the Defense Ministry and as deputy defense minister. Therefore, he understood the defense process, but he hadn't grown up through the military. Although he had supervised the defense establishment, where his own achievements were considerable, he'd let the chief of staff do almost anything he liked within the army.

When I came to the Defense Ministry, Gur had welcomed me with formal correctness, but he tried to safeguard his own position by putting me in my place. There were many areas—operational decisions as well as budgets and appointments—where I felt the final say belonged to the civilian authority. The covert confrontation between the military and political echelons ended with my assuming control—and that's as it should be in a democratic regime. Afterward, there were occasional misunderstandings between the two of us, but our relationship was reasonably good—until the publication of the interview.

A sharp rejoinder was called for. But what form should it take? A chief of staff cannot be punished. He could be dismissed, but I did not consider some vague offer from Sadat to come to Israel an adequate reason for giving Motta Gur the boot.

Gur returned to Israel. Straight from Ben-Gurion Airport, still wearing civilian clothing, he was summoned in all urgency to the Defense Ministry in Tel Aviv's Hakirya.

I awaited him impatiently, and on his arrival I gave him an angry reception. I wanted to let him have it, but I kept my voice down. Why had he done it? I demanded testily. What had gotten into him?

During his flight back, Motta had prepared himself thoroughly for his meeting with me. Encountering my rage head on, he now declared that he considered it his duty to forewarn Israel of the danger presented by Sadat's visit. He had not involved the Defense Ministry, he said, because the Yom Kippur War had taught him that accountability for defense ends with the chief of staff.

I told Gur that it would have been not only his right but his bound duty to come and tell me his opinions—but that he ought not to have expressed them to the press. Our exchange was tense.

Public demands in the media for the chief of staff's immediate dismissal evoked little response in me. One chief of staff had already resigned after the Yom Kippur War. I could not subject the army to a further body blow of the same nature. All the same, I clearly had to take some action. Accordingly, I told Motta Gur that I intended to cut short his term of office. Instead of April 1978, as had been agreed between us one week previously, he would leave his post in December of 1977.

Motta grew furious. He said: "Not the end of December—right now! You don't punish *me*. I can be fired, or you can demand my resignation today!"

I decided to lay the matter before Prime Minister Begin for his decision. A few moments later, my car was speeding toward Jerusalem.

On the Jerusalem highway, near Moshav Ganot, I suddenly noticed someone about to cross the road. "Itzik!" I yelled to the driver, "Look out!"

I was lying on the floor of a pickup truck when I was brought to my senses by a couple of slaps across the face from my bodyguard,

Shmulik. Itzik Azulai, my driver, lay nearby, unconscious. I couldn't grasp what had happened. Shmulik's voice sounded muffled. He said something indistinguishable about the car overturning onto the roadside. A black haze descended over my eyes, and I remembered nothing more.

The worried expressions on the faces of the doctors at Tel Hashomer hospital indicated that my condition was worse than I'd imagined. I was x-rayed, and all kinds of tubes and needles were stuck into my arms. I couldn't move. My whole body was racked with pain—my chest, my back. When I tried to make some jokes about my pitiful state, no one smiled. Then I knew it was bad!

That night, after the last of my visitors had departed, I suddenly realized that I might have been killed. I had missed death by little more than a hairsbreadth. What lousy luck that would have been— to die at a moment like this, on the threshold of a new epoch! It was like a soldier getting himself killed during the final hour of a war.

But it was not enough to console me two days later when Ilan notified me that Sadat would reach Israel on Saturday evening. As soon as that! Unbelievable! I chewed myself up in frustration. This would be the hash-up of a lifetime. I was furious—with myself, with my driver, with the whole world. Ilan was in a quandary. Every report he brought only sent my blood pressure soaring and added fuel to my rage. Sadat was to be escorted in by Israeli combat planes; he would be received by a military guard of honor, with the national anthems played and the flags of the two countries hoisted on high; he would stay at Jerusalem's King David Hotel; he would address the Knesset—and here I was, stuck in hospital.

In the meantime, my altercation with Motta Gur had been drowned out by the roar of impending historic events. Motta put it well in the note he sent me: "In these epoch-making days, of such great importance in the chronicles of our time, it would be unforgivable if two men like us were to engage in trivialities instead of rising to the occasion." With the prime minister's approval, I allowed the matter to sink into oblivion, where it was overshadowed by the great drama now unfolding.

The doctors stuffed me full of Valium to still my pains, which were getting worse. I couldn't get out of bed; I couldn't even budge inside the bed. I was attached to tubes everywhere, with one up my nose and another fitted to my arm. Every now and then, I grew dizzy. I tried to visualize what was going on outside, but that damned Valium deprived me of my capacity to think clearly. The imminent encounter between Begin and Sadat fascinated me, if I could only concentrate enough to imagine it.

Meanwhile, the intelligence branch was not wasting time. General Gazit brought together all the experts of the intelligence community—the intelligence branch of the defense forces, the Mossad (our equivalent to the CIA), the Foreign Ministry, and the Orientalists—for an exchange of views that went on far into the night.

The discussion was followed up by two detailed memoranda. One was an assessment of the situation. Its contents were unambiguous: Egypt had no intention of concluding a separate treaty with Israel, but she did intend to make peace. However, in return for her signature, Egypt was likely to make far-reaching demands.

The second memorandum was drawn up without anyone in the government requesting its preparation or expressing an interest in it. It dealt with the question of what to offer Egypt in exchange for a peace treaty. From an Israeli standpoint, its conclusions were very gloomy: we had nothing to offer Sadat. The Egyptians would accept nothing less than a complete withdrawal from the Sinai. This memorandum was promptly dispatched to the prime minister's office in Jerusalem, from which it was sent back along with some outraged comments: since when did the head of military intelligence dictate policy to the government?

As for me—I was lying prone on my hospital bed, far from the scene of these events. All my visitors could do was commiserate with me.

In moments of solitude in Ward 12, in the short intervals between the waves of visitors, I ate my heart out. "Weizman!" I said. "Everyone is going to be there at the airport on Saturday night to welcome Sadat—and you'll be lying here, attached to tubes and catheters."

The nights in the hospital were long as I fretted and seethed. God! What had I done to deserve this?

My morale was at rock bottom. I didn't know what to do with myself.

It was my close friend, Eliezer Zhorabin, who hauled me out of my despair. "You," he said firmly, "are going to go and hear Sadat address the Knesset even if you have to be taken there on a stretcher! You may get there more dead than alive, but you'll go!"

I didn't believe it was feasible, and I doubted whether anyone else would think so, either. I summoned the doctors. My original intention was to consult them, but I soon changed my tone. In a still feeble voice that was supposed to carry a note of command, I proclaimed: "Gentlemen, I'm going to the Knesset on Sunday—and I don't give a damn what you say!"

The doctors were taken by surprise. "We'll see how you feel Sunday morning," they told me.

"See—nothing!" I attempted to yell, but the yell came out faintly. "I'm going to Jerusalem. Get my legs in shape!"

On Friday morning, the doctors permitted me to watch television. I couldn't believe my eyes. An Egyptian plane landed at Ben-Gurion Airport, bringing the advance party to prepare Sadat's visit. Dozens of Egyptian security men strode down the gangway. Looking at their faces, I thought they seemed alarmed and frightened. I tried to imagine their thoughts. What were they saying as they caught their first glimpse of Israelis? Had they really come to believe we had horns sprouting from our foreheads? Were any of them former inmates of our prisoner-of-war camp at Atlit? I would have given anything to be able to exchange a few words with them, but here I was, completely helpless, enclosed in plaster, with fractures in my leg and three cracked ribs.

When Sadat landed at Lod, there were few visitors around me, mainly relatives and friends. Half of the Israeli people were glued to their television sets, and the other half were squeezing into the airport to shake the hand of our great enemy. Mesmerized, I stared at the television. Every now and then, those about me took their eyes off the screen to look at me. You could have cut the air with a knife. I totally forgot the pains coursing through my body.

But I was beside myself with envy. There were my cabinet colleagues strutting about the runway, rigged out like bridegrooms, sporting their finest plumes and feathers and blown up with their own self-importance. When the camera zoomed in on Motta Gur, clad in festive attire, I almost went out of my mind: pressed and polished, he was standing in line along with the rest, waiting to shake Sadat's hand.

I alone was condemned to be trussed up in bed.

The plane door opened. When no one appeared, I held my breath. But a fraction of a second later, I could make out the familiar figure of the Egyptian president. Our enemy set foot on Israeli soil. The unbelievable was happening.

Only after I had spoken with the Egyptian president did I grasp how vitally necessary it had been to make some dramatic step, some historic move of breathtaking uniqueness, in order to span the gulf that had widened and deepened over the years.

In the course of Sadat's three-day visit, I would often scrutinize the faces of his companions—ministers, advisers, security men. They appeared very nervous. Perhaps they had expected a different kind of reception. Sadat himself may have anticipated occasional hostile hisses or booing. Instead, Israel welcomed Sadat as though he were an old friend who had been given up for dead, only to reappear suddenly. The entire country stopped to greet him, wildly and enthusiastically.

I can easily guess how he felt in his heart because I know exactly how we felt on seeing the first Egyptians arrive here after so many years and after so much bloodshed. Many Israelis—including many of those who fell in battle—were born in the course of our war with the Arabs. They knew nothing of how matters had stood before the 1948 war. Those times were not free of enmity or bloody clashes between Jews and Arabs, but in the years before the war, the two peoples had lived as neighbors with far more social exchange.

In the course of the years and the wars, such memories were erased from my mind. Most Israelis—those who arrived after the creation of the state or were born after the fighting had begun— never experienced that kind of coexistence with the Arabs. As far as they were concerned, there was no such thing as a good Arab—yet another truism that everyone accepted. It was easy to see that the other side had adopted that attitude toward us with even greater alacrity. Israeli prisoners who fell into their hands learned it the hard way, from the harsh treatment to which they were subjected.

Like most of us, the Egyptians probably did not remember that there had once been an open border. As far as they were concerned, they were walking into the lion's den.

The doctors' expressions did not herald well on Sunday morning. I understood that my chances of getting to the Knesset were poor, but I wasn't giving in. Pulling rank, I tried to impose my authority. "Listen!" I said. "You're going to take your instrument cases, fill them up with heroin, cocaine, hashish, or anything else you like, and then you'll come along with me and make sure I can stay on my feet for at least twenty-four hours."

The doctors capitulated. They gave their consent—on condition that they remain by my side day and night. I naturally suspected them of trying to get on board the bandwagon to see history in the making, but what the hell? Just as long as I could be there.

I was washed and then dressed in a light-colored suit that had a zipper sewn in on one leg so that my cast could be set down comfortably—custom design for an invalid.

What I saw in the mirror was a mere shadow of my usual self. The pain did not let up. It was all I could do to seat myself in the wheelchair and allow myself to be pushed to the helicopter pad. Would I manage to hold out? I was on edge. The idea of Israel's defense minister being brought in a wheelchair for his first glimpse of the Egyptian president! I cursed under my breath. Dozens of patients came out of their wards to wave to me, and I tried to smile. But getting into the helicopter, I felt the smile freeze on my lips as a drop of oil fell on my light-colored outfit. What could I do? I was down on my luck even in the small things.

Outside the Knesset's main chamber, I halted. I was not going in there seated in a wheelchair! I hoisted myself to my feet, every bone in my body shrieking in agony. Clutching my walking stick, I entered the chamber. Many eyes followed me as I flopped into my seat at the government table, sinking into a drugged daze. From the corner of my eye, I could see my three doctors, poised and alert for any eventuality.

Sadat entered the Knesset chamber. My first impression was horrifyingly prosaic. He looked just as he did on television except that his complexion was darker than I had imagined. Still, I couldn't take my eyes off him. All of a sudden, I was seeing a dream come true.

I had no delusions about Sadat. He has never been enamored of us. However, there could be no doubt that the Knesset speaker's rostrum was now occupied by a man of extraordinary character, possessing a rare courage and great political élan. Only a man like that could have ventured a leap of such enormous dimensions. By taking it, he was risking his life: I hoped that every necessary precaution had been taken to protect him, considering the magnitude of the controversy on both sides. I shuddered at the thought of a possible assassination attempt in the courtyard of the Dome of the Rock, or in the Knesset building. Had I been a Lloyd's underwriter, I would not have risked issuing Sadat with a life insurance policy that day.

Sadat, as self-possessed as always, began to speak. He opened with a moving declaration, that "every person who meets his end in war is a human soul, irrespective of whether he is Arab or Israeli," but his subsequent words surprised me by their intransigence. There was a menacing undertone I didn't like at all. In effect, Sadat was restating the unyielding positions to which Egypt had adhered since 1967—complete withdrawal to the old borders, without compromise, and all the other lines I knew by heart. I had heard these views hundreds of times, and I'd always rejected them. Now, as I got my first sight of the most authoritative Arab spokesman, he was repeating these far-reaching demands without so much as blinking an eye. It was my impression that he had made no attempt to comprehend Israel's problems or meet our views.

"I did not come here to sign a separate peace between Egypt and Israel," Sadat said. "A separate agreement between Egypt and Israel cannot guarantee a just peace. Furthermore, even if peace is achieved between Israel and all the confrontation states, without a just solution of the Palestinian problem, it will not bring that just and stable peace for whose attainment the whole world is pressing."

The heat was stifling. I looked at my colleagues on the government bench and glanced at the Knesset members. I knew that almost all of them would be unanimous in their opposition to his demands.

"I have not come here to submit a request that you evacuate your forces from the occupied lands. Total withdrawal from Arab land occupied after 1967 is self-evident. We shall not countenance any arguments about it, nor will we go begging to anyone," Sadat went on.

Gradually, I felt myself sinking into disappointment and despair. I saw no bridge to span this mighty chasm. My nostrils caught the stench of battle.

"We have to prepare for war," I scribbled in a note that I passed to the prime minister. Begin read it and nodded.

Carried away by the festive atmosphere in the Knesset and hampered by the poor quality of the translation from Arabic into Hebrew, many people failed to perceive the traps that Sadat set in his speech. Everyone was too excited to pay much attention to details. I tried to keep in mind that in addition to the Knesset and the Israeli people, Sadat's speech was also aimed at the other Arab states—indeed, they may have been the audience he was addressing in the first place.

I did not believe that Sadat had come to Jerusalem to hoist a white flag. But I'd hoped he would be openhanded and that he would come to talk peace. What he had brought were the conditions for a new war.

In retrospect, that speech was a wise move on his part. Later on, whenever fierce arguments erupted, he would say—to me and others: "Everything I say today—I already said in my speech to the Knesset." And he was quite right.

More important—and this I only came to see later—was that Sadat's visit did represent a significant departure in one crucial regard. What Sadat offered in exchange for his unyielding terms was full peace, not an interim arrangement but a completely normalized relationship. Never in the past had such a possibility been acknowledged.

As Sadat came to the end of his address, I felt that he had sprung the surprise of a political Yom Kippur upon us. Leading off with a stunning piece of exhibitionism, he had taken the war out of the deserts of Sinai and carried it into the debating chamber of Israel's Knesset. In view of the whole world, he had forced us into a corner.

At moments like these, the political arena is the setting of great drama. This particular theater piece was marked by the participation of two men, both possessing a highly developed histrionic sense: Anwar Sadat and Menachem Begin. History did a good job of casting when it picked the stars for this occasion.

With his gift for drama, Begin was the right man in the right place when he had faced the airliner's gangway at Ben-Gurion Airport. But now, as he went up to the Knesset rostrum to reply to Sadat, Israel's prime minister was at a marked disadvantage. Having no prior intimation of the text of Sadat's speech, Begin's response was, of necessity, impromptu. The prime minister was dignified and reserved, but objective circumstances were against him. Sadat had grabbed center stage. The Egyptian president had blazed away with heavy artillery, while Begin had nothing to fire back with but a two-inch mortar.

I fell into speculation. What would happen now? Fate had been kind to Begin, granting him a historic opportunity. Would he let it slip away? During its first half year of office, the cabinet had functioned well. Would it now be shaken to its foundations? Where were we heading? If this visit produced no results, it could lead to dissension and disunity within Israel.

Beset by these thoughts, I took no part in the general jubilation. Aside from all else, my physical condition played its part: the pain was getting worse. I was being wheeled out in my chair when, unexpectedly, I received a summons to the prime minister's office. The Egyptian president wished to see me—possibly because I had missed the reception ceremony at the airport.

When I arrived in Begin's office, I could scarcely make out in my daze Israeli President Efraim Katzir, the prime minister, Knesset

Speaker Yitzhak Shamir, or the Egyptian president. All the same, I hoisted myself out of my wheelchair, and grasping my walking stick like a rifle, I swung it up in a quasi-military salute.

My gesture caught Sadat by surprise. He began to laugh, and the affinity we felt for each other at that moment was to characterize our future meetings, even when the going was tough.

3

MENACHEM BEGIN'S SCULPTURE GARDEN

With Sadat's visit to Jerusalem, Menachem Begin began to acquire an entirely new image in the eyes of both friends and foes. The superhawk, whose name was always associated with a policy of "not one inch"—not an inch of land given back—unexpectedly showed himself willing to take great, far-reaching steps toward peace. Before the elections that elevated Begin to power, anyone predicting that he, of all Israeli leaders, would be the one to take the first steps toward conciliation with Egypt would have been met with incredulity or laughter. Yet it was Begin who had matched Sadat's daring.

The party that Begin leads—Herut—had come to be perceived by three generations as an extremist movement. For decades, its members were denigrated as fascists and reactionaries. Herut advocated the unity of the land of Israel within its historical boundaries. At a time when Palestine was ruled by the British and the very creation of a Jewish state was still in doubt, Herut's fore-runners—movements inside Palestine and abroad as well as the anti-British underground—had already translated their aspira-tions into a political emblem: a hand grasping a rifle in the fore-ground, with the background showing a map of the territory on both sides of the Jordan River (including the present-day kingdom of Jordan under Hussein). The slogan underlining it was: "Only thus!"

Many Israelis saw Herut as the party of war. The Irgun underground—whose political successor was Herut—had advocated a hardhanded policy vis-à-vis our Arab neighbors. In the course of time and under the impact of changing circumstances, Herut's positions were gradually toned down. After the 1967 war, which gave Israel possession of the West Bank of the Jordan, Herut effectively abandoned the idea of conquering Hussein's kingdom. Begin, who had once written an article called "Amman too shall be ours!" now realized that this slogan had no hope of implementation. Herut remained content with safeguarding Israel's war gains, while the East Bank of the Jordan was relegated to its ideological museum.

The peace process adopted by Begin on taking office reduced his political rivals to stupefaction. The muse of history seemed to have played a diabolical trick on them—to my great glee. As the person who headed the campaign that brought Menachem Begin his first-ever election victory as prime minister in forty years of political life, I cannot deny that I drew particular satisfaction from the situation. Begin's opponents had always warned that his elevation to power would automatically entail war and bloodshed. What happened was precisely the opposite. For the first time, we were offered the possibility of breaking out of the endless round of hostility.

I blessed history for charging Menachem Begin with the task. I had faith in the prime minister. More than any of us, a man with his sharp historical sense was well equipped to realize the greatness of the moment and the enormity of the opportunity. Personally and politically, Begin was well prepared for a breakthrough—of this I had no doubt. All the same, I knew right from the outset that it would plunge him into a grave personal dilemma. I could imagine what had been going on in Begin's heart of hearts—every day, every hour—since the moment Sadat had set foot on Israeli soil to flaunt his obdurate demands.

On top of all the other barriers dividing Israelis and Egyptians, Menachem Begin had a further personal barrier to surmount. Throughout his years at the head of Herut, he had blazed the political and ideological trail to be followed by his adherents. I knew that Begin cherished the movement by means of which he had found political expression for all his aspirations and principles, for his personal philosophy and his life's work. All his energies and powers had been channeled into Herut. And now that party—the party of the hawks—was about to extend a welcoming hand to peace, and the turmoil was evident.

As for myself—I did not have to bear Herut's ideological millstone. The Israeli political arena is densely populated with parties and splinter groups, but ever since achieving political awareness, I had found Begin's party the closest to me in its positive national-ism, its attitude toward security and borders, and its emphasis on the land of Israel as the Jewish heritage. The Labor party looked for the socialism in Zionism. I was never a socialist. Even when I was a serving officer and therefore strictly forbidden to engage in politics, my views were well known. Moreover, several brief en-counters had given me the opportunity to express them to Begin himself.

On various occasions during my military service, members of the ruling Labor party—Herut's ideological opposite—approached me to join. It was even hinted that Labor party membership would facilitate my promotion in the army. My sister-in-law, Ruth Dayan, said, "Side with Herut? Are you crazy? You'll never make it to chief of staff!" Colleagues in the army advised me to keep a tighter rein on my tongue. I knew that my leanings toward Herut would prevent me from going far. Begin's followers were pariahs, outcasts, untouchables. The late David Ben-Gurion consistently adhered to the slogan he himself had coined: "Coalitions—without Herut or the Communists." Herut spent years in the political wilderness.

Because of the system of proportional representation, Israel is fractioned into two major political parties and a lot of splinter parties, and no single party can gain a majority of the 120 seats in the Knesset—the Israeli parliament. The government is therefore made up of a coalition between the party that has won the most seats and other smaller parties that are asked to join in order to make up a majority. This system has led to some strange mar-riages in Israel's political past!

In addition, the million and a half Israeli voters cast their votes for a party rather than for an individual candidate, as in the pres-idential elections in the United States. The number of votes the party gets determines the number of seats it will have in the Knes-set (15,000 to 20,000 votes win one seat). Each party draws up its own list of 120 members and runs that list as a slate. The person who heads the dominant party's list becomes prime minister, and the seats won by each party are distributed according to the set order of the list.

Apart from a brief membership in Golda Meir's cabinet, Herut had not only never been the dominant party but had never formed part of the government coalition. Thus, it had no experience with political power.

As commander of the air force, I was remote from the corridors of power because of being in the military, although when I occasionally speculated about the future, I did have long-term ambitions of entering politics. However, I never imagined that the path would be so smooth. I was awaited with open arms—as I learned one day in 1965 when I got a phone call from Elimelech Rimalt, one of the leaders of Gahal. (An alliance of Herut and the Liberal party, Gahal was a forerunner of the broader Likud alliance, of which it remains a component.)

Rimalt's message was simple: "Come and run with us in the elections." He was evidently aware of my political views.

Pleased and flattered by his invitation, I nevertheless turned it down, preferring to press ahead with my military career.

Paradoxically, that career came to an end just at the time when the views I had always held were apparently vindicated. In 1969, Israel was at the peak of her strength. Confounding the predictions of various fainthearted individuals, our forces were emplaced on the Golan Heights, along the Jordan River, and on the banks of the Suez Canal. With few exceptions, every Israeli was convinced that "things have never been better!"—a slogan we repeated day and night in a vain attempt to keep our minds free of forebodings about the future. More than ever before, stability characterized the political and military status quo, which the Arabs seemed powerless to challenge in spite of all their provocative declarations.

At precisely this moment, when my predictions were apparently validated, there was a progressive decline in my prospects of reaching the top of the military command. Evidently, the chief of staff's baton lay beyond my reach. No one said it in so many words—not in my presence, at least—but I could sense it in the air, in the attitudes of people around me.

At various stages in my military career, I had tried to visualize the day of my resignation from the service. I knew it had to come. Israel's armed forces have always depended on a system of rotation: as one officer leaves, another takes his place.

Even before the day I finally put away my uniform, I had a foretaste of the pangs I'd feel. In 1966, I had given up command of the air force, handing it over to Motti Hod. Although it was in a good cause—I was promoted to the number-two position in Israel's military command—my leavetaking of the air force was nevertheless painful. The force was an integral part of me. For eighteen years, its pilots and air crews were members of my extended family. I knew all the pilots by name, and I tried to remember the names of their wives. My subordinates told infinite jokes about the techniques I'd developed for this purpose—such as memorizing photographs of people I hadn't yet met, to be able to greet them by name. And now I was leaving all that behind me.

Whenever I had thought about the end of my military career, I'd tried to picture the following morning. It would be a dreary day. My telephone would not ring. The driver would not be waiting for me outside my house. I would probably get up without knowing how to occupy myself: I shuddered at the picture of me roaming the streets of Tel Aviv clutching a briefcase and thought: *Heaven protect me from that!*

What actually happened was totally unlike anything I'd imagined.

One day in November 1969, at the height of the Suez Canal War of Attrition, I was at a friend's house for a wedding reception when I was called to the phone. On the line was Yosef Kramerman, one of Herut's Members of Knesset. Kramerman wanted to see me that same evening. When I put down the receiver, I had no idea that a new career was about to open up before me.

That evening, I met Kramerman in Tel Aviv. He came straight to the point: "I've come to make you a proposition," he said.

A moment later, I heard one of the most astounding offers I have ever received. Kramerman invited me to join Herut and simultaneously take office as one of the party's representatives in Golda Meir's cabinet of National Unity!

I was thunderstruck. Almost without exception, my colleagues at GHQ were members of the ruling Labor party. Those who entered politics after leaving the army naturally preferred to head toward Tel Aviv's Hayarkon Street and the Labor offices. That was where they had come from, and it was only natural that they should return to the Labor movement. It was perfectly legitimate: this was the course adopted by most of my colleagues: Moshe Dayan, Yitzhak Rabin, Chaim Barlev, Motta Gur, and others.

I could have done the same. What would have been more opportune than adhering to the Labor party line when its members had been in power for so long and looked as if they were there to stay? But I refused to consider such a notion.

As far as I was concerned, the Labor party had gone off the rails. Its prolonged tenure of power had corrupted its members, from many of whom exuded the powerful stench of hypocrisy. While preaching socialism and egalitarianism, they themselves were hardly models of either. As I used to put it: being true socialists, they wore no ties with their sixty-dollar shirts.

At that time, joining Herut was political suicide. Admittedly, the Six-Day War had granted the party a measure of legitimization. The Israeli public saw the return to Judea and Samaria and to the Jewish holy places as a confirmation of Herut's vision, long dismissed by its rivals as a fantastic dream with no foothold in political and military realities. Begin saw the public celebration as his own personal triumph: the Israelis had not forgotten the far-off days of the biblical prophets when their people had taken shape. He could also regard it as a retroactive justification of everything he and his party had so passionately advocated, only to have it denounced by his foes as hollow chauvinist demagogy.

Amid the victorious revelries of the summer of 1967, Menachem Begin no longer appeared in the guise attributed to him by most Israelis during the fifties and early sixties. Under the changed circumstances, the ideas he had propagated for so many years were no longer ridiculous. Suddenly, the previously unbridgeable chasm—mental, political, and ideological—between him and his traditional rivals in the Labor movement no longer existed.

Now elevated to the post of minister without portfolio in Golda's cabinet, Begin was not only serving alongside those who were formerly his bitterest opponents, but also the principal plank in his party's platform had become a living reality—to the jubilation of many Israelis. Our renewed encounter with the biblical landscapes and with the ancient land of Israel—from which we had been cut off for nineteen years—set off a wave of burgeoning nationalism that engulfed the whole country, even the bastions of left-wing Zionism. This nationalist and religious tide cleared the way for Menachem Begin's rise to power ten years later.

On top of all this, anyone with any political awareness could notice—in hindsight, at least—that most of Begin's views had, in fact, been applied by the Labor-led governments, not only in foreign affairs and in dealings with the Arab world but also in domestic policies that progressively alienated the Labor movement from its socialist roots, bringing it closer to Begin's philosophy.

In mid-December 1969, a young woman officer came to my GHQ office and swiftly guided me through the formal procedures involved in my hasty resignation from the service. While clearing my office walls of the snapshots that had accompanied me throughout my military career, I received the last report to reach me as head of GHQ's staff section: the Egyptians had captured one of our officers as he was driving his jeep along the Suez Canal. The officer's name: Dan Avidan, from Kibbutz Ain Hashofet.

I closed my eyes. The name sounded familiar; so did the address. Suddenly, it came back to me: the summer of 1948, I was a young combat pilot at the Tel Nof air base. It was one of the most crucial moments in our War of Independence. A tired and distracted officer had appeared, urging us to take off without delay in a desperate bid to halt the Egyptian column headed for Tel Aviv. That was how I'd clambered into my Messerschmitt for my first combat sortie in the 1948 war.

The officer's name was Shimon Avidan, the commander of the Givati Brigade. Now, as I was about to conclude my military service, the wheel had come full circle with tragic force: the officer taken prisoner by the Canal was Avidan's son. The fathers had gone to war, and now destiny was sending the sons into battle.

My next call came from the Herut offices. The party's central committee was due to convene that evening at seven.

It seemed a long way to Jabotinsky House on Tel Aviv's King George Street. It had been ages since I'd last driven a civilian car. I glanced around at the pedestrians on the pavements, at the girls, at drivers halting before traffic lights. All of a sudden, I had time for an idle look at a Tel Aviv street on a weekday.

When I entered the hall, I was greeted with stormy applause.

The welcome stunned me. I was accustomed to military ceremonial; there is no applause in the army. Suddenly, I found myself surrounded by people of all ages, some very elderly, who were rising to their feet in my honor. Menachem Begin welcomed me as "my friend, my general, my companion." I was very moved.

From my seat on the platform, I could look around at the Herut members. They were all strangers. Few belonged to my generation. I had spent the best part of my life with officers my own age—on the whole, the army is youthful and dynamic. Without warning, I found myself now in the midst of bald pates and graying locks. I was alone. My eyes roamed the hall, seeking a familiar face—in vain. Everyone looked alien—even those whom I knew superficially from passing contacts or could identify from their pictures in the papers.

In fact, I had little time to study my new surroundings. One day after joining Herut, I was taking my oath of office as transport minister in the National Unity cabinet. Because of my military background, it was the most appropriate position for me, covering air routes, El Al, railways, and shipping. Getting the job was like skipping a class—overnight, I had sprung from general to minister.

Yet, however sharp the switch felt then, in retrospect, it was a natural step. The arena had changed, and so had the methods, but the aim remained the same. That aim had been clear to me, as it was to all of my generation, at a very early age. When I left my parents' home in Haifa, I was eighteen; since then, scarcely a day has passed in which I have not played some role in shaping the fate of my country. At first, it was in minor posts; in time, I rose to key positions within the principal prop of Israel's might—the military. My membership in the cabinet was, therefore, another step in the ladder of service, possibly, its high point.

At the same time, why pretend? In taking the job, I was fulfilling my personal ambition: I wanted to go into politics. I have no great regard for those who accept important posts merely "out of deference to party decisions"—supposedly offering themselves up on the altar for the people of Israel. Anyone who claims that his only aim in life is to serve his people is not telling the truth. Everyone has ambitions—and I am no exception. However, it is vital to find the appropriate balance between personal aspirations and the good of the country, and I have always been aware of how delicate that balance is.

A number of people in Herut hinted—and sometimes said openly and very loudly—that I owed them and their movement a great deal. I presume they were out to make political capital. I have never considered myself in debt to anyone in the movement, from Begin down. In joining when I did, I made an important contribution toward the legitimization of Herut because I was part of the establishment, having grown up in the military from the age of eighteen.

My name, however, was liable to arouse reservations on the part of Herut old-timers. They had witnessed the bitter, years-long rivalry between my uncle, Chaim Weizmann—later Israel's first president—and Ze'ev Jabotinsky, Herut's spiritual mentor, who, forty years after his death, is still regarded as the trailblazer of its ideological course. Weizmann represented the central, moderate trend in the Zionist movement, which followed a policy of conciliation with the Arabs as well as with Jews of different convictions and the British in Palestine. My uncle believed in the creative efforts of the Jewish community in the land of Israel, but he held that unless we also gained massive Western support, the Zionist project would not survive. Jabotinsky, on the other hand, was uncompromising in advocating a return to the biblical and historical Israel—the West and East banks of the Jordan.

Chaim Weizmann isolated Jabotinsky, forcing him out of the

Zionist movement and stigmatizing his followers as defectors. That stigma stuck to them, marking them as outcasts from the Jewish community in Palestine. For years, the two names—Jabotinsky and Weizmann—marked the two poles within the Zionist movement. The two camps were divided by fires of enmity. When I joined the movement that displayed such fanatical loyalty to Jabotinsky's political and ideological heritage, its elder members found it hard to forgive me for the name I bore. In their eyes, I was an alien idol in their sacred temple.

But they could not deny that Weizmann's nephew had always expressed his sympathy for Jabotinsky's successor. In consequence, as long as my relations with the party flowed in placid channels, my name had no significance beyond its paradoxical overtones. However, when a storm did erupt, the paradox took on entirely different dimensions.

Unwittingly, I added fuel to the flames. On joining Herut and being immediately chosen as one of the movement's representatives in the cabinet, I was thrusting aside several of its veteran leaders. They had spent decades weaving their dreams of the day when their hands got a grip on the levers of power. But when Golda Meir finally opened up a narrow chink of access to the control room, I was one of the few to get in, while they were left outside, disappointed and bitter. I could understand their feelings.

The spring of 1970 witnessed the first crisis in my relationship with Begin, when I voted in the cabinet in favor of Foreign Minister Abba Eban's mission to Germany at a time when official visits to that country were a matter of great controversy. What else could I do? I myself had visited Germany while serving as commander of the air force. I knew of the Bonn government's contribution to Israel's armament. Now, in 1970, long after the two states had set up diplomatic relations, opposition to Germany struck me as pointless and anachronistic. Knowing Begin would not like it, I scribbled a note to him, explaining the reasons for my vote. He wrote back: *"Vive la liberté!"* Would that be the end of it? Not for Begin. He does not enjoy having his authority questioned. I had stepped on my first land mine.

The second crisis blew up in the summer of 1970 when I came out against our resignation from the cabinet. In view of the government's adoption of the American peace plan (named for U.S. Secretary of State William Rogers), Begin regarded a continuing Likud membership in the cabinet as consent in principle to a withdrawal from the territory occupied in the Six-Day War. He was immutable in his conviction. "I'd rather chop off my right hand than sign this document!" he exclaimed dramatically at the end of his address to the members of our Knesset faction. Later, he was to say that as he made his decision, he was seeing in his mind's eye his mentor and spiritual father, Ze'ev Jabotinsky, who had not hesitated in 1933 to leave the Zionist movement because he did not approve of its policies.

I am not convinced that Begin's decision to leave the cabinet stemmed exclusively from his fundamental opposition to the Rogers plan. The urge to resign, whatever the cost, was equally a product of his long years in the opposition. All his life he'd been number one to his followers, and in Golda's cabinet he played second fiddle.

It may also have arisen from Begin's belief in words. He invests words with magical properties. In his eyes, a good speech is almost the equivalent of a great deed. At times, he finds it hard to distinguish between the two. In view of the supreme importance that he attributes to documents and formulations, Begin read the Rogers plan with alarm. In her efforts to torpedo the American initiative, Golda Meir used deeds. Begin opposed her—with words.

I was dismayed by Begin's oft-repeated declaration: "We will serve our people in opposition." Experience has taught me that the Israeli political system gives the most junior member of the government coalition greater weight than the chairman of the opposition. The only way the chairman of the opposition can exert his weight is by depositing it upon a chair in the Knesset cafeteria. I saw no need to return to the back benches. What would we do in the opposition? How could we combat the American initiative? How would we make our imprint on the shape of the country?

Many members of Herut shared my views. But, as I was to learn in time, they would invariably bow to Begin's wishes. In their eyes, Begin was and remains their commander in the pre-state Irgun underground. They even continue to call him by his former pseudonyms: "The old man," "the boss." Without consciously willing it, I found myself making comparisons with the army. The military is structured on a hierarchical relationship between superiors and subordinates. However, in the staff of every unit—and this is particularly true of the General Staff—before orders are issued, they are preceded by bitter, hard-hitting deliberations in which subordinates are never choosy about the terms in which they defend their views—even when they run counter to those of their superiors.

Those arguments were often characterized by their extreme heat. We said whatever was on our minds. At times, the terms we used were crude, worded in Sabra Hebrew with plenty of spice.

Now I suddenly found myself in a civilian organization headed by a "commander" whom everyone obeyed blindly, scarcely daring to argue with him and of course never going so far as to defy him. I observed an interesting phenomenon: one sharp glance from Begin suffices to eliminate any pockets of resistance. He narrows his eyes and furrows his brow; he says nothing, but the hint is obvious. "Before they raise their hands to vote, they glance at Begin to see how he is voting," said Gideon Patt, who was later to become a minister in Begin's cabinet.

There was no choice in the matter: Begin wanted to leave Golda Meir's cabinet, so leave we did. Our switch into the opposition took me to Jabotinsky House in Tel Aviv where I served as chairman of the Herut executive. I found myself at the head of the executive arm of an opposition party with very little to execute. Moreover, the "arm" was a short one. Herut could boast of a wealth of ideology, but it was impoverished in material possessions, and its organizational structure was tiny and underdeveloped. There was no hope of competing on equal terms with other parties; unlike them, Herut owned no economic enterprises and had no settlements (the Labor movement has many affiliated kibbutzim and moshavim); it had no ideological indoctrination center to compare with the Labor party's Bet Berl—it did not even have a party newspaper. Herut was a tiny preserve for an endangered species, the inevitable product of decades of consistent opposition to the official Zionist leadership.

No one was in any great hurry to join Herut. Naturally enough, fifty years of power had enabled the Labor movement to attract the better human material, the sort of person who wants to get things done. I looked around Herut, seeking in vain for the kind of person with whom I had spent the best years of my life—someone with initiative and energy. Those about me remained strangers. Their personal background was different, their mentality utterly unfamiliar. I did not know how to direct them and often asked myself: "What am I doing here?"

It was difficult. I was astonished at myself and at my situation. During my military service, I had enjoyed going "down below" to mingle with the lower ranks. I liked their company, found them interesting. As their commanding officer, I wanted to influence them and watch them rise. In politics, you also have to go "down below"—but there it's different: the aim is to gain popularity, to "sell," to persuade.

I found myself involved in give-and-take haggling over positions of power. That wasn't exactly my style. It wasn't what I meant by politics. I like to be involved in shaping policy. If there is any distinction between a politician and a statesman, let history judge which I am. What could I do? After years spent weighing fateful decisions, matters of life and death—whether in the army or in the cabinet—I found it hard to plunge into the squabbles and intrigues of a Herut branch in Zichron Ya'akov. It simply wasn't my cup of tea.

Some members of Herut would widen their eyes in astonishment whenever I opened my mouth. They were unaccustomed to my style. In the army, no one so much as blinked when I expressed myself in racy language. Even members of the General Staff used common military slang. Being with young people had its effect on us. But the nobly born gentry of Herut were struck dumb whenever I made some coarse remark. I, on the other hand, could not get used to the vocabulary of certain politicians, whose words did not reflect their true thoughts. Some of my friends had warned me about politics: "Are you out of your mind? Diving into those murky waters? You with your blunt, outspoken way of speaking—you'll drown!" I didn't drown; instead, I said precisely what I thought. In Herut, I was regarded as an outlandish creature.

But it left me homesick for the army and its familiar gallery of characters. Uprooted from that more native environment, I felt impotent in my new surroundings. I could blame no one, least of all my colleagues in Herut. So many years in opposition, with the mentality of a closed sect clinging to its past, had not made their movement particularly lively.

For them the past was more alive than the moment. To this day, they continue to live and function according to thought patterns shaped during their period in the underground. Not that I think it either possible or desirable to turn one's back on the past; without it, there is neither present nor future. The home I grew up in was filled with the living spirit of Jewish history. All the venerable ancestors of our people flitted down its corridors, bearing the burden and riches of bygone eras. But never have I seen people so immersed in the past as the Herut old-timers.

In an attempt to understand them, I reminded myself that, unlike the Labor party leaders, they had never gained power or won posts of which they were worthy. Their careers had come to an end somewhere in 1948.

Some of them got up every morning and asked themselves what Jabotinsky would have said about whatever minor step they were about to take. They could not understand how I could take over my office in King George Street without hurrying to hang up a portrait of Jabotinsky. Some attributed this delinquency to my name. What could I do? I have no mentors to idolize.

The closed sect of Herut old-timers, constantly prostrating themselves before the past, had in the course of time been reinforced by all those embittered by the injustices inflicted upon them by the Labor regime. This group had little charm. I looked around for those alongside whom I would be able to wage the great battle to shape the character of the state. I found many good and devoted individuals; a few were prepared to dedicate every ounce of strength and energy to this sacred task. However, they were like plants imprisoned in a padlocked garden.

Menachem Begin's sculpture park. In the center stood the largest and most imposing monument: the statue of Jabotinsky, which everyone revered and worshipped with great awe. It was surrounded by smaller busts, commemorating all those who in one way or another had taken part in mapping out Herut's course ever since its underground days.

Not unnaturally, the figures installed in this garden saw me as an alien transplant. An alien transplant stands out, particularly in a small, fenced-in enclosure. I wanted to open it up and broaden Herut's base of support; I wanted to spread out into the fields, alongside plants of every kind and species, in a living patchwork with its roots deep in the soil of reality.

I saw that I was wilting. I tried to turn up the soil, to plough it up. I had disagreements over organizational methods, over political views, and failed to convince my hearers. The statues in Herut's walled garden only huddled together all the more, begging to have the fence made even higher. That way, there was not the slightest hope of ever gaining power. They were warm and cozy in their little garden; I wasn't.

Behind my back, I could hear suppressed titters of malicious glee. Suddenly, I found myself alone. I sat at home and waited for someone to call me. Such are the moments when genuine friendship is put to the test; then you see who dives into a foxhole and who smiles at you, who phones—and who is out for your blood. Those are the moments when you can pick out the hyenas, the foxes, and the jackals.

The creation of the Likud alliance (uniting Herut, the Liberals, and State list and other groups) opened up the way for me to return to active political work in Herut, both because the Likud now included forces more in favor of my approach and because the controversy had mellowed since I'd become a private citizen. At the end of 1976, I was placed at the head of the Likud's election headquarters, which were to catapult Menachem Begin to power a few months later. I put everything I had into the election campaign. Frequently, I was troubled by doubts not only about our prospects of attaining power but also about whether the burden of power would change Herut and set it on a different course.

The triumph of May 17, 1977, left me with little time to ruminate about that. Our election victory put me back into the defense establishment—this time, at the very pinnacle of the pyramid. I flung myself into my new task, perceiving it as a double challenge. During my military service, I had come very close to being named chief of staff. I bore no one any grudge over being denied the post. But, as defense minister, I was now installed over the chief of staff, and I was determined to make a success of my job.

It was 8:30 in the morning of June 21, 1977—seven and a half years since I'd taken my leave of the defense establishment. Today, I was returning in great excitement to stand at its head. A large guard of soldiers greeted me on my arrival. At the entrance, I was awaited by the chief of staff and the director general of the ministry. The outgoing minister, Shimon Peres, was waiting for me in the office. On the table he had placed three volumes in blue bindings inscribed: *The Defense Establishment 1974–1977*. They contained all the most highly guarded secrets and plans.

An hour later, the ministry's conference chamber filled up with senior staff and high-ranking officers. I knew most of them well. I let my gaze linger on their faces, trying to gauge their precise opinion of me, of the political turnabout and its effects on the defense establishment. Not all of them looked overjoyed at seeing the Likud in power.

My eyes rested on gray hair and a tanned complexion. I could scarcely believe my eyes: it was Shimon Avidan, one-time commander of the Givati Brigade during the 1948 war, the man who had sent me and my fellow pilots off on our strafing mission against the Egyptian armored column and whose son, Lt. Dan Avidan, had fallen into Egyptian captivity during my last few minutes as an active general. Avidan was currently serving as the Defense Ministry's internal comptroller. The circle closed, yet again.

"Together with you," I told my expectant listeners, "I shall do everything I can to prevent a future war. I know that's a fine phrase—but I definitely believe it is possible. If it should be said that during my period of office war was averted, it would be one of the great achievements of my short career and in the history of the state of Israel.''

Even as I said those sentences, I was full of doubt as to whether I had anything to back them up. A few minutes earlier, in the minister's office, I had heard Shimon Peres's assessment: a new war was liable to break out within a few months.

One-half year later, all my military training and political skills as defense minister were going to be tested not by war but by peace.

4

A RAGING HAWK

Had anyone ever told me the day would come when I'd find myself confronting an Egyptian president, I would have laughed. If I occasionally gave it serious consideration, I calculated that such an event would only occur in consequence of a battlefield triumph. For thirty years, I had regarded Cairo as the capital of an enemy state. When I imagined revisiting the city I had frequented in the forties, I could only visualize myself swooping down on it in a combat plane or paying a courtesy call at the head of a column of tanks. In fact, in the course of my twenty-one years in the Israeli armed forces, I often thought about that possibility. After the Six-Day War, I referred unashamedly to my desire to take Cairo.

Everyone knew me as a raging hawk. My philosophy was well in tune with my military duties. Years of service had taught me to regard the Egyptian army as our principal foe. I won't say I hated the Egyptians, but I did seek out every opportunity to give them a thrashing. The Israeli army did a pretty good job of that. I saw the Egyptian army beaten, its morale shattered—and that never caused me to shed a single tear. On the contrary—I was proud of my share in our victories.

I even got a kick out of repeated examinations of the photographs of the Giza pyramids and the Cairo mosques taken by our air force at the end of the Six-Day War. I guessed then that the pictures—featured prominently in the Israeli press and abroad— would be a painful blow to the heads of the Egyptian administration and army by providing crushingly candid testimony to their great debacle. Who on earth could have dreamed that I would soon be there, beside those same pyramids, having my own photograph taken as I posed amicably alongside my Egyptian hosts, grinning from ear to ear?

Like most Israelis, I took an active part in the triumphant revelries that followed the 1967 war. I saw no reason to stand back. In fact, I crowed to myself: "Weizman! Did you say the air force could beat them in six hours? You did! Did everyone laugh at you? They did! And the air force did it in *three* hours. . . ."

It was only after my first meetings with the Egyptians that I began to grasp the mistake we had made. Whenever the Egyptians referred to their humiliation in the Six-Day War, their eyes grew moist. I suddenly realized how painful the blow had been and how it had spurred them on to redoubled efforts of revenge.

"Do you know what offended us most?" an Egyptian general explained. "That newspaper photograph showing your women soldiers standing guard over our soldiers, who lay face downward on the sands of Sinai."

Long before the Six-Day War, when Israel was constricted within the 1949 armistice borders, I vigorously expressed my feelings about those other portions of our homeland—Judea and Samaria. In my view, the West Bank was, and remains, our ancestral heritage, an integral part of *Eretz Yisrael*—the land of Israel, indeed, its heartland. Publicly—at the top of my voice sometimes—I expressed my longings for the Old City of Jerusalem, for the Western Wall, for Hebron's Machpela Cave, for Rachel's tomb in Bethlehem. These were the sights I remembered from my youth, the scenes of my native land. Whenever I got the chance, I would reminisce about trips with my father to the Casbah of Nablus, the marketplace in Bethlehem, Jenin, the Western Wall in Jerusalem. I believed with all my heart that the day would come when we'd return to those places and proclaimed my hope to anyone who cared to listen.

I may not have been unique in the army, but my views singled me out within the senior command. Particularly in those spheres I regard as vital to Israel's security, I had never kept quiet, although my uniform made it impossible for me to publicize my opinions. Nevertheless, they were known to my army colleagues, some of whom were quite disturbed by them. On one or two occasions, I managed to sneak them into the public domain, for which I was— deservedly—reprimanded.

On the other hand, the army is no different from civilian society;

it, too, has its quota of those who wake up every morning and check which way the wind is blowing so as to make haste and face in the right direction. Not everyone is like that, but there are some; the army has its professional yes men.

Yes men are a danger to anyone who holds a senior post, whether in the army or in government. They are sometimes hard to recognize. But there will always be senior officials, generals and political leaders, who prefer to shelter behind a solid cordon of yes men. It's a sure recipe for failure. During my periods of office—in the army and in the cabinet—I tried to avoid them. I would not say that my immediate circle has never contained anyone who hastened to agree with whatever bit of nonsense I happened to blurt out; I've had my share. But in the course of the years, I have learned to avoid this trap by consulting as many people as possible.

No one can accuse me of being a yes man. My political opinions were heartily disliked by many people. Every now and then, someone would hint that it might be worth my while to keep my mouth shut. I was given to understand that my views left me with little chance of going far—certainly not as far as the post of chief of staff. These warnings were counterproductive. I opened my mouth—wide! I've never found any difficulty in doing that.

As to the fulfillment of my hope that we'd return to those portions of our homeland that war had taken from us—I relied less on the Israelis than on the Arabs. In the course of the years, they have made so many blunders—and we have found ways of turning them to our advantage. That is precisely what happened on the morning of June 5, 1967, when King Hussein of Jordan decided to attack. There were a few kindhearted Israelis who tried to save his skin by counseling him to stay out. We sent him a cable, saying, "Sit still, and you don't need to worry. We won't go for you." But, thank heavens, he did not take the advice.

The unforgettable hours of June 1967 found me far from the scenes I so greatly desired to witness. When Motta Gur's paratroopers regained the Western Wall for the Jewish people and pressed against its stones with tears streaming down their faces, fate had me stuck a few hundred miles to the south, at Sharm el Sheik. The news of the liberation of Jerusalem came to me over our radio. Sitting alone on a wind-swept hill, I cursed my luck and rejoiced with the soldiers in spirit; my own eyes may also have been moist.

A day or two later, I stood among masses of people filling the space before the Western Wall. Their excitement was electric.

Looking about me, I saw some of those who used to laugh at me every time I said the day would come when we'd return to this spot. Now they were strutting about before the wall, posing for photographs and basking in the flash of popping cameras. Thank God we had no television at the time! I thought to myself: *Damn it all, it's only a year or two since they laughed when I told them that one day we'd get Jerusalem's Old City back.* But perhaps it was divine mercy that kept me from taking part in the storming of the Western Wall. My presence there might have spoiled the show for certain eminent and much-photographed individuals who had accused me of misleading our youth when I'd shared my dream.

Sha'ul Tchernichovsky, one of Israel's great poets, wrote that a man is nothing more than an image of his native landscape. If there is any truth in his words, it applies to me. I was born in the land of Israel. It was never an unfulfilled vision that I yearned for from afar. My love for it is intimate, simple, and very tangible. I know the country like the palm of my own hand. I have toured its length and breadth, I have flown over it from every point of the compass, I am familiar with its human landscapes.

Men are in the habit of bragging about their conquests or of their occasional lighthearted flirtations. But they will never boast aloud of their true loves, nor will they share their most intimate moments with anyone else. I know a number of people who talk of their ties to all sorts of places in Israel—places they could scarcely locate on a map. But I'd had a personal history in the places that were returned to us in 1967.

It was a tremendously gripping experience to renew my acquaintance with portions of my native land that I remembered from my childhood—like returning home. A homeland is no abstract concept. It can be sensed, smelled, touched. I love the East, with its smells and hues: I belong there. After the war, I strolled through the alleyways of Jerusalem's Old City, I toured Hebron, I wandered around Jenin, always on the lookout for familiar faces, hoping to find friends of my father.

And, like many others, I allowed myself to be carried away in the euphoria of triumph. With the Six-Day War, a wave of religious nationalism swept the country. Those who had made fun of me two or three years before, accusing me of being an arrogant big mouth, couldn't come to me and say: "Sorry, we were wrong." They did not have the time; they were too busy shuttling from one victory celebration to the next. And although I shared the satisfaction—I had advocated a united Jerusalem and the recovery of our holy sites—the fervor of these converts made me uncomfortable. It did not seem right to me that the source of their newborn convictions should be their physical contact with the Greater Israel, defined by its biblical borders. Religion seems to me a territory distinct from geography.

But I cannot claim to be sinless myself. I, too, was swept away by the sweet taste of victory and, perhaps, by the sentimentalism evoked by the scenes belonging to the history of my people, my family, and my youth. My voice was too loud by a couple of decibels. By the time I pulled myself together, it was too late. Defying certain predictions, King Hussein seemed to be in no hurry to make his long-awaited phone call to the Defense Ministry, saying, "I'm ready to talk." As the days passed, I realized that the Arab states were rebuilding their armies for a further round and that the war that had just ended in glorious triumph would not be the last.

The conclusion was clear: we had erred in failing to take advantage of our Six-Day War victory, whose momentum ought to have carried us into the Arab capitals. Arriving there, we would have put a stop to this bloody chronicle of endless war once and for all. We should have headed for Cairo, Damascus, and Amman. In June 1967, it would have been fairly easy. Our tanks had crossed the Allenby Bridge and were already racing across the east bank of the Jordan when they received their pullback orders. No one dreamed that it was feasible and profitable to go on. We were not prepared operationally and even less so politically. Our expectations had been so low that our success threw us for a loop. We were so relieved to have knocked out the threat and in such a "deluxe" war—not a single bomb dropped on Tel Aviv—that we went home to celebrate.

No one had imagined that the gains we'd made were possible. Legends notwithstanding, our GHQ did not have drawers full of detailed contingency plans ready for any eventuality that might arise on the battlefield. At least part of the Six-Day War's land operations were improvised, conducted according to the quick thinking of then Minister of Defense Moshe Dayan—because there was not always time to plan the next battle in advance. The war was a rapid one, and its final hours called for even greater haste in order to forestall the cease-fire until we'd done what we had to. Several of the most important political and military accomplishments were created by field commanders, some during the very last moments of the fighting.

As minister of defense, I tried to learn from that experience. My deputy, Mottke Tzippori, came up with the proposal that we make a first-ever attempt to define Israel's war aims. Nothing easier, I thought. We had all the data, and we knew what we wanted. But the General Staff's deliberations revealed that this was precisely the snag: we did not know what we wanted. Our discussions about war aims reached a deadlock just as the Egyptian president set foot on our soil. Then it was not the time to argue about whether or not to cross the Suez Canal again in the next war. The issue was deleted from our agenda. Peace stood on the threshold, and that was now at the top of our priorities.

I have been an expert on war all my life, but I had not the faintest notion about peace. On the day I first assumed my duties as minister of defense, I was prepared to prevent another surprise attack against us, but never could have anticipated that five months later I'd be facing the greater shock of a peace offering. The vagaries of history were on my mind as I set out for Jerusalem's King David Hotel and the ceremonial banquet honoring President Sadat the evening after his address to the Knesset.

On the way to the hotel, I got an injection to relieve my pain, but I made an effort to remain cool and clear-headed. I knew I'd need it. Entering the banquet hall, I was instantly dismayed: the table was much too large. The diners were seated far apart, and how could I work up a conversation at such a great distance? Nobody had paid any attention to such details; neglect of that kind can cause considerable harm.

Everyone seated at the table—Egyptians no less than Israelis—looked as though they had just returned from a funeral. President Sadat's speech to the Knesset had cast a gloomy spell over this first encounter around a table between the leaders of Egypt and Israel. They were staring into their soup plates as though the only reason for coming together after all these years of enmity was to test the skills of the chef. I had already heard that Sadat had brought his own personal cook and even his own mug. Was this a matter of eating habits, or did it testify to his total mistrust of the Israelis?

I tried to keep an eye on Sadat without his noticing. He looked despondent. Begin sat at his side, tense. Both men appeared withdrawn, distanced from each other by whatever thoughts filled their minds. Their speeches were banal. The silences around the table were long and very significant.

All these years we had been saying there was no one to talk to.

Now we had found Arabs to talk to—only there seemed to be nothing to talk *about*.

I glanced at the people seated beside me. Their eyes were glued to their plates, and they took great care to keep their heads down.

I had no appetite. There are meals where the food is terrible but the atmosphere is friendly. And there are the opposite kind.

Then I realized that I was staring at the Egyptians as though they were from outer space. What had I thought previously? Had I expected their way of eating and drinking to be unlike that of ordinary mortals? I found myself waiting to see whether they'd wipe their mouths on the tablecloth. What strange thoughts can run through a man's mind after so many years of hostility!

All the same, here we were, seated around the same table—Israelis alongside Egyptians, without mediators. In spite of myself, I couldn't take my eyes off them. I noticed the elegance of their dress. Their suits were well tailored. The scent of expensive shaving lotion mingled with the aroma of the food.

"Your prime minister's speech was disappointing."

It took me a long moment to grasp that the remark had been addressed at me. I looked at the speaker. His expression was sour. I didn't know who he was. Later, I learned that he was Osman Ahmed Osman, a former minister, a millionaire contractor and Sadat's father-in-law.

I remarked that Sadat's speech hadn't exactly made me dance for joy. He gave no reply. This first attempt at conversation was a flop.

I tried to catch Sadat's eye, far away on the other side of the enormous table. It wasn't easy. Grabbing at the first opportunity to draw his attention, I raised my voice to relate a few sporadic reminiscences of my time in Cairo. The Egyptians were all listening with great interest. I dredged up every possible memory of the Egyptian capital in an attempt to prove my familiarity with it. But I was out of date, as I learned from the bemused expressions of the president and his companions.

Playfully, I speculated: "I wonder whether I'd be able to buy a villa in the Ma'adi district?"

Somehow or other, the conversation turned to war. I recalled how I had shot down a British plane in 1948. A spark of gratification lit Sadat's face. I knew he had no great love for the British.

Osman came back with a story of another war. He told of the reconstruction of the Suez Canal cities devastated during the War of Attrition against us.

I looked around. Strange. There were two other generals seated at the table: Dayan and Yadin, men whose orders at various times had wreaked havoc in Egypt and inflicted losses upon its people. What was going through the minds of the Egyptian leaders sitting beside them? Did Sadat know of my part in the order that had sent the Suez refinery up in flames? Osman had referred to the reconstruction of the Canal cities; did he remember that the man seated next to him, listening intently, had a hand in the destruction of Ismailia? I recalled the Phantoms I had sent to set off supersonic booms over Cairo. Did the Egyptians have the same memories when they addressed me?

There was Moshe Dayan, who, perhaps more than anyone, personified our recurrent wars against the Arabs. Now the Egyptians sneaked glances at him, turning their eyes away guiltily whenever he caught their gaze. Sadat was the only one to treat Dayan with indifference—was it affected?

My thoughts raced on feverishly. I knew this was no time for contemplation, certainly not for daydreaming. This meeting was too important, and too fateful, to be allowed to slip by. Taking advantage of Osman's remarks about the Canal cities, I stressed my own acquaintance with that area.

"I know the Suez Canal well," I broke in. "One of your snipers shot my son in the head . . ."

Silence fell.

"All's fair in love and war," Sadat said. A moment later, he added: "We intend to make peace. I wish your son well."

My Egyptian neighbor took advantage of the opportunity to mention the president's brother, a pilot, who had been killed near Bir Gafgaffa in the 1973 fighting. I remembered the incident well. After the war, we had made a great effort to locate the body, which we then returned to Egypt through the offices of the UN.

Everyone was looking at Sadat. He remained silent.

Begin continued the bloody balance sheet. "Two of the ministers seated here with us had brothers killed in the 1948 war," he said. He was referring to Yadin and Dayan. The Egyptians knew nothing of this. I had known Matti, Yadin's brother, quite well. He had been a pilot, and we'd gone out on one or two sorties together. Matti had been killed in a bombing attack on Egyptian warships off the Tel Aviv shore. I had not known Moshe Dayan's brother Zorik very well, but my wife, Re'uma, was close to him. Without warning, the ghosts of two men who had found their deaths thirty years before returned to haunt the banquet chamber. For them, as for the rest of the fourteen thousand Israelis killed in battle, Sadat's historic visit was too late.

The awkward silence was breaking down, but our conversation was confining itself almost exclusively to the bloodshed of the past. Perhaps it was unavoidable. After so many years of antagonism, it would have been impossible to begin anywhere but in the past. All the same, I hoped that the past would not cast its shadow over our present meeting.

The waiters brought in the dessert; it was very sweet, but I was left with a bitter taste. I could not help feeling that the Egyptian president's epoch-making visit was about to fade into depressing exchanges about bygone conflicts with no tangible effect on the cycle of war.

Meanwhile, Sadat and Begin had closeted themselves for a private talk. I had no idea what they were going to discuss, even though I—like my cabinet colleagues—pretended to be in on it all. I tried to put myself in Sadat's place. He had taken an irrevocable step, with no way back. The Arab world might never forgive him. His choice now lay between striding forward on his chosen course or hurtling over the precipice of greater bloodshed. What was going on inside the man's head? In his heart of hearts? I tried to imagine myself setting out the following morning to Damascus to meet Hafez al Assad, as Sadat was scheduled to do. What would I, a fellow Arab leader, say to him? How would I look him in the eye? Just thinking about it made my stomach turn over. That evening, I did not envy the Egyptian president.

Although my pain was getting worse, I did not want to miss an opportunity for further conversation with the Egyptians. I wouldn't even have minded sitting there listening to them in silence—although I am hardly the silent type. More than anything, I wanted to hear, first-hand, how they perceived things and what they proposed.

It turned out that they were equally eager to listen to us, so that only a few moments later four of us found ourselves seated in one of the hotel rooms with glasses in our hands. Yigael Yadin and I were on one side; Boutros Ghali and Mustafa Khalil on the other. Ghali, a slight man, looked as though he bore the fate of the Arab world on his skinny shoulders. He had replaced two successive foreign ministers who'd resigned in protest against the unexpected tack adopted by their president. Khalil was the head of the Arab World Bank as well as the secretary of Egypt's ruling party, the Socialist Union.

In an attempt to break the ice, I tried a bantering tone. "Mustafa," I asked, "how does socialism go along with being the director of a bank?"

He did not even smile. "Let's not talk about that," he said dryly. "I'll explain some other time."

My wisecrack appeared to have been out of place. At the rate things were going, I wondered if he'd have another opportunity to give me an explanation.

But the night was still young, and I don't give up easily. I cast around for ways of prolonging the conversation and found nothing better than my memories of Cairo. Even I was getting bored with the subject, but I couldn't think of anything else, and I had to start somewhere. The two Egyptians listened patiently.

Finally, Khalil interrupted me. "Don't tell anyone," he said, "but Cairo isn't what it used to be."

Ghali nodded his agreement. "We're like Bangladesh," he said, "and Cairo is like Calcutta."

That was a disappointment. I had been in India during World War II and remembered well the sights of Bombay and Calcutta— the poverty, the neglect, the filth, the oceans of humanity. My memories of Cairo were quite different.

One of them—I don't remember which—remarked: "Every year, a million people are added to our population."

"And there are a million Egyptians working abroad," the other added. "In Kuwait, in Saudi Arabia, in Bahrain, we supply every- thing—from professors to plumbers."

Gradually, the atmosphere began to thaw until we were talking like old acquaintances, as if we had never faced one another in battle, never harbored the most evil intentions toward each other.

I thought of my father, who had loved to play host to his Arab friends. How he would have relished sitting here in our company.

Somehow or other, we got around to Israel's defense problems. I tried to explain it all in a brief, thumbnail sketch, talking about Israel's "narrow waist," a mere forty miles from the Mediterra- nean Sea to Jordan for a nation of three million fighting for its very life.

"If we lose a single war, we've lost everything," I said.

"What are you scared of?" Khalil demanded. "You have nothing to fear from us. We won't defeat you in war. We have no military solution against you—you have to believe the president on that."

They never referred to Sadat by name—he was always "the pres- ident," spoken in admiring and reverent tones.

I went back to the wars we had endured and their heavy toll.

"Our finest youngsters were killed in those wars," I said.

"Contrary to what you believe"—Khalil stressed each word— "we are not indifferent to our casualties. We are pained over every one of our men who gets killed."

This indeed ran against my thinking on the subject. Sadat had often declared he did not mind if he had to sacrifice a million soldiers on the field of battle. We Israelis had enjoyed swapping tales about the Egyptians' indifference to human life, from which we gained the great satisfaction of moral superiority.

The two men estimated that Egypt had lost between eighty and one hundred thousand men in its wars against Israel. The number surprised me. I remembered how our planes used to photograph their military cemeteries, trying to assess the extent of their losses. Strange that I never expected them to show such feeling in speaking of their dead.

Leaving the wars of the past, we went on to those liable to break out in the future.

"Is it true that you intended to go to war against us a few weeks ago?" they asked.

I pointed out their error, explaining that it had been no more than a training exercise. We knew that our maneuvers put them on edge and made them lose a lot of sleep. In fact, we enjoyed goading them. But now, all of a sudden, in face-to-face conversation, it became clear that our exercise could have ended in the worst possible fashion, with Egypt and Israel fighting a further round because of a mere nothing.

"What are you afraid of?" I asked. "Together with the Jordanians and Syrians, you have five thousand tanks—we have barely three thousand."

"Three thousand, five hundred," Khalil corrected me.

He looked at me as he said it, trying to read my expression. What could I say? Tell him he was wrong? I preferred to remain silent.

Khalil added: "Why are you so anxious about your security? After all, you have the atom bomb." Again, he stared straight into my eyes.

Our conversation went on until late into the night, and we decided to find some way of continuing the exchange. We also agreed on a method of transmitting urgent messages through mutual friends in a European country.

As I left my meeting with Khalil and Ghali, I had the feeling that we were standing at a turning point. I did not know where the new course ahead would lead, but I tried to use my imagination.

Fifty-seven years of my life have been spent in the shade of war. I was twelve when I followed the war between Italy and Ethiopia, raging in the distance. Two years later, I was trying to fathom events in the Spanish Civil War. Those conflicts were remote and unfamiliar and did not greatly concern me. But when the Second World War broke out, I was fifteen years old, and like many of my generation, I could not remain indifferent. In my eagerness to be on the side of the better part of the human race, I enlisted in the RAF as soon as I turned eighteen.

On my return from service, I no longer saw war in such romantic colors. I knew very well what a high price had to be paid for victory. At the same time, I had few illusions that mankind would learn its lesson: warfare is embedded deep in the human soul. History moves on from war to war. The land of Israel has always been a battlefield. Indeed, the entire Bible is filled with tales of war.

For many years, my mother kept a composition I wrote in my childhood in which I argued that a Jewish state in Palestine would only arise out of the storms of war. It may have been such views, held from my early youth, that made me choose a military career. In the course of long years in uniform, I came to regard war as the greatest challenge a human being can face, demanding all his physical and psychological resources, which find their supreme expression on the field of battle.

Pilots do not usually encounter the other aspect of war, although they constitute the spearhead of their armies. Fliers take off from a cozy rear base after a briefing in an air-conditioned operations room with wall-to-wall carpeting. To them, the enemy has no human countenance. At most, he is a distant target somewhere below. It is far easier, emotionally, to drop a bomb on a building that houses a thousand soldiers than to fire at one man from ten yards away. I experienced this remoteness both as a combat pilot and as commander of the air force. But I also witnessed the other side of war—the widows, the orphans, the bereaved parents. I always found great difficulty in meeting their gaze.

Yet, however difficult the hours I spent in their company, I never forgot for a single moment that the survival of Israel is the supreme value, towering over and above human lives.

Now I found myself in a luxurious hotel in the heart of Jerusalem, seated opposite the Egyptians—to discover that not only were they human beings like us but that, like us, they mourned the deaths of their young men on the battlefields, and they, too, wished to break out of the vicious circle of war. The question was, of course, how to go about it? It isn't enough to desire peace: one must strive to attain it.

Peace can be concluded only with an enemy, I decided. In the course of one century, France and Germany had waged three bloody wars. Germans and Frenchmen came to detest one another to such an extent that it seemed eternal hatred would separate the two peoples. But today they are fellow members of the European Common Market, as though there had never been an angry word between them. The foes of yesterday are the allies of today.

In Israel, we were at a crossroads, although I had yet to find a name for the new situation, nor could I define it precisely. For the first time, one of the components of our security might be peace. As our contacts with the Egyptians grew more frequent, the weight and importance of this component could only increase.

These thoughts flitted through my mind, the mind of an Israeli who had spent most of his life at war, the minister charged with safeguarding the security of his country. One route leading off from the crossroads was a little footpath winding its way into the unknown; its direction was indicated by an arrow inscribed with the biblical behest: "Seek peace and pursue it."

5

RESPECT AND SUSPECT

At about 8:30 the morning after the banquet with the Egyptians in Jerusalem, the telephone rang by the side of my hotel bed. In an uncustomary haze from the painkillers, I picked up the receiver and heard a voice speaking English with a pronounced foreign accent: "Good morning, this is Mustafa . . ."

It was Mustafa Khalil, calling from one of the neighboring rooms in the King David Hotel.

Having regained my senses, I remembered where I was and felt wide-awake. Mustafa invited me to meet President Sadat. I gathered that Sadat, who is in the habit of going to bed very late, had been briefed by Khalil on the previous night's conversation—probably right after its conclusion.

Why me? I asked myself. Why had the president picked me for a private talk? Years of suspicion had left their mark on me, making me skeptical. What did he want of me? The views I had expressed the previous evening—at the banquet as well as in private conversation with Khalil and Ghali—reflected the most intransigent Israeli positions. I would hear of no compromise on anything to do with the security of my country. Such opinions could never be acceptable to the Egyptians. In that case, what could President Sadat possibly expect from me?

My initial assumption was that Sadat felt concern over the attitude of our defense establishment, which was liable to oppose for security reasons any withdrawal from the occupied territories. It

occurred to me that he might wish to soften me up. Perhaps I had
been depicted as a hawk, a warmonger or expansionist. Maybe in
his present assessment of the situation I was the principal obstacle
in the way of whatever mysterious objectives he had.

I was very cautious. The course I would adopt in my talk with
the Egyptian president, from beginning to end, was: "Respect
him—and suspect him."

While preparing for my meeting with Sadat, I was somewhat
anxious about possible snags in communication due to language
difficulties. From Sadat's television appearances, I knew that he
did not speak English with swift fluency. His English is quite good
but slow. Later, I realized that it has a charm of its own, which has
earned him the affection of millions of people whose native tongue
is English. His pauses and hesitations have a warm human quality
that adds to his credibility.

I headed for the sixth floor of the hotel, to Suite 622. In its time,
this suite has housed some of the world's most prominent personalities, and now Anwar Sadat was there, awaiting me.

Sadat was dressed in an elegant dark-blue suit. At that first
moment, as we looked at each other, he appeared nervous.

I was equally on edge. Our two nations were separated by torrents of blood, and in our personal biographies, each of us could
show scars of the century-long conflict that had sent successive
generations to war, ever since the confluence of Zionism with the
Arab national movement. Returning home after two thousand
years of exile, the people of Israel had found another people settled
on its land. Two just causes were locked in mortal combat. In the
course of the years, there were very few genuine attempts to reach
understanding or seek a compromise. The calls to war always
drowned out the whispered prayers for peace.

Shaking hands with the Egyptian president, I said: "Before we
start our talk, there's something I must tell you." He stiffened, but
I went on: "As a professional, my compliments to you on the surprise of the Yom Kippur War."

I stressed the word "surprise." I saw no reason to compliment
him on the war itself. I thought of the 2,800 bereaved Israeli families who would find no grounds for praising the Egyptian president
for that.

It may have been my imagination, but I thought I saw a sparkle
in Sadat's eyes. My compliment had struck a chord. He gave me a
light tap on the shoulder, as if to say: "Let's not talk of war now." I
got the hint. I noticed three other men in the room: Mustafa Khalil,
Boutros Ghali and Osman Ahmed Osman.

Sadat led me to a small couch. I launched into a reprimand.

"Mr. President, your speech in the Knesset yesterday was very harsh. There isn't a government in Israel that could accept what you said and remain in office as long as thirty seconds."

The president's expression grew grave.

Anxious to soften the impact, I added: "But in my estimation, your step could take us along the right path. I must confess that neither I, nor anyone else in Israel, foresaw such a step. Last night, I told Osman that I hoped you made your speech the way people behave in business: You started with the price high, with the aim of coming down later."

Sadat briefly restated the main points of his speech to the Knesset the previous day. "Arab soil is sacred, and we cannot let you keep our land. But we do understand that you have security problems."

What was going on in the mind of the Egyptian president as he sat facing me? I had given orders that led to the deaths of thousands of Egyptians during the Six-Day War and the subsequent War of Attrition. Would he be capable of forgetting? How did he see me at this moment: as a man of peace or a warmonger? Would this be a one-time meeting, with our next encounter on the battlefield? How many more wars would our two peoples have to endure before we realized that too much blood had been shed? I would have given a great deal to be able to read his thoughts at that moment.

"Mr. President," I said, lightly touching his hand, "please come and look outside."

As I led him to the window, I noticed that the others had tiptoed out, leaving us to ourselves. Sadat pressed against the windowpane. Jerusalem was spread out below us in all its glory. The suite looked out over the most breathtaking vista of the city: the Old City walls, the shining Dome of the Rock, the Tower of David, Mount Scopus, the Mount of Olives. The sunlight flooded the ancient monuments, tinting them with a unique gold light.

"Look at Jerusalem!" I said. "Tell me, how can you divide it? Look at it all! You can't turn the clock back eleven years."

"But Arab soil is sacred," Sadat reiterated. "I wouldn't be able to look into the eyes of a single Egyptian if you remained in the territories you occupied in 1967."

Sadat tried to put on a bold face, but he failed. The foremost leader of the Arab world was uneasy—no less than I. His words were sparing. He was very cautious. There was a degree of surprise in his voice—possibly at himself and at his own actions. He had taken a historic step, with no way back—and he knew it. The hostile reactions of the Arab world told him so.

It struck me that at this moment I was fulfilling the dream of an entire generation of Israeli leaders, many of whom had spent years trying to arrange meetings with Arab rulers. A few were successful—although their encounters were always secret—but all attempts to reach an understanding had failed. Almost every Israeli leader has secretly met with King Hussein of Jordan. But no one had succeeded in meeting an Egyptian leader. The morning of November 21, 1977, was the first time.

Sadat spoke of his concern over the might of the Soviets and their expansionist designs. He knew them well; it was he who had expelled them from Egypt. I heard more than a shade of self-satisfaction as he described the day he'd summoned the Soviet ambassador and instructed him to repatriate the fifteen thousand Soviet advisers and officers then in Egypt. "I ordered them to leave within fifteen days—they did it in fourteen."

Sadat's decision to expel the advisers is etched in his memory as one of the most outstanding of his life. It sowed the seeds of the enormous error on our part that allowed our army to be taken unawares in the Yom Kippur War. As the last Soviet advisers left Egyptian soil, Israel adopted the view that without the Russians the Egyptian army was so weakened that it would be beyond its power to cross the Suez Canal.

"It's time for us to stop killing one another." Sadat set our conversation back on its course. "You have problems, we, too, have fundamental problems, and that's why I decided to come to Jerusalem." He spoke of the Arab-Israeli conflict in its various aspects, touching on the security problems of the whole region. I sensed that I was facing a man who, while racking his brains about his country's enormous difficulties, simultaneously allowed his vision to encompass half the world, from Gibraltar to the straits of Bab al-Mandab.

"I hope that, together, we shall inaugurate a new era with new possibilities," I said, adding something about the needless wars our two countries had waged. I noticed that he said nothing about our past conflicts, as though they were over and forgotten. He preferred to focus on the confrontations between the Great Powers and the role of our region in that conflict—his vision of the future.

"You must get to know the Egyptian people," he told me. "I know my people. They are a good people. If you convince them, they will follow you all the way. They have a sense of humor—but they also have fundamental problems of poverty and education."

I groped for a suitable response. Should I go back to the tales of my RAF service in Cairo to prove that I knew something about Egypt and its people? At the last moment, I decided not to weary him with all that, particularly as it was getting late. I knew that the time for our meeting was limited, even though Sadat possesses the gift of behaving as if he's got all the time in the world.

Instead, I gave him a detailed account of Israel's defense problems, stressing in particular the country's "narrow waist," the slim strip of coastal plain separating Netanya's beach from the pre-1967 border city of Tulkarem. "Mr. President," I said. "In 1948, I strafed Egyptian soldiers twenty miles from Tel Aviv, and I don't want to have to do it again!"

He repeated his stock phrase about the sanctity of Arab soil, going on to point out the benefits that would accrue to Israel if we could put an end to the cycle of war.

Throughout our talk, I looked straight into his eyes, as if to ferret out whatever lay concealed behind them. He noticed that I was not shifting my gaze, and he, too, fixed his eyes on me. We spent a long time in this covert facedown: which of us would be the first to lower his gaze? I did not give in.

The wheels were spinning wildly in my mind. Who was this man? I got the impression of an actor getting enormous enjoyment from the great drama, casting himself in the leading role. Was he playing out an act of deception unparalleled in modern history? Could one single man lead millions of Israelis astray, as well as tens of millions of Egyptians? President Sadat's eyes gave no answer to my queries. I could not help looking to the past for an analogous situation. Would this be like the Japanese delegation that had held talks in Washington at the precise hour that its air force was driving its fangs into Pearl Harbor? Nor could I forget that it was Sadat who had misled us in 1973.

The face before me bore a slight smile to cover up his unease and embarrassment. Two rows of white teeth stood out in contrast to his swarthy complexion. Sadat began to speak again, explaining that it was vital to make haste toward a peace treaty.

"The war between Arab nationalism and Zionism didn't start in 1967," I answered. "Mr. President, I've been fighting since I was young—you can't expect us to end it so quickly. I can only promise that I shall use all my imagination to reach an agreement."

Seated at his side, I still regarded him as an enemy. It never occurred to me that he intended to propose a full peace treaty with everything that entailed: embassies, airlines, the lot. For my part, I hoped for nothing more than some agreement that would prevent a renewed war.

"These past six months, we've been getting on your nerves in the Sinai," I told him. "You thought—wrongly—that we were about to launch a strike, and you concluded that you had to mount a preemptive attack." I reconstructed the events of recent days in the Sinai in an attempt to coax him toward some agreement that would, if nothing more, at least prevent a war breaking out by mistake.

"You're nervous and jumpy," Sadat said.

"Mr. President," I answered, after a moment's hesitation, during which I debated whether to reveal everything I knew. "You moved up your Fourth Division, you transferred Migs, you shifted SA-6 surface-to-air missiles, you called up reservists. Did you imagine we'd think you were doing all that on account of some minor exercise of ours?"

"You're nervous and jumpy," he repeated.

"What you say doesn't make sense. The whole thing in the Sinai could blow up, and that'll be the end of it! We have to make some arrangement," I said candidly.

Sadat paid scant attention to my account of the recent troop movements by both armies that had come so close to drawing Israel and Egypt into a war almost willy-nilly. These military details interested him very little; in his eyes, they were trivial and unimportant compared to the "big business" of his mission.

My gaze was still fixed on him, and he probably felt uncomfortable, but I didn't give a damn. I was trying to gauge his credibility.

The Egyptian president must have guessed what was on my mind. "I am a man who keeps his word. Believe me, you can trust me. I have said, and I repeat: no more war." He emphasized each word.

I wanted to believe him, but I couldn't—yet. Even if he meant every word he said now, tomorrow he might still draw his sword. And there was no certainty that his successors would follow the same course. I said that in so many words. "Mr. President, treaties are signed by nations, not by leaders." I gave him the traditional Jewish blessing: "May you live to be a hundred and twenty—"

"No, no!" He laughed. "Not that much!"

"All right, then may you live till a hundred and look like twenty. Look at me—the defense minister of the state of Israel. Last week, I was almost killed in an accident. You, too, might suddenly go, and what will our agreement be worth when your commander in chief, Mohammed Ali Fahmy, moves three thousand Egyptian tanks up to our border?"

"It would be an error and political suicide for Egypt—and for you." Sadat spoke dryly; apparently, my question came as no surprise, and his response may even have been prepared beforehand.

The room was air-conditioned, but in our agitation both of us were sweating profusely. The hands of the clock were advancing fast. Although no hints were dropped, I realized it was time to conclude. His schedule was tight.

The Egyptian president broke into my thoughts. "There's an Arab delegation from the West Bank waiting outside."

"All in all, you'll find we don't treat them too badly," I said.

"If they submit any request, can I make promises?" he asked.

I turned the matter over quickly. What could they possibly ask for? Nothing more than reunification of families or paroling a few convicts. At a moment like this, it would be generous on my part to meet him halfway.

"I'll do my best," I said in Arabic. Sadat smiled.

I left, with a sigh of relief as I went. Outside the door stood the delegation from the West Bank and Gaza. It was a small group—all the other leaders were boycotting Sadat's visit. Before his arrival, I had imagined that an event of this sort would draw all the notables of the occupied territories to the King David Hotel in a long line stretching from the hotel lobby to the Lebanese border. I was mistaken. The Arab leaders stayed at home out of fear of retribution by the PLO—a slap in the face to the president of the largest Arab state.

As I walked along the corridor away from Sadat's suite, my mind was weighing two conflicting possibilities. If the man I had just met was carrying out an exercise in strategic deception—as many of us were certain he was—our situation might be grim, though far from hopeless: I had faith in the might of our army. Should the Egyptians instigate a war, I knew we'd defeat them. Furthermore, I thought it would be politically stupid of Sadat to do it—he could not afford anything less than total victory, and that would never be.

On the other hand, I had a number of good reasons to believe him. I knew he hadn't come to Jerusalem for our good looks. First, he'd had to reach a very difficult decision—even more difficult than his decision to go to war in October 1973. At that time, the Arab world was solidly behind him, whereas his current visit to Jerusalem had begun to isolate him. All over the Middle East, from Damascus to Benghazi, in Amman and in Baghdad, he was being denounced as a traitor and burned in effigy, while his ambassadors were given marching orders.

If, in spite of all that, he had taken the fateful step—and taken it clearheadedly—it was for the good of his country. The burden of war was unbearably heavy. Egypt's economy was tottering. The high birthrate was dragging it down in internal strangulation. Rebuilding Egypt's economy and salvaging its social structure called for all available resources and all the nation's energies to be diverted into those channels.

Sadat must have concluded that he could not defeat Israel on the field of battle—certainly, he could not annihilate us, as he perhaps desired. He may even have feared an Israeli reprisal campaign that would thrust him still deeper into the quicksands.

Instead, Sadat had chosen the course that took him to Jerusalem.

The more I thought about it and the more I discussed it with experts and intelligence staff in the following days, the greater was my trust in him and the step he had taken.

Nevertheless, there was one question left unresolved. It is one that has been posed since the emergence of the human race: was any single individual capable of shouldering the entire burden of history? History books are strewn with the names of leaders, but not one of them could have shaped the course of events unaided. Sadat had broken through a psychological barrier single-handedly—one lone man against the entire Arab world. "I will lead the way, and they will all come puffing after me," he had said. Would he have the strength to hold out?

In coming to Jerusalem, Sadat was putting Israel to the test. He had every right to believe that should his visit fail to bear fruit, he would isolate Israel in world opinion, besmirch her reputation in the eyes of her friends, and sow dissension among her people. To this day, I do not know whether he foresaw the enormity of the problem he was about to place before us. He was unexpectedly confronting Israel with an Arab of a type quite unlike those we had grown used to over thirty years. The greatest enemy Israel had ever faced now stood in her capital, promising there would be no more war and attempting to convince her leaders of his genuine interest in peacemaking.

On leaving him after our meeting, even before I had time to fully digest everything I had heard, I could already sense the great change we would have to face. This premonition reminded me of my feelings after the Six-Day War: everything that had seemed unassailable truth suddenly had to be, if not dismissed as outdated and anachronistic, at least thoroughly reconsidered. And now, after we had always assumed that no Arab leader would be prepared

to talk to us at all—certainly not out in the open and even more
certainly not about peace—one morning, we woke up and found
him there. In our home.

A momentary wave of anxiety filled my heart. Were we genuinely prepared for this? Do we truly regard ourselves as an integral
part of the region in which we live? Do we see it as our natural
environment? Israel after Sadat's visit would not be the same as
she was one day before his arrival. In its light, we might suddenly
realize how wrong we had been throughout all these years that had
elapsed since the Six-Day War, when we'd sat with folded arms
waiting for the telephone to ring and the Arabs to plead with us.

Obviously, we would have to argue with Sadat, and the arguments would be tough, hard-hitting, and prolonged. If we went
along with him, we would have to make some undoubtedly painful
concessions. But how far were we prepared to go? To what extent
were we in agreement over concessions? Would everyone share my
view that it was vital to plunge into the bargaining—but with
great caution; that we should offer our shirts—but take care not to
lose our pants; that we should maneuver in such a manner that
Sadat might end up with all the cards in his hand—but we'd be left
holding the joker?

He was scheduled to leave in a few hours' time. I had missed his
arrival; I had to see him off. Who knew when we'd next meet or
how we'd communicate until then? At midday, when Sadat was
about to leave Jerusalem, I had myself wheeled down to the hotel
entrance. Sadat was already seated in his car, together with Israeli
President Katzir and Prime Minister Begin. I got out of my wheelchair and stepped toward him. Seeing me, he leaped out.

"Where are you going?" he demanded.

"I'm going to see you off at the airport," I told him.

"You go straight to the hospital!" he said in a voice used to
military command.

"*Allah ma'ak!* God be with you!" I said in Arabic.

Sadat appeared very touched. I was equally moved. Seizing me,
he gave me a resounding kiss—at the same moment, whispering in
my ear: "Our contacts will be kept up by way of Rumanian President Ceausescu."

6

LIGHT AT THE END OF THE TUNNEL

A day or two after Sadat's visit, the chief of staff, Motta Gur, undertook a tour of the Sharm el Sheik area. On his return, he told me of soldiers who had asked him when they were going to pull out and hand this wilderness over to the Egyptians.

This was precisely what I had feared.

I had been in India the day the war against Japan came to an end. Seventy-two hours after the radio announcer had heralded Japan's capitulation, discipline in the well-organized British army began to slacken. Suddenly, the soldiers no longer felt themselves on alert; all they wanted was to go home.

With this experience in mind, I summoned the chief of staff and a number of generals. Foreseeing that we were entering a new epoch, I wanted to hear the opinions of the army commanders on Sadat's visit. As a result of my accident and the rapid train of events, I had yet to learn what their views were. I hoped that their response would correspond to the one that came from Cairo: speaking on behalf of the Egyptian armed forces, War Minister Mohammed Abdel Gamasy had declared Sadat's mission "a courageous step toward a just peace."

I had a further reason for consulting the army chiefs: even if Sadat's visit marked a shift in the center of gravity of the Arab-Israeli confrontation—into the political arena—I knew that the strength of our army was our best guarantee, not solely as a bulwark against strategic deception but as a surety of Israel's political freedom of maneuver.

In addressing the commanders, I stressed the dangers liable to arise as a result of the visit. If nothing came of it, the whole world would likely turn against us. According to Western opinion, the picture would be clear: Sadat had made his great leap—and we'd failed to meet him halfway. Then, with the sympathy of the world bestowed upon him, Sadat would find it easy to go to war. If events did indeed develop in this fashion, my assessment was that war could be expected within a period of six months to a year.

Furthermore, I pointed out, the high level of motivation displayed by our soldiers—whether in training or on the battlefield—was one of the principal components of our national might. Ever since the creation of the state—and even earlier—we had gone to war and launched reprisal or preemptive raids buoyed by the conviction that we were fighting for our lives, for our very existence. We knew that on no account could we afford to lose a single war—because that was liable to be the end.

There was scarcely a person in Israel who failed to grasp the enormity of Sadat's move, and the great turnabout ensuing from his journey to Jerusalem, from the fact that he had addressed the Knesset, face to face with the enemies who had humiliated his army and sown devastation in his cities. Even if his demands were uncompromising, one couldn't help admiring his first step.

Should war break out after Sadat's far-reaching stride toward an understanding with Israel, it could undermine the motivation of many young Israelis. Whenever they had been called upon to go to war in the past, our men knew they had been summoned because there was no other choice open, because all other options had been exhausted. Now, for the first time, they were liable to ask themselves whether their national leadership had done everything in its power to prevent the war by setting the country on a peaceful course.

As defense minister, the immediate question I had to face was simple, although I did occasionally word it in a dramatic form: how could we look our soldiers in the face as we sent them into battle if we did not first make sure we had explored all the political options opened up by Sadat's visit? Contrary to the views of some of my political colleagues, this was no mere rhetorical question. With my responsibility for Israel's security, I regarded it as a matter of supreme military importance.

In addressing my General Staff colleagues, I was also frank about the other side of the coin. The dramatic impact of Sadat's visit could lull us all into a state of euphoria that might infect the army. My anxieties were reinforced by the report from the chief of staff about his talk with the soldiers in the Sinai. I feared that our troops' alertness would be reduced and that they would spend their training exercises in releasing doves of peace instead of firing off artillery shells. It's an unfortunate fact that without the tension of an enemy in sight, it's far more difficult to keep an army disciplined and motivated.

There was another military danger that could not be discounted. Throughout my term of office as defense minister, we had been holding extensive talks with the Americans, arising from their commitments to provide us with arms and military assistance. The new atmosphere created by Sadat's visit was likely to lead to a slackening off in this area, as the urgency appeared diminished. I instructed our purchasing mission and our military attachés to launch a full-scale blitz on our arms suppliers, to impress upon them that the end of hostilities was a long way off.

At the same time, we greatly reinforced our intelligence apparatus, which was directed to garner every possible grain of information about Egypt and the Arab world.

In the assessment of intelligence chief General Shlomo Gazit, the Arab states were in disarray—no less than Israel. Events had been swifter and more dramatic than their leaders' capacity to take them in. According to Gazit, Sadat was putting us to the test; he was prepared to wait, but not overlong.

But there were also contrary assessments stemming from the mistrust that had taken root in the course of thirty years. One senior member of the defense establishment made no secret of his opinion: Sadat had learned his lessons from Hitler. At the outset of his political career, Hitler had invited European leaders to see him, overwhelming them with displays of good will. It was much later before they realized it was a ruse. In this man's view, Sadat was well acquainted with Hitler's technique.

Chief of Staff Motta Gur adhered to the line he had taken before Sadat's arrival: Sadat would settle for nothing less than our return to the pre-1967 borders and a Palestinian state. Gur put it bluntly: "Peace without Zionism is something I don't want. Zionism without peace? That's feasible. Sadat wants peace, but on his own terms—and we can't accept those terms."

All of a sudden, we were forced to admit that the other side also wanted peace. The big question was: what kind of peace would it be? Sadat's demands, as formulated in his speech to the Knesset as well as in private conversation, were unyielding. On the other hand, it was equally clear that we had our own demands: 90 percent of the voters in the 1977 Knesset elections supported parties that saw the Jordan River as our defensible boundary—in other words, including the West Bank territories. The gap between Israel and Egypt appeared far too wide to be bridged overnight.

The wave of euphoria that swept the country threw up an intriguing paradox. Before the elections that brought the Likud to power in May 1977, voters were warned that Menachem Begin was liable to lead Israel into a new war by his inflexible attitude. There were similar undertones to the comments heard in Israel and abroad when he took up his duties as prime minister. All along his political path, Begin has borne the image of a doctrinaire hawk, a politician who knows no compromise. Even when he was firmly established in office, he continued to be haunted by his image as the former leader of an underground—and, indeed, the underground does remain more alive for him than for many since he still surrounds himself with cronies who served under him in pre-state days.

But I ought not to have been surprised by Begin's peace moves. Had I paid attention to his speech at the Herut conference in the winter of 1977, before he became prime minister, I would have heard him utter words quite out of keeping with his image. "Should the Likud be called upon to form a government," Begin said then, "our first concern will be to prevent war. The Likud government will undertake peace initiatives. We shall request a friendly state, which maintains regular diplomatic relations with Israel and with our Arab neighbors, to convey our proposal to initiate negotiations for the signing of a peace treaty. These negotiations must be direct, without any preconditions, and free from peace formulas produced from outside"—that is, America, Europe, or other countries. Begin laid down his terms for a peace treaty: the border would run through the Sinai and across the Golan Heights; Arab nationals in Israel would be guaranteed cultural autonomy.

The day after our election triumph, I went to congratulate Begin. As he shook my hand, his first words were: "Our government will do everything to prevent war." He repeated this on many subsequent occasions, possibly as a way of ridding himself of the image of warmonger.

However, the first harbingers of peace had made their appearance even earlier—only no one had noticed them. In effect, it is impossible to pinpoint the exact moment, the precise date or event, that marked the beginning of the peace process. All the same, there can be no doubt that the foundations were laid by the disengagement agreements that followed the Yom Kippur War, separating the defense forces of Israel and Egypt.

Far from the political spotlights, there were moments when those agreements appeared to be in danger. In 1975, for example, Israeli intelligence discovered that the Iraqis were making preparations to assassinate President Sadat.

Should the plot succeed, there was reason to fear that the resulting upheaval would sweep away the fragile structure of coexistence created by the disengagement agreements. It was therefore vital for Israel's own interests to foil the Iraqis' intention. The most obvious way to do so would be to forewarn the Egyptian president. But how was that to be accomplished?

Israel's leaders finally decided to entrust the information to Henry Kissinger, who was in the Middle East on a shuttle mission. Kissinger transmitted the warning to Sadat. Perhaps that was what persuaded Sadat to see us in a more benevolent light. Was it then that he started toying with the idea of an understanding?

There were other developments that foreshadowed the drama of November 1977. Eight months earlier, in March—two months ahead of the elections that were to bring Begin to power—a senior intelligence officer addressed the Knesset's Foreign Affairs and Defense Committee. In one hand, he held a sheet of paper enumerating signs of impending war that had been picked up from Egypt; in his other hand was a second sheet listing indications of peace. The peace list was longer.

Menachem Begin was not enthralled with the Yom Kippur disengagement agreements. The Likud had blasted them totally in its election program. In fact, before the elections, those agreements had reached a point of stalemate. At that time Israel's peace strategy rested upon two contradictory assumptions: that the Arabs would not be prepared to settle for less than Israel's returning to the June 4, 1967, borders and that Israel would never even consider a return to those borders. No Israeli leader wanted to find himself one day in the quandary of the late prime minister, Levi Eshkol, who had faced an Arab invasion in 1967 from the north, east, and south, within long, almost indefensible borders. The tempo of the Middle East arms race and the sophistication of the weapons supplied to the Arabs made a return to the pre-Six-Day War frontiers an impossibility—at least, in military terms. The 1973 war added even further poignancy to this conviction, as many Israelis asked themselves what would have happened had Sadat caught our army napping not on the Suez Canal but on the old international border. Just posing the question was enough to send shivers up our spines.

If public opinion fell short of unanimity on certain points, it was

mainly over the question of what Israel's final defensible boundaries ought to be. The old borders were not an option.

The Labor party leaders who had been in power until the spring
of 1977 never troubled themselves overmuch on this issue. Prior to
the Yom Kippur War, they had rejected the idea of an interim
agreement in the Sinai that would have Israel pull back from the
banks of the Suez Canal. Their refusal stemmed largely from their
conviction that Egypt would not choose to use its armed forces, for
its own political reasons. Ironically enough, the election campaign, cut short by the Yom Kippur War, had found the heads of
the Labor Alignment depicting the Suez Canal as the world's most
effective antitank ditch, a barrier that they claimed would deter
any Egyptian bid to alter the status quo.

In June 1967, there were few Israelis who believed that their
country could long hold onto the territories it had occupied during
the fighting. Everyone remembered 1957 and the Soviet-American
pressure exerted on the government of the late prime minister,
David Ben-Gurion, to withdraw from the Sinai. After 1967, the
Israeli army, haunted by this memory, had hastened to demolish
Jordanian and Egyptian army camps in the territories it had just
occupied—so certain did it seem that these areas could not remain
in our hands.

A few months later, when it became evident that the Americans
were in no hurry to insist on a withdrawal, the whole picture
changed. The United States acted according to a doctrine that
reached its high point during Kissinger's period of office, in which
Israel's battlefield successes were exploited to eliminate—or, at
least, to reduce—Soviet influence in the Arab states. At the same
time, there were growing demands inside Israel to hold onto the
territories as long as possible. The early-warning areas provided
by the Sinai peninsula and the West Bank soon became part of our
defense planning.

As long as it remained possible, the Labor governments adhered
to a policy of no peace, no war. Our situation along the banks of the
Suez Canal and the Jordan River seemed stable enough to be
under no threat from the Arab armies. This assumption was undermined by the Yom Kippur War, even though everyone continued
to adhere to it with regard to our new borders and the changed
political conditions.

When Menachem Begin had spoken of the necessity of achieving
peace, his words could have been interpreted as being directed at
Egypt. He knew the price would include large sections of the Sinai,
but Begin never regarded the desert peninsula as belonging to the

historical land of Israel. With the prospect of a peace agreement with Egypt, he was able to contemplate ceding portions of the Sinai not inhabited by settlements and not necessary for defense, without his political or historical conscience troubling him. But the climate awaiting the newly elected prime minister had not been one of peace.

Sadat's visit to Jerusalem marked more than a great turning point in the relationship between the two peoples and striking proof that a peace settlement was feasible; it was, first and foremost, the light at the end of the tunnel. With a single blow and in the most dramatic fashion imaginable, Sadat had erased what might be described as the greatest failure of the Zionist movement.

The history of the Jewish people's revival in its ancestral homeland is a success story in three principal spheres: resettling, defense, and worldwide recognition. Within a brief time, less than thirty years, during the most terrible period in Jewish history, the Zionist movement created something out of nothing in the land of Israel. Its goal was to solve the problem of Jews living as a minority, often oppressed, in foreign nations, deprived of a land of their own and all the ties that ensue—language, culture, a link between the past and future.

Zionism is, above all, an enterprise of creative construction. While the country was under Turkish and then British domination and in the face of growing Arab hostility, the Zionist movement established from the end of the last century extensive settlements, the rudiments of an industry, and scientific research centers.

At a certain point, it became necessary to shift the focus from construction to defense to safeguard Zionism's creations from destruction. When the menace of a Nazi invasion loomed on the horizon, young Jews—myself included—volunteered for the British army. When the British insisted on remaining in the country and denying it its independence, our young people took to the warpath in the ranks of four distinctive underground organizations. These later gave rise to the Jewish self-defense forces, which validated the 1948 Declaration of Independence and continue, to this day, to shoulder the burden of the state's existence.

In the course of all this, Zionism's political wing found ways of drumming up worldwide sympathy for the Jewish people's resurgence in its homeland. Theodor Herzl was the first to grasp the importance of that recognition. He met with the Turkish sultan in a bid to convince him to give his blessing and protection to the establishment of a Jewish national homeland in Palestine. My uncle, Chaim Weizmann, met with the world's greatest leaders, some of whom he coaxed into issuing declarations of support, such as the Balfour Declaration in 1917, which acknowledged the right of the Jewish people to a national homeland in Palestine, along with more concrete actions like the UN resolution of 1947 on the partition of Palestine and the establishment of a Jewish state.

These three courses of action—resettling, security, and political contacts with other nations—gave the Zionist movement a recognized status long before the establishment of the state of Israel. In effect, the proclamation of the state was nothing more than a formality. Even under the British Mandate government, the Jewish community in Palestine followed the directives of the Zionist institutions, which fixed the rates of taxation, drew up the school syllabus, and determined the quotas of recruits for the British army, or for the Hagana—the largest of the underground organizations, which came under their direct control.

There was only one sphere in which the Zionist movement remained unsuccessful: it failed to gain the recognition of the Arab world in whose vicinity it was staking its claim. Even though Palestine's Jews and Arabs had long lived side by side, on terms going beyond the formally correct, there were sporadic clashes between them that overshadowed their neighborly relations, providing a kind of bloody preface to the prolonged military confrontation between Israel and the Arab states. In 1929, the Arabs of Hebron massacred the Jews in their city. Similar incidents occurred elsewhere. In 1936, a nationalist wave engulfed the Palestinian Arabs, a sort of local reverberation from the great Arab revolt sparked off by British intelligence against the Turkish empire, which then held sway over the Middle East. Echoes of this national awakening were late in reaching the Arab villages in Palestine, but when the Arabs finally got the message, they turned on their Jewish neighbors. They assaulted Jewish wayfarers, attacked Jewish settlements on the outskirts of the large towns, and undermined security on the roads, obliging the Jews to fight back, blow for blow.

In effect, these bloody incidents went on incessantly, right up to the establishment of the state of Israel in 1948—though in varying degrees of intensity, depending on the fluctuating mood of local Arab leaders or stimulated by political events indicating that the world was coming around to permitting the Jews to set up their homeland in Palestine.

During this entire period, we never gave up our settlement work.

I remember touring the country with my father. "See that hill?" he would say. "At one time, we could have bought it for twenty-five bishlik"—about five hundred dollars.

"Why didn't you buy it?" I would ask.

"We didn't have the money!"

Spurred on by their national leadership, the Jews engaged intensively in land purchase. But they could not buy up all the land in the country. Had they done so, it is highly probable that the confrontation between Israel and the Arabs—in effect, a dispute over land—would have been lessened. One proof is that the land we bought then is not under dispute or the object of negotiation today.

Be that as it may, the fact is that the Zionist movement failed in all its attempts to gain the recognition of its Arab neighbors— and there were many attempts in the course of the years. My uncle, Chaim Weizmann, met with King Faisal immediately after World War I in an attempt to convince him of the common interests between the Jewish resurgence and the Arab national movement. Ben-Gurion met with many local Arab leaders. Golda Meir met with Jordan's King Abdullah before the 1948 fighting was at its height. After the Six-Day War, Israeli leaders met with King Hussein. Similar contacts— at a lower level—were conducted intermittently through the mediation of men of good will from Europe and the United States—without, however, leading to any face-to-face talks.

All these attempts failed—primarily because of the Arabs' belief that it would be possible to destroy the state of Israel. Some of them continue to adhere to that belief: Arab terrorist organizations refer specifically to their goal of Israel's physical annihilation, to be followed by the expulsion of its inhabitants to the countries from which they or their parents came. The Arabs are convinced that with the manpower at their disposal, their economic potential, and the support of their allies, they will one day overcome the qualitative disparity between their forces and those of Israel.

For twenty-nine years, the Egyptians held the same view. Time after time, they were trounced on the field of battle. In 1967, their air force was beaten in less than three hours. The sands of the Sinai saw their army humiliated as no other army has ever been humiliated—nevertheless, they continued to believe that they would one day succeed in overcoming Israel, in forcing her capitulation, in putting an end to her independent existence.

Paradoxically enough, the Egyptians may have begun to change their minds after 1967, and more strongly after the Yom Kippur

War, when their army managed to cross the Suez Canal. If under optimal conditions, with the advantage of total surprise, they had not been able to defeat Israel—on the contrary, they had been forced back on the defensive, with fighting ending 101 kilometers from Cairo—they must have concluded that they would never bring it off. At the same time, their partial success in battle had restored their trampled honor, so that they may not have had to prove themselves so urgently.

The seeds of the acceptance of Israel were sown after the 1973 war. When President Sadat landed at Ben-Gurion Airport, the Zionist movement could chalk up a success in the sphere that had seen nothing but setbacks: the Arab world's foremost leader had recognized it and acknowledged the necessity of peaceful coexistence with it.

The early feelers for an understanding with Egypt—our first important contact with the Arab world—centered about Moshe Dayan, then Israel's foreign minister. At the time of Sadat's Jerusalem visit, I knew nothing of Dayan's encounter with Egyptian Deputy Prime Minister Hassan Tohamy in Morocco in 1977.

The Moroccan monarchy maintains a tradition of warm patronage toward its country's Jews. Ever since the seventeenth century, Jews have occupied senior posts in the royal court. Well protected on the whole, the Moroccan Jewish community flourished. Its customs were adopted as part of the country's national culture. In the 1950s and 1960s, there was mass emigration of Jews bound for Israel. The king adopted a moderate policy on the conflict with Israel even though he sent units to the Golan Heights to fight alongside the Syrians during the 1973 war.

The year 1975 marked the beginning of Morocco's struggle for the western Sahara. Confronted with the Algerian forces and the Polisario Front's guerrillas, King Hassan sought international support and decided to employ the services of the Jewish community for that purpose. At the same time, he began to call openly for a fusion between "Jewish genius and Arab might." Hassan urged Sadat and the Saudi emirs to work toward an understanding with Israel.

I do not know King Hassan, but I have heard a lot about him. Hassan is a Muslim rooted in the Arab world but with pro-Western leanings. He was afraid of Soviet expansionism in the Middle East and hoped for an effective barrier to block it.

Moshe Dayan held his first meeting in September 1977 with the

Egyptian deputy prime minister in the royal palace at Rabat, in the presence of King Hassan himself and several of his senior ministers.

Tohamy spoke bluntly. Right from the outset, he stressed that Sadat regarded total withdrawal from all the occupied territories as a precondition for any peace settlement; there was no room for any further contacts unless Israel proclaimed her intention of evacuating those territories—Jerusalem included—right to the last inch.

In effect, Sadat's visit to Jerusalem in November forestalled a further meeting scheduled to be held between Tohamy and Dayan at the palace in Rabat. In time, the first meeting between Dayan and Tohamy came to be represented as paving the way for Sadat's visit, but that is not quite accurate. All the same, it provided Israel's political leadership with a sound evaluation of the positions Egypt could be expected to adopt. Clearly, Sadat would come to Jerusalem demanding withdrawal from all the territories. It was equally clear that the fate of the Sinai peninsula hung in the balance.

I have no complaints about not receiving advance notice of the meeting between Tohamy and Dayan. But, as defense minister, I was fully aware of the responsibility I bore with regard to the Sinai. Ever since the Six-Day War, the barren peninsula had constituted a cornerstone in Israel's military doctrine.

Prior to the 1967 war, Israel's strategy was defensive. Israel had no ambitions to expand its territory. However, in the event of an outbreak of war, our army would obviously be ordered to lose no time in carrying the battle into enemy territory—principally because of our lack of any strategic depth.

The West Bank was like a bone in Israel's throat. It was the ideal springboard for an attack on Israel. One of the first war games staged by our army was based on the assumption that the Jordanians and Iraqis had moved into the West Bank, from which they would launch their thrust into Israel. The war game was conducted in the area lying between Ra'anana, Herzlia, and Beersheba. We calculated that Jordan would occupy Ramleh and Lod. It was assumed that our forces would strike into the Sinai only if Egyptian forces entered in numbers we could not tolerate—or else if Egypt closed the Strait of Tiran, our maritime gateway to Africa and the Far East.

In view of our army's defensive strategy, we had no intention of occupying the West Bank. The generally accepted assumption—which I, however, did not share—was that Israel could achieve its national objectives within the 1949 armistice lines. Few of our military chiefs dreamed of occupying territories or annexation as a way of enlarging the area of the state. Prior to the 1967 war, our National Security College discussed what Israel should do with the West Bank after occupying it. The conclusion: UN forces would take over.

The Six-Day War completely altered Israel's strategy. The territories occupied in the fighting soon became an important component of our security. In my view, there is only one substitute for our military control of part of the occupied territories: a strategic alliance, with the participation of Egypt, Saudi Arabia, and Jordan, in a military alignment similar to the NATO alliance and with a political and economic structure resembling the European Common Market. I contend that this alternative would be more effective than clinging to all the territories.

Suddenly, without any such alternative being available, Sadat confronted Israel in his Jerusalem visit with the demand for a withdrawal from the Sinai peninsula—exchanging our security for uncertainty.

For many a long night, I found it impossible to close my eyes. I wanted peace, and I did my best to ensure that Israel would not let the opportunity slip by. But I had to prepare our army for war. As defense minister, I knew what a great strategic loss would be involved in giving up the Sinai and what an enormous risk Israel would be taking upon herself. The burden assumed by the loss of the peninsula would obviously fall upon the defense establishment and upon me as its chief. Ultimately, it was not I who decided to cede the Sinai—though I did participate in the decision.

Throughout Israel's existence, the failure of the Zionist movement in its contacts with the Arabs had deprived the state of the instruments required to foster an understanding or to lay the foundations for regional coexistence. Since Israel had come to observe the Arab world in warfare, everything connected to our relations with the Arabs had necessarily been under the control of the defense establishment.

Because of the defense establishment's involvement in formulating our political attitudes toward the Arab world and the paradoxical role it plays in attempts to reach an understanding with the Arabs and in shaping Israel's peace policy, it sometimes functions without coordination with the government bodies similarly engaged, such as the Foreign Ministry. At best, this results in duplication; at worst, it leads to blown fuses.

I do not justify this state of affairs. In the course of the years, some institution should have been established to handle this sphere. Yet the fact is that in anticipation of Sadat's visit, the necessary assessments were provided by the defense establishment, which had already played a dominant role in the political arena: after the Yom Kippur War, GHQ's planning branch, under General Avraham Tamir, prepared and processed Israel's disengagement agreements with Syria and Egypt.

As long ago as the years when Moshe Dayan and, later, Shimon Peres, ran the Defense Ministry, the planning branch had prepared files spelling out the various alternative steps toward peace with the Arabs. However, as the political echelons clearly refused to contemplate a return to the borders of June 4, 1967, the files did not contain any proposals for such an eventuality. The most daring plan appears in the "blue file": it shows our southern approaches and the town of Yamit remaining within Israel's domain; our northern defensible boundary would run across the Golan Heights; and the inhabitants of the West Bank and the Gaza Strip would be offered autonomy for an interim period until they decided on their future in a plebiscite.

All these proposals were based on one unassailable assumption: that peace between Israel and its neighbors was a matter for a future generation. It was likely to happen gradually, step by step, phase by phase, as the conclusion of a lengthy process. When Sadat came to Jerusalem, peace suddenly seemed to be close at hand. But it didn't take long for the euphoria of peace to make way for a more realistic evaluation; there appeared to be no need for a revision in our earlier assessments. Sadat's visit was an important step forward—an extraordinary step.

But no more than one single step.

7

THE BRIDGEHEAD

Sadat and I had taken to each other when we first met in Jerusalem. Now, after an eighty-nine-minute flight, here I was in Ismailia, Sadat's residence, for my second meeting with him. What was I to say? How should I conduct the conversation? Quite probably, our first words would largely shape the character of our relationship and almost certainly affect the atmosphere of the meeting itself.

In a way, this second meeting with the Egyptian president resembled a second meeting with a woman. The first encounter between a man and a woman is usually spontaneous. Afterward, each has had time to think about the other—likes and dislikes—and carefully plans the second meeting.

That's precisely what I did before my second meeting with Sadat: I prepared. I rehearsed. Trying to foresee the questions that might arise in the course of our talk, I composed my answers. For example, how was I to react if he boasted of the prowess of his army in the Yom Kippur War? Should I remind him that our forces had finally halted 101 kilometers from Cairo? Whatever happened, I thought it necessary to say something noncommittal about the wars and bloodshed of the past and to express the hope that they would never recur.

Acting as though we had been classroom buddies, Sadat placed one hand on my shoulder, waving the other skyward.

"How did you get here?"

I described our flight across the Mediterranean and up the Nile delta. I assumed that he knew all of this and was only asking out of courtesy.

"You came to Ismailia the long way. Why not return home directly, by way of the Sinai?

"And when there is peace between Israel and Egypt," Sadat added, as though nothing could be more obvious or self-evident, "El Al planes will also be able to come here."

The way Sadat immediately launched into aviation made me say to myself: *He's done his homework on me.* At this phase of lingering mutual suspicions, I guessed that his spontaneity was well prepared.

My face may have shown my skepticism about Egypt's granting overflight rights to our national airline because he added: "I mean it, seriously."

I didn't say a word. He was speaking as a man intent on full peace, the kind we had always hoped for. A song of Naomi Shemer, one of Israel's most beloved songwriters, ran through my mind, about battleships transporting cargoes of oranges. Just a few hours earlier, flying over Egypt, I had still looked down with the eyes of a combat pilot, still thought in terms of penetration routes for photographic reconnaissance sorties or ways for our combat planes to evade the ever-alert Egyptian missile batteries.

"You look smart," said Sadat, surveying my suit; I noticed he was looking me up and down.

"I've got to be smart to meet with the greatest of Arab leaders." I promptly fired back a compliment of my own.

From the beginning, the atmosphere was relaxed—helped, perhaps, by the climate: although it was winter, the weather was pleasantly springlike, with clear skies.

Sadat took an interest in the state of my health with a glance at my damaged leg. "I'm glad you came," he said, "and I hope you get another chance to see Egypt."

It was still strange to hear him say a thing like that. Apparently, my Israeli ears were as yet unaccustomed to such a note. I scrutinized the man whom I had last seen in Jerusalem. He looked a little more at ease here than at the King David Hotel—possibly because this time he was playing on home turf.

"Do you see that house?" Sadat pointed to the building bordering the lawn where we were walking. "I want to know the name of the officer who gave the order to bombard it in 1970." His voice took on a bantering tone.

"Mr. President," I said, "if you really want to know, I'm prepared to make inquiries in our artillery corps."

Sadat burst into laughter.

His home looked out on the Timsah lake, where Egyptian ships had remained stranded until after the 1973 war. On the other side, I could make out the remnants of our Bar-Lev Line.

"Do you see that fortress opposite?" I said, pointing to it. "Over there, I came under the worst shelling I have ever experienced. I barely got out alive."

Sadat laughed again. Strange how things that were once of supreme importance—literally matters of life and death—can become a subject for jokes. When I had been under that shelling, there had been nothing funny in the situation. But now, strolling across the lawn with the Egyptian president, I joined in his laughter.

Yet my heart was heavy at the sight of the Bar-Lev Line in ruins. Every now and then, I cast a surreptitious glance toward it. The price we had paid was a heavy one, I thought. But it would have been stupid on my part to refer to the past. Sadat himself drew a curtain over it. As far as I can remember, after this brief mention of bygone confrontations—no more than two or three sentences—he did not bring up the past.

And, indeed, he now went on to talk of the future, getting down to business. His expression grew serious. "From here, you will go to Janklis with War Minister Gamasy," he said. "Get together, talk things over, exchange opinions, make decisions—whatever you conclude with him can be regarded as if it has my approval. I want to move quickly. Above all: full relations, total normalization. Everything—and fast. We must achieve genuine peace as soon as possible."

"But there are stages—" I tried to interrupt.

"I don't want any stages. I'm ready to start with a civilian air route through Sinai."

"What about ambassadors?"

"Yes, ambassadors, too. I'm prepared to appoint an ambassador in Jerusalem. I just want you to tell Begin that for things to move quickly, he must proclaim his agreement in principle to withdrawal from all the occupied territories and a solution of the Palestinian problem."

"Mr. President, that's not so easy. The prime minister has difficulties of his own. You can't change everything so quickly, after so many years."

"I have changed things quickly! I want you to understand: something fundamental has changed. I suggest you start regarding my people not as enemies but as allies."

"Supposing we do reach an agreement with you," I said. "What about the Syrians? Don't forget the Jordanians."

"The Jordanians will follow in our footsteps. So will the Syrians. Things in the Arab world happen the way Egypt decides."

"At present, the Syrians are engaged in a military buildup."

"Remember what happened to them in 1973," said Sadat. That was an oblique compliment to our army on its success in blocking the Syrian attack in the Golan Heights and in later pushing back the battle lines by a counteroffensive.

Ignoring his flattery, I mentioned the Iraqis.

"They're tied down on the Iranian front," Sadat said. "And, anyway, what are you so worried about? You have a good army. You are well deployed, with reserves that can be mobilized quickly. You have a good air force, and your planes are better than ours."

The implication was obvious. As a way of defusing the military arguments by which we justified our retention of the occupied territories, Sadat was stressing the prowess of our armed forces to get us to make the maximum concessions.

Before my mission, I had been given overall instructions by the prime minister and the ministerial committee for defense. Begin had notified me of my scheduled meeting with the Egyptian president and his war minister, but I was given no specific details to discuss with them. At the same time, it was obvious that both sides wished to make an effort to reduce tensions. I had imagined that these talks could embrace anything, from idle chatter to a thorough consideration of the most fundamental issues. One thing I took into account: Sadat was liable to come up with yet another surprise, and there was no guessing what kind of rabbit he'd whip out of his hat this time.

When I met the Egyptian president, I wanted to be well briefed and ready for any conceivable proposal. Begin's instructions being of the most general nature, I had called together a group of experts—civilians and military men, Orientalists and jurists. I included people with whose views I disagreed totally. On the contrary, I wanted to hear conflicting appraisals. Having also invited Cabinet Secretary Aryeh Naor to listen in and report to whomever necessary, I asked the group for its views.

The facial expressions of the experts I had summoned revealed the uncertainty under which all of us were laboring.

One of them presented matters in a crude, oversimplified form, as though Sadat's visit had left Israeli-Egyptian relations unchanged. "The question is," he said, "whether we're interested in getting anywhere with him—or if we want to lead him up a blind alley. If we take the blind-alley approach, we have to operate in such a manner that the blame falls on the other side, so that the United States will accept our explanations."

I couldn't even lose my temper with him. I listened patiently to his presentation, which showed a total lack of faith in the Egyptians; he didn't believe a word Sadat had said.

My own views were clear. I said I was still not completely convinced of the sincerity of Sadat's moves. At the same time, there could be no doubt that his hands held the keys to war or peace. I was prepared to go a long way toward peace—or, at least, much farther than I had been willing to go in the past. I thought we could give up Sharm el Sheik at the tip of the Sinai and extensive portions of the Sinai as well. On the other hand, pulling back as far as the old international frontier was out of the question. We had not constructed the Rafah settlements on the border between Egypt and the Gaza Strip and Israel or our two big airfields in the Sinai for the purpose of handing them over to the Egyptians.

"If I were an Egyptian," speculated General Shlomo Gazit, "I would immediately demand the Rafah approaches—they're registered in the El Arish land registry as sovereign Egyptian territory."

The issue of the Rafah settlements arose in all its gravity. The more we considered the matter, the more we were forced to conclude that the Egyptians would insist on regaining the Rafah area. I considered the possibility of having to leave Israeli citizens under Egyptian sovereignty; still, it was better than evacuating them and losing the settlements completely.

At the end of that month, our forces were to hold a training exercise in Sinai. As usual, this was liable to put the Egyptians on a jumpy alert. I did not conceal my anxiety on that score.

"Our tanks might accidentally cross the Suez Canal and kill the peace," I said. After debating with myself whether to allow the exercise to go on or call it off, I finally decided that security needs came before anything else. "Should we invite the Egyptians to observe the exercise?" I hazarded an idea, which I myself promptly rejected: it was still early days. But the fact that such a proposal could even be voiced proved how much things had changed.

I liked the notion of giving the Egyptians advance notice of such exercises, possibly by means of a telephone link. For some reason, the idea of a direct line between Israel and Egypt had captured my fancy. I saw it as a symbol, testifying to the relaxation of tension. If ever I should decide to give the Egyptians a thrashing, all I'd need to do would be to call them up and say: "Good morning, we're having a war today." By the time I'd put down the receiver, Air

Force Commander David Ivry's planes would be over their heads.

"What about inviting Egyptian officers and men for a visit to Jerusalem?" This idea had occurred to me early in the conversation. "They could be brought in by the Egged bus cooperative or by Arkia domestic airlines—they'd go and visit the Mosque of Omar . . ."

"Will we be able to visit Egypt?" asked Motta Gur.

"We don't have a Western Wall down there," I reminded him.

Suggestions were tossed around. Supposing we were to propose peacekeeping patrols, like the four-man jeep teams in Berlin after World War II?

Every now and then, somebody would remind the group about the possible loss of our early-warning areas in the Sinai. "I wish the whole of the Sinai could remain in our hands," I said. "I also wish we could take up positions along the Euphrates in Iraq!"

Someone proposed that Israel should offer to buy parts of the Sinai from the Egyptians, the way the Americans had bought Louisiana from Mexico or Alaska from Russia. *What's the big deal? I joked to myself. I'd go to Sadat and say: "We want to buy, or lease, twenty thousand acres of land in Sinai."* Why not? For him with all his land, it's nothing; for us, it's a lot.

I thought: *If we demand a reduction of forces, that could be interpreted as playing down the importance of territory as a component of our national security.* I liked Motta Gur's idea for avoiding this difficulty. During his visit to Jerusalem, Sadat had asked Begin to permit the Egyptian army to move forward into the area of the Mitla Pass in the Sinai, which is easier to defend. This showed they were still very cautious with us. Gur thought it might be profitable to start talks by asking what they wanted in the way of security arrangements to ensure that we didn't catch them napping. That way we could find out what they were after.

Of all the proposals, I was most taken by that of Aluf Hareven, of the Foreign Ministry. Hareven suggested a formula for opening discussions—that our military government no longer administer the occupied territories and that it be replaced by joint arrangements between us and the Arab states, aimed at preventing war. This proposal offered several benefits. It could be applied in all areas, it boosted Israel's reputation for generosity on the most sensitive of issues, and it bypassed the problem of the borders.

Now, facing Sadat on the lawn alongside his house, I could confirm the accuracy of the predictions that Egypt would never let up on what it perceived as the main problem: an overall Israeli withdrawal. However, I could not overlook what Sadat was offering in return: full peace, with an exchange of ambassadors, with air routes, and complete normalization of relations between the two countries. I had not expected Sadat to speak with such commitment about full peace or to stress that he wanted to achieve it as quickly as possible.

With him now were his deputy, Hosni Mubarak, and War Minister Gamasy, the two men who are said to have planned all the phases of the 1973 war. As I gave them the gifts I had so carefully chosen, I wondered what was passing through their minds.

"Do people in Israel know that you've come here?" Sadat inquired.

"No," I said. "We kept it secret. We imposed censorship on the report."

"That's not at all a bad idea."

"Mr. President, it's up to you."

"We'll keep it secret," Sadat said.

Privately, I hoped it would leak out somehow. Israel's defense minister on Egyptian soil: the Egyptians would find it hard to wriggle out of that one! It would only reinforce their commitment to the peace process, which was just getting off the ground.

"Mr. President," I said, returning to the central issue. "You say we can't remain on Arab soil. What about our settlements at Rafah?"

"They'll have to go," Sadat replied firmly. His expression was grim. I felt as though I'd been hit over the head. Seated in my office in Tel Aviv, I had heard our Egyptologists predict that this would be the Egyptian demand, but I had hoped they were mistaken. Now, having heard it from the most authoritative source, there was no room for uncertainty.

Israel has never abandoned any of her settlements—or, at least, never willingly. That would run counter to the fundamental concept underlying Jewish resettling in the land of Israel. But this issue could make or break the peace. The Rafah settlements had been built up with much hard work and a lot of money. And now Sadat was saying we would have to leave . . .

"I should stress," the Egyptian president added, "that we are not discussing a separate peace between Egypt and Israel. After reaching agreement with us, you will have to hold separate talks with each Arab state."

His second sentence sounded like a most remote possibility.

At that moment, a full peace treaty with Egypt appeared to be well out of reach, yet Sadat was talking about negotiations with other Arab states! It sounded fantastic.

I tried to remain expressionless; I did not want the Egyptians to guess what was going on in my mind. I took my leave of President Sadat, determined to be optimistic in spite of the harshness of his demands.

On the way to Janklis, I pondered the difficulty of making such a sharp transition from war to peace. Would it indeed be genuine peace? The helicopter flew close to the Suez Canal. Down below, I could see the convoys of ships making their way along the water. On both sides of the Canal, tractors were at work. It was eerie to contemplate the remnants of our Bar-Lev Line from an Egyptian perspective.

It was very moving to land at the Janklis airfield. Thirty-five years before, on completing the RAF pilots' course in Rhodesia, I had returned to Palestine by way of Egypt. After a three-week delay, I had taken off for home from Janklis. Years later, I had caught a further glimpse of the field in aerial photographs taken by our pilots.

I looked about me. The antiaircraft positions were empty. There wasn't a plane to be seen in the surface hangars or in the underground shelters. *They've had a clean-out in my honor*, I thought. On seeing the empty shelters, I could not help recalling that it was our air force that had necessitated their construction, after we'd caught their planes on the ground on the morning of June 5, 1967.

Then I pulled myself up short. I had not come all this way to a place most Israelis could not even imagine for the purpose of conjuring up the past. I was here to feel our way, cautiously, toward the moment when we could turn over a new leaf in our relations with Egypt.

Peace lay in sight at the end of the road. Sadat himself had named peace as his objective.

But it looked as though the path leading toward it would be long and tortuous.

8

THE RED WINE OF JANKLIS

Lunch at the Janklis estate was the first grave test of the newly forged relationship between Israel and Egypt. With me now were Israeli Intelligence Chief Shlomo Gazit, head of the Southern Command, Herzl Shapir, as well as our bodyguards Raffi and Moshe: they had all flown in from Cairo International Airport. From the moment we sat down at the table, I watched how all the Egyptians, from General Gamasy down to the last of the waiters, subjected us to inquisitive stares. It may have been my imagination, but I thought I saw the questions in their eyes: Would we like their food? Did our tastes differ totally from theirs? Their attention focused on my chomping jaws and facial expression. The fate of the peace negotiations seemed momentarily to hang upon the flavor of the *bamia* (okra) gravy. Fortunately, *bamia* has been a favorite of mine ever since my mother used to cook it, and I tucked in lustily, praising the taste.

The first hurdle in Israeli-Egyptian relations had been successfully negotiated.

The curious glances of the Egyptians highlighted yet again the profound alienation created by years of enmity. I could understand the waiters looking at us as though we were strangers from another planet, but why did our hosts do likewise? After all, they must have been somewhat acquainted with us—from reading about us, at least, and probably from studying intelligence reports as well. It was astounding to see Gamasy and his aides watching

our every move, scrutinizing our expressions to see whether we
were truly enjoying the meal, and trying to read our minds.

But who was I to criticize? That was precisely what I had done
the first time I dined in the company of Egyptians at the banquet
held in Jerusalem to honor Sadat.

There was something symbolic about this mutual inspection
from opposite sides of the table. More than anything else, it testified to the groping uncertainty with which both sides approached
the present delicate stage in our relationship. If our minds were
occasionally assailed by doubts, the Egyptians must have had
similar misgivings.

Janklis lies at the heart of a green and lovely expanse of
vineyards. The great estate once belonged to a Greek millionaire
named Janklis, who had donated it to the Egyptian government.
The three-story building had been constructed some sixty or seventy years before, in a style evoking British colonial times. Its
atmosphere reminded me of buildings constructed in Palestine
under the British mandate: the large halls, the high ceilings, the
long windows and parquet floors that reverberated with the softest
of footsteps. It carried echoes of a world that had long passed
away.

At the conference table now, the Egyptians listened to us with
absolute attention, determined not to miss a single word, not a
syllable.

When it was their turn to talk, they went straight to the point.
They demanded our views on where the final borders should run
and asked when and how we intended to withdraw from Sinai.

My two talks with President Sadat had taught me that he
attached little importance to details. In Jerusalem, I had witnessed
the breadth of his vision, with its historical dimensions, though I
hadn't understood it then. His whispered assurance when I'd taken
leave of him outside the King David Hotel—that contacts between
our two countries would be maintained by way of Rumanian President Ceausescu—had puzzled me. As I came to know Sadat better,
I began to comprehend his political philosophy. Sadat sees things
in their overall historical perspective. In addition to the world's
current division—between East and West—he takes into account
the one looming on the political horizon and likely to make its
mark on the future: the division between north and south. In this
realignment into new blocs, a country like Rumania will play a key
role—due as much to Ceausescu's gift for maneuver as to its geographical position. While his country's internal regime is rigidly
Communist, Ceausescu has managed to win it a neutral status in

the tug of war between East and West. It was Ceausescu who had advised Sadat to trust Begin's word and to see Israel's prime minister as a strong leader capable of leading his people along an unconventional path.

Be that as it may, I was surprised when the Egyptian lower echelons—the war minister and his aides and advisers—similarly avoided any discussion of details and engaged exclusively in key issues and points of contention.

I repeated my proposal for a telephone link between the head of our Southern Command and the headquarters of their Third Army so as to forestall any possible errors or misunderstandings.

They granted the idea scant attention. "Why talk about that?" Gamasy wanted to know. "If there is peace between us, what will be the value of such a telephone link?"

We were transmitting on totally different wavelengths, but I doubt whether I realized it at the time.

Instead, I tried to point out their error. "We have come with open hearts," I said. "And I want you to know that we look forward to peace. I believe in your sincerity, that you want peace just as we do. But you must remember that we are a small country. If we lose one war—we've lost everything. In October 1973, you attacked us before we had time to call up our reserves. As I have already told President Sadat, we have a relatively large air force but only five or six airfields. You and the Syrians have forty."

I praised their president's peace initiative, expressing my understanding of his difficulties with the Arab world. But I requested similar consideration for the difficulties of Prime Minister Begin. "You should remember that peace treaties are concluded between nations, not between leaders. Leaders are transitory. In time, they vanish. Nations remain. In the year 2000, there will be 100 million Arabs facing 6 million Israelis. We have to safeguard the future of our children."

Whenever I went back to details, General Gamasy bridled.

"We're talking about a peace treaty," he said. "And you should know that it's on direct instructions from the president! We want to talk about immediate peace, full and genuine—not an interim agreement or anything of that sort. I am prepared to discuss an exchange of ambassadors, direct flights, whatever you want."

Once again, I gave a detailed account of Israel's security problems, as I had done previously with President Sadat.

"General Weizman," said Gamasy patiently, "we are aware of your security problems. The president explained them to us on his return from Jerusalem. At the same time, I should stress that we, too, have our security problems. You mentioned your large air force—obviously, we require protection from it."

As I had long been aware, the Arab military commands—Egypt's in particular—have a very healthy respect for Israel's air force; they retain painful memories of those fateful three hours in 1967 when our planes decided the outcome of the Six-Day War. Once, as I was driving along with General Gamasy, I saw Egyptian soldiers lining the route, standing almost shoulder to shoulder.

"You have a big army," I had commented.

"I'd be willing to exchange it for your air force," Gamasy had replied dryly.

In the course of the negotiations, Gamasy turned out to be a hard-liner. He was pleasant and even-tempered, always with an introspective, pensive look. He was an affable conversationalist but unwavering in his views, showing little inclination toward the slightest concession.

"Let me make it plain," he said. "We can't accept your proposal about border changes. If you retain your settlements and either of your airfields in the Sinai—even in exchange for some territory—it will be interpreted by our people as Israeli expansionism and annexation of Egyptian land."

Around six o'clock in the evening, Gamasy's aide entered and placed a note before him. Glancing at it, Gamasy made a face.

Turning to me, he said: "I am informed that Radio Cairo has just announced your presence here."

With the exception of my present visit and Foreign Minister Dayan's mission to Morocco, the whole drama had been played out on the airwaves, on television screens and on the front pages of the world press. As befits a historic event of the first order, Sadat's visit to Jerusalem had received unprecedented coverage, with American telecasters Walter Cronkite and Barbara Walters serving as its principal sponsors. It was possibly the first time in the chronicles of world politics that while both were still in a state of war, the head of state of one country had come to visit the other, and the whole pageant was watched by millions of viewers. History made an appearance on the small screen.

I tend to attach great importance to the media: electronic and print, in Israel and abroad. Experience has taught me that leaders everywhere—however much they try to avoid it—soon lose touch with their people and with reality. Leaders in every country are usually surrounded by people who avoid telling them what they need and deserve to know. That being the case, the news media are the true link between a leader and his people. They provide a way for him to break out of his isolation—just as long as he reads the papers, listens to the radio, and watches television without any prior sifting or selection. That is why I have never consented to read preselected newspaper clippings; I always insist on reading the whole paper, from readers' letters right through to the pharmacies' emergency numbers. I am convinced that the news media do give a correct picture of public opinion and therefore deserve attention. Knowing that I am open to them and respect what they have to say—even when it's against me—the news reporters over the years have given me an attentive ear. My relationship with the media has brought me considerable criticism, but that has never put me off.

With the report on Radio Cairo, Sadat had once again taken me by surprise. After agreeing that my visit should remain secret, he had authorized its publication. Sadat always directs affairs in such a manner that the final decision is invariably left to him—even on tactical matters of no apparent importance. On my return home, one of my first reports consisted of the single sentence: With Sadat, you must expect the unexpected.

As Gamasy reverted to the issue of our withdrawal from the Sinai, I contemplated the idea of returning Sharm el Sheik to Egypt. I attach military value to central Sinai rather than the southern tip, for whoever controls the center controls the entire peninsula—as exemplified by the wars of 1956 and 1967; no sooner had we broken Egyptian resistance in the Sinai desert than Sharm el Sheik fell into our hands like a ripe plum. Sharm el Sheik is a beauty spot; it has also become a kind of symbol. I was heartbroken at the prospect of its loss on that account. But I knew that there was no point digging in my heels; I had already come to terms with the notion that we would have to return it to Egypt in order to find ways of holding onto other portions of the Sinai—at the very least, the settlements of the Rafah approaches.

The murmurs within the conference chamber mingled with the undulating cry of the muezzin from the nearby village mosque, accompanied by the tinkling of bells, probably on the necks of water buffaloes. The whole scene had a somewhat surrealistic flavor.

I now turned to our chief of staff's proposal for a scaling down of the two armies. "Do you intend to reduce the size of your army when peace comes?" I asked.

Gamasy gave me an interrogatory look.

"In that way," I explained, "any movement of the Egyptian army, or any enlargement of its size, will serve as a kind of warning for Israel. Up to 1967, most of your army was positioned in the Cairo area. Now, you are positioned in the Canal Zone, and you would be able to cross the waterway in a few hours. Why can't the two countries agree on a pullback of the bulk of their forces to rear areas?"

"The Egyptian army has been on full alert since 1967," Gamasy replied. He seemed displeased with my question. "At present, we have 750 thousand soldiers," he added. "If there is peace, we won't keep the bulk of our forces beside the Canal. I can tell you officially that after we sign a peace treaty, our army will be reduced and its deployment will be changed so that it no longer threatens you."

"Can I notify my government of that?" I asked.

"Yes. But under no circumstances will that be included within the official treaty. We would never be able to explain it to the Arab world."

"I hope we succeed in organizing our reserves the way you do," commented General Graidli, head of the Egyptian General Headquarters' staff branch.

"We'll help you!" I promised cheerfully.

Gamasy proceeded to submit a further demand: Israel should consent to the stationing of Egyptian forces at El Arish as well as a squadron or two of planes in the Sinai; these, he explained, were matters of "prestige and honor."

"I must remind you," I said, "that President Sadat promised Mr. Begin he would not station military forces to the east of the Mitla and Gidi Passes."

"True, the president did promise," Gamasy conceded. "But he is not a military man."

His words were unexpected. I never imagined any Egyptian taking it upon himself to break a promise made by President Sadat in person.

Gamasy's demand sparked off a fierce argument. "In order to hold the passes," he elaborated, "we have to take up position to the east of them—and we must take up position in such a manner that we can defend them properly—"

"General Gamasy!" I broke in. "That way, you can get as far as Beersheba."

He ignored my comment. "It isn't enough for us to remain within the passes. The question I face is how to defend my country."

"I'd be glad to exchange your security problem for ours," I snapped. "I'll ask my people to draw you up a plan for the defense of the Canal!"

Gamasy took me at my word. He addressed the head of our Southern Command. "General Shapir, let us suppose you are the Egyptian commander and you have the task of defending the Suez Canal. How would you go about it?"

Spreading out a map, Shapir showed Gamasy how the Egyptians could secure the defense of the Suez Canal against any attack coming from the direction of the Sinai. His words gave Gamasy to understand that Israel intended to restrict the number of Egyptian troops stationed in the Canal Zone and to limit the types of armaments permitted there.

Gamasy said he would oppose any thinning out of Egyptian forces along the Canal, or demilitarization—either of which he regarded as infringing upon Egyptian sovereignty. "Not even the president could explain that to Parliament," he said. "They would make a 180-degree turn and withdraw their support. If you talk about demilitarization, that means it's not our land and that the Sinai is lost to us. You must help us safeguard our honor. I want an honorable peace. I want to live with you in peace."

"How can I tell an Egyptian pilot that he must not land at Bir Gafgaffa and Bir Tamada?" broke in the Egyptian military intelligence chief, Brigadier General Howeidi.

"If you want to be in Bir Gafgaffa," I fired back, "we have to be in the Etam and Etzion airfields."

"You defend your land from the very first meter," General Graidli pointed out. "We don't. Even more than you, we need security."

"Who from?" I asked, perplexed.

"From you!"

I was indignant. "The president said we must break through the barrier of mistrust. What Graidli just said belongs to the atmosphere of mistrust carried over from the past."

"Will Israel consent to demilitarization of Eilat and Beersheba?" General Graidli demanded.

"We have to know what's going on on your side," Shlomo Gazit stated. "We'll want the Sinai hills of Jabal Harim and Jabal Halal for intelligence purposes."

"Out of the question!" a chorus responded from the other side of the table.

Gamasy saved his good news for the end. He announced that he had no objection to leaving the Israeli settlements in the Rafah approaches and along the coast of the Gulf of Aqaba; the former would be under UN supervision, while the latter would come under the Egyptian governor. Speaking of the Sharm el Sheik settlers, he added: "They should understand that they must be willing to live under full Egyptian sovereignty, rather like the Jewish communities of Cairo and Alexandria. If they wish—they can remain. If not—they will have to leave. I expect they will want to return to their own country—with the possible exception of the inhabitants of Yamit in the Rafah area. In the long run, the same arrangement will apply to the Rafah settlements. But that is a political issue."

I regarded this as the lesser evil. Taking advantage of the favorable opening, I proposed a buffer zone along the international frontier, principally with the aim of retaining the two Sinai airfields, Etzion and Etam, in our hands. I explained that we had no substitute for these air bases. It seemed to me that Gamasy was listening without any show of objections. It was beginning to look as if they would agree that the two airfields and the Rafah settlements be allowed to remain—under UN supervision.

"We could agree on border changes." I threw out a revolutionary proposal. "The border was marked out by the British; couldn't we agree between us to change it? We could move a little way into the Sinai, and you could go a little way into the Negev."

Gamasy rejected the idea. "It is difficult for a political leader to change borders. The president and the Egyptian people will not consent to it, particularly after all these wars. A border change will be interpreted as annexation and expansionism."

Our talks were inconclusive. The Egyptians showed little eagerness to bring UN forces back into the area, they opposed the establishment of Israeli early-warning stations, they refused to permit our planes to carry out photographic reconnaissance missions, and, worst of all, they insisted on negotiations being completed by October 1978, when the interim agreement of 1973 was due to run out.

It was time for dinner. Removing the green cloth, the waiters spread out a white tablecloth on which they proceeded to lay out the dishes. As they did, I got a surprise: they were setting down bottles of wine. Alcohol is strictly prohibited in the Muslim religion. I had imagined that some of my hosts—even those who regularly attended mosques—drank alcohol at home. But I never anticipated that they would do so in the presence of strangers.

The Janklis area is famous for its vintages. I took a sip of wine, singing its praises. Later, on my return home, I found a gift in my baggage: two crates of wine.

From outside came the call of the muezzin, summoning the believers to evening prayers. The open window looked out on a typical Egyptian landscape, with its irrigation canals, beasts of burden, and villagers in their robes. Savoring the air of early evening, I took a deep breath of the land of the Nile.

After the meal, General Gamasy and I seated ourselves on a couch and began to swap reminiscences. We had a lot to talk about, having spent many years on opposite sides of the lines.

"What the hell did you want of us in 1967?" I demanded without so much as a preface.

He was silent. I thought I saw a sad look in his eyes.

"That May," I added, "it never occurred to me that war was about to break out. I won't say I didn't feel inclined to let you have it, but I didn't think you were heading toward war. Why did you move your army into the Sinai?"

"May 14, 1967, when our army began to advance into Sinai, was a black day for me." Gamasy's tone was gloomy. "I knew we shouldn't do it, but I had no choice. Orders are orders."

"Where were you on the morning of June 5?"

"At my divisional headquarters, at Bir Tamada in the Sinai. I knew what was about to happen. Nasser made many mistakes, but that was the worst of all. He made a mistake getting involved in the war in Yemen. I wasn't there—and I'm glad I wasn't."

I mentioned the surprise we'd sprung on them on June 5, 1967. He spoke of the surprise he'd sprung on us on October 6, 1973. His eyes sparkled, and his tone was proud; as we knew, he'd played a major role in planning their attack.

"On October 6, I was at my headquarters," he recalled. "At one o'clock midday, I contacted President Sadat to tell him that if your air force hadn't attacked yet, everything was all right. And, indeed, it was."

We exchanged views on the relationship between the army and politics. He came across as a professional officer with pride in his calling. "I try to keep the army out of politics," he said. "I did not belong to the group of revolutionary officers who carried out the 1952 revolution in Egypt."

The atmosphere was agreeable. Gamasy spoke as an uncompromising patriot, but I believed in his sincerity; he appeared to be sensible and open-minded. *If there are others like him in Egypt, there's hope of attaining peace*, I thought to myself.

Gamasy seemed very proud of his native land, whose history he related with great fervor. "We are Arabs and Muslims—but we are also Pharaonites," he said, reflecting the Egyptians' identification with their ancient history. He told me that when the Free Officers had seized power in the fifties, they'd renamed the streets for the kings of ancient Egypt—pointing to the role they claimed to play in shaping this region and its culture.

I told him of my son's injury on the Suez front and of the suffering he has had to bear to this day.

"My son is at university," said Gamasy. He appeared reluctant to go on, but our mood of shared candor drew him out. "He leans toward the Muslim Brotherhood. He is an extremely observant Muslim."

Once again, I caught a glimpse of the impact of Islam on Egypt. Another mark of the ubiquity of religion: the notepaper provided at Janklis bore the ornate inscription: *"Bismillah"* ("in the name of God").

We discussed the Arab states and their leaders. Gamasy spoke with great caution until we got around to the Libyan ruler, Muammar el-Qaddafi.

"He's crazy," Gamasy said. "We know that for a fact. His family is also abnormal. We could have finished him off."

"Why didn't you do it?"

"Algeria's President Boumedienne urged us not to harm him."

We found a common interest in books. "I'm reading Churchill," Gamasy said.

"He is one of my favorites," I told him.

We discussed Churchill, and the conversation turned to World War II. It transpired that Gamasy had served with the British army, winning a British decoration for his part in the desert war. I recalled my service with the RAF. Intriguing: there was a time when we'd fought on the same side.

I found in him the vigorous but not disagreeable qualities of a leader. More than others of his countrymen, he impressed me as being convinced of the need to "put things in order" in Egypt. He was deeply troubled by economic and social developments, referring to problems of food and housing and to the polarization of classes. And his principal concern was over the future of the younger generation. Egypt's historical and national objectives were the focus of his interest. He thought about the largest issues— over the long term. My admiration for him grew by the minute.

That night, I tossed and turned in bed, unable to close my eyes because of the cold. I begged my bodyguard, Amos, to do something to save me from freezing. After scouring the building, he ferreted out four electric heaters, which he placed opposite my bed. I barely managed to get any sleep before the call of the village muezzin woke me in the early-morning hours.

Despite the pleasantries of the previous evening, our talks with the Egyptians were going nowhere. On the way back to Ismailia, my only source of gratification was the lively conversation between General Gamasy and my bodyguard as they gazed out of the windows of the helicopter at the delta below. Amos—a kibbutz member and a captain in the Golani Brigade's elite reconnaissance unit—was telling Gamasy about Israel's agriculture and about his kibbutz in the Galilee.

On our arrival at the helicopter pad at Ismailia, I saw U.S. Ambassador Hermann Eilts. At the time, I attached little importance to his presence there because I was not yet as concerned as I would be about the extent of American involvement in the peace process.

Sadat was expecting us at his other Ismailia residence—he owns two in that city. This time, he was not awaiting me at the entrance; nor did he come to welcome me. I stood there a moment or two. The delay may have had no significance, but the anxieties plaguing me that day endowed it with symbolic meaning.

Sadat was with his deputy, Hosni Mubarak. The Egyptian president looked enraged and ill-tempered.

"You are persisting in your old methods," Sadat said very loudly. "You don't grasp the greatness of the hour! You don't understand what I did and the risk I took. If nothing comes of this, I am prepared to resign. Hosni will take over from me."

He looked very nervous.

"I am ready to conclude a contractual peace treaty," he went on, "with ambassadors, with freedom of navigation, everything. But you are getting out of the Sinai! That includes all the settlements. They've got to go! That includes the army. Not a single Israeli soldier is to stay in the Sinai. If you want the airfields to remain civilian, that's all right—but they will be under Egyptian sovereignty. If you want them to serve Eilat—that's fine, too. I don't mind. If you want us to plough them up—we'll plough them up. And if you think you and your air force need fields so far north, go ahead and build them on the other side of the border."

"They'll take a long time to build," I remarked.

"You are capable of building airfields in three or four months," Sadat snapped back. "Hosni here—he built me an airfield at Marsa Matruh in three months."

"It might be possible to transfer the Etam airfield, but not Etzion, near Eilat." I tried to save the situation. "We need Etzion to safeguard freedom of passage in the Bab al-Mandab strait."

Sadat shook his head angrily. "In addition, Egyptian troops will also take up positions to the east of the Suez Canal," he said.

I was unprepared for this. "Why do you need your troops there? What would they do?"

"Defend us from you," Sadat replied.

"Aren't we making a stupid mistake?" I wondered aloud.

As this disagreeable exchange continued, I realized that Sadat had been briefed on every detail of the previous day's talks. Gamasy must have reported to him in the course of the night.

"What do I need the UN for? What do you need the UN for?" Sadat wanted to know. "Whatever agreement we reach, we don't need the UN—not at Sharm el Sheik and not along the border. If we sign a peace treaty, we will keep the international waterway open—you can trust the Egyptian army."

I told him it was still early to trust the Egyptian army. Sadat did not smile.

I could not understand what had brought about this violent change of mood. Possibly having received reports about Begin's new peace plan for the Sinai—submitted the previous day to the U.S. administration—Sadat may have wished to make use of me to convey a brusque message to the Israeli prime minister.

I advised him to hold a private meeting with Begin.

"If you weren't in power," Sadat said, "I know you would be against this whole development."

His harsh tone came as a complete surprise; it was in glaring contrast to our affable conversation the previous day.

"I see that I have to keep after you," he said.

"I don't understand."

"If nothing comes of this—there could be an explosion." His tone was forceful. He was threatening us with war.

But I would not allow myself to be frightened. "We have already chased after you—in 1948, in 1956, and 1967. I myself strafed your column south of Tel Aviv. We wouldn't like to do it again. Look what happened to your air force in 1967."

I knew I had touched on a sore spot.

Sadat drew back. "Oh, yes . . . I don't want to talk about that."

There was a momentary silence before he went on in a more moderate note: "I am talking to you about total peace. Believe me, you have got to win the hearts of the Egyptian people. I know them. They are a people that does not desire war."

"What you want is a return to the 1967 borders," I said. "Suppose you disappear and someone else takes your place . . . ?"

Sadat's expression grew grave.

"What Nasser did shows what might happen," I added. "Without any warning, he sent seven hundred tanks into the Sinai, and closed the Strait of Tiran in 1967. I don't want us to have to repeat what we did in response. Today, we have a 'good' General Gamasy. But what happens when we have a 'bad' General Gamasy?"

"That's a risk," said Sadat. "You have to take that risk because I've done my part."

I expressed my regret at leaving him in a bad mood. He accompanied me to the gateway, and we kissed and embraced good-by. But it was out of politeness.

During the flight to Cairo, I did not speak. General Gamasy sat facing me, equally silent. The previous evening, we had met as friends. Noticing my mood, my military aide Ilan urged me to talk to Gamasy. I did not want to, but I apologized to the Egyptian war minister: "Sorry to be so quiet, but I'm thinking."

"That's precisely what I'm doing," Gamasy replied.

The helicopter flew over the pyramids.

At Cairo Airport, I met Eli Ben-Elissar and Abrasha Tamir, the first Israeli delegation to Egypt, who had arrived from Mina House in Cairo. Their business there had to do with yet another one of Sadat's surprises, this one sprung before I had left Israel on my way to Ismailia. Without consulting Israel, the Egyptian president had called an international conference in Cairo. The conference's principal purpose was to maintain the momentum and keep the peace issue on the international agenda; in addition, it was an opportunity for Sadat to persuade the Arab world that his strategy of direct negotiations fell within the framework of the Geneva Conference of 1974.

The Mina House conference had not been attended by ministers; its participants were officials whose job it was to "play for time" until my meeting with Sadat and Prime Minister Begin's arrival in Ismailia.

I was represented at the conference by General Tamir. Every day, Tamir would put in a call to me in Tel Aviv, describing his experiences with great excitement. Those early accounts from Cairo were instructive and fascinating.

My reunion with Tamir and Ben-Elissar was pleasant. Privately, however, I gave myself over to somber reflections, sensing that the peace initiative was liable to sink into oblivion. I wanted to know what had brought about the abrupt change in Sadat's attitude during the time that had elapsed between our first and second meetings in Egypt—although I guessed that those hours had seen him briefed by Gamasy and U.S. Ambassador Eilts.

There could be various reasons for Sadat's turnabout. With Prime Minister Begin due in Ismailia, perhaps Sadat had decided to start the negotiations from a tough position. The Egyptian president may have reached the conclusion that Israel did not want peace but only an interim agreement. He may have feared that Israel would not recognize Egyptian sovereignty over all of the Sinai and was stalling for time to create *faits accomplis* in the Rafah approaches, Etzion, the Gulf of Eilat, and Sharm el Sheik. That being the case, Sadat would not bargain—he would lay down conditions and stand firm.

I expected no major difficulties with regard to military arrangements, such as a thinning out of standing armies, withdrawal of forces from the Canal front, and the demilitarization of the Sinai. The thorny problem would be to coax the Egyptians into agreeing to leave the Etzion and Etam air bases under Israeli control for at least as long as it took to construct alternative airfields. Clearly, the Egyptians would not consent to leave the Rafah settlements under Israeli sovereignty. It was equally clear that Sadat would conclude no agreement unless he also achieved satisfaction on the issue of the West Bank and the Palestinian problem—even if, as I expected, he turned out to be far more flexible on these points.

I knew that we were going to lose the Sinai, and this caused me sorrow and concern. But I rejoiced because the reverse side of the coin was peace.

I consoled myself with an image from the future: a multitude of Israelis pouring down Kasser el Nil Street in Cairo and the Israeli flag fluttering over our embassy. . . .

9

TAKING STOCK

On the flight home, I reconstructed my first thirty hours on Egyptian soil. Despite the problems, I had enjoyed my encounter with long-forgotten landscapes and relished the new course of Israeli-Egyptian relations now being played out around the conference table instead of on the battlefield.

It was important to remember and note down every detail of my conversations. At times, each word can count. I reflected on something Gamasy had said—something to which I may not have attached the correct degree of importance at the time. His words now stood out in marked contrast with the rest of our conversation, giving the whole a new significance. As we were shaking hands, about to take our leave of one another, the Egyptian war minister had muttered: "You possess nuclear weapons—or, at least, a nuclear option. We should think about concluding a treaty for the nondissemination of such weapons."

I recalled that Mustafa Khalil had made similar remarks at the King David Hotel in Jerusalem. On each occasion, my Egyptian counterpart had looked straight into my eyes, as though trying to ferret out a secret.

"You talk about it with Libya and Iraq," I'd answered Gamasy.

"They don't have nuclear weapons," Gamasy had replied, not taking his eyes off me.

The Arab world—Egypt included—is very concerned over

the possibility that Israel has a nuclear option. It may have been one of the considerations that induced Sadat to undertake his mission to Jerusalem. Certainly everyone dreaded the appalling prospect of the Middle East entering the 1980s in the shadow of a mushroom-shaped cloud.

Even before Khalil and Gamasy had questioned me, it was obvious that the region's imminent entry into the nuclear age dismayed the Arabs. It could end, once and for all, their dream of annihilating Israel. Some of their leaders were beginning to realize that they must not force us into a corner where we might—albeit reluctantly—have no recourse but nuclear weapons. The Arabs may also fear that Israel would brandish its nuclear option for the purpose of political blackmail, along the lines of their own exploitation of the oil weapon.

On the other hand, assessments to the contrary were also current in the Arab world, discounting the likelihood of Israel ever developing a nuclear option. This school held that since Israel would be unable to use an atom bomb, its possession would not give her an absolute advantage; in consequence, the confrontation would be finally decided by conventional means or possibly by a popular guerrilla war. Even so, the Arabs were almost unanimously in favor of applying their powerful financial resources toward a concentrated effort to manufacture a nuclear bomb.

In effect, they were a long way off. Libyan ruler Muammar el-Qaddafi is reputed to have tried to buy nuclear weapons without success. However, recent years have witnessed grave developments in this sphere. In Iraq—standard-bearer of the "Rejectionist Front"—European experts, primarily French, are working alongside local technicians on manufacturing a nuclear bomb, under the pretense of "nuclear development for peaceful purposes." The Iraqis have pulled ahead of the other states in their atomic research and are on the verge of a breakthrough—bringing the Middle East closer to the age of nuclear weapons.

There are two topics that are not discussed aloud: cancer and nuclear weapons. People prefer to bury their heads in the sand when facing matters over which they have no control. But Israel cannot afford to behave in such an ostrichlike fashion. Nuclear weapons in the hands of Iraq, or any other Arab state, would constitute a danger of unprecedented gravity to Israel's existence.

A nation's nuclear might is not measured solely by the number of atomic weapons in its arsenals; rather, its strength depends on its capacity for withstanding a nuclear onslaught—its ability to strike a nuclear counterblow after having itself suffered such an attack. In any nuclear showdown, it is the second round that is almost certainly decisive. Therefore, China is one of the world's leading nuclear powers even though it may be unable to launch a large number of atom bombs at the United States or the Soviet Union. China's capacity for withstanding a nuclear attack is far greater than either of the other superpowers—principally because its billion-strong population is dispersed over a very large area and its territory contains almost no important strategic targets. Chinese industry is not so developed that its destruction could bring life in that country to a standstill.

At the other extreme, there are states like Israel, whose population is small and concentrated within a small area. A nuclear first strike could cripple such a state or at least destroy its living fabric. Israel's capacity for withstanding a nuclear strike is limited. From our viewpoint, the ideal solution would be a regional strategic alliance between Israel and the Arab states, with the backing of the United States. Then an Iraqi nuclear threat would not find Israel alone: instead, she would belong to an alliance comprised of Egypt, Saudi Arabia, and perhaps other Arab countries as well.

Efforts toward a nuclear alliance of this kind should give a renewed impetus to the peace process not only with Egypt but also with the other states in the region. Israel cannot remain alone. Not only must she strive for agreement with her neighbors; the nuclear age requires her to forge a strategic alliance to place her alongside them.

At the moment, this objective seems remote—almost unattainable. The peace with Egypt, which everyone wants to see as lasting, is buffeted by changing winds and, at times, by changing moods. But in the long run, Israel has no other choice open to her.

Ever since Khalil and Gamasy had asked me about Israel's nuclear capacity, I have given the matter much thought. Could the two men possibly have been thinking of a regional alliance when they stared at me? Behind the fear in their questions, were they thinking in the long-term?

I do not know. It is very hard to draw any conclusions from a single sentence, uttered at the end of an exhaustive discussion and colored by mutual suspicion. I prefer to believe that the question hinted at the possibility of cooperation someday.

As our plane approached the Israeli shore, I pushed atomic power out of my mind and began to prepare my report for the cabinet. The following day, it would be holding a special session in which I was to present my visit to Egypt. I saw myself in the role of the dove sent by Noah from the ark to see if the waters had abated on the face of the earth; I was the first Israeli minister to have left the beleaguered ark. My account would likely give my colleagues their first impressions—which could be lasting. How was I to begin? I could speak enthusiastically of the warm reception, the wonderful treatment, the friendly, emotional meeting with Sadat. Like other mortals, cabinet ministers love to listen to stories—and I'm a good raconteur. Or I could skip the radiant start and tell of the disturbing conclusion. I could begin with Sadat's statements about establishing diplomatic relations, about airlines and tourism, but I could also lead off with his demand that we give up the Sinai, including the airfields and settlements. I could start with my first conversation with the president and its mood of pleasant optimism or else with the second one and its distressing tension.

I could color my report bright or dreary; I could stress the great prospects—or the equally great risks.

I knew the responsibility I bore because I know the Israelis. They want peace. But they would not find it easy to relinquish the Sinai. With the possible exception of the Communists, not a single Israeli party is in favor of handing back everything, even for peace. For eleven years, we had believed that the world would recognize our security needs and accept our control of the Sinai. At most, we were prepared to pull back thirty or forty miles from the Canal. The commander of our armed forces, Motta Gur, would not hear of any greater concession, and I had agreed with him.

My own party, Herut, was even more extreme. It did not regard the sands of the Sinai as belonging to our ancestral heritage, but our election manifesto had declared that the border would run inside the Sinai. Who could have foreseen that it would fall to me to notify the cabinet that such a thing was totally unacceptable to the Egyptians? I could imagine the disarray likely to ensue in Herut. For years, the party had advocated one policy—and now it would have to do something quite different. In my mind's eye, I conjured up the faces of Herut's leaders: doctrinaire, dogmatic, unyielding. Decades had passed without their budging an inch in their views, even at the price of achieving power. How would they take it?

I thought of the prime minister. In 1957, when our forces had withdrawn from the Sinai under the pressure of the superpowers, tens of thousands of Begin's supporters had massed in city squares to hear his impassioned speeches against the withdrawal. Speaking with extraordinary fierceness, he had depicted it as a national disaster, if not an outright catastrophe. Now, he would have to struggle between reality and his own conscience; his was the choice between taking the peace process to its conclusion—or missing the opportunity. Above all, I was troubled by the question of whether Menachem Begin would manage to shake off the chains of his past and fling aside the axioms by which he had led his numerous followers from that very first moment in 1943 when he, a Polish soldier in the army of General Anders, had set foot on the soil of the land of Israel. Begin's lofty words had aroused his followers for decades, until finally they brought him to power. Would he remain in their thrall?

At the same time, I could not allow myself to be seduced in the other direction.

Weizman! I told myself. *Watch out! Don't fall for the sweet words you heard back there and don't allow yourself to be carried away by the intoxicating welcome or the landscapes or by suddenly seeing your enemies as human beings who don't have horns sprouting from the center of their foreheads. No one can guarantee that they aren't misleading you—and your country.*

The minister of defense was responsible for preserving Israel's might, for safeguarding the alertness of her army and for fostering its ability to win any war by rapidly carrying it into enemy territory. The Egyptian position, as voiced by Sadat and Gamasy, placed me in a difficult quandary. Hearing their views, any other minister—justice, for example, or foreign affairs—would hardly have had to face such a painful dilemma. After all, neither had to bear personal responsibility for Israel's security. After the Yom Kippur War, that responsibility was doubly significant. As defense minister, I could not acquiesce in the Egyptian demand that we give up the Sinai, with the airfields and the Rafah buffer settlements. However, as an Israeli who has taken part in all our wars, with a closeup view of the bloodshed, I also could not remain indifferent to the prospect of putting a stop to it and perhaps achieving close ties with those who were our enemies until yesterday.

I smiled to myself recalling our threadbare and overworked clichés. "There's no one to talk to!" we had said over and over again whenever we faced the possibility of an understanding with the Arab world.

After a few hours in the land of the Nile, I knew that was now meaningless. There *is* someone to talk to.

"Ezra!" President Sadat's words reechoed in my mind: "Pay attention! I'm talking big business. . . ."

I had come at him with a slingshot, proposing a direct telephone link between our Southern Command and the headquarters of his Third Army—and he'd bombarded me with his heaviest ammunition: exchange of ambassadors, total normalization, commercial relations, and tourism. There are states with whom we have never been at war, yet although we have fairly normal relations with them, we maintain no diplomatic missions in their capitals. Our relations with Spain are friendly, although there is no El Al route to Madrid and no Israeli embassy there. Sadat was proposing to take the hostile relations between our two countries—and transform them into closer ties than we had with many others. This was radically new. Even if his demands were unchanged, the fact is that he was willing to give us full diplomatic recognition.

The more I thought about it and considered the change in all its aspects, the more I grasped the full extent of the historic opportunity. I found myself believing in the optimistic version of my report.

At the same time, I knew I must devote even greater attention to stepping up the alertness of our forces and buttressing their strength. I would have to adopt a grotesque posture: while embracing peace with both arms, I would be looking around to make sure I didn't get stabbed in the back.

Sadat once told me that he had reached his decision to come to Jerusalem while flying over the Ararat mountains in Turkey. My companions would remember our one-and-a-half-hour flight from Cairo to Ben-Gurion Airport as subdued. I saw that flight as ninety minutes of taking stock—personal and national. It did not change me—but it convinced me that our world had changed and that we would have to get used to the change and act accordingly.

Whenever one sets out to storm some objective, it is vital to select forces suitable for the task. Mentally, I reviewed the forces that would join me in my assault on the "objective" of peace. The chairs around the cabinet table were occupied by men who had built their careers on Israel's isolation from the Arab world. There were some you could wake in the middle of the night and with their eyes still closed they could reel off the minutest detail of events in Plonsk in 1910—but they had not the slightest inkling of what went on in an Arab village within Israel last week.

There was, however, one minister on whom I pinned some hopes. He had spent his life fighting the Arabs, but he knew them well. He had made many turnabouts in the course of his life—

whenever the circumstances required it. Perhaps more than any other Israeli leader, he was afflicted by the trauma of the 1973 Yom Kippur War—and that may be why he had girded himself for the long haul that was to raise Israel out of the arena of war. The black patch over his eye had long ago become a symbol of embattled Israel, fighting for dear life.

I must confess that my relations with Moshe Dayan are complex and tortuous. I have known him for thirty-two years; during part of that time, we were related by marriage, as brothers-in-law. Our relationship has had its ups and downs. My elder by nine years, he was always a few steps ahead of me. When he served as chief of staff, I was a mere wing commander in the air force. That distance between us has been maintained over the years. I admire him for his individualism. Something about him makes him hard to pin down: he displays the wiles of a peasant and the deep roots of the Sabra—a blend of stubbornness, wisdom, experience, and considerable personal charm.

His biography parallels that of the state of Israel. He has become familiar to all, the whole world over: every child can identify him. Had he escaped the injury to his eye—I used to say—he would have had to inflict it upon himself to achieve the popularity that brought him admirers from Katmandu in Nepal to Asunción in Paraguay. However, I knew that his injury had also brought him great suffering.

I have always admired him as a soldier. He was the best chief of staff we ever had despite my disagreement with him about the outcome of the 1970 War of Attrition against Egypt. As defense minister, Dayan believed that his conduct of that war was correct. I contended that it had led directly to the Yom Kippur War.

Dayan was responsible for the shortcomings and failures of the Yom Kippur War—although I believe that he was saddled with too much of the blame. Many of the accusations against him were vicious and sharply worded. Dayan did not disown his responsibility, but, speaking for myself, I am more inclined to blame the military echelons.

I felt for Dayan after the war. Israelis love idols, but they also display an unrestrained lust in demolishing them. On the eve of the 1977 Knesset elections, Dayan was at an all-time low. The Labor party did not want him after the stigma of the Yom Kippur War; they would have been glad to get rid of him. I suggested that he join the Likud to broaden its popular following—but that came to nothing. He remained in the Labor party, which debated whether to swallow him or spew him out.

I was surprised and overjoyed at Begin's invitation to Dayan to join his cabinet as foreign minister. Dayan's inclusion, in spite of his not having been elected as a Likud candidate, would improve the cabinet's image in Israel and abroad as well as give it greater weight. I could not help admiring Menachem Begin for the offer, which testified to generosity and political astuteness.

There was not a single minister in the Begin cabinet so perfectly suited to the era of peace as Foreign Minister Moshe Dayan. Friends and foes alike describe him as more Arab than the Arabs. I foresaw that a man of his dimension could give the peace process the impetus it needed. I knew that Begin respected Dayan's views. Begin is perfectly capable of showering his veteran Herut colleagues with flowery compliments, but secretly he does not have any great respect for them—possibly because they have always bowed to his wishes. Begin gave Dayan almost unlimited credit, respecting his abilities and his political sensitivities. At the same time, the appointment did have its explosive implications. Demonstrations by bereaved parents outside Jabotinsky House—Herut's Tel Aviv headquarters—were a striking illustration of the widespread wish to erase the last political vestige of the Yom Kippur failures.

There were lesser drawbacks. Dayan can be compared to a demolition charge designed to bring down the wall of a house: placed incorrectly, it is capable of collapsing the whole structure. To tell the truth, I also bore him a grudge: Dayan could have appointed me chief of staff when he was defense minister. He may have refrained from doing so for fear of being accused of nepotism—we were still brothers-in-law at the time. Or did he have some other reason?

It was obvious to me that Dayan had not become foreign minister for the purpose of holding cocktail parties or lounging about in diplomatic receptions. From the very first, he focused his attention on two objectives: achieving a breakthrough with the Arab world and fostering our relations with the United States. I was in perfect agreement with him about achieving a breakthrough. But I had profound reservations about his attitude toward the relationship between Israel and America in the peace process.

Instead of taking this extraordinary opportunity to negotiate with Egypt directly, with minimal dependence on any third party, Moshe Dayan preferred to bring the United States in at almost every stage. He was convinced there would be no peace unless it was a Pax Americana, to which the White House would commit itself out of America's own interests.

My objections to excessive American involvement in the negotiations with Egypt stemmed from a simple consideration: I foresaw that U.S. interests lay closer to Egypt's than to ours, so that it would not be long before Israeli negotiators would have to cope with a dual confrontation as they faced a Washington-Cairo axis.

To understand why Dayan urged American involvement, it is necessary to remember his political heritage. Moshe Dayan was a great disciple of the late David Ben-Gurion. For Ben-Gurion and for his generation, certain things were axiomatic. B.-G., as we called him, always preached that we should be very, very careful not to be completely on our own, that we need one or probably two of the major powers in the world behind us. For example, in 1956, he didn't tackle the Sinai problem without France and England. (France and England were far greater powers then, and England was in the Canal Zone until the early fifties. In fact, Egypt was liberated from the British about five years after we were.) Again in 1967, on the eve of the Six-Day War, when we were on our own with the whole world taking the attitude to Israel of "very nice to have known you," we were considering striking first at Egypt. Rabin and others went to ask B.-G. what he thought of it, and he said, "Are you crazy, you're going to go without a major power to support you?" Yet we did do it on our own—Lyndon Johnson seems to have told the Russians, "You keep hands off and so will we"—and it was a beautiful Israeli operation.

At any rate, Dayan always worried about the reaction of the Russians to any military action we'd take. Similarly, in the case of the peace initiatives—a complete change in the Middle East through political action—he did not believe success was possible without the participation of the United States. Perhaps he was skeptical because he never thought Sadat would conclude any agreement with us on his own—a separate peace without the other Arab states involved in the conflict.

As I've said, I also knew nothing of Dayan's earlier contacts with the Arabs, which may have contributed to his attitude to Sadat's overtures. The prime minister had not seen fit to let me in on the secret. I was astounded when I learned that Dayan had been to Rabat in September and met with Egyptian Deputy Prime Minister Tohamy.

After Sadat had concluded his visit to Israel, contacts with Egypt did not cease. An Israeli emissary undertook a secret mission to Cairo. Moshe Dayan went to Morocco in December for a second meeting with Tohamy; this encounter was far more relaxed than the first because the intervening time had witnessed Sadat's visit to Jerusalem, when Tohamy had been a member of his entourage.

Ezer during the War of Independence, 1948

Left: Defense Minister
Weizman's first day in
office ARMY SPOKESMAN'S OFFICE
Below: Flying to
Jerusalem YOSSI ROTH
Right: Ezer's car after
the accident SHALOM BAR TAL

Left: Israeli children
welcoming Sadat, Nov. 1977
ISRAELI GOV'T PRESS OFFICE
Below: left to right,
Ehrlich, Begin, Yadin, Dayan
and Weizman applauding
Sadat in the Knesset   UZI KEREN
Right: First meeting in Egypt,
Dec. 1977   ARMY SPOKEMAN'S OFFICE

Left: Presenting Sadat with clock inscribed to
"the leader who moved the clock forward"
Top: With Gamasy at Ismailia convention
Bottom: left to right, Howeidi, Gamasy, Ezer,
Tehila, Ben Elissar, and bodyguard Amos at Cairo
International Airport

Above: Tahara palace,
site of military
committee meeting
ARMY SPOKESMAN'S OFFICE
Left: Sha'ul Weizman,
right, and Hisham, son of
Mustafa Khalil, in Egypt
Right: Ezer greeting
Egyptians on the streets
of Cairo DAVID RUBINGER

Above: Re'uma
and Ezer visiting
Cairo Museum
Left: Eating cakes
in the Groppi
Cafe, Cairo
ARMY SPOKESMAN'S OFFICE
Right: With Moshe
Dayan YOSSI ROTH

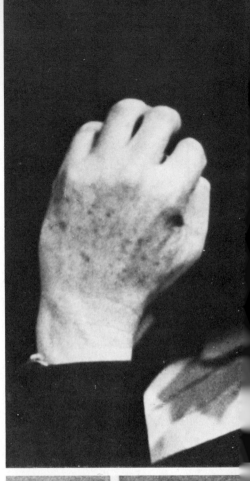

Top: Talking to
Menachem Begin
YOSSI ROTH
Bottom: Ezer between
the outgoing chief
of staff, Motta Gur, right,
and the incoming
Rafful Eitan, April 1978
YOSSI ROTH

Top: With Arik Sharon after a Cabinet
meeting ARMY SPOKESMAN'S OFFICE
Bottom: At a party with faithful aide
Chaim Israeli ARMY SPOKESMAN'S OFFICE
Right: Reviewing troops in March 1978
with Secretary of Defense Harold Brown
at the Pentagon WIDE WORLD PHOTOS

Left: At a training
exercise in the Negev
ARMY SPOKESMAN'S OFFICE
Below: Surveying damage
from a Katyusha rocket
at a northern kibbutz
ARMY SPOKESMAN'S OFFICE

Dayan brought Tohamy the proposals formulated in Jerusalem on the strength of Sadat's declarations to Begin: the Egyptian president had announced his intention of proclaiming the straits near the port of Sharm el Sheik an international waterway and stated his willingness to demilitarize the Sinai and keep the portions east of the Mitla and Gidi Passes free of troops.

Dayan submitted Israel's proposals: our forces would withdraw from the whole of the Sinai; the area east of the passes would be demilitarized, as Sadat had proposed; the Rafah settlements would be left in place, their inhabitants remaining subject to Israeli law as well as being permitted to maintain a defensive police force; Sharm el Sheik and the Etam airfield would become civilian installations, to be managed by Israelis under UN supervision; the fate of the Etzion airfield would be discussed in separate talks. Dayan proposed that the entire agreement come up for reconsideration in the year 2000.

It never occurred to me that Dayan, with Begin's backing, would discuss giving up the whole of the Sinai without so much as consulting the defense minister. Only later did I realize that Sadat's hard-line stance that so discouraged me in my meeting with him in Ismailia was, in fact, an outright rejection of Dayan's proposals to Tohamy—of which I was in total ignorance. Begin's inappropriate secretiveness in this instance was about to be repeated with graver consequences.

On my return to Israel, I was received with a blend of curiosity and suspicion. My cabinet colleagues swooped down on me, eager to hear my impressions of Egypt. In their excitement, some of them seized on the most trivial details, as though I had just come back from a holiday jaunt. I presented the situation exactly as it was, positive and negative. They responded to the negative. Their mistrust soon became evident in their characterizations of Sadat: bizarre, unstable, unpredictable.

Within the defense establishment, I set up a think tank, feeding its members with my impressions and all other relevant data. In the course of my years of military service, such staff work has become second nature to me. I hoped the cabinet would do likewise and summon all the available experts to exchange views and formulate a policy. After all, we were witnessing events of historic significance; as Prime Minister Begin, in his inimitable rhetoric, repeatedly stressed the historical dimension, I expected him to follow my example.

I was soon to learn my error.

In preparing his proposals for Arab administrative self-government in the West Bank, Begin had preserved the utmost secrecy, seeing fit to confide in no more than a handful of individuals. Others, such as his own adviser on Arab affairs, were not even consulted.

Begin does not work with a cabinet; he operates by means of an office. Leaders of his type need no advisers; they make do with aides. He is incapable of taking into account views or proposals that do not fit in with his own basic philosophy. The people in Begin's immediate vicinity do not submit different proposals or put forward a range of alternatives. This is partly the result of their past experience, which has taught them that such alternatives have no chance of being adopted; but mostly it is because Begin has chosen aides of a very specific human and political stamp. They think as he does. Having learned to guess what Begin wants, they try to outdo one another in proposing ideas that will be to the prime minister's liking and thus win his approval.

The executive branch of a Western-type state like Israel cannot function in such a manner—certainly not in the eighties. The problems confronting Israel are complex and intricate. Steering a state through our modern epoch calls for more than any one man can provide. He needs a team of advisers to feed him data and help him formulate his decisions. He needs to have command of thousands of items of information in diverse areas, beginning with economic and social problems through to technology, energy, and security.

When Begin took up his post as prime minister, I deluded myself into thinking the office would change him: suddenly confronted with the complexities of his task, he would have to alter his habits and rid himself of the behavior patterns acquired during the years in opposition. But as I soon learned, Begin is far stronger than the forces of reality. Every now and then, there was some microscopic signal that he was requesting advice. However, this was usually done with the aim of hooking the adviser into agreeing with the suggestion Begin had already put forward. As far as that type of political ruse is concerned, Begin has few rivals in Israel.

Several of Begin's self-declared admirers like to compare him to David Ben-Gurion: like Begin, Ben-Gurion did not share his decisions with others. This comparison ignores the fact that the level of activity in various areas was much lower and on a far smaller scale in Ben-Gurion's time. I myself found it hard to recognize the defense establishment on my return to it as defense minister—even though it had not been so long since I had resigned my post as head of GHQ's staff branch. In Israel—as in the other Western democracies—there is no return to the days of the Churchills and the de Gaulles.

Begin's mode of operation took its toll the moment Israel began to follow the course toward peace. His unshakable adherence to the perpetuation of Israeli rule over the West Bank and Gaza Strip led him into the autonomy plan. It may seem paradoxical that a man with Begin's unswerving commitment to the national-historical boundaries of the land of Israel could be the architect of a plan that some saw as the first step to a Palestinian state. In fact, Begin was being consistent. Rather than viewing autonomy as the beginning of Arab self-rule, Begin saw it as the way to prevent Israeli withdrawal. And he consulted no one who might seek to deflect him in his views.

On the eve of his departure for the United States in December 1977, where he was to present his plan to President Jimmy Carter, Begin sprang the surprise—not only upon the Israeli public but on his own cabinet as well. Scarcely any of the ministers had even heard of the plan. It was flung at the cabinet lock, stock, and barrel, making modifications of any of its component sections a difficult task. I was dissatisfied. No one had consulted the chief of staff, not even on the security aspects of the plan. Begin submitted the proposals—twenty-six points on what council should be elected on the West Bank, how resources should be controlled, and various other clauses—and promptly adopted his own recommendations.

"A plan of genius!" was the verdict of Deputy Prime Minister Yigael Yadin.

I did not share his enthusiasm. I knew the Egyptians would not accept the plan in its entirety. Neither Sadat nor Carter, for that matter, had talked about autonomy; they had spoken of a solution to the Palestinian problem. Nevertheless, I thought it might be better to bring a controversial plan, just as long as it led the parties to further talks. My assumption was a simple one: the more the two sides met, the more they looked one another in the eye and learned to listen to each other—the faster our mutual suspicions would melt away. I regarded the autonomy plan as the lesser evil.

Arik Sharon, minister of agriculture, did not agree. He said that the plan contained numerous dangers—it could be a declaration of independence for the Palestinians. But it might also be a plan we could live with, depending on what we did up to the time autonomy came about.

The prime minister took his autonomy plan to Washington and indeed presented it to President Carter as a temporary phase en route to annexation. When Carter's aides examined the plan, however, they came to a different conclusion. In their opinion, autonomy for the Arabs on the West Bank and in Gaza would result in the emergence of a Palestinian state. That may be why they hastened to commend it. Menachem Begin fell into the trap and returned from America jubilant, boasting of his success. "All who beheld it praised it," he repeatedly declared. Of Carter, Begin said, "I haven't met such an intellect since Jabotinsky."

What Carter had actually said was "It's a very interesting plan." Each misread the other—and the results of this misunderstanding were to emerge at Camp David.

A few days later, accompanied by Dayan and myself, Begin set off for Ismailia and his second meeting with the Egyptian president.

10

DEADLOCK

El Al's flight 447 from Tel Aviv to Ismailia, which carried Prime Minister Begin on his first visit to Egypt in December 1977, bore him a long way off the course traditionally followed by his Herut party. Next to Begin sat his aide, Yechiel Kadishai, holding a briefcase that contained the plan for granting administrative autonomy to the Palestinian Arabs.

No verbal acrobatics could conceal the truth—however awkward it might be. The Likud's election manifesto had mentioned the possibility of offering the Arabs living in the West Bank and Gaza cultural autonomy. But *administrative* autonomy constituted a far-reaching concession to the Palestinians. Herut traditionalists were shocked; they realized that such a program implied scrapping the party's dream of applying Israeli law to Judea and Samaria—the West Bank—and to the Gaza district. They mounted demonstrations against the plan—and against Begin himself. The prime minister spoke up in his own defense: "I, too, could be extremist, but I have to shoulder the responsibility with that degree of civic courage without which there are no political decisions." I imagine that he must have suffered great pangs of conscience before bringing up the idea of autonomy. In my eyes, the autonomy scheme constituted striking proof that Begin was capable of change—toward the internal affairs of Israel as well as the external. Despite his way of going about it—without consulting anyone—I was filled with hope.

In effect, I should not have been surprised. During the years that had elapsed since the Six-Day War, Begin had had several opportunities to demand an Israeli annexation of the West Bank and Gaza. Although he served in various cabinets, he had never submitted such a demand. Furthermore, in June 1967—a few days after our Six-Day War victory—Begin joined his fellow ministers in the cabinet of National Unity in agreeing to withdraw to the international boundaries in the Sinai and the Golan Heights—in return for peace. My subsequent disappointment in him was in this area: that he later backed off from implementing the autonomy agreements because his desire for annexation under the old Herut dream ultimately overcame the visionary in him that would strive for peace.

During the sendoff at Ben-Gurion Airport, my eyes followed Begin as he paced toward the plane. I could not suppress my admiration. That week, he had returned from a round of exhausting talks in the White House. The day before taking off for Ismailia, he'd presided over a long cabinet meeting—a tiring, nerve-racking affair that had dragged on till after midnight. This morning, his face bore the plain marks of his weariness, but he overcame his fatigue with the aid of his dramatic flair.

When the prime minister took his seat inside the plane, a moving incident occurred: unexpectedly, one of the stewardesses flung her arms around his neck, clinging to him and sobbing. Her husband had fallen on Egyptian soil during the Yom Kippur War. Begin almost burst into tears himself.

Just as on my previous flight to Ismailia, our takeoff was a stirring moment. We were flying toward a rendezvous with opportunity. Peace appeared to be within arm's reach even if plenty of obstacles still remained to be overcome. As the plane left the ground, I looked out the window one last time. Would we navigate the craft of peace to a safe landing?

A warm breeze greeted us on our arrival on the west bank of the Suez Canal. But our hosts' reception was chilly. In contrast with the warm and imposing welcome extended to Sadat on his arrival in Israel, neither the Egyptian president nor his prime minister was awaiting us at the airport. There were no flags, no band to play the national anthems—not even banners with messages of greeting. Nothing at all.

Our reception at the Abu Swair military airfield was a disturbing comedown after the high spirits that had marked the forty-minute flight from Ben-Gurion Airport. The euphoria of peace had engulfed the plane. Along with Begin were Moshe Dayan, foreign minister; Shlomo Gazit, head of military intelligence; General Abrasha Tamir, head of planning; Herzl Shapir, head of Southern Command; as well as others. Everyone had looked out as the plane entered Egyptian airspace in the Port Said area. (The Egyptians did me the honor of naming the route we were following "The Weizman Corridor.")

At Abu Swair, our mood had abruptly changed. There was something about the landscape that deepened our gloom. The airfield is in the desert, and while we were still in the plane, I spotted burned-out aircraft hangars, mementos of the wars of 1967 and 1973. Soldiers in khaki provided a drab welcome on the historic occasion.

Deputy President Hosni Mubarak was waiting at the foot of the gangway. He tried to smile, but his face soon reverted to a stolid, inscrutable expression.

Protocol does not require a president to come and receive a visiting prime minister. All the same, I had expected a gesture on the part of Sadat, and I was disappointed.

I knew Begin's sensitivity to his dignity and national honor. It is not merely an unslakable thirst for glory. For years he was a political outcast. On gaining power, he quite justifiably sought the deference previously denied him. On top of that, he is very partial to ceremony and symbolism. I have never underrated them myself, and I was even less inclined to do so after Sadat's visit to Jerusalem showed them to be so valuable in breaking down the psychological barrier. I hoped Begin would not mind the frosty reception, but I knew there was little chance that it would escape his notice.

To make matters worse, Moshe Dayan proceeded to pour oil on the flames. "Look!" he said to Begin as we made our way toward the president's holiday residence. "Not a single Israeli flag, not even a banner slogan to welcome us."

I was furious. I could not understand the Egyptians. Did they consider this visit of ours a matter of trifling importance? I wanted to vent my rage on someone: Egyptian War Minister Gamasy caught part of its force. "In Israel we received President Sadat with all due honor," I growled. "Look how you are receiving us!"

Gamasy almost certainly sensed the anger in my tone, but he pretended not to hear.

"Mr. Begin," Dayan said again. "Look, not a single flag. . . ."

We found Ismailia a riot of color. Motley arches spanned the main streets. On every side, festive portraits of Sadat—in naval or military uniform or in civilian dress—smiled at us in glorious oriental technicolor. Thousands of banners sang the praises of the Egyptian president in unqualified superlatives.

Without exception, the arches and banners ignored the appearance of Menachem Begin. It was a glaring omission, and an unwise one, in my opinion. The chilly welcome, the indifference toward Begin, the flouting of the most elementary rules of protocol and courtesy—all these could only be harmful to our talks.

On the way to Sadat's home, I tried to put myself in the shoes of the Egyptian president. There could be no doubt that Sadat had approved the instructions to refrain from hoisting Israeli flags or displaying messages of welcome to Begin. His intention was plain: he did not want to further antagonize the Arab world, which was already up in arms against him. He was cursed and vilified in Syria and Libya, in Jordan and Iraq. In Baghdad and Damascus, feverish consultations were underway with the purpose of putting an early end to Sadat's initiative—and to him, too, if possible. Arab ambassadors were leaving Cairo. Tourists from Arab countries were also departing. Arab airlines had closed down their offices in the Egyptian capital. Egyptian citizens became undesirable in other Arab countries. Without question, Sadat was in a difficult situation. I tried to take his problems into account, but I could not bring myself to waive the honor due to the state of Israel and to its prime minister.

Certain Israelis managed to put me in an even worse temper. The black official cars provided by the presidential office did not have enough room for the many visitors from Tel Aviv and Jerusalem, and some had to be taken by bus. One senior military personage, mortally offended, voiced his protest. *He's certainly found the right time*, I thought; *history is breathing down our necks, and he's got nothing better to do than defend his fragile dignity by demanding an upholstered seat in an Egyptian limousine.*

Right from the outset of our mission, I was surprised and disconcerted to find the prime minister's entourage including a number of figures whose presence in Ismailia I failed for the life of me to understand. I have no idea why Begin decided to take along business tycoons on this extraordinary mission. If it were up to me, I would have invited representatives of our bereaved parents, our veterans and military invalids—all those whose sacrifices, pains, and losses had made this moment possible.

No one had any foreknowledge of the agenda awaiting us in Ismailia. Certainly, no one could predict how our talks would end. Begin came armed with his peace plan—to concede parts of the

Sinai in exchange for retaining the settlements and oil—and the autonomy proposal. We did not know what rabbit Sadat would whip out of his hat this time. There was no doubt in my mind that President Carter had briefed Sadat on Begin's proposals. In my assessment, Sadat would be profoundly concerned lest Begin had succeeded in gaining White House backing for his peace plan. I expected to find him tense and nervous—at least, until matters became a little clearer.

The Egyptian president was awaiting us at the precise spot where he had received me a few days before. Contrary to my expectations, he was relaxed and at ease. Smiling broadly, he faced hundreds of cameras, joking with Begin about the heart ailments that afflict both men. Gusts of laughter arose from the small group surrounding them.

All the same, I was on edge. I knew that Sadat would propose full peace. What could we offer in exchange? What were we prepared to give? We had never thought through these questions. I could imagine the bitter disagreements in the Israeli public, possibly even within the cabinet itself.

We took our seats in a long, rectangular chamber. It was hot and crowded.

Sadat chose to inaugurate the proceedings in an astoundingly original manner. "I wish," he announced, "to swear in my new foreign minister."

Mohammed Ibrahim Kamel had received his appointment that same day, having been recalled from his post at the Egyptian embassy in Bonn to take over from Fahmy and Riad, who had resigned with such a resounding flourish in protest against Sadat's peace initiative.

Feeling like guests at someone else's wedding, we got up to leave the chamber, but Sadat signaled us to remain. He wanted to make us feel at home. With my love of spontaneity and my contempt for convention, I was delighted by the impromptu ceremony. Extending a Koran, Sadat administered the oath to Kamel, a close friend since they had been jailed together in the forties for political reasons. (Kamel had been released before Sadat: "His family was more influential," Sadat joked when telling me about it later.)

The swearing-in ceremony united us all—Egyptians and Israelis—into a kind of large extended family assembled to consider its joint future and the future of its children. At its conclusion, Sadat and Begin retired to an adjoining room, leaving the rest of us in confusion. I racked my brains to think of a valuable way to use the time. Suddenly, I got a brain wave.

"Could I call up Mustafa Khalil in Cairo?" I asked State Secretary for Foreign Affairs Boutros Ghali. Ghali was startled by the request, probably wondering what business I had with Khalil. He, too, was not yet accustomed to the changing circumstances. As for me, I saw Khalil almost as an old friend even though we had met only once, in Jerusalem, for that long conversation into the night.

I tried to telephone him in Cairo, but I could scarcely hear his voice. This was my first experience with one of Egypt's major problems: its telephone network. You can dial a number, but the lines simply do not function.

Begin and Sadat were not away for long. When the door opened, I thought I saw Begin beaming. Sadat appeared indifferent.

"We have agreed," Begin proclaimed, "to establish two committees—one political, the other military."

At first hearing, the idea did not strike me as particularly brilliant. I saw the Israeli-Egyptian peace treaty as a blend of political, military, social, economic, and cultural factors. I feared that the separation of political and military issues would bring in its wake a whole trail of difficulties, undermining the peace process. But I accepted the proposal—just as long as the talking went on and there was no letup in the momentum of the negotiations.

I was pleasantly surprised by Sadat's consent to Jerusalem's being the meeting place for the political committee. It augured well, implying some measure of recognition that Jerusalem was Israel's capital. I suppose my face must have shown my pleasure. Moshe Dayan's expression remained dour. He is not inclined toward emotionalism and certainly does not display his feelings.

"The Americans ought to be brought in," said Dayan.

I looked at Gamasy, and he looked at me. For what must have been the first time, we understood one another in a single glance, with no need to say anything.

"We don't need to bring in the Americans on the military side," I said. "We can manage on our own."

"Right!" the Egyptian war minister agreed.

Gamasy's response delighted me. Many of the Israelis present were convinced that the United States had a major role to play in the peace process. I differed, regarding this marked dependence on the friendly superpower across the Atlantic as a vestige of the mentality that characterized the Jews of the pale of settlement in Russia, where they lived under the protection and authority of their local overlords. I find it an alien attitude, reflecting a ghetto mentality.

I was convinced that meetings like our current one—face to face with the Egyptians—provided an extraordinary opportunity and an important precedent for resolving differences without recourse to outside mediators. For many years, we had yearned for the moment when we would find ourselves around the conference table with the Egyptians, as neighbors, without having to pin our hopes on some third party. I saw no reason why we should pass up the chance to try.

Dayan thought otherwise—and I cannot deny he had good reason. He foresaw the difficulties in store for us all along the way, at every stage of the negotiations. At cabinet meetings in Jerusalem, he had repeatedly voiced his prediction that nothing would budge without the assistance of the U.S. administration, and certainly not without its backing. He wanted to place the peace process under the full patronage of President Jimmy Carter. Dayan had been strongly in favor of presenting our peace plan to Carter even before its official submission to President Sadat. He had found an enthusiastic supporter in Secretary of State Cyrus Vance, who had visited Jerusalem a few days before our departure for Ismailia. Vance's support was understandable: he wanted to give the United States full control of the Middle East peace process.

Either way, the agreement on the two committees was a good start, and the atmosphere immediately improved. Before the day ended, I hoped we would startle the world with a communiqué heralding yet another swift step toward peace. My eagerness was based on an anxiety I still harbored. I was afraid that the peace talks could drag on endlessly: time was pressing for Sadat. From the moment he'd announced his intention of coming to Jerusalem, he had built up great momentum. "We must not allow it to slacken," I urged my colleagues. There must be a rapid transition to peace. I knew certain Israelis would mock me, denying the need for haste. "What's the hurry? We've waited thirty years, we can wait a little longer," they would say.

Yet every process has its own dynamism, just as every vehicle has its own cruising speed. Twenty-five miles per hour on a bicycle is very fast, but it's a snail's pace for a car. Driving too fast along an urban highway can end in disaster, but on the battlefield or under bombardment or in an assault, speed is of the essence: it can save lives. In 1967, I had joined my friend Motti Hod, then commander of the air force, in throwing all our influence at GHQ behind the plan to attack the Egyptian airfields, thereby determining the outcome of the war in three brief hours. On that occasion, swiftness played a decisive role. My job had changed; instead of a war room, I found myself in the negotiating chamber—and again I urged "full speed ahead" to take advantage of the momentum and strike at the chink in the psychological barrier for a speedy break-through.

I do not believe that this was an example of that foolhardiness of which I am sometimes accused. The opposite is true: having weighed all elements of the situation, I saw great advantages in a rapid thrust toward our objective.

As the proceedings went on, Sadat did his best to be affable. "Today is my birthday," he said, addressing Begin, "and so, this is a wonderful occasion on which to meet with you, here in Egypt, in an effort to put an end to the sufferings of our two peoples."

It was hot and crowded. Everyone squeezed around the table, apparently eager to huddle under the warm cloak of history. Every now and then, white-gloved waiters were summoned by hand claps to serve cups of green tea.

Sadat added: "This may be the first time we have sat together since the time Moses crossed the Red Sea, not far from here. We are sitting together to tell the whole world that we are working for peace and that we shall establish peace and love. Love will always guide our relationship—instead of the bitterness and hatred of the past thirty years."

Begin came right back on the same note: "Our heartfelt wishes on your fifty-ninth birthday," he said. "We know that you were born in a small village, in poverty, and that you attained your present position by your own efforts and sacrifices."

Sadat's expression displayed his unconcealed gratification. The Israeli prime minister was playing the game with great pro-ficiency.

"We have the most profound feelings of respect toward you as a man and as a leader," Begin continued. "In Jewish tradition, a man is congratulated on his birthday with the wish that he might live to one hundred and twenty. I know that might be difficult . . ."

Everyone smiled.

Following Sadat's lead, Begin went on: "When Moses led us out of Egypt, it took him forty years to cross the Sinai desert. Today we did it in forty minutes. Not only will we make peace—we will become friends."

The mutual courtesies came to an end. The two leaders resem-bled a couple of boxers who, having clambered up into the ring and exchanged warm handshakes, were now ready to trade punches.

Begin brought out the Israeli peace plan. Calling on all his rhetorical powers, he proceeded to expound upon it elaborately and at great length. Each sentence was read out clearly, in measured, stately tones. It was perfectly plain that Sadat had already received the plan from the Americans and studied it thoroughly. Furthermore, he had shown absolutely no inclination to address himself to the details, preferring to see the forest rather than the trees.

But Begin went on regardless. He was relishing the occasion. There were moments when he looked like a preacher, or a professor holding forth to his pupils. As on many other occasions during his career, he was demonstrating his faith in words and their capacity for initiating great changes—in addition to convincing his hearers.

His address engendered boredom all around. Dayan showed signs of irritability. I looked up at the ceiling and down at the floor, with occasional glances at Gamasy and Boutros Ghali. The Egyptians were courteously trying to listen to every word, but the crowding around the table began to take effect as various people fidgeted uneasily in their chairs. Sadat dabbed at his perspiring forehead, repeatedly calling the waiters to bring him cups of tea.

It was just what I had dreaded. Instead of discussing principles, Begin plunged into the smallest details, point by point, as though he and Sadat were to conduct every step of the negotiations, from beginning to end, at this preliminary discussion.

Now that Begin was fully launched, there was no stopping him. He went on reciting his homily, without blinking an eye—until he walked into the minefield. "I propose," he said, "that the Israeli settlements between Rafah and El Arish, and those between Eilat and Sharm el Sheik, remain in place."

Sadat looked impatient. He looked at me, trying to read my expression. Only a few days ago, he had told me that such a decision was out of the question and that the Sinai settlements as well as the airfields would have to be removed. His face showed his puzzlement, as though he were asking if I had briefed the prime minister on my talk with him. I gave him to understand that I had.

"Mr. President"—Begin ignored the rising tension—"the settlements will not infringe upon Egyptian sovereignty. I should point out that we cannot leave our settlements and our citizens without a means of self-defense."

I thought this was the end and expected Sadat to terminate the meeting. I knew he would not hear of such a thing. But I also assumed that Begin was stating his most extreme position, with the intention of compromising later on.

The prime minister reminded Sadat of the enormity of our concessions. "I want you to know that in deciding this, my government has abrogated the policies of every Israeli government since 1967, which demanded that the strip of land from Eilat to Sharm el Sheik should remain under Israeli control. I myself was minister without portfolio in the cabinet of Golda Meir, and I had a hand in that decision. Mr. President, we are now prepared to concede that position."

I cast a sideways glance at Moshe Dayan. Begin's words must have deeply affected him, even though he had given his prior approval to the prime minister's proposals. It was Dayan who had repeated, over and over again: "Better Sharm el Sheik without peace than peace without Sharm el Sheik." Dayan had thought up the idea of constructing the settlement of Yamit, and his initiative got the project launched. Dayan had headed the defense establishment while our forces were paying in blood for the conquest of the Sinai peninsula, including the Rafah approaches and Sharm el Sheik. What was going on in his mind at this moment? What about his supporters—how would he look them in the face? What would he say to those families that had responded to the appeals of the Israeli government to build their homes in the Rafah sand dunes?

"We have before us a peace treaty that shall last for generations." Begin's grandiloquent tone was in flagrant contrast to the edgy atmosphere in the chamber. His intonation gave me to understand that he was about to end his address. "I propose that the treaty remain in force till the year 2001—when we shall reconsider it," he added. I smiled to myself, doubting whether any of those present would live to reconsider it. All the same, it was the correct thing to say. I, too, had told Sadat that treaties are made between nations, not between leaders. Begin seemed to have read my thoughts: "We don't know who will be my successor or yours—and this treaty must survive for more than a single generation."

Everyone was convinced that Begin had concluded. We were all impatient. The chamber was thick with cigarette smoke. The Egyptians remained courteous, but I imagined they must be at the very end of their tether. A break now would have been timely, but Begin, ignoring everyone, ploughed right on. From the peace plan, he went on to detail the Israeli proposal for autonomy in the West Bank and the Gaza Strip.

"It is my duty and prerogative," he said in a firm voice, as though just commencing his address, "to state that Israel claims sovereignty by right over Judea, Samaria, and the Gaza district. We know there are other claims to sovereignty. To attain peace, we propose to leave the question of sovereignty open."

I knew how hard it was for Begin to make such a proposal. Ever since his youth, as a member of the Betar youth movement in Brest Litovsk, through his tenure as commander of the Irgun underground, and, finally, as the leader of Herut, he had never stopped believing in and promoting the unity of the land of Israel. Ever since the Six-Day War, Herut had advocated Israeli annexation of the West Bank and the Gaza Strip. Now he was proposing to grant the inhabitants of these regions self-government. It was the painful sacrifice of his dream, and he must have hoped that Sadat would appreciate the enormity of the concession.

But the Egyptian president appeared to be directing his attention elsewhere. The room was very stuffy, and everyone was losing patience.

Begin ignored the signs.

"Sadat is very nervous," I whispered into Begin's ear.

I must have broken his train of thought. Stopping his recitation, he looked at me in annoyance. "I, too, am very nervous," he replied, and read on. It was endless.

I scribbled an anxious note to General Tamir: "Are we going to leave here with our tails between our legs?"

"No," Tamir replied prophetically. "But we *are* going to spend a long time chasing our own tails."

On both sides of the table, the only ones to listen carefully to every single word were the representatives of the two foreign ministries and the jurists in each delegation. But while the Israelis, in deference to Begin, listened impassively, the other side displayed indignation. In addition to their disapproval of the substance of his address, their expressions clearly showed resentment of Begin's manner of presenting it without skipping a single item. Every now and then, Sadat glanced at his subordinates in an apparent attempt to gauge their reactions. Boutros Ghali was increasingly agitated.

Toward the end, Begin made another error in relating that the U.S. president as well as the British prime minister had praised his plan. There was nothing secret about that. Even before leaving for Ismailia, the prime minister had told the news media of the plan "that was praised by everyone who saw it." The statement was not quite accurate. Admittedly, Carter and Callaghan had commended the plan, but only as a good starting point for negotiations—and nothing more. Internal White House briefings had used far less flattering terms about the Israeli plan. Mention of the praise it had earned could only anger Sadat and his aides, who had no desire to find themselves in conflict with the United States, on top of their differences with Israel.

"According to the basic handbooks of international law, in the words of Lauterfacht and Oppenheim—"

Sadat clapped his hands, and a waiter appeared. "*Iftach al shubach*, open the window," the president commanded. A little air entered the smoke-filled chamber.

An audible sigh of relief came from all sides as Israelis and Egyptians stretched their cramped limbs.

Sadat began his reply, addressing Begin: "As I told you privately, Egypt has certain commitments to the Arab world. We are under an obligation to the Arab summit conference at Rabat on two points: withdrawal from the territories occupied in 1967 and a solution to the Palestinian problem."

As was to be expected, Sadat did not speak at length. He said that details would be discussed by the two committees—military and political. He repeated his reference to "big business" and suggested that the meeting conclude with a declaration of principles, which he, of course, phrased in accordance with his own views— withdrawal to the 1967 borders and a solution of the Palestinian problem.

As it entered its practical phase, the Ismailia conference took on the aspect of a dialogue of the deaf. Begin had brought a peace plan and an autonomy proposal, both of which he regarded as far-reaching, whereas Sadat merely wanted to issue a short communiqué, not more than two or three lines—but that was precisely what we could not grant him. The clash was unavoidable.

Dayan tried to salvage the situation, asking whether it might be possible to discuss principles, with the exclusion of the Palestinian problem. He had hit the nail on the head, and Sadat hastened to agree: "We don't have to go into details on their behalf, we won't go into that." But Begin refused to hear of this proposal.

"On Friday," I broke in, in an attempt to save the airfields and the Rafah settlements, "I spoke with American Ambassador Samuel Lewis in Tel Aviv. He said that President Sadat is offering us everything, for he is offering us peace. I agreed with him, saying that two months ago no one would have believed that such talks could be held. But I asked him: 'You, in the United States, do you have peace with the Soviet Union? Why, then, do you keep such a large army in Western Germany? Why do you keep the Sixth Fleet in the Mediterranean?' Lewis replied: 'To maintain the peace.' I said that to maintain the peace, the military men must trust one another. I spent twenty-four hours in the company of General Gamasy. Personally, I enjoyed every moment. But I wouldn't say I got anything substantive out of it."

Gamasy nodded his concurrence. Sadat looked at me like an old friend.

"Mr. President," I addressed him, "when you said you want a lot of troops and installations along the Canal, I asked you what you need them for. You said: 'To defend us from you.' To be honest, I don't understand that. Everyone says there is now trust, that a new era has begun. In that case, I propose that the further apart our armies are and the fewer weapons there are, the better."

"I agree with you, Ezra," Sadat replied. "I don't need a single soldier in Sinai. Up to 1967, we had only one battalion there. Believe me, when we have peace, we won't need that. But the fact is that this is Egyptian territory, and we have to keep forces there, as you have forces on your territory."

I was tired of all this talk. I was also hungry. It was out of the question to continue unless we at least took a short break. I hoped someone would suggest adjourning the meeting.

"Mr. Prime Minister and friends," Sadat said suddenly, "I propose that we suspend the meeting. I want you to see a little of the Canal."

The president led the way, and we followed. Without a word, Sadat seated himself at the wheel of a black Cadillac, motioning to Begin to take the seat beside him while Dayan and I got into the back.

All around us, chaos broke out. Dozens of security guards—Israelis and Egyptians—taken totally by surprise by Sadat's unscheduled step, momentarily lost control. Photographers surged forward to get a shot of the driver and his three riders. Once again, Sadat was showing the spontaneous, unconventional side of his nature. I appreciated these traits of his; they were very much to my liking. I speculated whether Begin would be capable of anything similar but rejected the thought outright—he can't drive!

We drove off into the streets of Ismailia. Gripping the wheel, Sadat explained what we were seeing, speaking with the ease of a professional tour guide. In his tone was a measure—not too pronounced—of pride: "A million refugees who left due to the War of Attrition have returned to the Canal cities. Ismailia was a pile of rubble, but we rebuilt it. Life here has returned to normal."

The black Cadillac completed its tour of the city and we came back.

During the hours of early midday, some of the Israelis wondered aloud when talks would resume. All eyes turned to me: my brief visit to Egypt a few days before gave me the status of an expert on Egyptian matters. As yet, I knew little about the land of the Nile, but my previous visit had taught me that the Egyptians devote their afternoons to repose. Like other Mediterranean peoples, the Egyptians never hurry.

I took advantage of the afternoon break to introduce El Al Director General Motti Hod to Deputy President Hosni Mubarak, who had commanded the Egyptian air force in the Yom Kippur War.

"Motti commanded our air force in 1967," I told Mubarak. "That was before your time, so I don't think you'll have any trouble making friends."

The two men shook hands.

"We should meet," said Mubarak. "We have a lot to talk about."

"We better be careful"—Gamasy, who was standing nearby laughed—"we have three former air force generals here, and they're liable to take over."

The talks began again in the early evening. A light breeze was wafting in from the Canal. The long break had been of benefit principally to the Egyptians; the Israelis had not rested for a single moment, taking advantage of the recess to discuss the substance of Sadat's address.

When we were reinstalled on either side of the conference table, Sadat hastened to eliminate any lingering doubts. "I had a talk here with Ezra last week," he said. "I told him frankly that my people will not consent to your conditions for the Sinai. At the same time, in a spirit of friendship, we are prepared to discuss between us what can be done—but without imposing a solution to the problem by military force. We have a complex from Ben-Gurion's theory about security. He wanted to impose peace upon the Arabs rather than reach an agreement with us. I was a journalist once, and I used to write articles about it."

"We have a lot in common, Mr. President!" Begin broke in jokingly. "Both of us have heart ailments, and both of us have written newspaper articles."

Sadat would not be deflected. "If I tell my people that my friend Begin said the Israeli settlements will remain in Sinai, with a defense force—they will stone me. Believe me, they will stone me!"

That remark let the cat out of the bag, highlighting Sadat's delicate position within the Arab world. He himself might possibly have consented to some concession or other on his own, but he could not afford it. After already denouncing him as a traitor, the Arab world was only waiting for some such concession to renew its onslaught with redoubled ferocity. Sadat had to convince millions of Arabs that he was capable of regaining the Sinai without firing a single shot. I thought I heard a beseeching note in his voice. If we were not to take the wind out of his sails, it was vital to go toward him as far as possible.

Begin took advantage of the mention of Ben-Gurion to reminisce about his own relations with Israel's first prime minister. He must have been aware of the enormous historic irony involved in discussing his greatest political opponent in the presence of the Egyptian president.

"Ben-Gurion and I were rivals for thirty years," Begin recalled. "But for the sake of truth, I must tell you there is a misunderstanding—Ben-Gurion did not wish to impose peace by force."

Subsequently, Begin brought up a topic he never missed an opportunity to mention: the Holocaust. "I lost most of my family then," he said. "That was the most tragic period in our lives. We had no state. The British ruled *Eretz Yisrael*—the land of Israel." Begin sketched out the principal events in our recent history. "In 1948, Ben-Gurion proclaimed our independence—and then on May 15 we were attacked. We had only a few rifles and machine guns. We faced annihilation. There are two men here who took part in the fighting—Dayan and Weizman."

Our talks went on into the night, but we made no progress on substantive issues. Each side dug in its heels. Attempts to span the gap by bridges of words produced nothing.

Long after midnight and again the following day, attempts were made to ward off a stalemate, but they were fruitless.

As we prepared to return home, our mood was heavy. In a bid to inject a brighter note, I approached the Egyptian war minister. "General," I said, "please give instructions to your antiaircraft batteries not to shoot us down, and let us have permission to fly low over the pyramids."

Permission was granted within minutes. After taking off, our plane banked toward the historic monuments, passing over them at an altitude of one thousand feet. We radioed a "thank you" message to our hosts and turned for home. As the pyramids vanished from sight, I tried to tell myself this would not be my last glimpse of them.

But the road to peace seemed to have turned into a blind alley.

11

DUMMY SETTLEMENTS
IN THE DESERT

On the flight home, our spirits were very low. The Ismailia conference had ended in failure. It had also highlighted the glaring differences between the leaders on either side.

Anwar Sadat had hoped the conference would bring about an
understanding in principle. He'd offered Israel full peace—in return for withdrawal from the Sinai and an understanding over the
Palestinians. In my view, what Sadat had wanted was an Israeli
declaration that he could then flaunt before the Arab world and
the Palestinians themselves. That desire was, I believe, no more
than lip service: he was probably the last person in the Middle
East—with the exception of the Israelis, of course—who would
have favored the emergence of a small Palestinian state between
Israel and Jordan, under PLO leadership. Sadat knows that the
PLO leadership is inclined to the Soviet Union. Having dismissed
the Russians from Egypt, he'd hardly welcome a Soviet foothold so
close to his borders.

As for Menachem Begin: he had ignored principles, plunging
into details instead, most of which scarcely interested the Egyptian president.

Anyone observing the two men could not have overlooked the
profound divergence in their attitudes. Both desired peace. But
whereas Sadat wanted to take it by storm, capitalizing on the
momentum from his visit to Jerusalem to reach his final objective,
Begin preferred to creep forward inch by inch. He took the dream

of peace and ground it down into the fine, dry powder of details, legal clauses, and quotes from international law.

A somber atmosphere prevailed in the plane. Begin alone was in high spirits. He was full of smiles and witticisms, exchanging jokes with the journalists who had accompanied us. Taking leave of our Egyptian hosts, I'd overheard him tell them he was going home "a happy man." I found it difficult to comprehend. Was he so divorced from reality that he'd failed to read the map? Was Begin so intoxicated by his own words, by the precepts of international law according to Lauterfacht and Oppenheim that he had quoted at such length, and by the Israeli position he'd expounded with such tiresome thoroughness, that he had once more managed to convince himself he'd succeeded? I preferred to hope that Begin was engaged in verbal sleight of hand, concealing the breakdown behind a thick mantle labeled "the spirit of peace." If that was his intention, it was indeed a clever play.

The day after Ismailia, Israel came down from the peace euphoria of recent weeks. Descending with a jolt from our former Olympian heights to the nitty-gritty of negotiations, we had seen our beautiful dream crumble, the cracks revealing disagreements within the Israeli public and its government. Many Israelis suddenly realized that peace did not grow on trees. It demanded a price—and the price fixed by the Egyptians was a heavy one.

Many of us had grown accustomed to regarding the Sinai as an integral part of the state of Israel. We had toured the length and breadth of the peninsula; the bathing beaches in the Sharm el Sheik area were regularly inundated by hordes of vacationing Israelis. Radio and television reported the weather forecast for southern Sinai and the Gulf of Aqaba in the same routine fashion as they quoted temperatures for the Galilee and the coastal plain. Furthermore, there was a new generation that could hardly remember Israel within the pre-June 1967 borders. For these young Israelis, the desert peninsula was part of their native landscape.

Suddenly, the Egyptians were confronting us with the demand that we give up the peninsula—whose size is much bigger than the entire country before 1967—in exchange for something abstract and intangible. This demand provided fertile ground for the seeds of mistrust that had lain dormant in the collective unconscious during the weeks when the peace euphoria was at its height. Many Israelis suddenly recalled that they didn't really have a great deal of trust in the Arabs.

Similar skepticism was expressed by members of the cabinet. I heard mutterings about the sinister intentions of the Egyptian president, about his cunning; he was leading Israel down the garden path. Everyone said we now had to beware of him because he had emerged as a clever man. This line of thought was particularly irritating. Sadat had indeed proved to be far wiser than certain individuals may have suspected, but I regarded this suspiciousness as a mark of contempt for ourselves, for our own wisdom, for our own capacity to correctly evaluate the situation and act accordingly. Whatever had become of our Jewish brains?

I am well acquainted with Israelis at moments of crisis when war clouds loom on the horizon. Once alerted, they step forward as one man to defend their country. I have never seen fear in their eyes. It was strange to see them afraid of peace.

All around me were manifestations of displeasure. Several of my cabinet colleagues asked—out loud—why I was so lavish with the embraces I had bestowed upon Sadat and his aides. They wanted to know why I displayed such open joy about going to Egypt. What did they expect me to do—wear mourning? Some made no secret of their indignation over the friendly relationship between the Egyptian president and myself. They were not overjoyed to hear that he was always pleased to see me and that he did not stint on tokens of his esteem. There were remarks about his buttering me up and inflating my ego.

I regarded all these naysayers as infected with more than a jot of pettiness—and, perhaps, a measure of jealousy. Dayan and I had stolen the show. Scarcely a day passed without either of us appearing on television or in the newspaper headlines—while our fellow ministers were shoved aside. Their lack of enthusiasm over the new prospects opened up by Sadat's visit to Jerusalem and their reservations about Sadat himself carried additional undertones of a personal nature.

I did my best to ignore all this. I concentrated instead on convincing those I could and on influencing the views of my cabinet colleagues. That was why I repeated my stories about Egypt over and over again until I grew tired of them myself. I described how I'd met with Gamasy in the helicopter on the way to Ismailia, how we'd drunk guava juice together as we gazed down at the scenes unfolding below. I reminded my listeners that I myself had given the orders that had sent tons of shells raining down on those same landscapes.

Without disguising the difficulties or concealing the obstacles, I wanted them to adopt a more balanced view. I'm not sure I succeeded—as I was to learn from the cabinet's subsequent moves, which came in direct response to the Ismailia talks and were inspired by the general mood in the country.

It was largely this mood of mistrust that made everyone seek ways of tightening our grasp on the Sinai before it was too late. As I learned later, Agriculture Minister Sharon—backed by Foreign Minister Dayan—now proposed that something be constructed in the Sinai without delay to create "facts on the ground."

I knew nothing of all this: when I found out, I exploded into a furious rage. This proposal struck me as a stab in the back of the peace process.

I would be the last to underrate the strategic importance of the Sinai. From the military viewpoint, the most valuable part of the peninsula is its central-eastern portion, the part nearest the Israeli border. Sharm el Sheik, at the tip of the Sinai, is of no more than political importance. In the past, it became a focal point for tensions because the Egyptians could easily close the Strait of Tiran, blocking free navigation to our port of Eilat. On two occasions, we have gone to war to preserve freedom of navigation in the strait. However, in the Yom Kippur War, the Egyptians outwitted us by blocking the Strait of Bab al Mandab, hundreds of miles from Sharm el Sheik. Not a single boat entered or left Eilat. With one fell swoop, Sharm el Sheik nosedived on the strategic stock exchange.

I was willing to give up Sharm el Sheik but not the two large airfields in the Sinai, Etzion and Etam. Etzion, near Eilat, would be even more important if the Strait of Tiran was out of our hands because of its relative proximity to Tiran and to the Egyptian heartland.

With such thoughts uppermost in my mind, I attended a meeting held a few days after Ismailia. Of all conceivable topics, the one chosen for discussion concerned the settlements along the Ras Mohammed-El Arish line, in western Sinai. Arik Sharon turned up, equipped as usual with his maps. He left us in no doubt as to his intentions: he wanted to lose no time in creating *faits accomplis* in the Sinai. I was up in arms against the whole notion, seeing it as a stumbling block to peace.

On the surface, my relations with Sharon were friendly. We had a lot in common: our roots, our style, our military past—even our mode of expression. But, in spite of our similarities, there was never any prospect of cooperation between us. Our characters are very dissimilar. This difference had found expression in clashes in the past and will probably reappear if we cross swords again.

I am, unmistakably, a scion of the Israeli bourgeoisie. My family belongs to the Mayflower generation of the old Israel, the elite of wealthy and well-born founding fathers. Many things in life have come my way with relative ease. I never had to trick or manipulate to achieve my goals. Although I've had my share of struggles in the army and in politics, they were never extremely fierce. I have had my share of setbacks, but they were not too painful.

Arik Sharon comes from a family of farmers, tillers of the soil, the product of socialism, Israeli style. His *moshav* family has deep roots in the earth; they are hard-working and stubbornly loyal to their work and their land. Many things in Arik Sharon's life were attained with great difficulty, due equally to his character and his manner of going about things. As a result, the passing of the years has seen him build up a complex strategy of trickery and ruses, indirect approaches and direct lunges. He has fought bitter political battles, has stumbled and gotten back on his feet, triumphed, and hastened to fling himself into the next battle. Striding through life, he tends to leave behind him a wide swath of bitter enemies, disappointed sympathizers, and fervent admirers.

Our paths had scarcely crossed while we were in the army. My bastion was the air force; his, the paratroopers. Sharon was the kind of military commander who leaves a deep imprint long after his service is over. Much of what he did in the army twenty years ago remains part of our basic military heritage, cherished and valued to this day.

Sharon and I stood out among the other generals. Unlike most of our colleagues, we had not served in the Palmach—the elite underground force—during the struggle for independence. I was something of an outsider in the company of Chaim Bar-Lev, Yitzhak Rabin, David Elazar, Sheika Gavish, and other former Palmachniks. Sharon may have been a little closer to the Palmach tradition, but he was excluded from the select group—which he, in turn, despised, downplaying its military skills.

As army officers, both of us caught the political bug. I was close to Herut; Sharon was an inactive member of Mapai, the original Labor party. He was a frequent visitor to the home of David Ben-Gurion, particularly at the time of the reprisal raids and the Sinai campaign in the fifties. Ben-Gurion's attitude toward Sharon was a complex one. In his diary, he wrote: "If he could rid himself of his fault of not speaking the truth, and [if he would] keep away from gossip, he would be a model military leader."

Both Sharon and I had hankered for the post of chief of staff. Having been appointed head of the GHQ's staff branch, I was nearer the top. Probably, both of us could have made chief of staff, each in turn, but timing and bad luck had us miss out. I had left the command of the air force about a year before the Six-Day War, the greatest and most successful of its engagements. Sharon had left the Southern Command three months before the outbreak of the Yom Kippur War. Had he been head of the Southern Command during the war, its outcome would have been very different according to some, and he would have won everlasting renown. Even so, the Yom Kippur War had brought Sharon to the peak of his popularity, as commander of a reserve division. He was a war hero—while I was left in the shade.

Dizzy with his successes in battling both Egyptians and Israelis, Sharon had left the Likud alliance, to which he belonged by virtue of his membership in the Liberal party. I went back into politics. Sharon then toyed with the idea of leading a mass political movement, which would revolve entirely around a single man. After a brief amount of time, he found himself in trouble, with the polls predicting that he would get few votes.

Finding himself in tight straits, Sharon approached various politicians and parties, including some whose outlook was not pre cisely identical with his own—as became known years later. Lova Eliav, a dove who favors talks with the PLO, heard Sharon say: "You'd be surprised how close my views are to yours." Eliav was indeed surprised. Yossi Sarid, who favors the establishment of a Palestinian state, was approached by Sharon and offered the second place on Sharon's slate in the Knesset elections. Sharon also tried to join up with the Independent Liberals, yet another dovish grouping.

Finally, Sharon broke off all these contacts, going ahead on his own in the elections of 1977, where his slate gained a scant two seats. Shortly afterward, he rejoined the Likud.

Sharon's return to the Likud did not bring me much joy. On one occasion, when Golda Meir was in power, she had startled me by confiding that Sharon had privately asked her not to appoint me chief of staff. Immediately after the Likud election victory, there was some influence brought upon me by Begin to appoint Sharon chief of staff. Although I bore him no grudge and respected his military accomplishments, I decided against it on the advice of friends because by then he was too political to return to the necessary neutrality of an army man.

Begin has a special regard for military men, and Arik Sharon has a particular place in his affections. Arik's grandmother was the midwife who brought Begin into the world. Sharon's grandfather, Mordechai Sheinerman, was the closest friend of Dov Ze'ev Begin, the prime minister's father; the two men were the first Zionists in their town in Poland, and on one occasion, they joined forces to break into the synagogue to hold a memorial prayer for the founder of the Zionist movement, Benyamin Ze'ev (Theodor) Herzl.

Arik Sharon is a great strategist; he may be the greatest combat commander of our times. In war, I'd follow him through fire and flood—as his former subordinates often proclaim. But political life has different values. Sharon has lost sight of the distinction between his own personal good and the good of the state. He was born in the wrong regime. When Begin recently expressed his fear that Sharon would one day send tanks to surround the prime minister's office, his subsequent denials had a somewhat hollow ring. Begin really believes Sharon capable of doing such a thing.

Sharon always had the knack of presenting his views in a manner that made them acceptable to most—if not all—of the cabinet's members. His fingers ran up and down the maps, which many of the ministers were incapable of understanding. There were occasions when I suspected that the markings on Sharon's maps were not totally accurate. In any case, not one of the ministers was prepared to concede that he had not the faintest idea what it was all about.

When our preliminary contacts with the Egyptians indicated that we would probably have to give up much, if not all, of the Sinai, Sharon expounded his proposal for the swift creation of "facts on the ground." In effect, he was proposing nothing more than token settlements. The idea was to station caravans, erect water towers, and dig defense positions—and proclaim it a settlement. My colleagues rapidly agreed with Sharon. The prevalent view was that if the Egyptians acquiesced to our "colonization," we would have pulled it off; if they refused to countenance the new "settlements," Israel could make a gesture and give them up in return for the right to retain the existing settlements.

I voiced my vigorous opposition. At most, I was prepared to strengthen the existing Rafah settlements. I could not refrain from making discouraging comparisons between the attitude implicit in Sharon's proposals and that exhibited by Sadat. The Egyptian president was talking "big business"—and we were engaging in trivialities. Moreover, they were pernicious trivialities, capable of foiling the whole peace process. This was worse than shortsightedness: I considered it a monstrous bid to "outwit" the peace process and deliberate blindness toward the new relationship emerging between Israel and Egypt.

Sharon's proposal contained an ironic element unconnected with the current peace negotiations. The settlement movement had always been regarded as Israel's backbone. The map of the state was largely staked out by settlements established along its borders, many of which found themselves in the front line, often under fire. The settlers struck deep roots in the soil, refusing to leave their homes for all the money in the world even if they had to face their attackers with nothing more than rifles, or sometimes stones. The chronicles of the War of Independence are full of tales of the heroism of the Jewish settlements and their resistance to enemy onslaughts. Kibbutz Negba in the south held out alone against almost the entire Egyptian army.

If Sharon's proposal were adopted, it would be the first time in the history of Jewish resettling in the land of Israel that anyone had suggested creating hastily erected dummy settlements, which no one planned to inhabit and whose only purpose was to obstruct peace or else to serve as bargaining counters in the negotiations. This gambit was supported by a government whose component parties have almost no foothold in the existing settlement move ment. Herut and the National Religious party have very few affiliated settlements; the other coalition partners have none at all. Many of them had never attributed the resurgence of the Jewish people in the land of Israel to the chain of settlements and to land purchase.

In contrast, the opposition Labor movement, having always regarded "another acre, another goat" as an important component of our national might, had brought up generations of youngsters on these ideas. Our ultimate surrender of the Sinai settlements was particularly painful to the members of the Labor movement despite their commitment to a policy of territorial compromise on the areas occupied in the Six-Day War. They were prepared to compromise by giving up territory—but giving up a settlement was a grievous loss to them.

I regarded Sharon's proposal as a sad parody of the history of Jewish resettlement in Israel; moreover, I considered it dangerous to our national morale and to the education of our young people.

Moshe Dayan gave his blessing to Sharon's proposal. He said there was no knowing how long negotiations would drag on nor how they would end. If the Egyptians kicked up a fuss, we would stop, he said.

Begin suggested inviting the Egyptians to tour the Rafah settlements, apparently convinced that their hearts would soften when they saw those green oases. I never believed it for a single moment. It was plain to me that we would have to give up the Sinai even though I continued to fight for the settlements in all our talks with the Egyptians.

"If the Sinai reverts to Egyptian sovereignty," I said, "another ten settlements will be of no use to us. Nor will they be of any military benefit. They can only damage our attempt to build a trusting relationship without bringing any security for the future."

Instead, I proposed that we insist that the airfields remain in our hands, reiterating that they were essential to our military defense. I also stated that Sharm el Sheik was not of military importance, thereby angering both Dayan and Sharon. Dayan was still standing by his catch phrase "it's better to have Sharm el Sheik without peace" and said that he considered an agreement with the Egyptians no good if it failed to give us a foothold there.

Sharon subjected me to a frontal attack. He criticized my proposal for mutual border changes, which would grant the Egyptians a bite out of the Negev in return for our being able to hold onto the airfields. He said that instead of talking about Ras Mohammed-El Arish lines, there was now talk of two indentations into the Negev. In his opinion, this was particularly grave. In the course of twenty-five years of military experience he felt he had never been wrong in his military thinking, and was astonished by this attitude toward Sharm el Sheik, wondering how anyone could say that Sharm was of no military importance.

Begin suggested that we adopt Sharon's proposal unanimously.

The balance of forces around the cabinet table made it a foregone conclusion. Begin, Dayan, and Yigal Hurwitz, then minister of communication and industry, united to endorse Sharon's proposal. Yadin, Simcha Ehrlich, then minister of finance, and I voted against it. Yosef Burg, minister of the interior, abstained. The die was cast.

With the help of a private contractor, Sharon had water-drilling derricks and old buses emplaced on various sites in the Sinai. They were erected in places that we had specifically told the Egyptians we were prepared to restore to them. The land around the sites was ploughed up to further underline our intention of staking a claim to the sand dunes. Bedouin guards watched over the sites.

There are no secrets in the desert. The local Bedouins observed the work in progress and hastened to notify their superiors in Egyptian intelligence. At the same time, the Americans found out what was afoot by means of satellite photographs. The Egyptians were still saying nothing.

But then Israeli radio gave away the secret, and pandemonium broke out. Egyptian papers asked questions. President Carter exploded in fury, firing off a fierce letter to Begin. The Americans demanded an explanation. World opinion held we were saying one thing and doing quite the opposite.

Inside Israel, too, the storm raged. Many people accused the government of trying to torpedo the peace process. Government ministers were depicted as nincompoops. Begin came under cross fire; most of the blame, however, fell upon Sharon. That was totally unjustified—the decision had been approved by the whole cabinet, with the backing of Begin and Dayan. But Begin held his tongue, allowing the news media to keep up their onslaught on Sharon. The prime minister's own credibility—with Egyptians and Americans alike—reached a new low. The propaganda damage was evident for all to see.

Before the world had fully digested that episode, a new outcry arose when a story was leaked to the news media about a plan to establish a further twenty-three settlements.

I was thunderstruck. No one had approved any such decision; it had not even been submitted to the cabinet for consideration. Had my colleagues failed to learn their lesson from the reactions in Israel and abroad to their previous move? I voiced my objections bluntly and without being choosy about my language. I told my colleagues that if we were out to create "facts on the ground," we could not tell the Egyptians that we were prepared to restore the Sinai peninsula to their sovereignty.

I still contended that our efforts should center on trying to save the Rafah settlements and the airfields. I saw this as an attainable objective—if we could channel our energy into the negotiations instead of wasting it on dummy "facts." Grabbing a little extra territory at the last moment was liable to weaken our bargaining position for the Rafah settlements, not strengthen it.

Calling on all my persuasive powers, I did my best to convince my colleagues. I tried to redirect the cabinet's deliberations back to our principal agenda: negotiating for essentials instead of endless wrangling about where in whatever godforsaken hole to place a couple of shacks and phony water towers. I told my colleagues that Israeli public opinion showed our citizens up in arms against their approach. The man in the street was beginning to ask why the hell we were pouring hundreds of millions of pounds into sand dunes that we had declared ourselves ready to give back to Egypt. I advised them not to dismiss the man in the street and his sincere aspirations. I read what the papers were saying—there was no point in brushing off their criticism.

Some of my colleagues differed, convinced they would be criticized in any case; whatever the Likud government did, the press would be hostile, they said.

I raised my hand to vote against the proposal, afraid we were about to bungle the chance of making peace—and that I would be an eyewitness and an unwilling partner to that appalling error. I was equally horrified at the contemptible image we would acquire in the eyes of the Egyptians and of the whole world.

I had seen the Egyptians displaying an extraordinary curiosity in all their encounters with Israelis. In the course of the years, they had come to see us as a power to be reckoned with. Hard pressed to explain how a small people had repeatedly routed them on the battlefield, they probably attributed their own setbacks to the superior traits of the Israelis. They may have regarded us as a breed of supermen.

And now we were about to adopt the guise in which the most venomous of anti-Semites have always depicted the Jews: crafty petty traders, slyly cashing in on every available opportunity and reneging on their own undertakings whenever it was profitable.

I was dismayed at the thought of our being portrayed in such a light. Unfortunately, my fears were not baseless.

The Egyptians hit the roof. Their papers vilified Begin, subjecting him to every imaginable form of abuse and publishing offensive caricatures with anti-Semitic undertones in which Israel's prime minister was portrayed as a Shylock.

The Egyptian reaction sparked off a counterreaction in Israel.

What I had most dreaded had come to pass. It became starkly evident how quickly—almost overnight—matters could shift into reverse gear. The peace process was still too fresh and fragile to survive events that either side perceived as provocative. Israelis were not unique in fearing Egyptian initiatives and in regarding almost everything Sadat did as an attempt to deceive their leaders. Many Egyptians were similarly convinced that behind every Israeli smile and every prayer for peace voiced by Menachem Begin and his men lurked a dire plot. Mistrust cast its shadow everywhere.

The Americans made no secret of their disappointment. Washington perceived the dummy settlements as a petty-minded and transparent bid to fool the administration no less than the Egyptian president. The White House deluged the American press with briefings unfavorable to Israel's settling the occupied territories.

In Western opinion, too, Israel found herself on the defensive.

The phony towers and rusty buses became a favorite subject for photographers, whose shots were transmitted by communication satellites into every home the world over. They appeared on television screens as monuments to Israel's obstinacy and to her leaders' inability to grasp the enormity of the opportunity offered by the peace initiative.

Once again, Sadat's generosity was highlighted. In contrast to the Israeli move, universally seen as provocation for its own sake, Sadat's unyielding demands for the Sinai seemed no more than a formality. His popularity in the West, particularly in the United States, forced Israel into a corner.

Under the circumstances, Sadat could afford to articulate his demands in the form of a sharp ultimatum: "Not a single Israeli settlement shall remain in the Sinai!"

If there were ever any prospect of saving the Rafah settlements from the talons of peace, that hope now faded almost completely. I saw no point in any further attempts to hold out or to convince the Egyptians. In the new atmosphere now prevailing, that would have been "mission impossible." I nevertheless prayed for a miracle.

While my spirits fluctuated from cautious optimism to bitter gloom, I noticed a strange glint in the eyes of certain of my countrymen. I saw it in various places: in the Knesset, in the corridors of power, even at the cabinet table. The vituperations against Begin published in Cairo were brandished as the genuine voice of Egypt and as testimony to the true countenance of its people. Some people said the Egyptians were not even capable of masquerading properly since they allowed their real intentions to be reflected in their newspaper editorials, in their cartoons and radio broadcasts.

I saw no point in arguing with them—possibly because of my own anger at the Egyptians for losing all sense of proportion in their reaction. They could have presented their point of view in a less volatile way.

"Both sides are letting peace slip by," I told my confidants.

Amid this atmosphere of mutual recrimination and renewed suspicion, we began preparations for the meetings of the military committee in Cairo and the political committee in Jerusalem.

12

"OPERATION AVUKA"

One ray of light had emerged from Ismailia: Jerusalem was picked out as the setting for the meetings of the political committee. I regarded this as a step of considerable consequence. Even friendly states, with whom Israel has long maintained normal relations, were in no hurry to do anything that might be interpreted as de facto recognition of Jerusalem as Israel's capital—yet the Egyptians did it without blinking an eye.

I found some consolation, too, in the fact that Egyptians and Israelis were to meet together around the same table, free of external pressures. And there was a measure of gratification in the fact that at least part of the negotiations were being entrusted to the ministry I headed, although it was somewhat ironic that a ministry charged with developing Israel's martial might should be placed in the vanguard of the battle for peace.

Naturally enough, the defense establishment in the past had done very little to prepare for peace, which was too remote a dream to justify the investment of any effort. Before the Yom Kippur War, a working paper had been drawn up by a team headed by General Aharon Yariv, then head of military intelligence. This document consisted of no more than five or six pages, which discussed peace in the most general terms.

In the midst of the gloom prevailing after the Yom Kippur War, General Abrasha Tamir had taken the initiative and prepared the first working papers dealing with a peace settlement. While the political echelons were at their wits' end, it was characteristically a senior army officer who had set out to prepare Israel for eventual disengagement, interim, or peace agreements. Abrasha Tamir, appointed after the 1973 war to head GHQ's planning division, was the right man at the right time. Throughout his military career, he was renowned for having a good head on his shoulders, and he now set his brain to work on considering the options that might make it possible for war to be traded in for its opposite. Tamir must have been one of the few people in Israel not caught unprepared by Sadat's lightning peace offensive. The moment the wheels of peace began their forward surge, the head of the planning branch kept pace with them.

Ordinarily, I would have expected a turnabout like the Sadat initiative to evoke a measure of suspicion on the part of a professional soldier. Chief of Staff Motta Gur was a good example of the skeptical military man. Yet Tamir launched a frontal assault on peace with the tenacity of a combat officer leading his men to storm a stronghold. One of the most brilliant military minds I have ever encountered, Tamir also proved open-minded in a sphere apparently unconnected to the army or warfare. Military men like him have a good idea of the price of war. Abrasha Tamir has never put on military airs. He has never had his photograph taken posing against a backdrop of tanks with a pair of binoculars dangling on his chest. Because he is not the commando type but the strategist behind the scenes that every good army needs, he has never gained full recognition for his share in our army's strategic thinking and planning.

General Tamir had clear views on the peace process. He regarded it as part of a broad overall strategic concept that would make Israel part of a defense alliance embracing the entire region. In effect, Tamir belonged to the third echelon of the constellation built up around the negotiations. This constellation was headed by Menachem Begin, at the peak of the pyramid, where the decisions were taken. Below Begin was the second echelon, taking the initiative in proffering advice and recommendations: it consisted of the ministers of defense and foreign affairs. The third echelon—made up of senior officers and civilian experts—put forward ideas, prepared alternatives, and submitted recommendations, but was not required to take any initiatives. General Tamir was an exception. In view of his experience in the talks that preceded the disengagement agreements of 1973 and his preparatory work well before anyone dreamed that peace was on the horizon, he became part of the echelon entrusted with launching initiatives. He proposed ideas, examined them, analyzed the intentions of the other side, and suggested gambits. His contribution to peace was weighty. When the time comes for the historians to rummage through the heaps of documents in an attempt to sketch out the process with the perspective of distance from the events, General Tamir will emerge as one of the architects of the Israeli-Egyptian peace treaty.

The first meeting of the military committee in Cairo was scheduled for mid-January 1978. Its purpose was to discuss Israeli defense arrangements in the southern sector—but no one could foretell how matters would unfold around the conference table.

My quest for peace and my efforts to achieve an all-embracing view free of past grievances did not make me forget that I headed the establishment charged with protecting my country. I regarded peace as the highest guarantee of our security, but I did not overlook the military risks involved in abandoning early-warning electronic installations for the sake of achieving that guarantee. My position was clear: Israel must demand security arrangements that would protect her against any Egyptian overland surprise attack.

I had often felt that we went too far in proposing to surrender the Sinai. However, on hearing the reactions all around me, I was equally concerned about the risk of our revoking our stated willingness to withdraw. That would have pushed Israel into a dead end, showing her in a negative light as obstructing peace. My cabinet colleagues looked as though they had just sobered up from some dream. A few of them racked their brains trying to think up some gimmick, some magic formula that would give them peace without demanding the whole of the Sinai. I considered that at this stage this was a delusion. Some Herut leaders feared that after our withdrawal from the Sinai, we would someday find ourselves in a renewed confrontation with Egypt, who would continue to demand our withdrawal from all or most of the occupied territories: since those Herut members were opposed to an overall withdrawal, they saw no point in sliding into the whole process. I did not share this view, but I could not deny it had its own inner logic.

The opposite approach, which I advocated, saw the Sinai as a lever by which Israeli-Arab relations might be shunted onto a totally new track. Sadat's linking of the Sinai with the Palestinian question could provide the opening for a complete political metamorphosis. If we proclaimed a "new deal" for the Palestinians, the

Israeli-Egyptian agreement might provide the cornerstone for a comprehensive agreement. I regarded this as a national objective of the highest order.

Many of my countrymen come out in a rash whenever the Palestinians are mentioned as partners to negotiations. Our neighbors and foes, the Palestinians have long been portrayed as a nation of terror organizations and murder gangs. For years, it's been a matter of "them or us." But the Israeli-Palestinian conflict is the focal point of the Middle Eastern conflict, both cause and effect. A dispute over a tract of land—it's as simple as that: the modern version of an age-old territorial dispute.

Menachem Begin did not argue about relinquishing the Sinai but promptly plunged into a renewed confrontation with the Egyptians over the Palestinian issue. Begin's position was clear: he was giving up the Sinai to protect himself against any eventual concession in the West Bank. I was afraid that this attitude could ultimately drag us into another showdown with Egypt—at a time when the Sinai would no longer be in our hands as a bargaining tool.

During the preparations for the meeting of the military committee, Chief of Staff Motta Gur suggested that we adopt Henry Kissinger's technique, shuttling home for consultations after each day of discussions in Cairo. I approved the proposal, smiling to myself as I did: the distance from Cairo to Tel Aviv had shrunk considerably in recent weeks. Gur also proposed that whatever the topic on the agenda, we take along the officer concerned: the air force commander would attend the discussion about the airfields; the navy commander would come to talk about the Strait of Tiran. This idea also earned my approval: I wanted as many senior commanders as possible to go to Cairo, to feel the pulse, to meet the Egyptians. It could only help break down barriers of anxiety and suspicion.

In preliminary discussions held within the defense establishment, I outlined my views about the military issues arising from the peace process. I stated my opinion about Sharm el Sheik, saying that many of us were inclined to overrate its importance. Some members of the General Staff looked dismayed. Their reaction was predictable. I knew these men well. They included a number of seasoned desert foxes, familiar with every stone and canyon in the Sinai. They felt at home in the desert: many of them had fought there in three wars, going into battle at the head of the cream of Israeli youth. They had lost some of their best friends among its wild rocks and its endless expanses of sand and viewed those expanses as an integral part of Israeli might. I could well imagine what went on in the minds of air force and armor officers on hearing their defense minister tell them that our army would have to do without the vast wilderness of the Sinai. As an air force man, I knew precisely what was involved in surrendering the peninsula's airspace.

"Gentlemen," I said, "I would be very glad if anyone can come along and show me a way to hold Sharm el Sheik and the eastern Sinai—and also achieve peace."

I did not see any such way. My own military priorities were the Rafah settlements and the two large airfields. I was almost certain the government would not survive if it were to cede the settlements: the public was that committed to them. As military men, those I was addressing may not have needed to take that political factor into consideration. But as defense minister, I felt it my duty to tell them so candidly.

I cast around for ways of safeguarding the settlements should Israel indeed be required to restore the area to Egyptian sovereignty. The problem was far from simple. The Egyptians would evidently not consent to the presence of Israeli forces in the settlements. If there had been the vaguest prospect of their agreement, the episode of the dummy settlements had destroyed it.

"Then who will defend the settlements?" Motta Gur demanded. The question was to the point. I thought of my niece Diana, who had gone with her husband, son, and daughter to settle in Neviot, on the coast of the eastern Sinai, to build their house and grow melons. What would become of her? Would she be forced to leave for the north? Would she stay there? And if she were to stay—under Egyptian sovereignty—who would protect her?

Recognizing the military risks behind the peace process, I obviously could not advise the generals to underrate them.

"A peace settlement will shape the character of the state of Israel for many years," said one of the generals. "What's called for is to draw it out as long as possible—there's no sense in being overhasty. That could provoke crisis and dissension." His words typified the prevailing suspicion.

The discussions at GHQ were intensive. We tried to assess the reaction of the Russians; we analyzed the effect of the oil weapon on the impending stages. My deputy, Mottke Tzippori, flung out an idea that might have come from some science-fiction fantasy: we should propose that the Egyptians channel their Nile water to our Negev!

There was not much I needed to tell our generals about the Egyptian army. They knew plenty from intelligence reports. The

Egyptian air force was suffering from a severe shortage of spare parts. In my view, Sadat's haste in offering peace was reinforced by sound military reasons: having cut himself off from his previous suppliers, the Soviets, he was eager to milk the American cow.

After floating around in discussions that were somehow quite abstract, I was brought back to earth by our quartermaster general, Aryeh Levy, requesting an assessment about the evacuation of the Sinai. Only a few days after Sadat's visit to Jerusalem, the quartermaster branch's planning teams had already sat down to plan the eventual evacuation. It was too early for me to tell General Levy anything by which he could work out even the haziest timetable. But withdrawal suddenly became a practical likelihood.

Cairo had fired everyone's imagination—including the greatest skeptics. My office was deluged with calls from people volunteering for any imaginable task, just as long as they could be among the first Israelis to set foot on Egyptian soil. I decided to take along Mottke Tzippori and Motta Gur to the meeting of the military committee. Gur's participation was particularly important, primarily because of the unfortunate interview he had given on the eve of Sadat's visit to Jerusalem. I foresaw that he would naturally attempt to justify the pessimism he had expressed then and thought it was therefore essential that he meet the Egyptians himself.

"Motta," I told him, "you're coming along with me."

He was thrilled. His reason for wanting to go may have stemmed from a desire to convince himself and others how right his first instincts had been, but I hoped that the outcome would be the opposite.

I also took along General Herzl Shapir, head of the Southern Command, and General Abrasha Tamir; Moshe Sasson of the Foreign Ministry and Colonel Zvi Efrat from the military advocate's office; and my military aide, Ilan Tehila. I appointed my friend David Kolitz to be my spokesman for the mission.

As is the custom in military matters, this mission was given an operational code name: "Avuka," torch—in the hope that it would light our path to peace.

As the time of our departure approached, there was a growing agitation within the defense establishment. We were determined to do our homework thoroughly so as to enter discussions equipped with all the available data necessary to quickly conclude the military codicil to the peace agreement. So detailed were our preparations that on being notified that the military committee would be meeting at Tahara Palace, I hastened to request our intelligence branch to provide an aerial photograph of the building, which lies in Cairo's elegant Heliopolis quarter. Our intelligence chiefs told me it was there, at this palace, that Sadat had conducted the Yom Kippur War. I studied the enlarged photograph at length, trying to commit every detail to memory.

We took off in an air force Boeing 707, along with a large band of journalists. I wanted the Israeli papers to write about Egypt as accurately as possible, to capture for their readers the essence of the country.

We flew to Egypt by way of the "Weizman corridor." As on previous flights, everyone pressed against the windows, drinking in the sights. There were moments when I felt like a guide, keeping an eye on my charges to make sure they were all content.

I glanced at Motta Gur. Something about him bothered me. I looked again and realized what it was: whereas all the other members of the delegation were smartly dressed, as befitted the occasion, Motta Gur was the only one to appear in a sports jacket of brown suede, which was not even particularly new and far too casual. I was surprised. Having spent years as our military attaché in Washington, he should have known the ways of the world. I found it strange that he, of all people, should turn up in unsuitable clothes. After further thought, my wonder changed into anger as it dawned on me that his casual dress was no oversight. Was this his way of showing disdain for the whole affair? I know him well. Motta Gur likes to stand out. Was that why he had dressed in a manner that would instantly draw everyone's attention? Be that as it may, I was annoyed. I did not say a word, but I held it against him.

But flying over Egypt was exhilarating. Now well acquainted with the vistas along the air corridor, I looked down at them with a sense of familiarity, almost of a homecoming. My enthusiasm was no longer over the sights but because this mission was all mine. My first flight to Egypt had taken place under a veil of secrecy. Only after my arrival did Sadat reveal that the Israeli defense minister was on Egyptian soil. On the mission with Begin, his companions played second fiddle, as all eyes focused on him. This time, it was my show.

In a few moments' time, I would be shaking hands with the commanders of the Egyptian army, the men who had been our greatest and bitterest enemies. I was arriving as the senior representative of Israeli military prowess. Around me sat our generals, each of whom had made decisions that had given the Egyptians some anxious moments. We were coming to turn over a new leaf, to talk about peace—but we were backed up by the strength of Israel's armed forces. That certainty filled my heart with pride, giving me great confidence. I saw our army as a mighty lever for attaining peace; it was also a powerful crutch to lean on in the unfortunate event of a breakdown in the peace process.

Our army is the Jewish people's most original creation since returning to its homeland. That I was a former general and the civilian minister presently in charge of it made me glow with pride.

I terminated my military service in 1969, at the height of the War of Attrition along the Suez Canal. I was a worried man when I doffed my uniform. The somber mood in the civilian sector had infected the army. We were down in the mouth. Almost every day, the newspapers carried pictures of soldiers killed in action along the Bar-Lev Line. There was a spirit of despondency in the country. Tel Aviv was deluged with sick jokes about the last Israeli leaving the country and switching off the light at Ben-Gurion Airport. A TV show called "Queen of the Bathtub" hurled barbs of satire at our army's self-confidence.

In contrast, the day of my appointment as defense minister will always linger in my memory for the pleasant surprise it afforded me. During my years outside the defense establishment, I had tried to keep up my connections. But these links were principally of a social nature, and I had no reason to imagine that the army I had grown to know so well would, within such a brief period of time, change almost beyond recognition.

It had been with a degree of anxiety that I'd anticipated my renewed encounter with the armed forces and the defense establishment. I was on the lookout for the scars of the Yom Kippur War and the "war of the generals" that had accompanied it.

To my delight, the reality bore little resemblance to my expectations. The army I took over was large, strong, well equipped, and better prepared than at any time in the past. The senior command now consisted largely of officers who were still unknown when I had commanded the air force and later GHQ's staff branch. I got to know those commanders well; they were the best men we had.

Above all, I was surprised by the size of our forces. When I'd left the service, we had no more than a dozen antiquated armored personnel carriers (APCs), captured from the Jordanians. On taking over the Defense Ministry, I learned that we now owned APCs by the thousands. The numbers of tanks and planes were astounding. If anyone had told me during the time when I commanded the air force that we would one day have the kind of planes I now found, I would only have laughed in bemusement. And I was considered overly optimistic about the air force in those days! But the present reality far exceeded any fantasy I could have had.

However, the navy proved to be an even greater surprise. After its creation in 1948, it was invariably shunted aside. In view of the particular features of our battle arena, it never achieved top priority—justifiably, I believe. Its equipment was antiquated, picked up largely from the scrap yards of Western fleets. But the navy I found in 1977 was a modern force, well equipped, proportionately small compared to the army and the air force, but possibly one of the most advanced in the world. Its morale was high, in direct consequence of its successes in the Yom Kippur War.

I hoped the Egyptians would never again encounter our forces on the field of battle—I wished them that with all my heart. When fully mobilized, our army is enormous; it has more tanks than Britain and France combined. Beyond being one of the best in the world, our air force is also one of the largest, exceeded in size only by the air fleets of the two superpowers. And our navy, too, could now compete with anyone's.

As we approached the Cairo Airport runway, a sweet sense of satisfaction came over me. We could without a doubt defend ourselves if need be. But peace was the target now, and I could not dismiss the problems we faced. Israel's geopolitical situation is highly problematic. Any error in our military thinking could result in a national catastrophe. Israel is a tiny country, with most of its population concentrated in the Jerusalem-Haifa-Ashkelon triangle, which is one-quarter of its overall surface area. This triangle also contains almost all of our military, economic, and technological infrastructure.

Unlike other small states, Israel is not part of any political or strategic alliance that could come to her aid in times of war. No superpower has undertaken a specific commitment to safeguard her existence. These basic facts are unlikely to change and force Israel to build her security exclusively upon her own forces.

Furthermore, Israel has very little physical room to maneuver, to permit her to survive a powerful onslaught. That makes it vital for Israel to think twice—ten times!—before taking any step likely to further restrict her area of maneuverability. From that point of view, surrendering the Sinai was no trivial matter.

Right from the early stages of our negotiations with Egypt, it became evident that the other Arab states were in no hurry to join in the peace process. In fact, Syria, Iraq, and Libya stepped up and redoubled their military efforts. In my assessment, the next ten years will witness no significant reduction in overall Arab military might. The Arab states will continue to maintain forces of a size exceeding those of the NATO alliance in Europe.

The Middle East is an unpredictable region. No one here would take the risk of granting unlimited credit to treaties and agreements. Leaders and regimes rise and fall; there are some whose first act on taking power is to renounce every commitment undertaken by their predecessors.

While laboring tirelessly for peace with Egypt, we have to bear in mind that the Arab world remains the arena for radical elements operating with great vigor. Their declared intention is to bring about a deterioration of the situation, leading to a renewed war between Israel and her neighbors. Their internal conflicts notwithstanding, the Arab states have proved their capacity for coordination among themselves whenever it is a matter of war against Israel.

There is another force at work in the region: the Soviet Union, which played an active role in the escalation that culminated in the Six-Day War, may try to bring about a renewed flare-up if it permitted them to regain their former standing in the Middle East.

In view of all these factors, five basic principles guided us at every stage of our negotiations with the Egyptians:

• Any Arab-Israeli agreement had to rest upon the basic assumption that Israel would be prepared to confront all strategic threats, even in times of peace.

• Egypt (or any other Arab state trying to establish genuine peace) would have to prove the credibility of her intentions by her forebearance from any bid to exploit the agreement to gain strategic advantages over Israel.

• A starting point for calculating the strategic threat to Israel would be the land depth we possess for protecting our vital interests in comparison with the strategic depth of the Arab states. (From the Mediterranean Sea to the border of Jordan is only forty miles, and before the Six-Day War Israel had six miles with which to protect herself!)

• The most effective way to reduce the danger of such threats is to create an alliance with as many neighboring countries as possible for the purpose of averting war.

• One of the greatest dangers to peace lies in the cooperation between the Soviet Union and the radical Arab states, which have the common interest of pushing the West out of the area.

These and other thoughts were buzzing around in my head, but preparations for our landing at Cairo Airport cut them short. General Gamasy was awaiting me, and I suddenly felt a great closeness toward him. I rejoiced to see him striding toward me in his elegant suit. Motta Gur's sport jacket was particularly irritating in contrast.

Gamasy's expression was grave. He tried to smile, but it was forced. We shook hands, and he drew me aside, away from the others.

"General Weizman," he said, "before anything else, we must fly to Aswan for a talk with the president."

Next to the Israeli air force Boeing stood an Egyptian Falcon Mystere-20 executive jet. I glanced at the insignia of the Israeli and Egyptian air forces, side by side. It was still hard to remain indifferent to the sight—it always thrilled me.

Accompanied by my military aide and my spokesman, I boarded the Falcon. The plane was comfortable. A stewardess stood ready to serve us. Gamasy sat opposite me, quiet and thoughtful. I sought a way of drawing him into conversation, but we took off, and the sights beneath us deprived me of the power of speech. The Nile delta was spread out below in all its glory, linked to the meandering course of the great river that has been Egypt's artery of life ever since ancient times. On both sides of the waterway, the desert stretched into the distance. The water, a silvery gray, was flanked on both sides by stretches of green broken by brown patches—fields under cultivation. The belt of green gradually faded as though the endless desert was slowly swallowing it up. The strip of land between the river and the desert has witnessed the rise and fall of civilizations, eternally subject to the whims of the two. At times, the river burst its banks to flood the layers of culture; at others, the desert swept in to bury that strip of green and choke the life out of it.

Gamasy broke into my train of thought.

"The president doesn't understand you," he said in an aggressive tone. "You Israelis are making things impossible. On our side, it is believed that you are misleading us."

I had known it would come. Our recent deeds in the Sinai had done nothing to dispel the crisis atmosphere generated at Ismailia.

Sadat was not trusted in Israel; therefore, certain Israelis wanted to create "facts on the ground," whether Sadat liked it or not. Of course, the dummy settlements whittled away Egyptian trust in Israel even more.

I tried to divert the conversation into another channel. I knew matters called for clarification—there was no avoiding that—but I preferred that it take place under more appropriate circumstances. Gamasy seemed to understand. Leaving aside the main issue, our conversation followed associative links to delve into the past, in which each of us had played a part.

Somehow or other, we touched on the Six-Day War. Again, I saw a cloud cross his face. He did not enjoy recalling the days of early June 1967, and I saw no reason to press him on that point. All the same, there was one enigma that intrigued me—Abdel Hakim Amer, who had served as Egypt's minister of war during the Six-Day War and committed suicide immediately after the hostilities ended. He was a riddle to us. We could not figure out whether he was a complete fool or a wily character. Amer was in the air during the morning hours of June 5, 1967, when the Six-Day War broke out with our planes swooping down to destroy the Egyptian air force on the ground. Amer's plane had scarcely managed to find a place to land.

"What sort of man was he?" I asked brazenly.

"What can you expect of a major who is promoted to field marshal?" Gamasy retorted. His tone held more than a little contempt. I smiled to myself. The Egyptians, too, have their "wars of the generals."

Once again, he recalled how the fighting had found him at Bir Tamada, in the central Sinai, with bombs falling around him. In passing, he told me something I had not known: he had resigned from the army immediately after the war. I believe this to be a characteristic act on the part of such a proud man. He could not stand the disgrace of the debacle and the humiliation it conferred on the Egyptian army. His expression grew bitter whenever he spoke of it. He had sought revenge and found it—in 1973.

"We made a stupid mistake in 1967," he said dryly, "and we paid dearly for it. But what the hell did you want of us in 1956? Why did you go along with the French and English to try and take the Canal away from us?"

My recollections of 1956 were hazy, perhaps because that campaign had no tangible results. The tempo of Israeli life is swift and dynamic, and events follow one another in rapid succession. As far as I was concerned, the 1956 war was a matter of history.

But it is different for a man like Gamasy. The British ruled his country right up to the fifties. His generation dreamed of the day when it could get rid of them. It is no accident that youthful Egyptian nationalists made heroes of the two young Jews—Eliahu Hakim and Eliahu Bet Tzuri, both members of the Lechi underground—who went to Egypt and assassinated the British minister, Lord Moyne. Many young Egyptians drew inspiration and encouragement from their deed, which was, however, subsequently forgotten in the inferno of Israeli-Egyptian enmity. Members of Gamasy's generation have never been able to forgive the British and French for their abortive attempt to regain control of the Suez Canal and again trample Egyptian national honor into the dust.

I reminded him of the guerrilla forays into Israel during the fifties, mentioning the Egyptian military attaché in Amman who had directed the raids into our territory.

"If we made a mistake," I said, "it is balanced out by yours."

I tried to give Gamasy a brief account of Zionism, describing our ties to the land of Israel and stressing that we had never viewed ourselves as colonialists—on the contrary. But even as I said it, I remembered those Israelis who still retain the mentality of the eastern European pale of settlement, seeing themselves as planted in a strange and alien region. Given half a chance, they would gladly pack up the state of Israel, lock, stock, and barrel, and put it down somewhere between Minsk and Pinsk.

The plane was coming in to land. I looked out the window at the Aswan Dam and recalled its inauguration by the former Soviet leader, Nikita Khrushchev, during the Soviet-Egyptian honeymoon that had culminated in the 1967 war against us.

The lineup of antiaircraft missiles ringing the dam surprised me, and I recalled the books and newspaper articles that had proposed the fantastic notion that we would bomb the dam and bring devastation on the surrounding region. I hastened to banish these thoughts from my mind. I was about to meet Sadat, and I felt uncomfortable even thinking about such things.

We landed at Aswan. The whole area was marked by a strangely pastoral tranquillity.

THE GATHERING STORM

Sadat was awaiting me at his Aswan home. He greeted me with a smile, but his eyes reflected a sadness blended with severity. He shook my hand warmly, but his expression was earnest. He had obviously been looking forward to my arrival; he had something to say to me.

Since our first meeting in Jerusalem, I have come to know Sadat quite well. Not that he was ever a totally unknown quantity to us: even before he set foot in Jerusalem, we had made efforts to find out all about him. War is more than a struggle on the field of battle; at times it becomes a contest of minds. Each side makes a close study of the key figures on the opposite side, trying to get inside their skin and grasp their thought patterns. After our initial miscalculations in comparing him unfavorably with Nasser, we had investigated him carefully. All the same, in the flesh he did not quite resemble the portrait sketched out by the intelligence reports.

My previous meetings with him had already taught me that he is very isolated at the pinnacle of power. The full burden of responsibility rests on his shoulders. I have the impression that some of his most fateful decisions were adopted without his sharing his thoughts or calculations with another soul. From that point of view, Sadat bears no resemblance to the "executive" leader who has fought his way up the bureaucratic ladder. Unlike that of Western technocrats, his thinking has never been swamped in an ocean of papers, nor were his decisions reached in smoke-filled back rooms. Almost all his decisions were the fruit of inner contemplation. That may explain his periodic withdrawals to one of the many homes he has scattered throughout Egypt.

Thus, Sadat's character is in harmony with the regime he heads. By contrast, Begin, like other Western leaders, can never withdraw within himself entirely to weigh fateful decisions even if he greatly wishes to do so. In addition to taking into account every last Knesset member of the Herut faction, he also has to consider his coalition partners and sometimes even the leaders of the opposition. Begin can make his own decisions and often manages to impose them by virtue of his dominant personality, but in every case they require approval and ratification. He may not consult, but he has to consider others. To a great extent, the regime Sadat heads frees him of such constraints.

Western democratic eyes can soon pick out the defects inherent in this mode of decision making. However, democracy has a totally different meaning in the Third World. It denotes very little to the millions of laborers living on the banks of the Nile. By itself, democracy cannot propel a country like Egypt into the twentieth century; it certainly cannot solve Egypt's pressing social and economic problems or deal with its population explosion. In a land like Egypt, democracy is an abstract concept.

Fortunately for the citizens of Egypt, Sadat's personality is a rare blend of simple folk wisdom and exceptional political sophistication. My meetings with him and my analysis of his tactics have taught me that he is not a man to fumble with details—those he delegates to his aides. In effect, Sadat sets down the main line, leaving his advisers to deal with its ramifications. I have never seen him working with papers or referring to figures or memoranda. Unlike superbureaucrats, he works with his personality and his grasp of principles.

That may explain Sadat's weakness for people like the late Golda Meir or Menachem Begin. Right or wrong, Sadat sees them as his own kind—individuals with an overall view of historical dimensions who are capable of reaching agreements in matters of principle while leaving the details to the lower echelons. It may also explain Sadat's attitude at Ismailia, where he could hardly conceal his disappointment or keep his patience as he listened with visible discomfort to Begin's nitpicking exposition of the Israeli peace plan and the autonomy scheme. His expression indicated that he had no tolerance for such trivialities.

Many Israelis, including some senior political figures, misunderstood Sadat's moves, scrutinizing every statement or act of his for some hidden trap or pitfall. They never realized that Sadat does not engage in such things; they do not interest him. I can understand those who contend that his entire peace initiative was nothing more than an act of strategic deception—though the better I got to know him as a man and a statesman, the more firmly I rejected this conjecture. On the other hand, I find it hard to comprehend the rationale behind the more petty suspicions directed at him. I do not believe that Sadat had any evil designs in coming to Jerusalem, but if he did—as is alleged by Israel's extremist fringe—they were to do with something far greater and more momentous than winning some minor advantage for one of his armored battalions in the Sinai.

"Your suit is well tailored." Sadat greeted me, looking me up and down.

"You look well," I replied, trading compliment for compliment. Noticing that he had grown thinner during the three weeks since I last saw him, I asked whether he had been on a diet.

"No, of course not!" he replied. "I make a custom of fasting once a week—on Thursday, usually. When I fast, I don't smoke, not even the pipe you gave me."

A smile spread across his face, but his expression remained tense. I imagined he was disappointed with the outcome of the Ismailia meeting, even though he did not say so, and that the dummy settlements in the Sinai also cast their shadow over our present encounter.

"I hope you enjoyed your flight," Sadat said as we paced along, "and that you managed to see a little of Egypt."

I seized on his last remark to move to more practical matters. "You have a large country," I said. "It took us an hour and a quarter to get here. I felt that we could fly forever, that there is no end to Egypt. I represent a country that is great in values and spirit—but it is small and underpopulated and surrounded by enemies. If I had flown an hour and a quarter in an easterly direction from Israel, I would have reached Baghdad! In our country, everything is so small that we sometimes get claustrophobia. That's why the Rafah approaches, for example, seem such an enormous area to us. For you, it's one half of one percent of Egyptian territory."

Sadat did not leave matters dangling in uncertainty; he hastened to reply—from his own point of view. "I know my people well," he said. "Believe me, I know what you can demand of them and what you can't. I will not be able to persuade my people to consent to a solution that offers less than the return of the whole of the Sinai, including your settlements and airfields. I might be able to get it passed, but believe me—that would be the seed of the next war."

"You've got to understand the Israelis," I said. "Many of us live very close to the border. For example, Beersheba is only twenty miles from the border. Before the 1967 war, Kfar Shuba was right on the border. It's only natural that we are more sensitive than you to land security. There's not a single Israeli who doesn't bear the burden of security, in one way or another, whether it's kibbutz members in the north or south or civilians serving in the reserves or with sons in the army. For thirty years, you fought against us, you threatened to throw us into the sea—you can't now expect all the Israelis to come running toward you with open arms. Israelis can't shake off the awareness that they belong to a people of three million, surrounded by one hundred million enemies. For us, the question of security is a question of life and death."

"You are right," Sadat said. He showed some understanding of our security problems but would never relinquish his demand for a total withdrawal from the Sinai, including the settlements and airfields. The phony settlements and the fuss that accompanied them in the Israeli and foreign press only reinforced his position. I had no hope that we would succeed in getting over this hurdle in the deliberations of the military committee. Sadat seemed set in his view; even his expression testified to his resolve.

"Mr. President," I said in an attempt to bypass the obstacle by a lunge at his flank, "I want to speak frankly. You have no idea what a measure of affection and admiration you enjoy in Israel. Everyone regards you as a leader of courage and stature. Only a few days ago, I was passing through Tel Aviv, and I saw a shop decorated with your picture alongside the portrait of Begin. Do you know what the shop is called?"

The Egyptian president was listening intently, a questioning look on his face.

"The shop is called 'Sadat Fashions'!" I answered after a dramatic pause. Sadat responded with a faint smile.

"It would be a pity if you lost the affection of the Israeli in the street," I added. "Here and there, incidentally, there are already voices complaining that you demand far too much. There are people who say: 'What is this? Just because he came to Jerusalem—do we have to give him everything?' "

Sadat's swarthy features broke into a scowl. He is not a man to keep his feelings to himself: they are immediately evident in his expression as well as in his voice and gestures. I thought he was about to interrupt me, and I ploughed on.

"Believe me, Mr. President," I continued, "we appreciate your deeds. Yesterday, in the Knesset's Foreign Affairs and Defense Committee, I compared your journey to Jerusalem to man's first landing on the moon."

The president's face showed his gratification. The comparison flattered him. To my regret, I was obliged to mar his pleasure.

"You must be careful," I said, injecting a stern note into my words, "because the first man to set foot on the moon also came down to earth."

Sadat's deputy, Hosni Mubarak, seated beside us all this time without uttering a word, listened with an impassive expression. Gamasy, too, was silent. I had previously observed some marks of tension between Sadat's two senior aides. In the past, Mubarak had served under Gamasy as commander of the air force. Now he stood above Gamasy in the hierarchy of power, and I imagined that the war minister found it hard to live with the situation.

"Mr. President," I went on, keeping up the pressure. "You are a courageous man; you have already proved yourself capable of making courageous decisions. I am sure that you can explain this to your people."

Sadat shook his head in the negative. "No, no," he said, raising his voice. "I know what I am talking about. My people will not accept Israeli settlements in the Rafah approaches."

"You say the Egyptian people won't make the concession," I persisted. "But I find it difficult to shake off the depressing knowledge that we have lost one-third of the Jewish people in the past forty years. We have been through five wars with you. You tried to annihilate Israel on the day she was created. We had no intentions of occupying the Sinai in 1967. If you had asked me then whether there was going to be a war, I would have said no! On the way here, I was talking with Gamasy. He said that moving the Egyptian force into the Sinai in May 1967 was a gamble and a political error. With all my admiration for you and my hope that you remain president for many years, you must understand that we can't afford to take risks or gambles.

"This is our fifth meeting," I said. "When I come to Egypt, I feel at home. Each time, I am glad to meet you and talk to you, out of my appreciation for your intelligence and courage. We all admire the step you took, but you must consider that Begin has a problem, too. His problem may be more difficult than yours—it is much easier for you to push decisions through."

I tried to put it tactfully without offending him. But the implication was obvious. Sadat continually spoke of agreement or disagreement on the part of the Egyptian people even though he was clearly able to ensure the adoption of almost any decision he wanted, whereas Begin had to consider many others, in his party and out.

Israelis somehow have the impression that Sadat is often compelled to take into account the opinions of his ministers and advisers whose views are apparently more unbending than his own. I do not believe this is true. Sadat stakes out the main principles of policy, leaving their practical application to his assistants. When those principles go against reality, the outcome is friction, naturally enough. The more one delves into details, the greater the friction—hence, the apparent intransigence of Sadat's aides, contrasting with the seemingly more flexible approach of the president.

On the Israeli side, the opposite often happened. Begin got bogged down in details, engendering the greatest possible friction—while Dayan and I tried to work out principles, which permitted us to gallop ahead.

Sadat did not appear to be particularly overawed by the difficulties facing Begin. He may have believed that only a strong man like Begin—an authoritarian prime minister, a superhawk—could afford to make concessions without having to defend himself against charges of abandoning Israel's most vital security needs.

"Don't push too hard!" I advised Sadat. "You must also understand the enormity of Begin's step. He is regarded as the hawk of hawks. All of us—myself included—were considered warmongers. Remember, the Begin cabinet is seen as a hawkish cabinet, and its views about withdrawal from the occupied territories are well known. All the same, it went a long way to meet you. We have reached the limits of our capacity for concessions. I have explained our security problems and our anxiety about them. If this government does not seem to pay enough attention to security problems, it will lose credibility in the eyes of the Israeli people. Security isn't just territory and equipment—it's also a people's faith in its leadership. And you can't undermine the Israeli people's faith in its direction."

Once again, I sketched out the military problems Israel faces. I did it from every possible angle with all my rhetorical power.

It was in vain.

Sadat repeated his view over and over again, using almost the identical words and making it plain that he would not give an inch.

"What are we talking about?" I demanded, raising my voice. "The settlements and airfields do not constitute more than four percent of the surface area of the Sinai and about one-half percent of the area of Egypt. I want to ask you: are we going to destroy the peace over this? I'm not asking you for a reply this second. You are a wise and brave man. I beg you, use your intelligence."

"I know my people, and believe in their devotion to peace," Sadat said. "And you must understand that I am talking about full and genuine peace, with ambassadors, commercial relations, everything. You will receive genuine peace, but first—I must get back that part of my land that you took from us."

"Mr. President, ambassadors are very important, but it isn't so long since you recalled your ambassador from Iraq." Ambassadors come and go, I was thinking, and are not as significant as military guarantees.

Sadat frowned. My words obviously displeased him, and I pretended not to notice his annoyance.

"We are talking about peace with security," I said. "You must remember that the problem is not only between us and Egypt. We have a difficult problem with Syria, too."

"You finished the Syrians off in three days in the Golan Heights!" Sadat retorted with a contemptuous wave of his hand. "Assad himself came and told me you finished off twelve hundred of his tanks. What makes you worry about the Syrians?"

"We have problems with Iraq, too. Tomorrow morning, they could move two thousand tanks up to our eastern border through Syria. As long as we haven't solved these problems, how can you expect us to relinquish the airfields in the Sinai?"

My words irritated him even more.

"You and President Carter talk about your giving up the West Bank and Gaza Strip but leaving behind security forces. Now you mention retaining the Sinai airfields because of the Syrians." There was irony in his voice.

"I am also concerned over internal security problems," I said. "Only a few days ago, a bomb went off in Jerusalem. There were casualties. Today, I can send policemen and security agents to pursue the perpetrators everywhere—to Ramallah, Hebron, Nablus. We have to be able to do that in the future, too. Mr. President, you would ask the same if you were in my place."

The conversation at Sadat's Aswan home lasted an hour. The

house stands on a hill overlooking the old dam. The building itself is not ornate, but its view is splendid. Nevertheless, in my mind the true background to our exchange was the Ismailia conference and, even more, the dummy settlements.

I wanted to reach some agreement with Sadat, even if it were only in a narrow sphere, because in the absence of some progress, however minor, there was almost no purpose to the deliberations of the military committee in Cairo.

"I have invited Gamasy to come to Israel," I told Sadat. I did not mention Gamasy's cautious reply that it was "too early yet." "I suggest you send a military mission to Israel. I want them to take a close look at Israel's security problems. We will receive them with all due respect and listen to their opinions. I want to know how they would go about solving our problems if the border were to return to where it was in 1967, as you propose."

"That's not a bad idea," Sadat commented. "On Saturday, I will be in Cairo—I will give you my answer there."

I left Sadat unsatisfied. Our conversation had not taken us forward. My spirits lifted slightly when I noticed an Israeli journalist among the crowd of newsmen, photographers, and television teams at the gateway. I was astonished to find him there. A peace agreement was nowhere in sight, yet Israelis were already penetrating every remote corner of Egypt.

The way from Cairo's international airport to the city itself brought a new excitement. On my two previous trips to Egypt, I had not entered the city proper. This was my first visit to Cairo in thirty-five years, and I couldn't take my eyes off the route. I tried to read the advertisements, calling on the fragments of Arabic I remembered from home and school.

"Smoke Cleopatra cigarettes!" I said in halting Arabic. "Fly with Saudi Airlines!"

Every now and then, I recognized portions of our route. "We are on our way to Heliopolis!" I told Gamasy loudly, as though I were letting him in on a big secret. He nodded politely: I thought I saw him smile.

"Oh, here's the Almaza Airport!" I leaped up in excitement. "Almaza!" It was from there that I had taken off in 1946, in a four-engined bomber headed for Lod airfield on my way home from my RAF service in India.

I could hardly recognize Heliopolis. It had been one of the city's most luxurious neighborhoods, housing the richest families of Egypt and the Arab world. I did not take in the change at first. But then I caught on.

The elegant houses had grown shabby. Cairo was no longer what it had been. The oriental splendor had disappeared. The Egyptian capital resembled a faded old lady, whereas I remembered a beautiful young girl.

But underneath were traces of the same city. Heliopolis still displayed the traditional Egyptian style of building, with elements of French influence—the balconies with their iron railings, the curved roofs. As we drove along, I caught the aroma of Cairo I remembered, the scent of spices blended with dust and smoke.

A large iron gate opened before the car, and we entered the Tahara Palace. All around, everything was green, clean, and carefully tended, in sharp contrast with the city.

King Farouk had given the Tahara Palace to his first wife, Farida, forty years before. The palace consisted of a complex of buildings surrounded by a wall. The architecture was in the colonial style: marble floors, broad stairways, crystal chandeliers, oil paintings, parquet floors, and heavily ornate furniture.

My hosts led me to a room that was a kind of palace-within-the-palace.

"This was King Farouk's room," said my guide.

Like most of my generation, I had heard a lot about King Farouk and his corrupt exploits, about his passion for luxury and the splendor with which he loved to surround himself. I had always enjoyed tales about his vices—about which countless jokes are told in Israel.

But never, in my wildest dreams, had I imagined myself sleeping in his bed!

14

IN THE SHADOW OF THE PYRAMIDS

History does not acknowledge concepts such as "if only," even if historians do occasionally toy with speculations about what would have happened "if." I am not in the habit of indulging in conjectures of this nature. Nevertheless, I believe that if we had not erected "settlements" in the form of old buses and secondhand drilling derricks and if we had conducted the Ismailia negotiations on matters of principle, with greater sensitivity toward our partners, it is possible—though far from certain—that the Sinai settlements and perhaps the airfields would have remained in our hands, one way or another. No one can judge the point with any degree of certainty. But whereas I had always found the Egyptians open to persuasion, particularly in the form of military arguments, when I spoke with President Sadat at Aswan I understood that it was no longer feasible. With all their understanding for Israel's concern about security, the Egyptians perceived our twelfth-hour attempt to create "facts on the ground" as a brutal provocation. The Arabs have always alleged that Israel takes advantage of every possible opportunity to establish *faits accomplis* at their expense. The dummy settlements of the Sinai gave them additional fuel, precisely at a time when we ought to have been doing everything in our power to convince them otherwise.

The Cairo daily paper *Al Ahram* wrote that hostilities between Israel and Egypt might be renewed sooner than anyone expected. I hoped that this prediction did not originate with any of our Egyptian counterparts in the negotiations, although I was aware the newspapers there do not print anything the authorities might not approve.

Still, I was in total agreement with Mustafa Amin, who wrote in *Al Akhbar:* "Sadat has gambled on his presidency, his life, his everything. If he fails, the fanatics will rule for a thousand years. The situation today makes it look as though Sadat is bestriding a rocket, while Israel plods behind him on a donkey. If Israel does not restore the territories, those same Egyptians who today call loudly for peace will change overnight and fight again."

At the same time, there was some consolation in my conversation with Sadat at Aswan early that day, which had left me with the impression that he was determined to advance toward peace in spite of all the obstacles.

"If the Egyptians expect us to give up everything we have attained in thirty years, they're mistaken!" I told a journalist in the courtyard of the Tahara Palace. "We won't consent to pull back to the old borders. If we did, the next demand could be our withdrawal to the partition borders of 1947." Everyone in Israel knew that within those narrow, outdated boundaries, the state could not survive a single day.

I had lunch with Gamasy. He looked gloomier than ever. "I pray for peace," he said.

"*Inshallah!* May it be the will of God," I replied.

Gamasy tasted the *bamia,* cooked with mutton in tomato sauce—he must have remembered how I enjoy the dish.

"General Gamasy," I asked. "Why are you called 'minister of war,' whereas my title is 'minister of defense'? It's about time you changed the name of your post. It's not much, but it would improve the atmosphere."

Gamasy made no response.

A waiter with Sudanese features approached our table. Setting down a bowl, he learned toward me. "Sir," he whispered in my ear, "do you know the Weissman family?"

I turned toward him, thunderstruck. "The Weissman family?" I said. "From 13 Kasser el Nil Street?"

Now it was the waiter's turn to be amazed; his eyes opened wide.

I stared at him. He looked about fifty, a typical example of the Sudanese waiters, some of whom had also served in Palestine at the time of the British mandate.

The Weissman family, although we were not related, had been a prominent Jewish family in Cairo; 13 Kasser el Nil Street had been my home away from home during my RAF service in World War II.

"I worked for the Weissman family," the waiter whispered, looking around in all directions. He must have been considerably
alarmed: such a conversation with Israel's defense minister was
open to misinterpretation by those around him. "They were like
brothers to me."

A small world. Out of forty million Egyptians, he was the one
picked by fate to serve our table.

"How is Miss Aviva?" he whispered.

"She is now the wife of the ambassador, Emil Najar," I told him.
"Sit down, write her a letter—I'll take it to her."

He shook his head, his eyes showing concern. I hoped for the day
when letters would flow in both directions between our two countries; for the moment, however, that was no more than a dream.

The last time I had seen an Egyptian with Sudanese features was
in 1967, immediately after our occupation of Sharm el Sheik, when
I came across a group of eight prisoners. To my anger, I saw that
our boys had tied their hands behind their backs, and I gave orders
to untie them instantly.

One of the prisoners was Sudanese—tall and extremely handsome. I called him over; he looked scared. He showed me pictures
of his wife and daughter, and I tried to cheer him up a little.

Before leaving, I called the commander of our men. "These are
unarmed prisoners," I told him. "Give them food and water. And
take care not to harm a hair of their heads."

Two or three months later, I toured the Atlit POW camp in the
company of the chief of staff and several other generals. There,
among thousands of Egyptian captives, I again encountered the
Sudanese prisoner from Sharm el Sheik. Feeling as though I had
discovered a long-lost son, I asked to have him brought over. The
Sudanese approached me, halted momentarily in amazement, and
then, without warning, flung himself into my arms. It was only
bashfulness that kept him from kissing me.

"Sir," he mumbled, "sir."

Deeply moved, I asked him what he was doing in the camp. He
said he would like to work in the kitchen. I pulled some strings on
his behalf and took my leave of him with a handshake.

Memories of that other meeting rose in my mind as the Sudanese
waiter made greater efforts to gratify my every desire. "What
would you like to eat?" he asked. "Ordinary bread, or *khubez bala-
di* (the local Arab bread)?"

It is fleeting encounters like these, of trifling importance as they
occur in the shadow of great historical events, that nevertheless
give the latter their peculiar flavor. When all is said and done, both

sides of the conference table are made up of human beings whose minds are not engaged exclusively with the main purpose of their meeting. Each one looks about, picking up impressions, trying to learn something about the individuals he chances to meet. I wanted to learn more and more about these people.

However, historic occasions can also reveal a great deal about people one supposedly knows well. Had I not seen it with my own eyes, I would probably have refused to believe it, but behind the scenes there was a fierce guerrilla war in progress between various members of our delegation, as each one sought to bask in the rays of glory and grab himself some extra slices of honor. Among other points at issue, there was a covert but very bitter tussle over the privilege of sleeping at the Tahara Palace. Those required to take up quarters in the neighboring building were mortally offended by what they perceived as a blow to their prestige. Some of them would have been glad to sleep in the corridor and eat breakfast off the piano—just as long as they could stay at the palace. I didn't like it at all. We had not come to Cairo to squabble over matters of rank or status.

There were similar confrontations over places at the conference table. One or two people fought for a good seat in the middle—as if they were buying movie tickets. I was told that certain individuals sneaked into the conference chamber and checked on the name plates set out on the table to ensure that they had been seated in a place befitting their dignified station.

The talks began in the early evening. The two delegations were seated on either side of a large dining table in a wood-paneled chamber. Crystal chandeliers were suspended from the ceiling. Security guards bustled about, fighting off dozens of journalists and photographers trying to record the event.

I believe there is greater mutual respect among military men on either side of the front line than among the politicians of their respective countries. Soldiers are more open toward one another—possibly because they have learned the dreadful price of war.

I would not say the mood was friendly. There were still suspicions lingering on both sides. All the same, the atmosphere was warm—even though it was periodically marred by disagreements.

I glanced about me. On one side sat Deputy Defense Minister Mottke Tzippori, who had commanded an armored brigade in 1967, and on the other—Motta Gur, who'd liberated Jerusalem in that war. Farther away sat Intelligence Chief Shlomo Gazit and

Herzl Shapir, the head of our Southern Command, whose son was badly wounded during the Yom Kippur War. Confronting us were Gamasy, the architect of the Yom Kippur War, and Mohammed Ali Fahmy, who'd commanded the antiaircraft defenses that had wreaked such havoc on our planes during the War of Attrition and in the 1973 fighting.

Before leaving for Egypt, it had been agreed that our military personnel would appear in civilian clothes. We thought it would help improve the atmosphere if we tried to avoid anything that could evoke bitter memories. I gave orders that we were to wear uniform only at the ceremony for the signing of the peace treaty.

The men facing me also wore civilian clothes, although they, too, were military men, the top commanders of the Egyptian armed forces. I tried to visualize them in uniform but found it difficult.

"Welcome to Cairo." Gamasy opened the proceedings later that day. There was silence in the chamber as he spoke softly. "We are convening to resolve the military problems, including the question of the Sinai settlements, in order to achieve a just and lasting peace."

Reference to the settlements in his opening sentence was not a good omen.

"I pray for the success of the conference," Gamasy concluded.

It was my turn. I spoke straight from the heart, and it was the hearts of those on the other side of the table I was aiming to reach.

"All my colleagues here are military men, like you," I began. "We have all taken part in battles. Unfortunately, some of us have been left with scars. But that also has its advantages. Military men comprehend the gravity of war and can achieve a better understanding—better even than the politicians."

The Egyptians were listening intently. I praised President Sadat, pointing out that he had moved the hands of the clock forward and expressing the hope that they would never again stop. Right from the start, I tried to enlighten the Egyptians on Israel's defense problems by giving them something of the beleaguered feeling we experience. I reminded them of the proximity of our settlements to the border, referring to our claustrophobic sensation and mentioning that the ordinary Israeli, who is called up for reserve duty all his life, perceives himself as a soldier with eleven months' annual furlough. They listened without a sound, and seemed interested in this glimpse of Israeli life. I wondered if it resembled their intelligence reports.

It had been agreed beforehand that our deliberations would be conducted without a permanent chairman; nor would there be a fixed agenda. I'd hoped this would provide an opportunity for each person to express himself in a free and relaxed manner, without constantly glancing at the hands of his watch or at the chairman's upraised gavel. As the conference proceeded, a dialogue did evolve from both sides of the table.

"I'm convinced the settlements aren't as important as you portray them," Gamasy said, raising his voice. "How many inhabitants do they have? Very few. There will be no difficulty in transferring them. Anything else will not be acceptable to our side."

"I don't agree with you," I said. "The border in the Sinai was never fixed. Is it such a big problem to give up so small an area? The airfields cost us tens of millions of dollars. It would be very stupid and wasteful to dismantle them."

In a bid to get the Egyptians off balance, I repeatedly spelled out Israel's defense dilemma—but they remained unimpressed.

"I propose Egyptian sovereignty over the Sinai, that the settlements remain, and a special status be given to the airfields," I said.

"What is the importance of the airfields?" the Egyptian commander in chief broke in.

"To defend Eilat," I said.

"Against whom?"

"Against Jordan and Saudi Arabia," I said. "Not against General Gamasy, I hope."

"We shall defend Eilat for you."

"We shall defend the Suez Canal for you," I jested. The joke did not improve matters.

The Egyptians' insistence on the point of the airfields was not arbitrary. Israel's security rests largely upon her air power; not for nothing had we cultivated our elite air force. I was afraid that the Egyptians, realizing the importance of the fields for our air force, would use them to undermine its strength. The Sinai contains ten airfields—some in full operation, others on standby for emergencies. The peninsula's airspace is very useful for training flights; it also provides an early-warning zone against air attacks on Israeli population centers. Control of the Sinai also made it possible to distribute our planes over several airfields, diminishing the potentially fatal effects of a surprise attack. Relinquishing the Sinai would force us to squeeze hundreds of planes into a small number of airfields—an enormous risk.

"If we give them up," I remarked smilingly, "we shall have to buy an aircraft carrier."

I proposed that one of the Sinai bases be converted into a civilian airport and the second be retained by the Israeli air force in an area that would remain under UN supervision till the year 2001.

Right from the start, it was evident that the military arrangements would constitute a salient feature of any agreement to be reached with Egypt. I was convinced that the discussion over the details of the military agreement would lend momentum to the overall negotiations. There would likely be a measure of deadlock in the autonomy talks, whereas discussion of a military agreement could be concluded quite quickly.

The principal problem to be solved by the military agreement was reduction of possible points of friction between the two armies to improve the atmosphere—while paying scrupulous attention to our security needs. In giving up the Sinai, Israel would have to ensure that the peninsula could never again serve as a springboard from which the Egyptian army might someday launch a renewed onslaught. It was vital to demilitarize the Sinai in order to provide us with an early-warning zone. Our military experts calculated that a wide demilitarized zone would give us sufficient time to mobilize our reserves—our principal forces—in the event of an Egyptian move to attack us. Of course, Egypt might be able to move its armored divisions into the Sinai and deploy them eastward. However, they would have to negotiate a broad area of empty desert without the guarantee of that logistic support that is essential for the secure progress of an armored force—backup fuel, ammunition, and materiel. No such logistic infrastructure could be constructed without violating the demilitarization agreement. Demilitarization could not prevent an air attack, but it would hinder the establishment of airbases in the Sinai like the ones that had been there before the Six-Day War.

We were particularly interested in working out inspection techniques to enforce the military agreement. Our experience of UN supervision has proven bitterly disappointing. In 1967, the UN forces stationed at Sharm el Sheik and Gaza were sent packing by Nasser without anyone in the world blinking an eye. We have never regarded the UN forces as capable of blocking an attack: a few companies of lightly armed soldiers cannot check the advance of armored divisions. However, an inspection system can provide information about the situation on both sides of the border, and that is its principal function.

In view of our disillusioning experience with UN supervision, my preference from the beginning was the creation of a joint Israeli-Egyptian inspection structure. The size of the supervisory forces was of secondary importance next to the central fact that they would be mixed units of Israelis and Egyptians. On top of everything else, it would necessarily have a strong psychological impact.

In light of these ideas, Gamasy's opening address seemed rigid and inflexible. He reiterated the hope that the 1973 war would be the last one, but in the same breath he stressed that no one in Egypt would be prepared to give up any land. "We want peace," Gamasy declared. "But first, we must get back our property—and then we can agree to all necessary security measures. You say that we are discussing one percent of our native land. It is easy to talk of one percent, but we cannot consent to border changes. The most difficult problem is the settlements."

"And the airfields!" I broke in loudly.

In the dialogue that ensued, there was one point on which I found myself bested. Gamasy was cleverer than I in his references to the politicians. In response to my remark that military men like us were more capable of achieving an understanding than politicians, he said, "We shall help the political leaders to achieve peace," raising his voice to stress the word "help." I was embarrassed. He was right on target—much more so than I. I could not forgive myself for my blunder.

"This morning," I said, "I told President Sadat that he is a wise man. Wisdom and courage go together, and he has both."

"You, too, are a wise man," Gamasy promptly fired back on the same note. "You are 'wise-man,' " he quipped.

The pun on my name evoked peals of laughter from both sides of the table. Once more, the atmosphere was relaxed, and I seized the opportunity. "I'm sure that when you heard that Begin, Weizman, and Sharon were in the cabinet, you thought that war was going to break out the next day," I said.

The Egyptians did not respond. I was convinced I had scored a direct hit.

"We look like a cabinet of hawks," I added.

The Egyptian commander in chief smiled. Gamasy remained poker-faced.

"The previous government spoke of Sharm el Sheik the way it spoke of Jerusalem," I went on. "We have done things no previous government did. At the same time, you can't come to the Israelis and say, 'What's past is past, and what we said wasn't said.' "

I observed signs of disagreement. Having undergone a fundamental change, the Egyptians could find no reason why we should not do the same. A day or two earlier, Sadat had told an

Israeli journalist: "The spirit I created by my peace initiative has had no effect on Israel—it lives only within me." Clearly, my negotiation partners felt that the past had to be erased.

"We are worried that in a few years' time there won't be any General Gamasy to talk to," I said, looking at him. "And then, the fear is that we shall again meet on the field of battle."

I thought Gamasy looked a trifle irritated.

"Would the Sinai settlements give Israel security?" he demanded.

I tried another way of bypassing the issue. "Israelis living on the border would bring about a normalization of life. People would live together, the way they do now on the Jordan bridges. That gives everyone a good feeling."

Gamasy and his colleagues shook their heads.

I feigned anger. "What would you do in my place, as defense minister?" I asked the Egyptian minister of war.

"I would remove the settlements without delay," Gamasy replied quietly. "If there is peace, but we give up land, it will mean war in the next generation—even if the loss of land is part of a territorial exchange."

Gamasy's statements that evening gave me to understand that the Egyptians did not accept the proposal we had submitted at Ismailia: they did not share our views on the settlements and the airfields or about an area under UN supervision—certainly not on giving Israelis free access to the buffer zone.

I did not accept Gamasy's counterproposal: a buffer zone on both sides of the international border—in Sinai and in Israel— with Israel demilitarizing a part of her territory as well and no limitations on the Egyptian forces to the south and west of the demilitarized zone.

"The gap between our positions is wide," I summed up dolefully. "Thorough study is essential."

"We are deadlocked on every point," Gamasy concluded.

He was right, and I could not conceal my disappointment. My face must have shown it vividly. That evening we had failed to take a single step forward.

15

KING FAROUK'S BED

My room was only a few yards from what had been President Sadat's subterranean war room. I had a tremendous urge to catch a glimpse of it, but of course I could not subject my hosts to such an embarrassing request. In fact, I never even referred to it out loud. Assuming the Egyptians may have planted microphones everywhere, I said aloud only what I would have uttered freely in their presence.

Before going to bed, I made calls to several of my friends in Israel. It was still something of a miracle for me to be able to dial their numbers from Cairo. The Israeli post office and our army's electronics and signals corps had equipped me with an advanced type of telephone receiver that enabled me to contact Israel without recourse to Egypt's telephone system.

"Hello! This is Ezer calling. From Cairo!"

I got quite a kick out of starting my calls in that fashion and tried to visualize the expressions on the faces at the other end.

"I'm lying on the bed of King Farouk," I told them. Amazing how people can be impressed by trivia when it's about places they had not dreamed of reaching. Israeli newspaper readers were as carried away as I was. A superficial account of daily life in London or New York would scarcely interest a soul in Israel, but such descriptions from Cairo became smash hits.

In my report to the prime minister, I tried to sound confident while presenting the facts realistically: as long as Sadat's attitude remained unchanged, there was no hope of progress in the deliberations of the military committee. At the same time, I again stressed the value of the meetings. Even though the talks were reaching an impasse, we were still talking face to face around the conference table—and in the Egyptian capital.

In the following day's discussions, Chief of Staff Motta Gur stole the show with a well-constructed and previously prepared discourse on Israel's security problems and the dangers we faced.

"When I graduated from school"—Gur began his address—"my teachers expected me to become a teacher. Indeed, I won a scholarship to study in England. Later, in 1947, I thought of making law my career, but that precise year we were faced with the necessity of fighting for our lives, and so I had to renounce my ambitions. Instead of becoming a teacher or a lawyer, I became an army officer."

I love speeches that carry a personal note; dry lectures have always bored me stiff. Gur's words came straight from the heart, and I noticed that the Egyptians were following him with a close and growing interest.

On further thought, it struck me that Motta Gur's opening sentences could be seen as a compact collective biography of his generation. Most of our generals had not dreamed from youth of a military career; some wanted to become scientists or businessmen; others planned to join a kibbutz or go into politics. Foreign generals, on their retirement, hang up their uniforms and go fishing. When their Israeli counterparts leave the army, they launch themselves on a second career, in which they can fulfill their true dreams. Officers of this type are yet another element of Israeli strength. Israel's military thinking has never gotten itself into a rut, nor has it depended on theories drawn from professional literature. It has always stood out in its originality and freshness, which is probably why it often succeeded in taking the Arabs—and the whole world—by surprise. Our military theorists are potential professors and frustrated scientists, obliged to dedicate their lives to defending their country and safeguarding its existence. They give the army the best years of their lives—because there is no other choice. Security demands the best, and they respond to the call.

"After the 1948 war, I went to study at the university," Motta continued. "About that time, the armistice agreements were concluded. In Israel, we saw them as the first step toward peace. I myself went into Middle Eastern studies because I dreamed of a diplomatic career in one of the Arab capitals. Unfortunately, a few months before completing my studies, I was obliged to return to the army—because Arab guerrillas were attacking us from every side, making life intolerable along our long borders. Instead of becoming an ambassador—I hope I will make it yet—I had to go back to being a soldier."

The Egyptians were transfixed. I'm not sure that they grasped the Israeli tragedy so exemplified by Motta Gur's biography, but they were obviously impressed and listened with a fascinated attention.

Motta was equally candid and incisive in depicting Israel's military situation. He did not take refuge behind elegant words or polished phrases. I have always admired him for his powers of articulation even when disagreeing with the substance of his ideas. It is no accident that he is a writer in his spare time.

"One of the principal questions we face is to what extent Egypt will be able to remain outside the hostilities should war break out on Israel's northern or eastern borders," the chief of staff explained. "We live in the shadow of our past experience, especially since we have not yet been able to resolve our problems with the other Arab states and with the PLO."

I looked at Gamasy and his colleagues, studying their faces to detect their reactions to Gur's words—in vain. They remained inscrutable.

Motta Gur also managed to inject a personal note into his political, strategic, and tactical observations. "In 1956, I was a battalion commander with the paratroopers who were dropped into the Mitla Pass," he related. "We ran into an ambush of yours. For five hours, we were pinned down in a narrow space. When we noticed a group of Egyptians leaving their position and trying to take up a new one, we made the mistake of shooting at them instead of letting them get away. They returned to their former position—and continued to fight."

Across the table, the Egyptians looked pleased. They took the words of our chief of staff as a compliment, and I rejoiced at Gur's success in winning their hearts.

"My conclusion from the battle of the Mitla," he went on, "is strategic: the other side must be allowed to get out of its predicament—unless you are set on killing and being killed. In my view, each of the sides must make concessions to achieve a peace agreement."

Motta Gur went on to talk about the Sinai airfields, stressing their key role in the defense of Israel. "It is a matter of the utmost importance," he said. "The distance between Israel and Syria is ten to fourteen minutes' flying time; between Israel and Jordan it's no more than two minutes; between us and you it's ten to twelve minutes. We have six active airfields—and we are encircled."

"You have fifty airfields," said Gamasy, anxious to prove his expertise.

"You're wrong," I remarked.

"You operate six airfields," Gamasy insisted, "but you have fifty. You may not consider them airfields, but they are landing strips."

I was surprised by his misinformation, but for the moment I thought it better to leave him in ignorance. The error may have stemmed from Egyptian respect for our air force, whose power they probably overrate.

"I have to give a bad mark to General Shaukat," broke in General Shlomo Gazit, head of our military intelligence, referring to his Egyptian counterpart. The remark was out of place. Gazit should have known that the Egyptians—with their sensitivity about their dignity—do not like to hear patronizing comments.

"I swear we don't have more than six active airfields." I addressed Gamasy. "You operate twenty-five airfields and the Syrians fifteen."

It was obviously superfluous to remind the Egyptian military leaders of the dangers inherent in concentrating large numbers of airplanes in a few airfields, but Motta Gur went into the issue, wishing to make it clear beyond any shadow of a doubt that we were insisting on nothing more than our most vital needs.

"If you look at the Golan Heights," he continued, "you can understand how great the temptation was for the Syrians to attack us there. I once took my father on a tour of the heights. He looked down at our settlements below. Do you know what he said? 'No wonder the Syrians sat up here and fired down at the Israeli settlement!' "

While Motta Gur was giving this personal account of Israel's security problems, someone entered the room to place a note before General Gamasy, who gave a grimace of annoyance. Making his apologies, he left the room, to return a few moments later, an angry expression on his face.

"General," he addressed me, "the president has just contacted me to inform me that yet another 'settlement' is being erected in the Sinai."

I was outraged, though I could not vent my anger in public. Here we were, discussing security arrangements, trying to give the wagon of peace one more little shove forward—and my colleagues in Jerusalem, instead of learning the lesson of the phony settlements, were erecting yet another one at the very hour that negotiations were in progress. I refused to believe that someone in Jerusalem was trying to torpedo the prospects of peace—but that was probably the way matters appeared.

Requesting an intermission for consultations, I made telephone contact with the prime minister's office in Jerusalem. A few minutes later, I got a message from Menachem Begin, which I was glad to transmit to General Gamasy: "The prime minister wishes to declare that we are not constructing new settlements in the Rafah approaches and requests that this message also be conveyed to President Sadat."

I was relieved: my colleagues of the Israeli delegation also looked greatly cheered. We could return to our deliberations. It was now the turn of Egyptian Commander in Chief Fahmy to respond to Motta Gur. "We are talking too much about the past," Fahmy began. "We should concentrate on the future. History teaches that the enemies of the past strive to become the friends of the future. We must plan the future in such a manner that each side can defend itself without attacking. Your proposals are at the expense of our lands and our sovereignty. I heard what General Gur said about the importance of early warning. We refuse to have this at the expense of our land. I understand the importance of strategic depth, but Egypt, too, has such problems. We have no early-warning system from the direction of the sea, and are vulnerable there."

Again I heard beneath his words that fear of the Israeli air force.

"I have heard that even Tripoli is within the range of your air force," said the Egyptian commander in chief.

I did not answer. I take great pride in our air force, but singing its praises would have weakened our bargaining position. The Egyptians could then argue that our air force was an adequate substitute for other defensive measures.

"Our demands are minimal," I said. "The Etzion airfield is the only one in the vicinity of Eilat, which is a very isolated town. The only force capable of protecting Eilat is the airfield. It will also be the only airfield within range of Ras Mohammed, when that is in your hands."

As I was speaking and carefully noticing the impact of my words on the men facing me, I had a brain wave. "You say our air force needs are no reason to take land away from you. But they may be a good reason for holding joint training flights over the Sinai."

"We'll do that," said Gamasy.

I was delighted by his response, even if I had my doubts about the feasibility of putting the idea into practice. All the same, I tried to take advantage of this minor success. "Our settlements in the Sinai are of military importance," I explained. "The settlers there are soldiers in civilian clothes. You might also establish settlements there, and the two sides could live together."

The Egyptians had no need to say anything: their objections were written on their faces.

We went on to discuss the limitation of forces on both sides of the border, trying to find some sphere in which agreement would be possible. It was not going to be easy.

History is more than the product of isolated volcanic outbursts; rather, it is the accumulated fruit of processes unfolding and crystallizing over prolonged periods—and the statesman directs his policies accordingly. The United States did not come into being through the Declaration of Independence of July 4, 1776; the Soviet Union didn't turn Communist in October 1917; neither did the state of Israel come about by the proclamation of its independence on May 15, 1948. Israel's creation was the outcome of a long and complex process, which began with the Zionist Congresses at the end of the last century, continuing through Zionist resettlement in Palestine and culminating in the creation of sovereign Jewish military and political institutions in our country.

More than other states, Israel is constantly undergoing transitions—political, strategic, economic, technological, social and ideological. At the state's proclamation, there were six hundred thousand Jews, mostly of European origin. Within thirty years, Israel absorbed nearly two million immigrants, over half of whom came from Africa and Asia. In the course of those thirty years, everything changed. Consequently, no Israeli leader is entitled to underwrite the future form of the state in years to come. We must be guided by our long-term objectives, but our decisions and actions have to be adopted in the full awareness that we are in a period of transition.

The principal feature of the period we are in now is our attempt to integrate into the Middle East. This attempt calls for various compromises but is also marked by an insistence on several basic conditions, the most important of which is Israel's continued existence as a Jewish and Zionist state. I hope and believe that when this transition period ends, we shall be an integral part of the region surrounding us. Even before this process reaches fruition, we will be in the midst of another period of transition, whose problems and difficulties will be intrinsic elements of the new situation; however, in creating solutions, we will be able to depend on a stronger and more positive base than our present one.

My awareness of being in transition toward a goal of integration into the region guided me at every stage of our negotiations with the Egyptians.

I asked them frankly: "What will happen in a few years' time when Gamasy and I are old—and you move four divisions into the Sinai?"

"And what are we to do if you move your army into the Negev?" Gamasy answered.

We came to an understanding together that limitation of forces on both sides of the border was the best solution and thus laid the foundations for our first point of agreement—and for the military appendix of the peace treaty in the future. From there, we went on to debate details, but our deliberations were drawn to a close by the hands of the clock. Midday was approaching, and the Egyptians wanted to take advantage of the lunch break to show us around Cairo.

I summed up the points on which we appeared to be approaching agreement. The Egyptians proposed a thinning out of forces on both sides of the border, based on three elements: a buffer zone between the armies, a demilitarized zone, and possibly a thinning-out zone, too. I expressed my satisfaction with their presentation.

"I'm glad that we have concluded the principles for a buffer zone and a demilitarized zone on both sides of the border," Gamasy responded.

"Just a minute—" I broke in. "We did not agree to demilitarization on both sides. We spoke only about the principle. On our side, there is no room for demilitarization. What can we demilitarize? Beersheba?"

It was my impression that at least on this point the Egyptians understood us. They had so much more territory to play around with. Our agreement therefore remained in the realm of principle rather than in concrete details of lines and battalions, but Gamasy did not let me rejoice in it for long. He brought up the Palestinian issue, which was scheduled for discussion at the political committee meeting in Jerusalem. Nonetheless, not wishing to miss the opportunity, I explained our unswerving views on the matter, clearly and incisively.

"Nothing will budge without a solution of the Palestinian problem." Motta Gur expressed his opinion in a note he scribbled to me. He then addressed the conference.

"For two years, I was the military governor of Gaza," recalled the chief of staff. "I spent hours interviewing dozens of terrorists in my office. I got the impression that they had not abandoned their ambition of wiping Israel off the map. As long as that is their ambition, it will take time to resolve the Palestinian problem."

I had given Gur permission to express himself freely despite the fact that we did not at all agree.

"It would be very good if we could sign a full peace treaty as quickly as possible and make peace an established fact," said the chief of staff. "But on the other hand, I don't think we should run too fast—and expose our flanks. In my opinion, we should sign quickly and implement slowly."

However, the most abrasive point of view came from our military intelligence chief, Shlomo Gazit, the man who was supposed to know the Arabs better than anyone else and whose former post as coordinator of our activities in the occupied territories had brought him into almost daily contact with them. Nevertheless, Gazit erred seriously in the tone he adopted toward the Egyptians.

"I'm a man who doesn't know how to negotiate," he said, "as my wife can bear witness. I understand that our negotiations are being conducted the way things go at the market of Khan al Khalil—starting high in order to come down later."

A sudden hush fell over the ornate chamber. You could have cut the air with a knife. The Egyptians were profoundly offended at the suggestion that they had been haggling in a *suk*, and it was only with the greatest difficulty that they swallowed their rage. Gamasy's eyes flickered nervously, but Gazit did not even notice the impact his words were having.

"In our case," he added, "it's not a matter of bargaining but of basic principle. You can't expect us to withdraw to the old border and forget everything that's happened. There's no point in repeating that we shall trust one another from now on. It takes time to build up mutual trust."

The Egyptians glared at him angrily, but Gazit blindly continued. "My friend Moshe Sasson tried to pick up the Israel Radio broadcasts in Arabic from here, but he failed. You interfere with the broadcasts."

"That isn't so!" Gamasy broke in.

"I saw a booklet called *Egypt Today* issued by your propaganda institute," the intelligence chief went on relentlessly. "It contained

a map of the Middle East. The name Israel does not appear—
what's written there is 'Palestine.' In Israel, Egypt appears on
every map. Trust is more than just words. Trust is created by a
process, and that takes time."

Our talks had always been conducted in a friendly spirit even
when there were fundamental disagreements. Gazit's words,
backed up by the examples he mentioned, jarred on the ear and left
a final note of discord.

"I will return home and discuss our points of agreement with the
prime minister," I concluded.

There were a few hours left until we were due to fly home, and
I toured Cairo with the Egyptian intelligence chief, General
Shaukat.

Shaukat is an affable man, pleasant but very restrained. He
chose every word with great care, and I decided to draw him out.

"In the 1973 war, you didn't know we'd crossed over to the
western bank of the Canal, did you?" I challenged.

He was embarrassed, unsure whether or not to reply.

"As head of intelligence," he said, "I did have reports, right from
the early stages of the war, that you were conducting bridging
exercises in the wadi of El Arish. I thought that if you were practic-
ing bridging, you must be intending to cross the Canal. I reported it
to my superiors, but they paid no attention.

I burst out laughing. Once again, I was hearing a familiar tune:
it was precisely what happens in Israel.

Our column of cars, escorted by police vehicles and motorcy-
clists, edged its way through Cairo's traffic jams. Suddenly, an old
memory flashed across my mind.

"After this bend, there should be a railway station," I recalled
aloud.

"Right!" Shaukat confirmed. "This street is now called Ramses
Street. Following the officers' revolution, many Cairo streets once
named for modern kings were renamed after ancient pharaohs."

"In 1942, just by this railway station, I had an accident," I told
him. "I was driving in a convoy and fell asleep, and I ran into the
vehicle in front of me."

Shaukat smiled.

I did not take my eyes off the route. The population explosion
was immediately evident. The sidewalks were teeming, and many
of the pedestrians were forced to walk in the roadway. Our cars
could scarcely inch forward through this human sea. For the first

time, I had a concrete sense of the burden imposed by Egypt's population density.

The people in the street had yet to identify me, but a few smiled or waved. I could scarcely bring myself to wave back. I was stunned.

I asked to see the house of my relatives, at 26 Al Gazira Street, where I had spent many hours and days in the forties. Shaukat ordered the security guards to take me there, on the way to the pyramids. To my disappointment, the first thing I saw was the sign at the entrance of the house: "Tunisian Embassy." I dropped the idea of visiting the building.

The way to the pyramids was familiar, but something was missing. "Just a moment!" I cried. "Where's the tram to the pyramids?"

Shaukat laughed. "We scrapped it a long time ago," he said. "But I see you have a good memory."

We reached the Giza pyramids. Tourists were scurrying about, darting in between the camels and piles of garbage.

Near the Sphinx, I got fed up with the security regulations that forbade me to leave the car. "Stop!" I told the driver. "I'm getting out!" My bodyguards—Egyptian and Israeli—hurried toward me in an attempt to block my path.

"Come on, fellows. I want to see Egypt. Let me out."

Within moments, there was a crowd. Schoolchildren greeted me.

"You have brought light to Egypt." Their teacher welcomed me in the traditional Egyptian manner.

American tourists were on the verge of tears. Russian tourists sprang forward to snap pictures of Israel's defense minister in the midst of a group of Russians at the foot of Egypt's pyramids. I took the opportunity to say a few words of the Russian I remembered from home.

In the meantime, I was surrounded by a group of European tourists. Before I took my leave of them, one approached me. "Shalom," he said in Hebrew. I was not surprised: Shalom has become an internationally recognized greeting.

But the man went on—in fluent Hebrew! "My name is Efraim Proper," he said. "I am a graduate of the Max Fein technical school in Tel Aviv."

I could not believe my ears. For one brief second, I toyed with the idea that he was an Israeli spy who had chosen this spot, at the foot of the pyramids, to reveal his identity to me. I'm sure that was what the Egyptian security men thought: they seemed bent on hustling him away.

"Who are you?" I demanded. "What are you doing here?"

"I came to Palestine as a young boy," said the man, who looked about sixty. "I settled in Degania. During World War II, I joined the Czech army to fight against the Germans. My family disappeared in the Holocaust. I went to search for them, but I couldn't find them. Then I got stuck in Prague. I married a gentile woman and started a family. I speak Hebrew to this day. My brother was killed in the battle against the Egyptians at Yad Mordechai in 1948."

The twists and turns of Jewish destiny. A Jew comes to Palestine from Czechoslovakia, settles in Degania, returns to Prague, his brother is killed fighting the Egyptians—and now, here he is, talking to Israel's defense minister at the foot of the pyramids.

The drive back through the streets of Cairo resembled a retrospective tour of my youth. With great excitement, I picked out the places I remembered. I asked the driver to stop at the Groppi café, the haunt of Egyptian society during the forties and a meeting place for British soldiers during World War II. I had spent a lot of time there and wanted to see it again.

I got out of the car. A large crowd gathered from all sides. People clapped or pressed against me to shake my hand. At the same time, I saw the concern in the eyes of my bodyguards, who were afraid someone would try to knife me. I took a seat in the café in great anticipation, but the place bore no resemblance to its past. It was a dismal establishment, shabby and without a remnant of its former glory.

When too many people gathered outside, the security guards urged me to leave the café. They pushed the crowd back in a manner I did not like.

"Nobody will do me any harm!" I shouted, but none of the bodyguards from either side paid me any attention.

We drove to the airport. The way to Israel was short—shorter than the way to peace.

16

WAR CLOUDS

Before the elections that elevated Begin to power, anyone predicting that he would ever give up the Sinai peninsula would have met with scorn. But he proceeded to do just that—to everyone's astonishment.

Begin's most extreme opponents—those who continually subjected him to scathing criticism, often reinforced by deep personal hostility—were suddenly falling all over themselves to praise him for the flexibility and generosity with which he welcomed the new era dawning in the Middle East. At the same time, some of his most loyal followers were in despair: the man they had trusted, more than any other Israeli politician, the man they had relied upon as a bulwark against any eventual surrender of our Six-Day War conquests—overnight declared himself willing to give up the whole of the Sinai.

But those—like me—who had followed events from an inside vantage point and from a close acquaintance with Menachem Begin knew that he had not changed. I have not the slightest doubt that renouncing the Sinai was highly painful for Begin. However, behind the willingness to give up the peninsula was the true Menachem Begin, alive and active. He must have decided to reach a compromise with the Egyptians in the south as a way of perpetuating some form of Israeli rule over Judea and Samaria. Whereas the Egyptians saw the Sinai agreement as the model for similar understandings with Jordan and Syria over the West Bank and the

Golan Heights, Begin saw it as the precise opposite. As far as he was concerned, the withdrawal from the Sinai would be the end of the story.

After a short time, Begin himself woke up to the pitfalls latent in the autonomy scheme. What was meant to be the first step to annexation could equally be the mandate for a Palestinian state in the future. Ultimately, fifteen modifications had to be inserted in the plan—some of a major nature. The amended scheme bore little resemblance to the plan that had been presented by Begin to Carter and transmitted by the latter to the Egyptian president. The White House seethed with anger. Sadat was beside himself with fury. On top of being made to look foolish by the White House and Sadat, Israel seemed to be finding every possible tactic to impede the peace process—which was finding the going rough enough before the alterations in our autonomy plan.

Certain moves took me unawares; in decisions about the West Bank and in our relations with the Americans, it soon became evident that I was not privy to everything going on. Astonished, I reacted at the top of my voice. After all, I did bear responsibility for the cabinet's most sensitive portfolio: any possible agreement with Egypt had far-reaching implications for my sphere of duty, yet I was not fully briefed.

Questions dangled in the air, and I pointed them out to friends and companions. I did the same with some of Begin's own friends and sympathizers. They could not provide me with any clear answers. However much I puzzled over the reasons for my being excluded, I could not believe that it was only because of Begin's mode of decision making or his intolerance of any opinion that does not conform to his own. There were also grudges from the past. Begin has never forgiven me for my actions in the early 1970s, when my activities to try to open up the Herut movement did not meet with his approval. Menachem Begin is good at harboring grudges. The annals of Herut are strewn with the charred accounts of those who dared to act in defiance of his ideas.

I soon learned that I was not alone. Other ministers, similarly denied inside knowledge, used to hang around in the prime minister's office in Jerusalem in an attempt to ferret out whatever they could. Others consulted one another by telephone to find out what was going on behind the scenes.

During Golda Meir's term of office as prime minister, there were countless jokes about her political "kitchen," where she hosted her senior ministers for consultations and exchanged views on new political constellations. Even though the matriarchal undertones gave rise to wisecracks and criticism, I have always been a firm believer in letting people in. Golda's great gift was that she held together a cabinet of different and volatile personalities—Begin, Dayan, Sapir, Allon, myself—and she controlled it well. She ran a tight ship, and we often used to say: "She's the only man in the cabinet."

Begin's cabinet was the opposite. Starved of information, the ministers fell prey to suspicions of Sadat. Each minister made his own attempts to interpret the Egyptian president's statements and deeds. The temporary deadlock in negotiations—as well as the dummy settlements and the modifications in our autonomy plan—had all combined to push the Egyptians off balance and make them respond emotionally. Losing their tempers, they now subjected our prime minister to a stream of abuse. Begin was offended—with some justification: even a man less mindful of his dignity would have been wounded to the quick. He wisely restrained himself from giving public expression to his feelings, but in cabinet meetings he repaid the Egyptians by fostering the atmosphere of mistrust toward them. Influenced by this mood, several ministers began to emulate Begin. The fact that the peace initiative had come from Sadat put the Israeli government on the defensive, and some petty behavior resulted.

Unlike some of my colleagues, I considered myself under no obligation to Begin. I felt no gratitude to him for making me defense minister. I have little doubt that given half a chance, he would have denied me the appointment. But I did not find the job in the gutter, nor did I gain it by the grace of Begin's benevolence. Among other reasons, I won it because I had headed the election campaign that brought him his first-ever election victory.

Be that as it may, when the political committee convened in Jerusalem, I was effectively excluded from its proceedings: the Defense Ministry views were represented by Mottke Tzippori. But even from the outside, I could not help noticing the change from the tone that had previously characterized contacts between the two sides. The Egyptians adopted a harsh and unyielding position, and Israel responded in kind.

This state of affairs stemmed largely from Sadat's predicament in the Arab world. From talks with him and his close advisers, I got the clear impression that for all the importance they attach to the Palestinian problem, it is not at the top of their priorities. The tone of their demands grew appreciably harsher whenever the talks touched on the Sinai settlements and airfields. At the same time, I realized that Sadat could not afford to abandon the Palestinians—

that would have turned the Arab world even more against him, leading to the complete rejection of his country by its neighbors in the region. We Israelis, who have made such an effort to fight our way out of the isolation so long imposed upon us, ought to have been the first to comprehend his dilemma.

That was why I favored meeting Sadat halfway on all those matters where a concession on our part was unavoidable. I thought we should do it with the greatest possible speed—taking a calculated risk—lest unforeseen events in the Arab world block our path to peace. Certainly, the political committee's meeting in Jerusalem could have given the Arab world a pretext.

The threat of finding themselves isolated within the Arab world incited the Egyptians to demand that the political committee begin its deliberations with the Palestinian issue. Israel rejected the demand. Dayan hastily recruited U.S. Secretary of State Cyrus Vance, who came up with a compromise formula—that the discussions deal with "issues to do with the West Bank and Gaza Strip." Everyone knew it was a rose by another name.

In view of Sadat's fears of a final drop in his standing in the Arab world and the current hostility between Jerusalem and Cairo, it was evident from the first moment that the committee's deliberations were doomed to failure. As though to make that doubly sure, Menachem Begin added fuel to the fire.

A dinner for the Egyptian delegation at the Jerusalem Hilton gave the Israeli prime minister an opportunity to display one of his less admirable traits. Hosting the banquet in honor of Egypt's then Foreign Minister Mohammed Ibrahim Kamel constituted a gesture of good will on Begin's part: protocol required nothing more than a banquet given by Dayan, Kamel's opposite number. But Begin's good intentions led him somewhere else altogether.

Begin is absolutely convinced that he holds the truth in his back pocket. Consequently, in addressing others—including the heads of great nations—he adopts the manner of a teacher talking to his pupils. There is something overbearing about his manner, and I suspect it has infuriated certain key figures in Washington, Cairo, and elsewhere.

The prime minister began his address to the banquet with the words: "My young friend." The Egyptian minister, who is in his fifties, was mortally offended. After that auspicious opening, Kamel had to listen to a long sermon in which, on top of a lecture on Jewish history, he was also given a lesson in statesmanship. Begin then presented the Israeli position in a forceful, uncompromising tone.

Leaving his prepared text in his pocket, the Egyptian foreign minister rose to respond. The verbal clash between eastern Europe and the Middle East sent the sparks flying.

The political committee began its deliberations.

Kamel had brought along a draft declaration of principles. Its main point was the full implementation of Security Council Resolution 242, in all its parts—in other words, Israel's undertaking to withdraw from all occupied territories. Like Resolution 242, the declaration called for recognition of the principle of non-acquisition of territory by force. It also proposed mutual defense arrangements, such as demilitarization and arms limitations. However, the chief pitfall lay in the phrase: "A just solution of the Palestinian problem in all its aspects, on the basis of self-determination, by means of talks between the representatives of Egypt, Jordan, and Israel, and representatives of the Palestinian people."

I knew Kamel to be the originator of the "wilting" theory: he was the first to propose peace with Israel as a way of erasing her from the map by peaceful means. I see no prospect of that. The Jews have managed to survive for two thousand years as a minority dispersed over five continents; during the British mandate over Palestine, we were in a minority in our country. There is no reason why we should not hold out as a minority in the Middle East without being overwhelmed.

Israel then submitted her own plan for administrative autonomy, as presented by Begin to the president of the United States and submitted for discussion at the Ismailia conference.

The committee's deliberations were deadlocked.

Even though I had no particular reason to be there, I headed for the Jerusalem Hilton to seek out a few of my Cairo acquaintances. I took one of them—intelligence chief Brigadier General Howeidi—to the Knesset building. For years, the Egyptians had been told that in the center of the Knesset there is a mysterious map on display that depicts an all-powerful and all-conquering Greater Israel stretching from the Nile to the Euphrates. I wanted to show him that there was no such map and that the whole story is part of a years-long campaign of fabrications. In the Knesset building, I introduced Howeidi to two of our former chiefs of staff, Yitzhak Rabin—chief of staff during the Six-Day War against the Egyptian forces—and Chaim Bar-Lev—chief of staff against them in the War of Attrition. His eyes sparkled.

During the tour, Howeidi complained of an earache.

"What's the matter?" I demanded.

"It's an old story," he replied. "In 1956, I ran over one of your mines at Rafah!"

Early that evening, I returned to the Hilton where the political committee was continuing its meetings. Going up to the room of Egypt's secretary of state for foreign affairs, Boutros Ghali, I found him perplexed and in despair.

Right from the outset, from our very first meeting during Sadat's visit, I had felt a great admiration for Ghali. He is a kind of "negative print" of Zionist history. His grandfather served at the beginning of the century as Egypt's prime minister, and as such he met Theodor Herzl, the seer of the Jewish state; the Egyptian had rejected Herzl's proposal for Jewish settlement at El Arish.

Ghali was the heart and soul, the conscience and compass, of the peace process from the Egyptian side. He is a professor of political science, widely educated, with an enviable command of languages. With his ascetic features, he looked as though he carried the full burden of history on his fragile shoulders. He is emotional and inclined to pessimism. In Israel, he was portrayed as "the bad guy." I had frequently heard him voice his concern over the possible failure of the negotiations. He was anxious about his own personal safety as well as that of Sadat and his intimates.

"We've received orders from Sadat to return to Cairo without delay," Ghali said as I entered his room.

I was thunderstruck. I took a very grave view of this turn of events, regarding it as a perilous setback for the overall process. Of the two committees decided upon at Ismailia, the military body had started its talks in Cairo, and the sides were firmly resolved to reconvene for a renewed attempt to spring the hurdles. By contrast, the political committee meeting in Jerusalem experienced a total breakdown. Not only had the talks failed to chalk up the smallest achievement, but the breakdown would further darken the already murky atmosphere. I was furious at the Egyptians. Sadat's decision to recall his people from Jerusalem made me fear that he had given up on his attempts to reach a peace settlement with Israel.

Throughout those days, official proclamations coming from Cairo carried the menacing sound of saber rattling. No one said it in so many words, but that war that everyone had vowed to avert now cast its sinister shadow. Egypt was hardening her position— and, simultaneously, vilifying Israel's prime minister. Sadat himself stated that should Israel insist on leaving her settlements in the Sinai, he would personally set them ablaze. Begin repaid Sadat by referring to him as "Nero." Israelis from the extremist fringes, constantly lurking in ambush to discredit the peace process and point up its faults, suddenly emerged from their lairs to pounce upon Sadat's step as further proof of the age-old Israeli gripe that "there's no one to talk to."

For the first time since Sadat's arrival in Jerusalem, the horizon grew dark with war clouds.

17

FLYING SPARKS

The sharp setbacks to the peace process—marked by the break-down of the political committee's talks in Jerusalem and by the mutual recriminations between Jerusalem and Cairo—made me lose a lot of sleep. My worry was a double one. I was afraid we were losing the historic opportunity to construct a bridge of under-standing and good neighborliness between Israel and the biggest and most powerful Arab state. However, as defense minister, I had another cause for concern: that we were facing a further round in the thirty-years' war between Israel and the Arab states. I was under no illusions. The switch from peace to war could be sharp and swift. Sadat would not have to retract a single word; even his famous declaration in Jerusalem: "No more war!" only needed repunctuating to read: "No more! War!"

Convening the members of our General Staff, I advised them to prepare for the worst. War was a possibility—and not just because of Egypt's disappointment in her attempt to regain peacefully what she had failed to regain on the battlefield. There were other data of various kinds, which taken together were disquieting.

The October 1973 war had fortified the Arabs' self-confidence; above all, it had reduced the deterrent capacity of our armed forces. Previously, we could expect the Arabs to think twice before allowing their fingers to curl around the trigger; but in the Yom Kippur War the Arabs learned that, under certain conditions, they were capable of achieving some battlefield gains. They must have realized they lack the strength to crush Israel—certainly they cannot erase her from the map, as a few of their leaders would like. However, they are capable of a renewed onslaught; they might lose the war, but they could exploit their own downfall as a political lever to isolate Israel in the international arena and force her to withdraw with her tail between her legs, relinquishing her most vital interests.

In addition to heightening the Arabs' confidence in themselves and in their armed might, the 1973 war also decimated the myth of Israel they had once held. Gone was their view of Israel as a powerful fortress state, lavishly endowed with high-quality manpower; instead, they perceived us as a society in disintegration. More and more, they viewed Israel as a modern version of the medieval Crusader state, an alien transplant that crumbled internally before being demolished by the army of Saladin. They saw post-1973 Israel as beginning to fall apart, borne down by economic burdens, wrenched by constant and nerve-racking military alertness, torn by social tensions and intercommunal friction, with her leaders and parties constantly at one another's throats.

For many years, the Arabs had believed that in the overall confrontation with Israel time was on their side. For the first time, the years following 1973 showed their belief to be not unfounded. The oil weapon has turned the Arabs into an economic power to be reckoned with. It has greatly enhanced their political clout and boosted their strategic muscle: the military might confronting Israel since 1973 is incomparably greater than anything we had faced previously.

At the same time, in view of their new standing in the international arena, the Arabs changed their tactics in the conflict with Israel. During the period preceding the Six-Day War, we benefited from the overt and unabashed manner in which the Arabs proclaimed their aggressive intentions. Television viewers and newspaper readers everywhere took note of Arab vows to hurl Israel into the sea. One did not need to be out-and-out pro-Israel to be put off by that rhetoric. After the 1967 war, the Arabs moderated their tone to a very large extent. But their fine phrases were belied by the famous "Three Nos" adopted at the Khartoum summit: no peace, no recognition of Israel, and no negotiations with her.

After the 1973 war, the Arabs launched a feigned peace offensive. Taking advantage of their oil and their economic power, they depicted Israeli policies in a harsh light and their own as moderate and reasonable. Those with an inclination to blame Israel for piling obstacles on the path to peace forget that the Arabs have not, in fact, modified their underlying intention. They still hope to erase Israel from the map—if possible. All the same, the Arabs did succeed in convincing Western leaders that the establishment of a Palestinian state in the West Bank and Gaza Strip was vital for the fulfillment of Palestinian national rights.

The West somehow believes that solving the Palestinian problem will bring peace. But the Western world has not been blessed with an overlong memory. As Shimon Peres once put it, the West forgets that the West Bank, the Sinai, the Gaza Strip, and the Golan Heights did not fall into Israeli hands by means of a rigged poker game: Egypt, Syria, and Jordan had attacked Israel, openly proclaiming a war of annihilation—and that was well before the Palestinian problem appeared on the agenda. Furthermore, long before the West Bank and Gaza Strip fell to Israel, thousands of Palestinian refugees had been left to rot in the inhuman conditions of refugee camps scattered throughout those areas. No Arab leader lifted a finger to help rehabilitate them—not even on humanitarian grounds.

It was my duty to take account of the likelihood that the West would display understanding—if not sympathy—toward an Arab attempt to overturn the Middle Eastern status quo by military means. Sadat's popularity in the West after bringing his peace offer to Jerusalem might help the Arabs in convincing the world that force was the only remaining way of inducing Israel to give up what she had refused to hand over at the conference table.

Even though there was no doubt of our ability to inflict a decisive defeat on the Arab armies, Israel's international predicament was likely to hinder her from implementing the military option. We needed to be free to exercise that option: to have that freedom we had to launch our own political and propaganda offensive, which, in addition to enlightening the world about our fundamental positions and the military problems overshadowing daily life in Israel, would expose the roots of our conflict with the Arabs. Such an offensive would benefit Israel, whether she continued her snail's-pace advance along the path toward peace with her neighbors or once again found herself at war with them.

Although I am adamant about Israel's right to call on her military forces if necessary, I also believe the time has come for Israel to break out of the circle of enmity that has encompassed her—as long as it is feasible and as long as she maintains her military strength. Peace would enable Israel to devote herself to her domestic problems, to rebuild her economy and salvage her social fabric, in keeping with the dreams of the Zionist founding fathers. Above all, the striving for peace is vital for perserving the national consensus, which has been so weakened in recent years.

Even before Sadat's visit to Jerusalem, many Israelis were asking themselves whether their government had done enough to put an end to the long-standing confrontation with the Arabs. Questions of this nature tend to arise during periods of stress, such as the height of the Suez Canal War of Attrition, when Israel appeared condemned to fight for her existence till the end of time. Israel's younger generation has been brought up to believe that there is no other choice open to them other than to fight to defend their country. I believe that this "no-choice" conviction is an essential constituent of our strength. However, recent years have seen it riddled with question marks. During the War of Attrition, high school students due to enlist for their military service wrote letters to Prime Minister Golda Meir in which they subjected her to some incisive questions. It is our duty to convince such youngsters that we are doing everything in our power for peace. Should we fail and again be obliged to send them to the battlefield, we would be able to meet their eyes with a clear conscience; if we make genuine efforts to achieve peace and do not succeed, that can only boost their fighting spirit. Outsiders may not understand the importance of the morale and determination of Israel's citizens; in wartime, these factors carry as much weight as several divisions.

I do not know whether defense ministers in other countries involved in fierce, ongoing confrontations with their neighbors permit themselves to talk to their soldiers about peace. I did so; even as I prepared for war, I saw peace as the ultimate objective.

In July 1977, long before Sadat set foot in Jerusalem and before anyone even dreamed of such an event, I addressed a group of pilots who had just won their wings.

"You are joining the air force in a very interesting year," I said to the young fliers and their families. "This may be the first year that there's a chance for an understanding with the Arabs—possibly even for peace. Some believe that Israel is not interested in an agreement with her neighbors. We shall strive to prove that the reverse is true."

Unfortunately, the desire for peace is different from the up-and-down process of hammering out the details of its implementation. The Egyptian delegation to the political committee left Jerusalem on Sadat's orders. As on previous occasions, the mood in Cairo was evident in the comments of the Egyptian newspaper editors, who expressed their disgruntlement over the Israeli position in harsh terms. Egyptian anger was directed mainly at Begin. Cairo newspapers again subjected Israel's prime minister to unbridled attacks—harmful above all to themselves and to the prospects of peace, in my view. These verbal onslaughts sprinkled salt on Israel's open wounds of mistrust.

All the same, the Egyptians were on the lookout for a suitable opportunity to renew negotiations, and they went out of their way to bring this to our attention. They no longer required the services of any third party to do so. Cairo's Tahara Palace was now the seat of an official Israeli military mission to maintain communication, which we referred to by its code name, "Zahava" ("Goldie"). At that point, it was the principal achievement of the peace talks between the two countries—and not one I underrated. A few months earlier, the idea of an official Israeli military mission in the Egyptian capital would have been unthinkable. After the breakdown of the political committee's talks, I could find some consolation in the fact that at least we had representatives in the land of the Nile; their presence there could help ward off any further misunderstandings.

The delegation was headed alternately by two colonels from our military intelligence corps—Ya'akov Heichal and Eliezer Rimon—who relieved one another every two weeks. In the delegation's signals room in Cairo, there was a duty clerk on the alert twenty-four hours a day to reply to telephone or Telex calls, directly or in code. The telephone line from Cairo was connected straight to my office and my home.

I have a great weakness for telephones and signals equipment, and I love playing with them. When I was commander of the air force, I was the first to have my car fitted with a two-way radio. One day, after a long session with the then prime minister and defense minister, David Ben-Gurion, in which we discussed military allocations running into tens of millions of Israeli pounds for the purchase of planes, I was driving the stenographer home. On the way, in what may have been a bid to impress her, I used the two-way radio to contact air force headquarters and inquire whether there were any messages for me. I was hoping for something momentous.

"Yes, sir"—a voice came over the air waves—"your wife wants you to call her at home."

I did not always have something to say to our delegation in Cairo, which did not prevent me from calling them almost every day. I was greatly taken with the idea of such easy communication and enjoyed surprising visitors to my home by showing off this wonder.

In fact, the members of our delegation in Cairo did not have much to report, either. They spent much of their time in sports contests with the Egyptians and got thoroughly bored. Even so, there was one function they fulfilled well: they served as a kind of barometer for the state of Israeli-Egyptian relations, registering the fluctuating Egyptian attitudes. At first, they were given friendly treatment. But there was a sharp change when the Egyptian delegation stalked out of the Jerusalem talks. All of a sudden, the Egyptians became cool and withdrawn.

I left General Abrasha Tamir in Cairo for a long time, where he grew quite expert in his dealings with the Egyptians. I counted on his instincts and on the wisdom of his assessments. However, even his sensitive antennae were blunted by the wall of alienation dividing the two countries. Abrasha soon got to know the Egyptians, but he must have brought along his own prejudices, the bitter fruit of years of enmity. Such preconceptions emerge in minor incidents. He told me of one occasion when he had dined at a fish restaurant in the company of General Taha Magdoub. Abrasha stuffed himself on two platefuls of cheese "as salty as the sea." That night, he returned to his room at the Tahara Palace and lay down on his bed, where he was overcome by a terrible thirst. He opened the fridge in his bedroom; it was empty. Leaving his room, he headed for the kitchen on the top floor. The door was locked. He went down to the second floor, where the committee held its deliberations, but hearing the snores of the Egyptians, he was reluctant to wake them. Still afflicted by thirst, he continued down to the ground floor and tried to open the exit door—only to withdraw in alarm. Not knowing the password, he was afraid to go outside lest the Egyptian guards open fire on him. With no other choice, he returned to his room, where he found some orange peel that he sucked until his mouth was afire. He described the hours that elapsed until dawn as "terrible torture."

In the morning, General Magdoub turned up, and Abrasha told him what had happened.

Magdoub was astonished. "Why didn't you drink from the faucet in your room?" he demanded.

After hesitating whether or not to tell him, Abrasha finally decided to be candid. "Our doctors gave us instructions not to drink tap water in Cairo, saying you have endemic *Bilharzia* here."

"Sir!" General Magdoub replied. "We have had water disinfection installations for the past ten years. We do not have *Bilharzia*, and everyone drinks from the faucets!"

*   *   *

I reaped the first fruits of "Zahava" courtesy of General Gamasy. By way of our people in Cairo, Gamasy invited me to fly over immediately for a confidential meeting with him at the Janklis estate, where we had first met. After weighing the matter, I put forward a counterproposal: renewal of the work of the military committee. My proposal was accepted. It was a good omen: in spite of everything, the Egyptians were willing to continue talking.

All this time, Moshe Dayan had been demanding the recall of our delegation from Cairo. He held that we must not allow the Egyptians to carry on negotiations as the mood took them; we should not permit ourselves to be at the mercy of their changing fancy. Dayan proposed that we suspend the meetings of the military committee in Cairo as long as the Egyptians refused to renew the deliberations of the political committee in Jerusalem.

I had not the slightest doubt about Dayan's commitment to peace: peace was his goal when he'd joined Begin's cabinet. Moshe Dayan is a mythological figure, but his legendary image was shattered on October 6, 1973. The Yom Kippur War left a black stain on Dayan's splendid military and political record. Dayan hoped to erase that stain by some act of great, dramatic impact, which would restore him to his former position in Israeli public esteem and guarantee him a place in the history books. He knew that peace would serve that purpose.

But he had his own views about peace. His version of a peace settlement had the border running inside the Sinai, along the El Arish-Ras Mohammed line. As defense minister in Golda Meir's cabinet, he had played a greater role than anyone else in urging the erection of the two large Sinai airfields, Etzion and Etam; he was also behind the construction of the town of Yamit and of the Rafah settlements. He wanted to create "facts on the ground" similar to those that had been the foundation for the establishment of the state of Israel. He believed that such "facts" were capable of providing defensible boundaries. He also had his own views about the West Bank, where he wanted to let Jordan regain control of civilian affairs, with security remaining in Israeli hands. He did favor giving the Jordanians some token security function to allow them a sense of being involved in the preservation of security and bound to its maintenance.

Begin ruined Dayan's hand by surrendering the whole of the Sinai. (It is said that he would be capable of handing over part of the Golan Heights, too, as long as he could preserve our control of the historic land of Israel in its entirety.) Dayan attempted to salvage his plan, at least in part, by trying to graft its main features on to Begin's proposals: when it became evident that Begin was willing to cede the Sinai—and do so with an unexpected promptness—Dayan demanded retention of the Rafah settlements as Israeli entities under Egyptian sovereignty, with an Israeli force to defend them. It may have been Dayan who encouraged Sharon to erect his dummy settlements while negotiations were in progress.

Throughout, Dayan adhered to his position that the Egyptians were not a party to negotiations over the West Bank. I disagreed. In my assessment, Sadat—however reluctant to grant the Palestinians an independent state—could not afford to abandon them completely. Events bore me out.

Be that as it may, Dayan demanded that we recall our delegation. He held that there would be no difficulty in maintaining contact with the Egyptians by way of the United States. In any case, the Americans were intimately involved in every phase of the negotiations.

"We'd better recall the delegation," Dayan said, "before the Egyptians humiliate us by expelling it."

I replied: "All these years, we've said repeatedly that we want direct negotiations—and now, when we get the opportunity, we go looking for an American mediator!"

Begin supported my view. However, there were misgivings in the cabinet. Ministers accused me of having too much faith in Egyptian good will and in Sadat's commitment to peace. On occasion, doubts were cast upon the veracity of the reports from our delegation in Cairo—and even on my own.

As we prepared to renew the Cairo talks in March 1979, I decided it would be better this time to take a small delegation. Anyone with anything to say had already said it at the previous meeting, where Motta Gur had put forward proposals that did not harmonize with cabinet decisions. I notified the Egyptians that I would be accompanied by my intelligence chief, General Shlomo Gazit; General Abrasha Tamir; my military aide, Ilan Tehila; and my spokesman, David Kolitz. At General Gamasy's invitation, I also brought my wife, Re'uma, and my son, Sha'ul.

I was glad to take Sha'ul along, but I did have some anxieties about him. Sha'ul bears the scars of war. He was born in 1951, into a home where the prevalent atmosphere was military. When he grew up, he wanted to follow in my footsteps by becoming a pilot. But the medical board found a defect in his eye, and he was refused acceptance to the pilots' course. Instead, he became a paratrooper. At the height of the Suez Canal War of Attrition, he was posted to a stronghold on the banks of the Canal, 150 yards from the Egyptian positions where snipers were on the constant lookout for Israeli heads projecting above the sandbags. Sha'ul took great care to keep out of their telescopic sights.

In the summer of 1970 when I was minister of transportation, the then chief military rabbi General Shlomo Goren, on a morale-boosting tour, visited the strongpoint where Sha'ul was serving.

"I'm not scared," Sha'ul told Rabbi Goren. "I might start being scared if I ever stop a bullet—"

"Don't open your mouth to Satan!" Goren subjected him to the traditional Jewish rebuke for mentioning a misfortune and thereby running the risk of incurring it.

Sha'ul spoke his mind freely. "There are times at night when I'm alone in my position and I imagine that at any moment some chance Arab might appear out of the darkness. I always picture him as an enormous giant, and I hold my grenade tight and wait for him."

Aware that this young soldier was my son, Rabbi Goren listened intently, possibly trying to pinpoint resemblances and differences between father and son. He encouraged Sha'ul to say whatever he had on his mind.

"I don't hate the Arabs," Sha'ul said. "Hatred stems from fear. We don't fear—therefore we don't hate. That may be where our self-confidence comes from."

Two days later, a bullet fired by an Egyptian sniper penetrated Sha'ul's skull.

Badly injured, Sha'ul underwent brain surgery at Jerusalem's Hadassah medical center. For several days, he hovered between life and death. Together with Re'uma and with my daughter Michal, I spent days and nights by his side. In a glass bowl at the bedside, the doctors laid the bullet splinters they had extracted from his head. I was beside myself with anguish. Every morning, I woke from a night of half sleep to face the uncertainty. Would I ever see my son alive again?

When Sha'ul finally opened his eyes, I heaved a sigh of relief.

However, he has never fully recovered from his injury. Every now and then, it returns to afflict him. It has altered our whole way of life. Sha'ul is still in need of treatment and may require it for many years. Consequently, our family life hinges upon him, as we waver between hope and despair. The horrors of war have taken up quarters in our home, casting their painful shadow over our lives.

*   *   *

I thought twice before inviting Sha'ul to accompany me to Egypt, not knowing how he would respond.

He accepted the invitation in a simple matter-of-fact way that took me by surprise. "Of course I must go," he said. "If they see that I, whose injuries at their hands have changed the course of my life, am willing to reach out to them, perhaps they will believe how strongly we desire peace."

During the flight, I watched him out of the corner of my eye, particularly when we flew over the Suez Canal. Not a muscle in his face moved. Only his jaw worked. I could imagine what was going on within him.

I did not take my eyes off him in Cairo, either, afraid that his encounter with the Egyptians might put him under stress.

At the reception at the Tahara Palace, I noticed Sha'ul surrounded by Egyptian generals: Shaukat, Graidli, and Magdoub. Seeing them immersed in conversation, I joined the circle to listen in.

"I shall bear the horrors of war on my body all my life," I heard him say. "But I have never hated you."

The Egyptian generals did not conceal their amazement. I was proud of him.

"Is there anything special you would like to see?" Magdoub asked. "Just tell us—there will be no difficulty."

Sha'ul fell silent. I could sense his uncertainty. I guessed what he would want to see, and I waited, wondering whether he would say it. The Egyptian generals—possibly thinking him bashful—encouraged him to express his wishes.

"I would like to return to the place where I was wounded," Sha'ul said finally.

The fortress where Sha'ul was wounded had fallen to the Egyptians at noon on October 6, 1973. I imagined there was little left of it.

"There is no difficulty about that," the Egyptians said. Later, it transpired that our stay would be too short to permit Sha'ul to go to the Canal. Our hosts promised to take him there on our next visit.

At General Gamasy's invitation, Mustafa Khalil brought his family to the banquet, including his wife Malk and his son Hisham. Seated together at the table, Sha'ul and Hisham got into conversation.

"Have you been in the army?" Sha'ul asked.

"No," Hisham replied.

"He is an only son," Mustafa Khalil broke in. "That's why he was released from military service."

"You don't know what you're missing!" Sha'ul told Hisham.

"Go on, tell him!" Gamasy cried.

It was yet another of those strange moments where the world as I'd once known it was turned on end. There was my son, wounded by the Egyptians, telling an Egyptian his own age that the army was the experience of a lifetime!

To my joy, Re'uma shared my views about peace. As the mother of a badly wounded soldier, she could have had a very different reaction. But Re'uma was delighted at the chance of being able to talk to the Egyptians person to person and was thrilled at the prospect of making peace with them. Floating in a dreamlike trance, she toured Cairo's streets and the city's vicinity: the marketplace, the museum, the pyramids.

On the eve of our marriage, I had promised her the day would come when I would show her the pyramids. Now I found myself with her facing the emblems of Egypt's historical culture, one of the seven wonders of the ancient world. It was wondrous to me that I could fulfill my promise to her!

Ever since that trip, Re'uma has been coming to Egypt with me and has become an excellent ambassador of Israeli-Egyptian relations.

When we took our places at the conference table, I was surprised to find our own reduced delegation confronting the Egyptian team at full strength. Gamasy proposed that we start with the tough problems: the Rafah settlements and the airfields. "With regard to security arrangements," he said, "I don't foresee any great difficulty."

I took up the challenge of starting with the points of dissension. I reiterated the Israeli position: the Sinai peninsula would return to Egyptian sovereignty, but to avoid threatening Israel's security, the settlements would stay in place and the airfields would also remain in Israeli hands.

Gamasy repeated the Egyptian view: Israel's security needs could not be met at the expense of Egyptian land. He proposed that evacuation of the Etzion and Etam airfields be left until the final phase of our withdrawal.

I could not agree with him. At most, Israel was prepared to reconsider the status of the airfields in the year 2001. All the same, I left myself an out.

"We will examine the feasibility of a solution on a time basis," I said. "But you might as well know that it will be a long time."

Our disagreements on the settlements were even fiercer. I asked them to submit a proposal based on the assumption that the Rafah settlements would remain in place.

Gamasy scowled. He said again that if the settlements remained, they would prove to be the seeds of future difficulties. "It's Israel's problem," he said, "and Israel must solve it."

I reminded him that we saw the settlements as a component of our security.

"There are two principles I cannot alter: land and sovereignty," Gamasy insisted. "You must propose an alternative that will facilitate a solution."

The principal danger in handing over the Rafah settlements was the obvious possibility that it would serve as a precedent for surrendering our settlements elsewhere. Gamasy must have read my mind.

"We do not regard evacuation of the Sinai settlements as a precedent for other sectors," he said.

I wanted to hear him repeat that. "Do you mean it won't be a precedent?" I asked.

"Yes!" Gamasy stressed.

"You have a very small number of settlements in the Gulf of Aqaba, and you can evacuate them easily," he continued. "The problem is the Yamit region. We are ready to accept any Israeli who wants to come and live with us here in Cairo or anywhere else in Egypt—but not in the Rafah area. If there are Israelis in Rafah, that will spark the next war."

"You must learn Israel's problems," I urged him, "the way we are trying to understand yours. We can't change our position on the settlements. General Gamasy, you argue that allowing them to remain might be the spark of a fire in the future. And I tell you that dismantling them could block our efforts to build peace at the moment."

There was no response from Gamasy. I did not get the impression that he was particularly alarmed by my implied threat.

I went on: "Even Abba Eban, who is regarded as a dove, insisted on a strip of sovereign Israeli territory to run from the Rafah approaches to Sharm el Sheik. When President Sadat addressed the Knesset, I was very worried. I thought: *What will happen now? If this is your opening, if you want us to return to the 1967 borders, if you want a Palestinian state and the repartitioning of Jerusalem—then your demands are the stumbling block on the path to peace, not ours. I'm sorry, I have no other proposals.*

All the same, so that this exchange with Gamasy not be the last one, I tried to leave the door open. "Try to find a solution," I said.

"What do you prefer—taking a risk for the future or endangering the talks today?"

"We are prepared to consider the settlers as individuals but not as settlements." Gamasy did not give way. "We shall treat them like any other foreigner in Egypt, in accordance with our laws. In the course of time, it will be possible to evacuate them in a good and fair manner."

"All you mean is a longer timetable," I said. "We can't maintain a civilian settlement and develop it when we know that we're going to give it up at some time. We have agreed to a reevaluation in the year 2001; 2001 isn't that far away."

"I think the issue will come up in a year or two," Gamasy predicted. "And then we really will have problems."

"But it's also possible that everything will work out well in the course of the years, and there will be normal relations between us—as there are between Belgium and Holland. Another example: did you know that Basel airport is built on French territory and the agreement is extended every few years by agreement between the two countries?"

"But they don't have a buffer zone," Gamasy pointed out.

"The whole Rafah problem will appear in a different light in another fifteen years' time," I reassured him. "Believe me, we are flexible, and our proposals are equally flexible."

"The problem will be more complex in fifteen years' time," Gamasy retorted.

"You don't operate on an appendix till it hurts! Everyone's eyes are on this forum, hoping for a settlement. If I return home with your present position, that will endanger negotiations," I warned.

We continued to argue about the time factor. I told Gamasy that everything could change in the course of the years. "Three months ago, could you ever imagine yourself sitting with Ezer Weizman and holding a discussion with him?"

"No," Gamasy conceded.

"Then why do you think the things I said are impossible?"

Gamasy did not reply.

The issue remained unresolved. But he did leave a chink of hope. "I don't want the military committee to reach a deadlock the way the political committee has," Gamasy said. "We must help our political leaders solve the problems. We must find a way."

I took advantage of the intermission in our talks for a short tour of Cairo. Having had a few glimpses of the city, I was beginning to feel at home. I wanted Re'uma and Sha'ul to see it, too. For myself, I wanted a tour that would permit me to draw a little closer to the Egyptian people. On my previous visits, I'd observed that the tours organized by our hosts were rather sterile and impersonal. I wanted a taste of Cairo's chaotic turmoil, where I could wander about spontaneously.

In Adly Street, an enormous crowd assembled, roaring: "Ya Sadat! Ya Sadat!" Somebody hauled me into his shop, which was filled with sweets. "You must taste my delicacies," the proprietor said. I sampled his cakes, which resembled the ones I am in the habit of eating in Nablus.

The shopkeeper embraced and kissed me, his bristles scratching my face. He hastened to introduce me to all the members of his family. The crowd outside was still shouting.

"There will be peace," I promised the shopkeeper. "You can come and visit us."

His eyes lit up. "But Mr. Minister, tell me"—said the storekeeper, who was, I discovered, a Palestinian refugee—"can I get back my house in Jaffa?"

One session of the military committee was devoted to the early-warning stations in the Sinai. Over the years, we had set up very advanced stations, at a cost estimated to run into billions of Israeli pounds. The station at Um Hashiva was sensitive enough to detect troop movements far away, in the heartland of Egypt. When we withdrew to new lines after the 1975 interim agreement, we insisted on maintaining the station.

"There is an interconnection between intelligence and our willingness to run risks," began military intelligence chief Gazit. "The more extensive the security and intelligence arrangements, the more risks we'll take."

Gazit proposed that Israel retain three early-warning stations in the Sinai until it became evident that peace was going to be lasting.

"How long?" Gamasy demanded.

"Fifteen years," Gazit said.

Gamasy scowled. He did not like the idea. "Who will operate the stations?" he asked.

"I prefer the technicians manning them at present," Gazit said. "But they could be Israeli civilians, too. Not Americans or the United Nations."

"How would they receive their supplies?" Gamasy wanted to know.

"There will be a corridor, like the ones to the existing stations—yours and ours—in the Sinai buffer zone."

"What happens if they are attacked?" Gamasy asked, smiling.

"That's less serious than if they are attacked in the streets of Cairo, when they come as tourists," Gazit said.

"Fifteen years?" Gamasy pondered. "After a peace settlement? In another fifteen years' time, you will possess new and advanced technological systems and electronic devices to give you advance alerts in place of the early-warning stations. Why complicate matters by insisting on keeping what will soon be out of date, anyway?"

"We have no alternative," said Gazit. "We have no objection to your maintaining an early-warning station in our territory."

Gamasy did not buy the idea. "There isn't a state in the whole world that keeps early-warning stations in another country," he pointed out.

"Even today, the American embassy in Tel Aviv covers various spheres in Israel," Gazit revealed, "and Israel has no greater friend than the United States."

"That's legal espionage," Gamasy replied. "You propose illegal espionage. When you have an embassy in Cairo, you can equip it with all the installations you need."

"I think early-warning stations on a mutual basis could be a good idea"—I broke into their exchange. But Gamasy did not like the idea.

We went on to discuss security arrangements. Abrasha Tamir presented the Israeli view. "Our armies should be a hundred miles apart." Tamir explained the considerations of time and distance: a hundred-mile gap between the armies is vital for Israel's security.

I reminded Gamasy of our prime minister's midnight conversation with President Sadat in Jerusalem. The two leaders had agreed that east of the Gidi and Mitla Passes there would be no Egyptian forces, and the area would be demilitarized.

"That was a misunderstanding," Gamasy said, trying to go back on points already agreed upon by Sadat and Begin. "When the president said there would be no Egyptian forces to the east of the Mitla and Gidi passes, he did not mean that the whole area to the east of the passes would be demilitarized—just that our principal forces would not go beyond that line. Between that line and the international border, we will have certain forces. Their size is open for discussion. I will not station more than a division there, possibly less. But I don't want the written agreement to impose restrictions upon that area because that would embarrass our armed forces."

"Do you think Begin misunderstood Sadat to such an extent?" I asked skeptically.

"They were talking about principal forces," Gamasy repeated. "But there could be a battalion there, or a brigade—that shouldn't cause any concern to the Israeli forces."

"That won't do," I said. "I don't think our prime minister could have been that far off in understanding your president's words."

At this point, Gamasy unexpectedly changed the subject. "Let us now discuss what is more important to Israel's security," he proposed. "Total demilitarization of the Sinai—or the Sinai with armed forces and the Rafah settlements and the Etzion airfields? I want to understand how much we have to pay for Israel's security."

I did not fall into the trap. "The Rafah settlements are a separate problem," I said. "If the Sinai could be totally demilitarized, that would be ideal for both countries."

"Without settlements or airfields?" Gamasy asked.

"I didn't say without the settlements," I corrected him.

"We will solve the problem of the defense of Eilat by placing the Eilat area under Egyptian sovereignty," Gamasy said. To this day, I do not know whether or not he was joking.

"You don't want Eilat," I said. "If you want a link with Jordan, we can consent to an international highway between the Sinai and Jordan."

Gamasy bought that idea. "In Europe, there are many routes between states," he said.

"But there are no Palestinian terrorists!" I fired back. "No Syria, no Iraq, no Saudi Arabia."

"We are paying a lot," Gamasy concluded. "You demand too high a price from us for Israel's security."

"We are withdrawing from the Sinai," I reminded him. "And recognizing Egyptian sovereignty over the peninsula. That's no small price to pay."

The Egyptians brought out a map of their proposals for our withdrawal. It showed a narrow demilitarized zone within the Israeli Negev, paralleling a wider zone in the Sinai.

To make it quite clear that the idea was unacceptable, I refused to take the map back to Israel with me.

18

THE BATTLE FOR THE LAND OF ISRAEL

In June 1948, one month after the creation of Israel, the state had hovered on the threshold of civil war. Largely due to the restraint and responsibility displayed by Menachem Begin—whose Irgun fighters had just emerged from the underground—the confrontation was fortunately avoided; otherwise, the newborn state fighting for survival against external enemies might have drowned in the blood of its own citizens.

As the Arab armies hurled themselves at Israel's borders, threatening her population centers, a landing ship made its way toward the Israeli coast. The ship, which had formerly served in the American navy during World War II, went under the name *Altalena*—Jabotinsky's literary pseudonym. The *Altalena*'s holds contained the most precious cargo Israel could pray for at a time when she was fighting for her existence: arms and ammunition. The munitions had been purchased with money raised from Irgun supporters in the Jewish diaspora, with a further amount donated by the French government.

To this day, there is disagreement in Israel as to the assigned destination of the *Altalena*'s cargo. Menachem Begin stands by his claim that the arms were intended for the Israeli army, with some set aside for Irgun forces fighting in Jerusalem. David Ben-Gurion, who had just proclaimed the independence of Israel and was to be the state's mentor throughout its early years, was equally vehement in believing that Begin was capable of using the arms to launch a coup d'etat. Because of the long-standing rivalry between the various anti-British underground groups and the hostility of most Israelis toward the minority that followed the commander of the Irgun, few people believed Begin's word in 1948—thereby doing him a great injustice.

The man who would later serve as deputy prime minister in Begin's cabinet—Yigael Yadin—was at that time chief of operations in the Israeli army's GHQ, under Ben-Gurion. Yadin ordered his subordinates to enter into negotiations with the Irgun command.

The clash might yet have been avoided, but after many years of differences, neither side was very good at reading the thoughts of the other. Ben-Gurion's men saw Begin as a "fascist," capable of almost any antidemocratic act. It was only in retrospect that they realized how wrong they had been, when Begin subsequently proved himself to be a humanist and a strict adherent to the letter of the law.

Be that as it may: owing to a misunderstanding, the *Altalena*, with its cargo of weapons, approached the Tel Aviv coast. Ben-Gurion gave the order to open fire on the vessel, Yadin passed the order on, and the army acted upon it.

The smoke from the burning ship wafted in across the Tel Aviv beach and hangs over Israel to this day. Several people on board the vessel were killed; others suffered injury; the rest leaped into the sea and swam ashore. The survivors never forgave Ben-Gurion—not even after his death. The *Altalena* wound still festers.

When the regular army had started shooting at the ship, Begin's adjutants, on board with him, had urged him to respond without delay. For a short time, it looked as if he would not succeed in making his men hold their fire. However, as in previous confrontations between his troops and the other underground organizations, Menachem Begin's sense of national responsibility came out on top. Whatever the price, he was determined to avoid a fratricidal war.

Along with many others, I, too, chanced to be on the Tel Aviv beach while the shooting was in progress. I find it hard to blot out the memory of Jews firing at other Jews at the height of the battle for the very existence of the Jewish state.

The muse of history is not in the habit of using carbon paper. Events never repeat themselves exactly. On the surface, the circumstances in the late seventies bore little resemblance to those of the original occurrence. Ironically, the man falsely suspected in

1948 of planning a *Putsch* now stood at the helm of power—while others were plotting to undermine his position. Even more ironically, the latter were previously Begin's most outspoken supporters, who had only recently looked to him as their savior and messiah. Yet the tension that surfaced within Israel a few weeks after Sadat's visit threatened the community internally in as serious a way as the *Altalena* incident—and continues to do so.

When historians come to trace Menachem Begin's rise to power, they will conclude that it did not happen overnight. Some people see the Likud's victory in May 1977 as the fruit of a process set in motion on October 6, 1973, when the outbreak of the Yom Kippur War sullied the luster of glory surrounding the Labor leadership. That is partly true. However, the shakeup that transfigured Israel's political scene in the election of 1977 had its roots in another upheaval—of a far deeper nature—which remolded the collective unconscious of the Israeli people.

It began with the Six-Day War. Before June 5, 1967, Menachem Begin was dismissed by his political rivals with a mixture of scorn and abhorrence. No one foresaw that he would be invited to join the National Unity cabinet formed under Levi Eshkol and bequeathed on his death to Golda Meir. The idea of Begin's ever achieving power was considered a threat of national dimensions.

In addition to being a politician with a highly developed sense of national responsibility, Begin is also a perfect gentleman. He showed both traits on the eve of the Six-Day War, when the knife was at Israel's throat: thrusting aside the petty interests that still preoccupied his rivals, he stood out by placing the welfare of Israel and its people above any other consideration. Begin proposed that the fate of the state be entrusted to his greatest foe, the aging David Ben-Gurion—the very man who had ostracized him. The proposal was not adopted, but it showed Begin in a new light.

After the 1967 war, Israel's government found it hard to lay down a long-term policy for the newly occupied territories—particularly the portions that were more densely populated. At the same time, the fringes of the political map began to fill up with groups and individuals resolved that, whatever the cost, the biblical lands must never again fall into alien hands. Among them were people who had never made any secret of their longing for east Jerusalem, Hebron, and the historic landscape of Judea and Samaria. Others were motivated by profound religious feelings; but the nationalist tide also carried along people hitherto renowned for their moderate views, who now emerged as "more Catholic than the pope."

Most of these groups and organizations took on the character of

debating clubs. They conducted lengthy symposiums, issued declarations, published newsletters, and founded a lobby to exert
pressure on the political parties. On the whole, that was as far as
they went.

However, one organization stood out by its refusal to rest content with mere rhetoric. Beyond urging that the newly occupied
territories be settled by Jews as a way of creating "facts on the
ground," the group drew its strength from the single overriding
fact that its members backed up their demands by personally
volunteering to establish settlements beyond the "green line"—the
pre-1967 border.

This organization is called Gush Emunim—the Bloc of the Faithful. Its founders are dedicated young Orthodox Jews, graduates of
the national-religious educational network and of the religious
youth movements, where they have been imbued with the
national-religious ideology. Gush Emunim members have an additional source of strength: they represent a revolt—against the
older generation of Orthodox Jews and against the religious
establishment.

At that time, the religious establishment was an appendage of
the existing political regime. The religious leaders occupied themselves exclusively with defending the status quo between the
religious and secular elements of the population. The religious
establishment had always controlled the balance of political power between the rival secular parties: because the coalition government needs their votes to gain a majority, the elected members of
the religious party wield far more power than their numbers
would indicate. Nevertheless, the religious establishment had always permitted the secular parties to decide all major political
issues as well as everything to do with defense and foreign policy.
In contrast, the younger generation of Orthodox Jews wanted a
share in blazing the trail to be followed by the state. The Six-Day
War and its outcome gave them their opportunity.

At that time, my views were very close to those of the Gush
Emunim. Well before the 1967 war, I had declared that the day
would come when Israel would regain Jerusalem and the other
sections of our homeland lying beyond the armistice borders with
Jordan.

However, the nationalist-religious wave that now engulfed the
country was not to my liking. I could sympathize with the feelings
of religious Jews who poured into the newly liberated Old City of
Jerusalem, wandering in a daze through its alleyways and clinging
to the stones of the Western Wall. But I was disgusted by certain

nonobservant Jews who desecrated the Sabbath and ate nonkosher food, yet did not hesitate to use religious arguments to justify their indifference to the fact that the population of the Promised Land includes Arabs, who also view it as their own country. National-religious mysticism became a political card. Being a professional soldier at the time, I was not active in politics, but I was disturbed by this pseudomysticism, which obscured the serious problems confronting Israel.

In subsequent years, I retained my sympathy for Gush Emunim, although I always distanced myself from their tactics and their overbearing contempt toward the Palestinian Arabs. Throughout the 1977 election campaign, while still viewing Gush members as idealists, I made it clear that I would not tolerate their illegal activities: "I shall use force to dismantle any unauthorized settle-ment," I declared. Later, backing up that commitment, I earned myself a compliment from Gush Emunim leaders: "You didn't mislead us," they told me. "Back in the election campaign, you already said you'd remove us by force."

At the height of the peace process, I found myself in a showdown with Gush Emunim. At that time, I met a friend—a distinguished pilot and a *moshav* farmer—who asked what had happened to make me change so much. I'm not sure that I changed: the cir-cumstances had changed.

A few days after the Likud's election victory in June 1977, I had a meeting with Menachem Begin at his home. He was in a trium-phant mood.

"I'm going to visit the Elon Moreh settlement tomorrow," he informed me.

"I suggest you don't," I said. I left it at that—possibly out of a desire to avoid dampening his high spirits.

Elon Moreh was Gush Emunim's best-known settlement. It had acquired most of its renown from the Labor government's attempts to dislodge its members from the site they had occupied without authorization near Nablus. These attempts had failed; steadfastly adhering to their objective, the settlers and their sup-porters showed an uncompromising determination to stay put even if it involved clashes with the law and with the army. On top of that, they had supporters within then Prime Minister Yitzhak Rabin's cabinet.

Toward the end of Rabin's term of office, there were moments when Gush members seemed set on a collision course with their government. Not content with settling beyond the "green line," in defiance of government policy, they threw the full weight of their influence against the 1973 interim agreements with Egypt. From their own point of view, they read the signs correctly before the course of peace had even been finally charted. They calculated then that the interim agreements in the south were liable to result in a withdrawal from the Sinai, which, in turn, could lead to possible withdrawals in other sectors. In addition to attacking the government that had signed the interim agreements, Gush Emunim also directed its barbs against their architect: U.S. Secretary of State Henry Kissinger.

Whenever Kissinger set foot in Israel in the course of his shuttle missions between the capitals of the Middle East, Gush Emunim members greeted him with stormy demonstrations marked by violence. Seizing upon Kissinger's Jewish origins, Gush leaders accused him of ingratiating himself with the *"goyim"* by selling out Israel's most vital interests. Some of them highlighted the fact that his wife is non-Jewish in order to depict him as a renegade—a Christianized Jew. All these attacks carried a tone that could best be described as anti-Semitic. On at least one occasion, Gush members welcomed Kissinger with cries of "Jew boy!"

As Israel approached the moment of truth when she would have to decide whether to remain in the occupied territories and settle them or convert them into a bargaining counter for achieving peace with the Arabs, Gush Emunim grew in power. Operating as an extraparliamentary body, they undermined the rule of law in the country.

It is still early to judge what role—if any—they played in toppling the Labor government, although there can be little doubt that they eroded the cabinet's self-confidence and its public standing.

On the face of it, if there was one body whose support the Likud government should have been able to count on, it was Gush Emunim. Its members had welcomed Begin's election victory with jubilation. They could think of no one who would so resolutely carry out their aims as the newly installed prime minister: Menachem Begin, the man with the hawkish image, who is so careful to cultivate a piously godfearing appearance and who has never ceased to swear his fealty to the historical boundaries of the land of Israel.

Hearing Begin announce his intention of visiting Elon Moreh, I saw that he would have to get used to being prime minister, shouldering overall national responsibility. He could no longer afford to fire off declarations or take steps that may have been appropriate during his years as the head of the opposition. I was afraid Begin would be carried away by his visit to Elon Moreh, and by his own rhetoric. My fears proved to be well founded.

On his arrival at Elon Moreh, Begin was given a hero's welcome. Beside themselves, members of Gush Emunim cheered him wildly.

"There shall yet be many Elon Morehs!" Begin proclaimed with a tremor of emotion in his voice.

The Gush Emunim members applauded enthusiastically. But when their acclamation died down, the rest of the world reacted angrily. Overnight, Begin's image as a hawk was reinforced in the West. His proclamation also sowed confusion within Israel. The extraparliamentary Gush Emunim, perceived by many Israelis as a threat to democracy, had suddenly received the stamp of official approval. Cracks disfigured our national consensus.

During the months that followed, I tried to the best of my ability to prevent the government from being identified with Gush Emunim, without success. Paradoxically, the facade of unanimity between Gush Emunim and the Likud was smashed by an outsider. His name: Anwar Sadat.

As Israel's government began to walk the path of reconciliation with Egypt, it progressively distanced itself from Gush Emunim. On several occasions, relations between Gush and the government were on the verge of breaking down. Menachem Begin, once the idol of young men in skullcaps, now became the target for the same accusation—"Traitor!"—once hurled at Yitzhak Rabin. I saw Begin in anguish; he never missed an opportunity to complain to Sadat and Carter about "my colleagues who demonstrate against me."

Begin's willingness to relinquish the Sinai alarmed the members of Gush Emunim no less than Herut's old-timers. Their opposition was not just a refusal to give up the territorial gains of the Six-Day War; what they feared even more was that such an agreement in the south might lead to similar territorial deals on the West Bank.

Back in the 1977 election campaign that preceded Begin's rise to power—at a time when Gush Emunim looked like a natural ally of the Likud—I formulated aloud my policy of settling in the occupied territories. I did not deny the right of Jews to settle all over the land of Israel—but I said that right should be exercised in conformity with government policy and according to a fixed set of priorities. It was with great concern that I heard the extremist utterances of certain Likud leaders who—totally carried away by the no less extremist demands of Gush Emunim—spoke as if the

West Bank were an uninhabited region. Their mystical zealotry greatly troubled me.

At the height of one of our gravest confrontations with Gush Emunim over Jewish settlement in Hebron, I received a phone call from Miriam Levinger, wife of Gush leader Moshe Levinger.

"Last night," she told me, "as I was dreaming, I heard the voice of King David. He said that you, Ezer, will be greatly blessed if you work for the settlement of Jews in Hebron."

On hearing her words, someone else might have laughed. I was appalled at the thought of our senior political echelons being led and influenced by such fanatical dreamers.

On top of that, David is not one of my favorite biblical characters. He rose in rebellion against his anointed king, goading and humiliating him; later, having gained the throne, David coveted the wife of one of his own military commanders and sent the man to his death to get her. All the same, the Bible sings hymns of glory to his name—which probably proves that King David controlled the media in his time!

Over the years, I have held frequent talks with Gush Emunim leaders. They did not conceal their dissatisfaction with me, although they did praise me for not having led them astray. Even at the height of the honeymoon of Gush members with the Likud government, I had never promised them heaven and earth, and I'd never disguised my reservations. Now, as the peace process gained momentum, they saw me as an outright enemy.

In September 1978, when Gush Emunim members set up an unauthorized settlement on Hawara hill near Nablus, I went to try and talk them into dismantling it. The exchange highlighted the differences between us. I reminded them of the past; as they well knew, there had been times when I, too, had advocated a Greater Israel.

"But my aim today is—above all else—peace with the Arabs!" I said. "That's why I've come to persuade you to leave this place."

"You are living under an illusion!" Rabbi Levinger said angrily.

"Maybe," I conceded. "They told me I was living under an illusion when I was the first to dream of reaching the Jordan and the Canal. Before 1967, when we were living within the old borders, most people felt: 'How goodly is our land!'—that's a fact. What would have happened if Nasser had come along in 1965 and said: 'Let's make peace!'? Everyone would have danced for joy without having Judea or Samaria or Gaza, but I wouldn't have been content. Now, when I want peaceful relations with them, you tell me

I'm living under an illusion? I think we've got to find a way of living in the Middle East, and I believe the path I propose offers a high probability of coexistence."

I tried to be candid. I told them that we had apparently let our opportunity slip by. Immediately after the Six-Day War, we could have annexed Judea, Samaria, and Gaza, just as we did Jerusalem. I regret that we failed to do so then, taking advantage of the stunning impact of our victory. Now it was too late. The autonomy scheme was a step toward a surrender of Israeli sovereignty over the West Bank.

"The solution offered by the Israeli government is the lesser evil," I told them. "As a Jew and an Israeli, I would like to see us controlling all of the land of Israel, right up to the Jordan River; I would like Samaria to be like Galilee—but what we failed to do all these years we can hardly do now."

"Are we talking about castles in the air?" demanded Chanan Porat, another Gush leader. "Have we given up the prospect of extending our sovereignty to Judea and Samaria?"

I was obliged to disappoint him. "It's more likely that we've lost them than that they will be under Israeli sovereignty," I replied.

They shut their ears and hearts. They saw peace as no more than a scrap of paper—and they said so unabashedly. Several expressed their heartfelt hope that Sadat would either give up trying to reach an understanding with Israel or else lose power.

"Damn Sadat!" one of them said. "I hope he stops a bullet!" This settler actually saw peace as the pursuit of an easy life without any challenges rather than as the greatest possible challenge.

I tried to persuade them to preserve due democratic processes by ending their defiance of the government. They tried to persuade me that settling the length and breadth of the West Bank was of the highest value and that nothing else was of equal importance.

There was an enormous gap between us.

"At least you didn't call me 'traitor,' " I said.

"But that's what we think!" someone pressed forward to yell at me. "These agreements you're going to sign are a betrayal of the people of Israel and of the land of Israel!"

I was deeply hurt by that. Ever since I came of age, I have been taking part in our country's military efforts. I have never brandished my military record; it has never occurred to me to make a big deal of it or use it as something to hang my hat on. I knew that the Gush people used the word "traitor" wholesale, flinging it at anyone who declines to agree with them. I had seen others offended by being stigmatized that way. Now, for the first time, I was feeling it in my own flesh.

Before Sadat even set foot on Israeli soil, I had realized that the cabinet could not avoid a thorough and extensive study of our settlements in the West Bank. The Likud government—just like its predecessors—tried to dodge the issue, but it loomed around almost every corner. Beyond being tied up with the problem of our security, our settlement policy is equally linked with the future boundaries of Israel.

Begin's views on the matter were straightforward: the West Bank is part of our historic homeland, he felt, and must therefore be open for Jewish settlement. Sadat's visit did not change Begin's mind.

"The battle has begun for the land of Israel," he said with profound emotion. "This is the battle of the entire Jewish people for its historic homeland."

He went on: "I told Sadat: 'We took into consideration your statement that the soil of the Sinai is sacred to you. I want to tell you: Our land too is sacred, and that goes for Judea and Samaria no less than for Tel Aviv—more, perhaps. Tel Aviv is seventy years old, but Jericho is nearly six thousand!' "

However, shortly after taking office, Begin had faced constraints that prevented him from gratifying his dreams of Greater Israel by annexing the West Bank or at least opening it up to massive Jewish settlement. It turned out that to settle Jews in the West Bank was easier said than done. The component parties of the Likud alliance have never had any foothold in the settlement movement. Despite its eagerness to settle the historic land of Israel, the Likud differs from the Labor movement in that it lacks the organizational infrastructure—sources of income such as factories and banks as well as existing "movement" settlements—that could have provided the necessary momentum.

However, Gush Emunim had the advantage of being represented within the cabinet by one of its prominent members, Agriculture Minister Arik Sharon. (Generally, it is the minister of agriculture who is responsible for developing settlements.) Like many Gush Emunim sympathizers, Sharon is not religious. I do not know whether he observes religious precepts or traditions, but he did forge a political alliance with the young men in skullcaps.

The cabinet never did conduct an intensive discussion of the settlement issue. Whenever something made it necessary to bring up the matter, however, Sharon emerged as a reliable ally of Gush Emunim. Such deliberations sometimes began with a soft-spoken introduction from the prime minister: "The Agriculture Minister has something to announce about the settlements. . . ."

As a rule, these announcements took the other ministers by surprise. No one was ever given notice to prepare for the debate. Few knew precisely what was under discussion. I was often astounded to find the cabinet being called upon to give its retroactive stamp of approval to *faits accomplis.*

True to character, Sharon could lend an imposing note to these deliberations. This teddy-bear-shaped human bulldozer, who is perfectly capable of crushing whatever lies in his path, would turn up with a grim expression and the look of a man ready at any moment to launch his onslaught. Under his arm, he'd hold a roll of maps, which he'd enjoy displaying before people who had never learned to read maps and could scarcely distinguish north from south. Sharon would charm them into submission, aided by his aura of a glorious and heroic strategist—the man who had crossed the Suez Canal, "Arik, king of Israel," as his soldiers had called him during the Yom Kippur War. Whenever Arik told the ministers that some road junction was of vital importance or that some settlement or other was of supreme military value, his words were taken as divine gospel.

Most of the seats around the cabinet table were occupied by persons of that caliber. Incapable of comprehending the military significance of what they were being shown, they automatically bowed to Arik Sharon's views whenever he uttered the word "security."

When Sharon launched into one of his expositions, Menachem Begin would listen in silence, resting his chin on the palm of his hand. Should anyone interrupt Sharon—particularly when he was holding forth on "security matters"—Begin would expel his breath in long sighs as though the burdens of the whole world rested upon his shoulders. More than anything else, those sighs typified the mood with which the cabinet welcomed the peace process.

Being in charge of the Defense Forces, I was obliged on occasion to have soldiers remove settlers from unauthorized sites, disrupting some of Sharon's plans.

During one meeting, I argued that Sharon was not giving an accurate account of the facts.

In response, he attacked me as a saboteur.

In Israel, the word "saboteur" can also mean "terrorist." It was a deplorable moment.

Sharon ploughed on to say that the army was out of line and the defense establishment was out of line.

"If I'm a saboteur," I bellowed at the top of my undeniably loud voice, my face probably flushed with anger, "I have nothing more to do here."

The prime minister's face turned pale. The war of the generals was in full swing before his eyes. This was not the first time I had clashed with Sharon over his settlement programs.

"Withdraw!" Begin shouted. "Withdraw what you just said!" The prime minister rarely raised his voice in meetings. "What's going on here?!" He slammed his gavel down on the table top.

"If he doesn't withdraw his words," I threatened, "I'm leaving!"

In the end, Sharon proffered a semiapology, and I stayed.

The seat next to Begin's was occupied by one of the greatest disappointments in Israeli public life: Yigael Yadin. The arguments about the settlement program showed up Yadin in all his pitiful weakness. It was a painful surprise to see the world-renowned archaeologist, who had served as Israel's second chief of staff, suddenly lose his wits, leaving him at a total loss. Yadin was against the settlement plan, but in cabinet sessions he wriggled and squirmed—about himself no less than about the issue—abjectly incapable of standing by his views.

Settlements are more than a matter of our security; they are part of the Israeli myth. What had enabled the state to withstand the invading Arab armies were the settlements. Israel's borders were largely marked out by the settlements. For many years before, under the British mandate and even further back, under Turkish rule, agricultural settlement all over the country had become one of the Zionist movement's principal objectives—perhaps the most important of them all. The era of pioneering settlement is regarded as the heroic epoch in the chronicles of Zionism. The conquest of the soil and its cultivation were viewed as national projects of the first order.

The dream of a Jewish renascence began to take concrete form late in the last century when agricultural settlements were built on land purchased at its full price in compliance with the commercial regulations in force under various successive regimes. However, the interplay of big-power interests between Turkey, Britain, and France, alongside growing Arab opposition, soon obliged the Jewish settlers to concern themselves with problems of security. "Wherever I settle—there I guard!" was the slogan of Hashomer, one of the first Jewish self-defense groups in Palestine.

This historical background fueled the public debate about the settlements: it also gave impetus to the settlers themselves. Overlooking the fact that time does not stand still and that the circumstances of the seventies and eighties in this century are incomparably different from the pioneering days, the settlers demanded to know why whatever had held good at the outset of Jewish settlement in Palestine no longer applied to current settling in the West Bank. The members of Gush Emunim saw themselves as the successors of the early settlers. By adopting this line of argument, they succeeded in drawing a considerable measure of sympathy because the average Israeli's admiration for the early settlers is imbibed together with his mother's milk.

For all our differences, there was at least one area in which I agreed with Gush Emunim. Unlike those individuals whose support for settling the West Bank was wrapped up in the cloak of "security needs," the leaders of Gush made no bones about declaring security a secondary consideration. Their motivation was and is Zionist: the West Bank is part of the land of Israel, and it is unacceptable that, of all places, this area should be *Judenrein*—free of Jews. If Jews have the right to live in Brooklyn and the Bronx, in London and Paris, why should they be denied a similar right in that tract of land that was, beyond any doubt, the cradle of our nation? There is a lot of justice in this argument even though its proponents, refusing to take into account the inherent limitations, treat the local Palestinian population as though it had no desires or aspirations of its own.

I regard the land of Israel—the whole of it—as my native land. No one can give up his native land or divorce himself from portions of it. "Otherwise"—as I once told some Gush Emunim members—"what am I doing here? I could go and live in California!" On the other hand, we have historical rights to the Jordan River's eastern bank, too—but we have long since relinquished the idea of exercising those rights.

I accept the fact that political conditions may require that the land of Israel—Palestine—be partitioned along lines that do not coincide with its historical or geographical boundaries. I do not regard this as a catastrophe. The Jewish people controlled the whole of their country for no more than a brief period of history; its borders have always fluctuated according to changing political circumstances.

I do not imagine there will ever be an Israeli government that will consent to the West Bank being Jew-free. Consequently, I believe that Jews should be allowed to settle in the West Bank just as long as they do not dispossess or displace the Palestinian Arabs already living there. Under the Labor government, dozens of Jewish settlements were established in the West Bank—and it was only rarely that they evoked any interest in the outside world. When the Likud government took office, the eyes of the whole world, and of the Arab states, suddenly focused on the settlements. Arik Sharon did his work to the accompaniment of noisy trumpeting—and countless television cameras focused on his tractors and bulldozers. "Arik, my friend," the prime minister once remarked at the height of one particularly great outcry, "why is it necessary to bring such enormous objects, which simply beg to be photographed?" However, the keen interest of the world did not arise solely from our unnecessarily vainglorious declarations; the principal cause of the world community's heightened sensitivity was the anxiety over the possibility of Israel's annexation of the West Bank.

With regard to settling the West Bank, Israel cannot be guided exclusively by military or political considerations. It is quite correct for us to take into account the future boundaries we desire, using them to mark out the areas to be settled, but I see no disaster in Jewish settlements remaining beyond our borders. It would be better for Israelis to live in settlements on the other side of the border but still within their ancestral homeland—than pack their bags and head in the direction of New York. I hold that these considerations, together with economic factors, should guide our settling beyond the "green line."

While objecting to Gush Emunim's arguments in favor of settlements on the West Bank, many Israelis nevertheless fall into the trap of "security reasons." That term is negotiable currency in the state of Israel. The lesson to be learned from all the wars we have suffered is the reverse: border settlements have never been a substitute for the army. Even those settlements that held out against the Arab armies in 1948 usually did so with the help of the army. Moreover, Israel was obliged to evacuate its Golan Heights settlers during the Yom Kippur War when they were stranded in the middle of the battlefield.

Security considerations favor large and well-established settlements, which—in addition to standing on their own financially— have the manpower to defend themselves or to be an integral part of our regional defense system. Weak and isolated settlements are a burden and a nuisance in military terms. A large proportion of the settlements in Judea and Samaria fall into this category. Every morning the men go to work in the coastal plain, leaving behind the women to be protected by the army, which is also charged with defending the access routes to the settlements.

If it is desirable to settle in the West Bank, the settlements should be in places where a Jewish population can live irrespective of the ultimate political solution. Large clusters of settlements should be constructed where there is no Palestinian population, and therefore no need to dispossess Arabs or to confiscate private land. There is no lack of these areas in Judea, Samaria, and the Gaza district. The defense establishment has pinpointed at least six such vacant areas, at key points, on state-owned land.

It is also essential to extend the borders of Jerusalem and bring more Jewish inhabitants into the city. By its strategic position, Jerusalem divides Judea from Samaria; consequently, the city ought to be broadened. This would prevent Judea and Samaria from becoming a single continuous geographical entity that might provide the springboard for an attack on Israel.

In the Judean hills, too, there is room for meeting the needs of both security and settlement—independent of any future political solution and without confiscating Arab land.

I object to the confiscation of Arab land because the most important component of our security is the feasibility of peaceful relations with the Palestinians and with the rest of the region. Our future depends on it.

Even though the cabinet never held an extensive discussion of the settlement issue as a whole, I submitted my proposal for six clusters of settlements to the ministers. The concept was approved, its principal support coming from the economic ministers, who could appreciate its financial benefits. However, in spite of the decision on settlement in clusters, Arik Sharon overlooked the defense establishment proposals and helped create "facts on the ground" in the form of dozens of small settlements. With the aim of forestalling a flood of such settlements throughout Judea and Samaria, I approached him to work out a coordinated plan for the sites on which he wished to establish additional settlement points. Drawing up a joint plan of military and settlement sites, we presented it for cabinet approval. But Arik Sharon was crafty and rallied the entire cabinet behind him. In my view, these shenanigans inflicted severe harm on Israel.

More than almost any other topic, the cabinet's attention was engaged by Elon Moreh. By my reckoning, the subject of that settlement came up in over twenty sessions, taking up dozens of hours of discussion. "Elon Moreh is a continuous burden on my mind," Begin would sigh.

"The Middle East is on fire," I complained loudly. "Khomeini has taken power, the Russians are entering Afghanistan, there are riots in Syria, coups in Iraq, battles in Saudi Arabia. Our economy is in a state of collapse—and what do we busy ourselves with?"

"Gentlemen!" Begin pronounced in festive tones. "When my time comes to face the heavenly tribunal and I am asked: 'What is the good deed you have done which makes you worthy of entering paradise'—I shall reply: 'Elon Moreh.' "

In recent years, the Elon Moreh group of Gush Emunim had been quartered in a military camp at Kadum, between Nablus and Kalkiliya. This was a compromise arrangement forced upon the Labor cabinet after the group's attempt, in 1974, to set up a settlement without government approval.

Following an understanding with the Americans that allowed military settlements to be established in ex-Jordanian army camps—since they already existed—the Elon Moreh group was offered settlement sites in military camps at various spots in Judea and Samaria. However, the group's leaders rejected the proposals outright. "We shall settle in Sh'chem [Nablus]," they said, "only in Sh'chem."

Over the years, the Elon Moreh group made eleven attempts in secret to settle in the Nablus area; on each occasion, they were removed by Israeli soldiers, frequently obliged to use force. These disgraceful scenes were witnessed by scores of journalists and photographers.

"Our soldiers are nail-booted thugs!" Sharon bellowed when we were considering the forcible eviction of unauthorized settlers. I was angry and dismayed. Begin asked Sharon to apologize.

Begin saw the Elon Moreh affair as the focal point of the battle over the future of the land of Israel. Whenever he had to deal with the issue, his face would break into a grimace of pain. "What will become of the land of Israel?" he would groan.

I said: "This man, and this Gush, are forcing the cabinet into situations that endanger its survival. This is a cabinet that doesn't make decisions; instead, it is dragged along."

"Who is 'this man'?" Begin demanded in dour tones.

I mentioned him by name.

By his deeds—overt as well as covert—Arik Sharon encouraged Gush Emunim members to steal out under the cover of night and establish a foothold at their various settlement sites. These exploits were planned like full-fledged military operations, with a precise timetable and a logistic backup. However, for all the military trappings in which they were enshrouded, the so-called "security settlements" failed to gain the blessing of most of the cabinet's ex-generals: Sharon found himself in a minority against

Yadin, Dayan, and myself, all of us contending that Elon Moreh possessed no military value.

At the time, it was claimed that I disagreed with Sharon because our backgrounds are different. Sharon is a paratrooper, an elite foot soldier, to whom every hillock and each path can be the key to victory or defeat. I, in contrast, am a pilot. As far as I am concerned, every mile is no more than a tiny fragment of an enormous vista. The sky's vast expanses contain no hillocks or paths, nor do they have historical associations like the tale of the sacrifice of Isaac or of Abraham's covenant with God.

The situation at Elon Moreh was to grow even more complicated when the inhabitants of a nearby Arab village, taking advantage of the disagreements within the cabinet, appealed to the Supreme Court of Justice in the spring of 1979 for Elon Moreh to be removed from the land confiscated from them.

We might have won the case, had I—as defense minister—declared the Elon Moreh settlement vital for security. But I could not perjure myself. I had always argued that Elon Moreh had no military value, and I could not change my views.

One day in June 1979, I got a call from the prime minister requesting that the chief of staff submit an affidavit in court regarding the military importance of the Elon Moreh settlement site.

Begin was attempting to bypass me, thus undermining my authority as defense minister. Swallowing hard, I sent a note to the chief of staff: "Prepare an affidavit as requested."

The chief of staff did as he had been asked. "I have reached the conclusion that Elon Moreh is vital for military reasons," Rafful Eitan wrote in a lengthy and well-argued affidavit. He said that settlements in Judea and Samaria sited on traffic routes and commanding positions constituted a further guarantee for Israel's defense.

I did not intervene in Rafful's preparation of his affidavit; despite my belief that it was a perilous precedent for the army to take sides in a political disagreement, I remained silent. But I gave vent to my opinions in a letter I attached to the affidavit when conveying it to the prime minister. I wrote to Begin that the military purpose could be achieved by the military presence—not by settlements.

My fury over Begin's ruse resulted in a personal confrontation. I told him that situations could arise that would make it difficult for me to continue at my post. And then, I would resign. I did not want to find myself in conflict with my own conscience.

Begin had nothing pertinent to say about the matter. What could he say? "Ezerkeh," he murmured. "You're a nice fellow. You're a good defense minister."

"Mr. Prime Minister," I retorted, "the settlements are not the principal component of our security."

"What is?" he asked.

"Peace, the might of our army, the moral fiber of the state."

My reply went right over his head.

The Supreme Court now proceeded to place the government in an embarrassing predicament, showing up the prime minister and his colleagues in a ludicrous light. "If the defense minister sees no need for establishing this military settlement," mused Judge Alfred Vitkon, "who am I to argue with him?"

The decision by the deputy president of the Supreme Court, Judge Moshe Landau, that "the Elon Moreh settlers be removed within thirty days!" unleashed an emotional upheaval. My own views were reflected in the verdict: "I am convinced that were it not for the pressure of Gush Emunim, and the political and ideological considerations guiding the political echelons, it would not have been decided to set up Elon Moreh."

Instead of blaming themselves, the cabinet ministers vented their anger on me. Yigal Hurwitz advised me to resign.

Begin was in a dilemma. As a man who acknowledged the supremacy of the law, he was required to obey a verdict that ran counter to his most cherished principles. "My old age shall not bring shame upon my youth," he said, a mournful expression on his face. "I was born believing in the Greater Israel, and I shall die a believer. On that conviction I won't make the slightest concession even if I am called a traitor."

I found him borne down by a sense of despondent helplessness, casting about for a solution to a predicament that he should never have allowed himself to be dragged into in the first place. "They are already living in houses," he sighed, highlighting the fact that this time the Elon Moreh settlers had set up house with government approval—and with the aim of never again abandoning the site. Begin would not even entertain the idea of forcible eviction. "In the underground, I avoided bloodshed," he said. "We won't raise our hands against Jews."

The solution was costly and provoked a blend of indignation and ridicule. Helicopters hauled houses up to a site of publicly owned land at the peak of Mount Kabir, near Nablus. Many millions of Israeli pounds were spent on a few dozen settlers—making the prime minister and his cabinet appear as empty-headed ninnies.

* * *

Throughout the ups and downs of the peace process, the West Bank settlement program provided a somber backdrop to the reconciliation efforts with Egypt. "Facts on the ground" in Judea and Samaria were a kind of compensation to certain Israelis for the loss of the Sinai and particularly for the inescapable necessity of surrendering the settlements in the Rafah approaches and on the Sinai coast. The growing misgivings over Sadat's true intentions toward Israel were an added incentive to make all possible haste in settling at any available spot beyond the "green line"—the pre-1967 border—without forethought, without prior planning, without taking into account the international quandary into which Israel was maneuvering herself, without considering the peace process. Many Israelis felt compelled to hurry up and grab anything they could get their hands on. These impulses were further encouraged by the hitches in the negotiations with Egypt.

Although the settlement schemes bombastically proclaimed from Jerusalem often had nothing to back them up, they nevertheless infuriated the Egyptians and angered the West. As a result, Menachem Begin and Arik Sharon were forced into a corner, issuing ever more strenuous calls for immediate settlement of every possible site.

The protests of the world community, the denunciations from Cairo, the grumbling from Washington—only assisted the Greater Israel zealots and the advocates of settlement throughout Judea, Samaria, and the Gaza Strip in clinging ever more desperately to their unyielding positions.

Noting that the West agreed with Egypt in regarding the settlements as a provocation against peace, Gush Emunim and its sympathizers were not at all displeased. Such reactions only encouraged them to adopt even more extremist views. To them peace was an abstraction—perhaps no more than an act of formal politeness.

While the negotiations were in progress, one of their more fanatical supporters, Moshe Shamir, expressed his support for peace with Egypt!—but only when the Egyptians recognized Israeli sovereignty over the Sinai, including its oil fields, and submitted to the presence of our forces on the banks of the Suez Canal. Having been head of GHQ's staff branch in 1967, I was in a position to tell Shamir that when we'd attacked Egypt on the morning of June 5, 1967, our planes had bombed the Egyptian oil fields because it had never occurred to us that we were going to occupy the whole of the Sinai. He was not persuaded. As Shamir could well imagine, not a single Egyptian would accept his peace terms. But for people like him, any other form of peace—aside from not being worth the paper it's written on—is not even desirable.

These actions were a threat to Israel and her security and a menace to the Jewish people's renascence in its own land. The more I considered the matter, the more convinced I was that the true danger lay in those who turned their backs on peace, refusing to believe in its possibilities or rejoice in its arrival, those doing their utmost to make sure that Israel missed the opportunity of attaining it.

In the winter of 1978, the settlements became the central issue in the battle for peace, as provocative in Washington as in Jerusalem or Cairo.

19

FROZEN TRUMPETS

On Wednesday morning, March 8, 1978, the temperature in Washington was minus three. The sky was gray, and snowflakes were gently covering the rooftops and broad avenues of the U.S. capital. It was only two days since I had basked in the warm rays of Israel's wintry sun, and I was disgruntled to have to wrap up in a thick winter overcoat.

On my first official visit to the United States as defense minister, I was flying into an icy headwind, which emanated from the administration with frosty blasts coming from all its branches: the White House, the State Department, the Pentagon. The same evil wind, funneled through the communications media, was chilling the hearts of the American public. I was there to ask for more weapons for Israel and particularly to explain the peace process from our point of view in order to win Washington's support. It was not going to be easy.

At the impromptu press conference I held at New York's Kennedy Airport, the erosion of Israel's credibility in the United States became evident in the very first question:

"Sir," a journalist asked, "why isn't Israel prepared to do its part in the peace effort by halting the settlement program at least temporarily?"

I cast about for an answer. My views on the settlements were well known in the United States, and it never occurred to me to lie. Ultimately, I evaded the issue with a few noncommittal remarks about "productive talks." Then, seeing the sour expression on the journalists' faces, I tried to squeeze a smile out of them: "I'm going to my hotel room now to see Errol Flynn at the age of twenty-one in a TV movie."

If there is any political significance to facial expressions, they taught me at that moment the gravity of our situation: not one of the journalists even smiled.

That impression was reinforced when Israeli ambassador Simcha Dinitz and other senior Israeli representatives briefed me: even Israel's friends in the administration and in public opinion could not understand her policies. Every evening, millions of television viewers saw Israel portrayed as a country seeking every possible ruse to sabotage the peace efforts. Superstar Sadat was presented as the man who had taken the historic step forward, while Begin was shown trying to trip him up. Sadat had conquered the United States with a few banal sentences uttered in his faulty English, while Begin told stories. Satellite pictures transmitted from Judea and Samaria showed every tractor at work, each stake being driven into the ground. Briefed by administration officials, the media placed us in the dock.

Outside the main entrance to the Pentagon, my host, U.S. Secretary of Defense Harold Brown, awaited me. Opposite, on the snow-bedecked parade ground, two hundred men and women soldiers of the American armed forces stood in ceremonial order in my honor.

Try as I might to keep myself from going overboard about ceremonial parades and bugle calls, I always get carried away. I can't imagine a politician or any other public figure who can remain indifferent to such displays. A parade, with its wealth of multicolored uniforms, with the roll of drums and the thunder of artillery salutes—all these flatter the ego of any leader, great or small. Mine, too.

The soldiers—detachments from the U.S. army, navy, air force and the marines—presented arms with admirable precision. The cannon roared. The band's instruments glinted in the cold light, like the officers' swords. "Weizman!" I said to myself. "Take care that you're not dazzled by the glitter of the swords or deafened by the cannon—and guard your flanks!"

The television cameras filmed incessantly. My pulse was racing.

Meanwhile, snow and rain mingled into a icy sleet. One glance was enough to show me that the soldiers on parade were not wearing overcoats. The women soldiers had nothing on their legs but thin stockings. As a military man with some experience of parades and ceremonies, I knew the soldiers must have taken up position at least half an hour before my arrival at the Pentagon. I felt uncomfortable. *Those soldiers must be freezing*, I thought. *If this parade were being held in Israel, I would take off my overcoat as an act of solidarity with them.* I wanted to fling off my thick winter coat as a way to win the hearts of the men and women on the parade ground. But what of the U.S. defense secretary, bundled up like me in a heavy overcoat? If he emulated me, the secretary might catch pneumonia; but if he kept his coat on when I took off mine, it could appear that I was trying to show him up.

Should I take it off or not?

I kept it on.

The ceremonial parade outside the Pentagon was briefer than usual. "I beg your pardon," Brown murmured just before I paced through the soft snow to inspect the guard of honor. "The band won't play the anthems today; the trumpets have frozen up!"

Harold Brown looked to me then like a history professor taken by surprise from his lecturer's rostrum to fill a post he had never sought. His soft bespectacled features, like his crumpled overcoat, seemed out of keeping with the time and the place—and were in acute contrast to the uniforms of the military commanders who had dignified the parade with their presence. There was not a trace of a smile on Brown's face.

Admittedly, relations between states depend primarily on interests, but I have always been inclined—excessively so, according to my critics—to attach importance to personal relations. Brown was not the sort of man I could treat to a playful slap across the shoulders.

If this Brown fellow is anything like today's weather, we're in big trouble! I thought as the defense secretary led me and my colleagues to his office on the third floor of the world's largest office building.

My memory does not usually betray me. Moreover, public life has obliged me to try and keep it as sharp as possible: some of the most uncomfortable moments I remember as a public figure occurred when I failed to identify people who were most eager to be recognized. Consequently, when Brown told me that we had already met, I was surprised to find myself with no more than the haziest recollection of the encounter.

"We met in the 1960s when I was secretary of the air force," he reminded me. In the mid-1960s, while serving as commander of the Israeli air force, I had conducted the negotiations to purchase American combat planes.

Brown sat down at his desk, which had once belonged to the

legendary General Pershing. Again I reflected that he would look more in place as dean of some university faculty than at the head of the mightiest army in the free world. The U.S.'s fourteenth defense secretary—the grandson of a Jewish immigrant from central Europe—had spent twenty of his fifty-one years in the Pentagon before reaching the top. Throughout his career, whatever post he held, he was always the "child prodigy." He was only thirty-three with a career as a nuclear scientist and as director of the U.S.'s hydrogen bomb project already behind him when Defense Secretary Robert S. MacNamara placed him in charge of the military research programs where he controlled multibillion dollar allocations. Subsequently, he went on to become secretary of the air force.

Befitting a man charged with the security of the free world, the American defense secretary had an impressive office: rugs, models of ships and aircraft, pennants.

And a single picture.

The only portrait to adorn his office was that of the first defense secretary, James Forrestal. Forrestal had come from Wall Street to his post, where he was required to coordinate the activities of the army, navy, and air force and impose civilian authority on the various branches and their commanders as well as contending with Congress. He had pitted his strength against the formidable obstacles until, giving way to the burdens and pressures, he leaped to his death from the window of his hospital room. That portrait may have been there, I speculated, as a cautionary lesson on the difficulty of controlling the Colossuslike defense establishment without falling apart.

"I am pleased to welcome you here with us today." Brown addressed the Israeli delegation in the routine manner. There was still a frozen expression on his face. His eyes were earnest and severe. I began to feel concerned. We had to break through to Brown; we could not afford to fail.

In recent years, with the lengthening list of foreign affairs setbacks suffered by the United States and the growing aggressiveness of the Soviet Union, I had come to fear that the United States was a broken reed for the free world to lean on. Yet Israel had no other choice: as an open society, humanist and democratic, Israel's fate is bound up with that of the West; the Soviet Union's enmity toward Israel only reinforces that tie. During the early years of our independence, we had made some hesitant steps toward a neutralist policy, but those attempts failed—possibly because they were not pursued wholeheartedly.

Many Israelis are anxious about historical developments that indicate an accelerated decline of the West while the Soviet bloc seems to gain strength. Their concern is more acute than that of citizens of the West, for Israel is one of the few countries in the world that has cause to fear physical annihilation.

Yet I wonder how true it is that the West is in decline. Some cite the Vietnam War and the American hostages in Iran as proofs. Both episodes do represent humiliating setbacks to the world's mightiest military power. In contrast to these American defeats, there are the Communist successes—real or imagined—which are seen as testimony to the growing power of the Soviet Union.

For almost as long as I can remember, I have heard about the concept of "The Decline of the West"—as set forth in the historical and philosophical treatise of that name, published in the early 1920s. The German author Oswald Spengler claimed that human history records the rise and fall of empires according to the phases of a predictable process and that the West was sinking. The Nazis adopted Spengler's theory and saw themselves as the founders of the Third Reich, the empire that would rule the world after the fall of the West.

Despite the West's victory in World War II and the enormous economic and technological power it now wields, the talk of the declining West continues. This outlook is anachronistic and groundless. It overlooks the situation created since World War II, particularly since the appearance of atomic and thermonuclear weapons, which has convinced the two principal power centers— the United States and the Soviet Union—that neither can hope for the physical annihilation of its rival without running the risk of its own destruction.

After World War II, the old imperial concept also collapsed. The true might of a power is no longer measured by the size of its colonies. Physical control of territory can sometimes weaken colonial power, as happened in the 1950s when France stubbornly tried to cling to her hold on Algeria. A large portion of French resources were channeled into the war in North Africa. Today, France draws great economic benefits from her special relationship with Algeria—precisely because the latter is now independent. France's military budget is relatively small compared to what it used to be, and—more important—the French people are no longer torn by the dissension that divided them during the Algerian war.

True, there is an opposite example: the Soviet invasion of Afghanistan. The Soviet Union is being forced to divert considerable resources to the war in Afghanistan, where large Soviet forces are tied down—while suffering harsh economic reprisals from the United States. In the long run, the Soviets run the risk of internal stresses arising from the frustration caused by their military setbacks in Afghanistan. From a Soviet viewpoint, it would be preferable to have Afghanistan under a stable and loyally pro-Russian government rather than under Soviet military occupation. The Soviet military incursion is a mark of weakness rather than of strength.

In modern times, the might of a state is measured not by its physical size but by its impact upon its regional constellation. The West possesses the advanced means suited to this new era, whereas the Soviet Union differs in being forced—by its economic and technological backwardness—to use imperialist means, which are less sophisticated. In the long run, the resilience of the West and its fitness to compete and contend in the modern world far surpasses that of the Communist bloc.

The current state of affairs may lead to the emergence of an extreme school of thought within the Soviet Union that will call for violent action before it falls even further behind. This is where atomic and thermonuclear weapons come in: use of force is liable to result in the final and complete pulverization of both sides. The Soviet Union has therefore charted a crafty course: its leaders have developed a mode of operation whose principal aim is to inch forward and change the situation to their advantage without allowing themselves to be drawn into action that could detonate the whole world. The Cuban missile crisis in 1962 taught the Soviet Union where the red danger line is, and how far it can advance without risking a third world war.

Overall, the reserves of the Western world are much greater than those of the Communist bloc. The ideological might of the West rests upon a far sounder and more solid foundation: man's desire for liberty, as exemplified by the strikes and unrest among Polish workers in 1980. That is why the West can endure setbacks, disappointments, and traumas that the Communist bloc is unable, or afraid, to undergo.

The man who, in 1978, held the key to the West's strength and weakness had many attributes, but popularity was not one of them. In Harold Brown, I discovered my own opposite: reserved and shy, he has great difficulty in forging personal relationships.

Harold Brown is a brilliant man; his mind is swift, always running ahead of others and therefore reducing him to boredom and
impatience much of the time. He dislikes discussions, preferring to
sit alone in his office from 6:30 in the morning, issuing written
instructions. As far as possible, he tries to avoid face-to-face meetings and is almost incapable of small talk.

I was told of one occasion when he was on a tour of Korea and
had to inspect an American unit stationed there. Stopping in front
of one young soldier, Brown asked weakly: "How do you feel
here?"

"Feel fine, sir!" the soldier replied.

Brown smiled, glanced down at the ground, then back at the
soldier, finally giving a nervous little laugh and concluding:
"That's about all I have to say." Later, he explained: "All kinds of
styles can work, but not the attempt to be what you aren't. I have
never been particularly affable. It's too late to start now."

"What is your impression of the state of the peace talks between
Israel and Egypt?" Brown now asked me.

I was not a bearer of good tidings. The peace talks had run
aground and were in imminent danger of foundering.

I traced Sadat's moves since his Jerusalem visit. "Sadat believes
that just by coming to Jerusalem and doing something no one
expected of him, he has contributed the maximum that could be
demanded of him, leaving him with nothing more to add. Sadat's
journey to Jerusalem did not, of itself, alter Israel's security problems and needs." No particular intellectual effort was required to
understand that the last sentence was directed at Washington.

"What is Gamasy like?" Brown asked. I was surprised by this
unusual display of curiosity on his part.

"First class!" I told him.

It did feel strange to be speaking so enthusiastically about the
Egyptian war minister before the American defense secretary. But,
as is my wont, I proceeded to illustrate the sentiment with personal anecdotes. I told Brown of my first flight over Egypt, with
the American plane winging its way over the Egyptian missile
systems; of my warm reception in the streets of Cairo; and of how
"I sat in the Groppi café in Cairo and remembered all the sins of
my youth . . ."

This highly personal glimpse of the peace talks ignited a spark of
interest in the frozen features of the defense secretary. I thought he
was beginning to shed his hard outer shell. He smiled, made comments. The warmer atmosphere was having its effect on him. Now
was the moment to launch my attack.

"Sir," I said, "our region has witnessed many fundamental

changes in recent months. Both sides in the conflict, Israel and Egypt, have altered their traditional policies. Sadat came to Jerusalem. Israel has agreed to Egyptian sovereignty in the Sinai and to establish autonomy in Judea and Samaria."

Brown could guess what was coming. His expression returned to its former sternness.

"The United States is the only party that has not changed its traditional attitude," I went on, raising my voice. "In spite of these historic events, the United States still adheres to a policy aimed at bringing about an Israeli withdrawal to the 1967 borders with only minor changes."

The White House had a clearly defined policy whose main ideas were taken from a report drawn up under the auspices of the Brookings Institute by a group of experts, most of them active members of the Democratic party. This report had provided President Carter with chapter and verse for his notions on resolving the Middle East conflict.

The Brookings report had recommended urgent efforts toward an overall settlement in view of the fact that the interim agreements were incapable of resolving the problems underlying the conflict. One of these problems—designated as the key to the conflict—was the Palestinian issue. The authors of the report believed that the Palestinians' right to self-determination would ultimately find expression in either an independent state that would undertake to fulfill the commitments arising from the peace agreement or in a Palestinian entity with a federative link to Jordan. In return for a comprehensive peace agreement, which would include diplomatic and commercial relations, freedom of travel, and an end to the Arab boycott, Israel would be required to withdraw to what amounted to the 1967 borders with only minor changes—even those conditional upon mutual consent.

The report proposed that the Soviet Union be invited to take part in the peace process. It also proffered a solution to one of the touchiest problems: the status of Jerusalem. In its view, the Holy City should not be repartitioned; there should be freedom of movement between its various sections and free access to the holy places—the latter to be under the supervision of religious bodies. Each national group within the city's population would be entitled to political autonomy within its own neighborhoods.

On the surface, the Carter administration's adoption of the Brookings report ought to have been gratifying to Sadat. However,

Washington's attitude had worried him because Carter had declared that the Arab *quid pro quo* to Israel would have to be full peace, with everything that entailed. This did not accord with the ideas Sadat had held before coming to Jerusalem, when he'd felt that full peace and normalized relations were something to be left to "the next generation."

Sadat was also worried about Washington's overt attempts at a rapprochement with Syria. Since their objective was an overall agreement, the Americans sought contacts with the Soviets, the Syrians, and the more moderate elements within the PLO. Sadat, on the other hand, wanted no cooperation with his pro Soviet rivals and was doubly apprehensive over Moscow's attempts to undermine him. He had not expelled the Soviets from Egypt so that they could return by the back door.

Egypt saw the American courtship of Syria as an attempt to shift the center of gravity from Cairo to Damascus or, at least, to make Damascus into an additional focal point. Sadat was convinced that the Americans were making a mistake. Furthermore, he claimed that this approach would not lead to agreements within the framework of the Geneva Conference but rather to its collapse. Damascus had opposed the Egyptian idea of dividing the Geneva Conference—first convened in 1974—into working groups chosen on a geographical basis, insisting instead on working groups organized according to topics. The presidents of Egypt and of Syria had also disagreed on Palestinian representation at the Geneva Conference. From the beginning, Israel had rejected the idea of PLO participation, while the Syrians had made their participation conditional on it.

Sadat had been taken by surprise by the joint U.S.-Soviet communiqué issued at UN headquarters in September 1977 in which Washington had granted the Soviet Union equal status in the peace process. The two powers had called for the reconvening of the Geneva Conference no later than December 1977. Both Israel and Egypt were alarmed at the Carter administration's assistance to the Russians in buttressing their standing in the Middle East. A few days later, after negotiations going on into the small hours of the morning between President Carter and Foreign Minister Moshe Dayan, the two men had published a "working paper." In this paper, Dayan gave his consent to the participation of anonymous Palestinian representatives in a united Arab delegation; those representatives would attend the opening of the conference and later join the working groups whenever topics that related to the Palestinians were up for discussion.

Perplexed by what he perceived as bizarre behavior on the part of Washington, Moscow, and Jerusalem, Sadat had upset the apple cart by setting off for the third of those three capitals—and stealing the show.

My conversation with Harold Brown returned to more placid waters. The defense secretary spoke at length about Sadat's predicament in the Arab world. "Sadat needs the support of the Arab world, particularly of Saudi Arabia," said Brown. "Therefore, the United States cannot avoid taking a position with regard to the situation on the other borders. From our perspective, it is very important for the peace settlement to relate to other sectors, too." Brown's words represented the traditional American viewpoint, but the decisiveness of his tone was surprising, implying that there were no other options. I had the impression that he was very insistent on this point—more so, perhaps, than Sadat himself.

"None of the parties in Israel except the Communists will agree to a withdrawal from Judea and Samaria," I said. "The Labor party's program also specifies the Jordan River as Israel's defensible boundary. Consequently, the United States cannot expect Israel to agree to a withdrawal from the West Bank."

Brown did not like what he was hearing. "I can agree," he said grudgingly, "to a number of security measures in Judea and Samaria—a few vital radar stations but no more, and those to be decided within the framework of the peace treaty."

The gap between Washington and Jerusalem had left the Americans free to act without reference to matters that had been agreed upon in the past. On the eve of my departure for the United States, the administration had taken us by surprise by an extraordinary decision, when it had linked delivery of the F-16s promised to Israel in the framework of the 1975 interim agreements to the supply of planes to Egypt and Saudi Arabia. I went on to discuss this point. "Your understanding in 1975 was given in writing and was not made dependent upon any further conditions," I pointed out.

Brown was silent. I had made things uncomfortable again.

"Your position is incorrect, and it could harm the peace process," I remarked severely. "We are not interested in seeing F-15s in Egypt and the Sinai and Saudi Arabia, near our southern border. That would endanger Israel by tipping the balance of forces to her detriment."

Brown tried to reassure me. "Delivery of the planes to Saudi

Arabia won't begin until 1981, and by that time there could be fundamental changes in the Middle East," he said. With the skill of experience, he applied the argument that the best form of defense is attack. "What do you want—that Egypt receive planes and military equipment from the Soviet Union? We have to provide the Egyptians with planes to safeguard the United States' position in the Middle East."

Brown's rejoinder had its own inner rationale. I myself was of two minds about this issue; during confidential discussions in Israel, I had already declared that we could not have our cake and eat it, too. The Egyptians, having taken a historic step toward peace, would be our enemies no longer; they had expelled the Soviets. Like the Egyptians, we were eager to reinforce the U.S.'s position in the region—so what was the point of objecting to Egypt's acquiring American arms? The Egyptians could not be expected to defend their country with clubs and knives. All the same, it was a perilous precedent; it was therefore important to lodge our protest.

Brown's point reminded me of the mercurial character of the Middle East, how fluid and unpredictable it is, with anything liable to happen. Who could have foreseen a few years ago that the Egyptian army would equip itself with American arms? Nasser must have turned over in his grave. Together with Nehru and Tito, he had sponsored the formation of the neutralist bloc, which, after its launching at the Bandung Conference in 1955, later developed into what is known now as the nonidentified bloc, encompassing most of the states of the Third World.

For political, military, and economic reasons, Egypt was progressively drawn away from her neutralist stance to adopt a pro-Soviet position. Egypt became dependent on the Soviet Union, no less—more, perhaps—than any East European country of the Warsaw Pact. This is a process the Soviet Union attempts to duplicate in its relations with every Third World country. In recent years, the Soviets have chalked up some marked successes in this sphere, with the help of one of its most prominent and dangerous satellites: Fidel Castro's Cuba.

However, Egypt was also the first to break out of the clutches of the Russian bear. In 1972, following a series of well-considered political moves, Sadat expelled the twenty thousand Soviet military advisers serving in his country. The years since the Yom Kippur War have witnessed a political rapprochement between Egypt and the United States, which also found its expression in arms supplies: 1975 saw the conclusion of a contract with Egypt for American Hercules C-130 military transport planes—a deal that aroused considerable indignation in Israel.

The president's approval of a three-way arms deal with Saudi Arabia, Egypt, and Israel was consistent with U.S. policy of the 1970s. How the world had changed! Less than ten years after the dogfight in which Israeli Phantoms had shot down five Soviet-piloted combat planes over the Gulf of Suez, Egyptian pilots were being trained to fly Phantoms under the supervision of American flight instructors.

Even if I did not agree with those who protested against the supply of American arms to Egypt, I could understand their point of view. Egypt was the largest and most powerful of our enemies. It is hard to get used to new ways of thought or to the new terms and concepts that emerged from the circumstances prevailing in the region after the Yom Kippur War and particularly since the launching of the peace initiative.

Realistic thinking should lead the architects of Israeli policy to the conclusion that the supply of American arms to Egypt and to certain other Arab states is a positive factor in the region—on condition, of course, that it is done in a well-considered and controlled manner. An Arab state that receives American arms will no longer turn to the Soviet Union. Russian arms are usually accompanied by Russian influence, Russian pressures, and a pro-Soviet political orientation—all of which lead to confrontation with Israel. By contrast, American arms bring American influence and a pro-Western political orientation, encouraging the stabilization of the Middle East and a policy of nonconfrontation.

In retrospect, our cries of protest when the process began lacked credibility and probably did us harm. In the future, instead of sponsoring demonstrations in Washington, we should advise the United States to operate in a deliberate manner. Instead of objecting to the arms deals themselves, we should emphasize that deliveries of weapons serve as a means of achieving peace in the region and request that preference be given to states willing to make peace with Israel—in the same way that the Soviets exploited the weapons they supplied to foster the confrontation with Israel, a confrontation they viewed as forwarding their interests.

The defense secretary was gradually becoming more cordial. He recalled that while serving as secretary of the air force in the

1960s, he had recommended escalation of the bombing raids into North Vietnam. In time, he'd changed his view. Now he discussed it in a contemplative way. "As a private individual, I learned a lesson that the nation ought to learn, too. We have to be very prudent in extending our foreign policy commitments beyond our own vital security interests. A further lesson: the limitations of military force in a situation of political indecision."

As the atmosphere grew warmer, the conversation turned to that regular favorite of the Pentagon repertoire: requests for arms. This time, I sensed things would be easier. Before I'd left for the States, I had decided to break with past tradition, where the success or failure of a mission to Washington was gauged by the contents of one's "shopping bag." This time, I'd set out with a list short enough to avoid knocking Brown out of his seat with stupefaction. There were no grounds to demand more. Since the guns had fallen silent at the end of the Yom Kippur War, we had received U.S. military assistance of stunning proportions, far exceeding what our forces had possessed in the Six-Day War. By my reckoning, some 20 percent of our defense system is maintained by the American taxpayer, to the yearly tune of a billion dollars in military aid to Israel.

The enormous volume of this aid and the undeniable fact that ours is one of the world's strongest armies inhibited me from presenting additional demands. A similar thing had happened in 1965, when I had gone to the United States to ask for a large number of planes for our air force. I had sought counsel from then Prime Minister Levi Eshkol.

"To get them to sell us planes," I'd said, "I have to present our air force as somewhat weak despite the fact that I believe it can cripple the Arab air forces within three hours. What should I do?"

"No problem," Eshkol had replied without hesitation. "Present yourself as *Shimshen der nebichdiker*—Samson the weakling!"

"On our eastern front, we could find ourselves facing five thousand tanks and a thousand planes," I now proceeded to tell Brown, afraid he was going to say that the peace agreement would make it possible to reduce the size of our forces. "Syria is under strong Soviet influence; there are three thousand Soviet advisers and technicians, espionage vessels . . ."

Brown was well acquainted with the facts. Every Tuesday, he went to the national military command center on the Pentagon's second floor for a security briefing with top commanders of his staff, while electronic display panels flashed the minutest details of the global military picture on 'top secret' screens. He knew the sites of intercontinental nuclear missiles, the flight routes of a hundred bombers on air alert, the positions of missile submarines, and the deployment of armored divisions in Europe and the Far East.

"The agreement with Egypt," I said, "does not permit us to reduce our forces."

In place of the elaborate documents submitted by Israel's Defense Ministry in the past, one single sheet of paper now sufficed to list our total current requests for military supplies: an increase in the number of F-15s, and F-16s, speedup in their delivery, and approval for the purchase of helicopters.

"We will consider the matter," said Brown without promising anything. That is the kind of answer I am in the habit of giving when I don't have an answer—or don't want to give one.

The close cooperation and mutual trust and appreciation between Israel and the United States and the military establishments of the two countries found expression later when I was taken along the endlessly long corridors of the Pentagon and its interminable labyrinth of rooms, chambers, and basements.

"You could be born and die here without ever leaving the building," I remarked jovially to my guides, who came right back with the story of the pregnant woman who approached one of the Pentagon employees demanding to know where the maternity ward was.

"Madam," the employee rebuked her. "In your condition, you should never have come in here."

"When I came in here," the distracted woman fired back, "I wasn't in this condition!"

My trek ended in the situation room, which I entered alone; none of my companions could be admitted. The intelligence officers gave me a long, comprehensive, and fascinating exposition on Soviet military might and its deployment. The extent of the information available to U.S. intelligence was remarkable.

I had a renewed opportunity for an exchange of views with the secretary of defense at a ceremonial—and strictly kosher—banquet. In the informal atmosphere, Brown came across as more relaxed, displaying a sharp sense of humor. Then it was time for serious discussion.

"How can the obstacles be overcome for a renewal of negotiations?" Brown asked me. Without anyone saying it aloud, I understood that the Americans saw Begin as the obstacle to peace. The press, radio, and television repeated the charge incessantly.

"You do not show sufficient appreciation of Begin's step," I told Brown. "You don't understand what a turnabout he has made in comparison with his former views."

I tried to penetrate Brown's soul. As a descendant of the Jewish people, who had grown away from his roots, what did he think of us? I refrained from asking him. Although he said nothing outright, I thought I caught a pained expression on his face. It was the grimace of a wise man attempting to convey a message: what are you doing? Why are you making things difficult for the United States and for its Jewish community?

I returned to my attack on American views as expressed in President Carter's speeches.

"The president says that he is continuing the policies of Johnson, Nixon, and Ford," Brown replied. "All of them demanded a return to the 1967 borders, with minor changes."

"Forget it! That will involve danger to Israel. A hundred and ten out of a hundred and twenty members of the Knesset will never consent to an Israeli withdrawal from the West Bank. There isn't a single MK who won't insist that Israel's defensible boundary lies on the Jordan River, with Israel retaining footholds in the West Bank. How can Israel be defended ten miles from the sea?

"When I meet the president next week, I shall advise him to drop his demand for a return to the 1967 borders; I'll suggest that he encourage an Isracli-Egyptian agreement and leave the Jordanians to come to the conference table in a few years' time."

"Out of the question," Brown retorted. "You can't ignore the problem of the West Bank. The world will not accept the retention of territory acquired by force. It now favors a return to the former borders within the framework of a peace settlement."

I repeated what I had heard Begin say at Ismailia about the distinction between wars of defense and of aggression. I refreshed Brown's memory: Latvia and Estonia exemplify situations where the principle of restoration of conquered territories was not applied. "If the Arabs of Galilee, who are Palestinians, live in the state of Israel, why can't the Arabs of Judea and Samaria?"

"There is a difference between the wars of 1948 and 1967 from the different perspective of the times and the development of nationalist feelings," Brown commented.

"I can assure you that the nationalism of the mayor of Nazareth, which is within the old borders, does not fall short of the nationalism of the mayor of Nablus."

Brown disagreed.

"You should help us find a solution to guarantee coexistence between Jews and Arabs in the West Bank rather than insisting on our withdrawal from there," I said.

"Begin's peace plan marked a considerable advance," Brown conceded. "But it all depends on what your point of departure is.

Israeli credibility in the peace process has been eroded by various steps you have taken—first and foremost, the settlements, which give the impression that Israel wishes to create permanent facts while negotiations are still in progress. Public opinion welcomed Sadat's step as revolutionary, and it does not consider the Israeli response adequate."

"Sadat's step was most dramatic," broke in Simcha Dinitz, Israel's ambassador to Washington. Hard-working and efficient, Dinitz—formerly bureau chief to the late Prime Minister Golda Meir—now participated fully in the political maneuvers of the Likud government. "We cannot compete with Sadat for drama, which had to be greater because he started out from an extremely negative position. We did not start from such a negative position. Every Israeli government to date has repeatedly called for meetings with the Arab leaders, but those calls evoked no response."

The exchange grew fairly heated, but the atmosphere remained free and easy. I was enjoying every minute of it and was sorry to take my leave of Harold Brown. I expressed my hope that there would be further opportunities for us to meet.

"We will meet at the White House," he promised.

Outside, it was still snowing, but in the Pentagon the thaw had begun.

20

COFFEE ON PENNSYLVANIA AVENUE

In my temporary headquarters—a suite on the ninth floor of New York's Regency Hotel—I had to conceal my own views as I fended off the onslaught of critics directing their fire at me, as the senior representative of the Israeli government. Everyone—administration officials, heads of the American Jewish community, media representatives—berated me in the harshest terms.

Several of the American Jewish leaders who came for talks looked at me with tear-filled eyes. One of them said worriedly: "Israel is liable to spark off a wave of anti-Semitism with these settlements." In his anguish, he may have missed the tragic irony implied in his reproach: Israel, the state established as a sanctuary for persecuted Jews, could cause Jews additional persecution.

The offensive against the settlement program was pressed home on all sectors simultaneously. In Washington, it was led by the president in person. Carter defined the settlements as "illegal"— and public opinion applauded his comment. From his image in the newspapers and on television, Carter struck me as tough and far from friendly—the sort of man I would not like to meet in a dark alley.

In Tel Aviv, the onslaught was spearheaded by Sam Lewis. The U.S. ambassador to Israel was a regular visitor to the prime minister's office. Almost none of our ministers had the privilege of seeing Begin in private as frequently as the American representative. Acting on behalf of Carter, Lewis showed himself very inquisitive on the subject of the settlements. Not content with mere talk, he

sent embassy officials to tour the West Bank and report back on
what they had seen with their own eyes. Lewis acted with great
vigor—excessive, at times. He seemed highly conscious of the enormous political and military might of the superpower he represented. His aggressive approach made some people call him "the
high commissioner"—the title of the British governors of Palestine
in mandate times. I'd tried to defend Lewis, reminding his detrac-
tors that he was an American first and responsible to his country. I
was afraid of Israel's jumping on the deplorable bandwagon of
various countries in Europe, Asia, and Africa that eagerly take
American dollars and then attack her behind her back.

Statements by administration officials in Washington, press
stories, and telecasts all presented a most unsavory image of a
state once viewed as upright and attractive. In a confidential briefing to American Jewish leaders, presidential adviser Zbigniew
Brzezinski called the Rafah settlements an obstacle to peace.
Within the administration and in the Senate, outspoken pro-
Israelis like Sen. Henry Jackson tore their hair in despair: "Why
are those ten settlements so vital to you?" Israel's behavior was
inexplicable and incomprehensible. We were depicted as a rabble
of tricksters and scoundrels, petty hucksters from the international
flea market, the direct descendants of Shylock.

I read, listened, and watched—and wrung my hands. I told my
close friends that we were letting the opportunity of peace slip
by—and that I might feel compelled to resign in protest. Out-
wardly, I held my tongue, but within I was storing up a growing
measure of bitterness.

I never believed in the dismal refrain that "the whole world is
against us." Most of my anger was directed at my colleagues in the
cabinet. New York only reinforced the impression I had brought
with me from Israel—that when the peace train had chugged into
the station, it found most of the ministers in an exhausted sleep in
the waiting room. On hearing the engine's whistle as it set off on its
way, they woke up in a panic. I may be exaggerating, but some of
them acted as if peace had come at the wrong moment, bringing
with it unnecessary headaches. Who needed it?

Peace was a couple of sizes too large for some of them.

Members of the cabinet, from the prime minister down, looked
back with longing to the recent past, to their first months in office
before Sadat's arrival in Israel. How idyllic it had all been! They
bewailed their fate. The Egyptian president had spoiled the show

for them. Internal disagreements—personal as well as political—were now revealed in all their sordidness. The Israeli public saw its government torn by bickering dissension and infested with mistrust and jealousy.

After regaining the Sinai for next to nothing, Sadat had raised the price of peace. He had put forward demands about the future of the West Bank, acting mostly out of pressure from the Saudis, who, as the press wrote, were "sitting on the fence." (I said they were sitting beside it and squinting through the holes.) Begin was trying to woo Jordan by offering to refrain from exercising our right to impose Israeli sovereignty over the West Bank and by stressing the temporary nature of the five-year autonomy plan.

But Sadat did not seize the bait. Encouraged by the sympathy of the Americans, he attacked on every front: in his visit with Carter in February 1978, he had demanded our withdrawal from the Sinai within eighteen months; the right to move his army into the peninsula, beyond the passes; and a Palestinian solution for Judea, Samaria and the Gaza district.

That was too much.

With the backing of the United States, Sadat's steps forced our government into a corner. After renouncing the Sinai, it would be difficult to explain that peace could not come about owing to other problems. The ministers were afraid of being blamed for missing a historic opportunity. Begin was agitated; Dayan became irritable.

Sadat's behavior sparked a crisis of confidence in him and in his integrity. I proposed that we maintain an attitude of trust toward Sadat—while simultaneously preparing the armed forces for war. My proposals were rejected out of hand.

"If Sadat remains unyielding," said Dayan, "there won't be an agreement."

In the midst of the discussion, I asked Foreign Minister Dayan: "Moshe, do you believe that Sadat genuinely wants peace? Or is it all a trick to weaken Israel?"

"I believe," Dayan answered, "that he genuinely wants to end the conflict—but not at any price. And if the negotiations break down (because we don't accept his conditions), he will not hesitate to use force so that the United States will have to exert pressure on us to accept his conditions."

Of the other ministers, some—though not all—continued to disregard Sadat and his peace initiative as though nothing had happened. Their mental calendars simply did not record the day of his arrival in Jerusalem. My reports on my talks with Egypt were greeted with skeptical nods and shrugs.

"Ezer," I was told several times in a tone of commiseration, "the Egyptians have managed to lead you down the garden path."

The suspicion of Sadat gave rise to a phenomenon that began to characterize our cabinet meetings: almost every minister found a reason to comment on every single detail to ensure that his words were recorded in the cabinet minutes—and promptly leaked to the press. More and more, cabinet meetings began to resemble sessions of the Knesset: they became long, boring, and pointless. I regarded them as an intolerable weekly imposition. The cabinet devoted dozens of hours of discussion to trivial details—unimportant and unnecessary—while failing to hold a single discussion to formulate an overall strategy or to think about what the future would hold. All my demands for such a discussion were immediately rejected.

Between the lines—between the words and phrases poured out in torrents by the ministers—there were repeated displays of that oldest of human traits: envy. The peace negotiations were making Begin, Dayan, and me into international figures whose features appeared in closeup on television screens the whole world over. As the pageant of peace dominated the stage, the other ministers felt like extras—and as is the habit of extras, they sought ways of upstaging the principal stars and stealing the show.

"Ezer's in fashion now," one minister remarked mockingly at a time when he thought I was getting too much attention.

In the middle of one meeting, Arik Sharon told me: "Ezer, I have a wonderful mare that once, in a moment of weakness, I fed on high-quality oats. Having had a taste, she insists on eating them every day now, and that causes extraordinary difficulties. You must understand the cabinet (which resembles another beast belonging to the same family). Having savored the intoxicating taste of conducting peace negotiations, the ministers are no longer prepared to do without it."

It was a tragic misunderstanding, augmented by unnecessary battles of prestige. Everyone was affected simultaneously: Sadat, Begin, Carter—at loggerheads with each other.

"I have to go shuttling from Jerusalem to Cairo and back over every comma," complained U.S. Assistant Secretary of State Alfred Atherton, who was attempting to mediate between the sides.

"Your shuttling could go on for months," I told him. "If we could meet with the Egyptians alone, we could tie it all up." This barb was directed equally at Begin and even more so at Dayan. The two men were determined to involve the Americans in the peace talks out of concern that the administration would otherwise join in the confrontation against Israel. Ironically, the Egyptian president was afraid of the precise opposite: when Begin reported the American president's praise for his peace plan, Sadat was immediately on the alert, afraid that the American horse would be harnessed to the Israeli chariot. But he soon learned that Carter's sympathies inclined toward him.

Sadat had wanted to bring the Americans into the negotiations almost from the start. He foresaw—correctly—that no one but the U.S. administration was capable of delivering the goods. Only Carter would be able to force Israel into withdrawing from the occupied territories. While in Egypt, I had heard of Sadat's fear of the Jewish vote in the United States and its potential for foiling his aims.

Had the Egyptians done their homework thoroughly, they would have learned that Jewish influence in the United States is not powerful enough to forge close links between Washington and Jerusalem. Admittedly, the United States had supported—somewhat hesitantly—the establishment of the state of Israel; however, when our founding fathers courted the United States in subsequent years, the Americans did not respond. Left with no other choice, Israel's leaders had turned to Europe. In three of our major wars—1948, 1956, and 1967—our soldiers were equipped mostly with Soviet, French, and British arms, while the Americans remained on the sidelines of the Arab-Israeli conflict.

Various developments—primarily, Soviet attempts to penetrate the Middle East as a new sphere of influence—threw Israel into the arms of the United States. This was at a time when, after a long period of isolationism, the United States was again opening up to the world. Perhaps more than any other state, Israel had reaped the fruits—political, economic, and military—in the post-1967 era.

Sadat understood that he could chalk up no political or military gains without the help of the White House, the State Department, and the Pentagon. He had expelled the Russians in order to find a way to the Americans, but the latter were already committed to Israel. The Egyptian president proceeded to direct events in such a manner as to force the United States to steer its course between its commitment to Israel's security and its desire to gain a position in the Arab world.

The only way for the United States to achieve both aims is to unite Israel and Egypt within a single strategic structure. In addition to military cooperation, a strategic constellation also depends on a solid economic foundation, as I realized the day I saw the first bottle of Coca-Cola in Egypt. Economic successes can provide a shot in the arm for Egypt without necessarily harming Israel.

I have often been told that Israel is too dependent on the United States. I do not agree. In my view, there is no such thing as total independence in the present-day world. Even the United States is not independent; it lives on imported oil, whose delivery largely depends on the mood of some Arab sheik who possesses no army but does have the bill of ownership to the oil fields. Nor is the United States free to employ its army to the same extent that it could have forty or fifty years ago.

Fortunately, Soviet Russia is not independent, either. The Soviets live on American corn and wheat and will soon need to import oil. There is nothing to be done about it. The only genuinely independent people are the African tribes who live on the birds they trap and the water they draw from the river.

The United States, Egypt, and Israel share a common enemy: the Soviet Union. Friends of mine within the Egyptian leadership have often expressed their concern that the Russians may try to pay back Sadat for their humiliating expulsion from Egypt. One of their scenarios is that the Soviets would try to get Syria embroiled in a war with Israel in an attempt to worsen Egypt's predicament within the Arab world. But past experience has shown that the Soviets act very prudently.

The Soviet Union needs the Middle East for its own defense because of the region's geographical proximity to its borders. A similar reasoning guided the Soviets after World War II when they built up their western defensive cordon by annexing the Baltic states and by creating the Communist bloc in Eastern Europe. On the Soviet Union's southwestern flank, Communist regimes were installed in most of the Balkan countries. However, the Truman Doctrine foiled Soviet attempts to wrest control of Turkey and Greece by including them in NATO, and 1948 saw Yugoslavia's break from the Soviet strategic alliance. The Soviet Union's only immediate neighbor not forced to adopt a Communist regime was Finland, which was, however, totally neutralized in political and military terms.

After the Communist revolution in China, the Russians hoped to achieve security on their southeastern border, too. Some years later, in the 1960s, this hope proved illusory, as the rift with China turned into a menacing rivalry.

In the past, the Soviets have run into snags in trying to penetrate the Middle East. Because of the distances involved, they can't march their army into the Middle East the way they can in Afghanistan. In addition, the Communist ideology is not an easy product to peddle in the Arab countries, where the Communist parties are small and marginal. With the current emergence of radical Islamic movements, those parties will dwindle even further. In the economic sphere, the West has the upper hand.

Soviet strategists have always found the Middle East a tricky problem. The region is unstable; it serves as the arena for radical forces aspiring to alter the status quo. It is always possible that one of the sides in a conflict will invite the Russians to intervene, giving them a chance to get a foot in the door. That is why the Soviet Union will continue to be a potential menace to stability and detente in the region.

In fact, the Soviets operate very cautiously. As far as possible, they avoid any confrontation with the West over control of the Middle East. Even the temptation to gain control of the oil fields will not entice the Russians into a military showdown with the West. Admittedly, oil is of growing importance to the Soviet Union. By 1985, the Soviets will, apparently, switch from exporting oil to importing it. However, buying oil—from Iraq, Saudi Arabia, or Iran—will still be cheaper than war, even a limited war. Soviet ideology may talk of a life-and-death struggle between the socialist and capitalist camps, but the Soviet regime is very pragmatic by nature.

The Middle Eastern goods Sadat had to sell to the United States were better than ours: he could offer the Americans a strategic alliance of a number of key countries that would join in blocking Soviet expansionism. As he told tens of millions of American television viewers: "We will be the spearhead of the anti-Soviet campaign in the Middle East and Africa."

It was the sharp rift between Begin and Sadat that had induced the latter to go meet Carter in the winter before my March visit. The Egyptian president had taken the United States by storm. His personal charm had worked overtime. In American public opinion—of such vital importance to us—we began to be perceived as tricksters.

To my dismay, the American administration had sided with Sadat. I believed—erroneously, perhaps—that agreement could be reached more quickly with Boutros Ghali than with Alfred Atherton. Dayan, whose views differed so completely from mine and who wanted American involvement so badly, went to Washington for talks; he returned empty-handed.

Left with no other choice, Begin himself now prepared to go to the United States to try and salvage the peace process. He decided to attach Dayan and me to the team that would conduct the White House talks; perhaps he wanted to commit the two of us to any conclusions reached there and possibly demonstrate, too, the unanimity of views within the Israeli cabinet. Awaiting his arrival—scheduled for the second week of March—I stayed on in the United States, serving in the meantime as the lightning rod for the storm surrounding the Israeli government. It was not a pleasant task.

I was sitting in my New York hotel room when my military aide, Ilan Tehila, brought me the news that Sharon and Dayan had talked Begin into permitting preparatory construction work on the settlement of Neveh Tzuf (Nebi Saleh) in Samaria.

"Just one bulldozer . . ." I was told.

As far as I could recall, Neveh Tzuf consisted of no more than ten families, quartered in an abandoned Jordanian police station. But that made no difference. Before the evening was out, television screens all over the United States would be featuring that lone yellow bulldozer; once again, I would hear Walter Cronkite and John Chancellor being indignant over Israeli provocations.

It was not the strategy I objected to; it was the tactics. I knew that it was not a question of one bulldozer; the issue was our right to the land of Israel. But I could not understand the need for this display before the eyes of the world, with cameras zooming in from every conceivable angle at our bulldozers' piling mounds of earth over the grave of the peace initiative. Ilan tried to calm me down—in vain.

I dialed a Jerusalem number. "Good morning, Mr. Prime Minister."

I did my best to be respectful and courteous. I asked Begin for details, and he confirmed the veracity of the report.

"Sir"—I raised my voice—"if the bulldozers go to work on the site, I shall cut short my visit to the United States and return to Israel."

There was silence at the other end.

"My dear sir!" I went on. "You can't come to the United States in this way—" Begin was scheduled to arrive in Washington in a week for his talks with Carter.

In one call, I fired off the explosive charges I had been storing up for so long. From the ninth floor of New York's Regency Hotel, thousands of miles away from the scene of the crime, I poured out my anger at the prime minister and his colleagues for being too thick-skinned to grasp the gravity of the situation. Unless the bull-dozers were removed, I told him, I would resign.

My ultimatum had its effect, though at the cost of my being attacked in the Israeli media as impulsive, trigger-happy, irresponsible—the usual charges!

Two days later, when I moved to Washington to prepare for the impending meeting with the president of the United States, I took up quarters in a hotel that was part of a large complex of office and residential buildings. Only a few hundred yards from my room was the setting of the affair that ultimately put an end to the career of the man then occupying the world's highest political office: Richard M. Nixon.

The hotel was the Watergate.

The night before my meeting with Carter, I spent hours tossing and turning in my bed on the third floor of the Watergate Hotel, trying to envisage various situations liable to arise in the course of my conversation with Jimmy Carter. What should I say if he asks for my views on the settlement program? Or about the future of the Rafah settlements? About the airfields? Or the peace process? I had been told that Carter occasionally takes a guest aside and, having got him alone, demands to know his personal opinions about issues. He had done it with Prime Minister Yitzhak Rabin when Rabin visited him in March 1977—resulting in the first rift between the Carter administration and the Israeli government. Carter had invited Rabin up to his private apartment, apparently hoping that the Israeli prime minister would reveal his true thoughts. Rabin did not fall into the trap.

My own opinions were an open secret. They had been splashed across six columns in *The New York Times*. On a number of matters they were not identical with those of my cabinet colleagues. What was I to do if the president asked me for my private point of view? I did not want Carter to take advantage of our meeting in order to sow dissent between my colleagues and myself. The widespread publicity surrounding my stormy telephone conversation with Begin had shattered my image at home—but not in the eyes of the American administration. Americans—government officials as well as journalists—saw me as moderate and sane: "A fresh breeze after Begin's legalistic tone and Dayan's inflexibility"—as the media expressed it.

"Just imagine how far things have gone"—I grinned at the Israeli journalists crowding around me—"if I am regarded as the only one who is sane!"

I had never before seen President Carter except on television.

Begin had been the one to meet with Carter over the autonomy plan.

My only involvement with the American president had been during the 1977 election campaign when I'd attacked Carter for inviting Yitzhak Rabin to the United States shortly before polling day. "The president of the United States is wasting his time," I said then. "In any case, Begin is going to be the next prime minister; he's the one the American president should be meeting."

Now the president of the United States welcomed me in the White House's oval office, standing beside the couch where we were to sit. The television spotlights flooding the room showed up his pinkish complexion.

Carter is shorter than I had imagined. His face is marked and scarred like the face of a sailor who has spent many hours in the sun and taken a lot of salt spray. I was impressed by his physical robustness.

The following day's newspapers reported that my agitation had made me play with the buttons on my jacket.

Carter noticed my nervousness. Flashing his famous trademark—two rows of gleaming white teeth—he responded to the entreaties of the cameramen by gripping my right hand again and again. I was very curious to find out what sort of man this was.

"Welcome," he said. "I hope you are enjoying yourself here."

I mumbled a few polite nothings.

I had been in the White House only once before: shepherded along the roped-off walkways in the company of hundreds of tourists from scores of countries, I had listened with impatience to the lengthy explanations of the guide who was leading us through the six rooms open to the public.

This time, I entered the presidential residence by a different entrance in a different status. From the very first, I was surprised. In visiting the palaces of rulers, I am accustomed to encountering guards in an assortment of clownlike costumes, with swords—even horses—at times. But the White House has no chocolate soldiers stationed at its portals. Everyone was wearing ordinary, fairly unembellished clothing.

The oval office was crowded. Carter had gathered the heads of his administration, possibly as a political gesture to demonstrate his appreciation and sympathy for me. Some I knew from earlier contacts; others I recognized from their pictures in the press or on television.

"Do you know Professor Brzezinski?" Carter asked.

I shook his hand. "I have heard a lot about you," I said politely.

"I can imagine what you've heard," he said with a smile.

National Security Adviser Zbigniew Brzezinski had been portrayed in Israeli circles as the evil spirit of the White House, the *éminence grise* behind the administration's vigorously anti-Israel actions. Israeli government figures and journalists kept him under running fire. That week, the papers had published details of a briefing he'd given American Jewish leaders in which he'd attacked the Begin government. Brzezinski noticed my reserve toward him.

"I suggest you get together with Brzezinski for a talk," the president said in a bid to reduce the tension.

"Sir," I fired back, "that would be like two pilots in a dogfight."

Suddenly, I felt uneasy. I had just discovered that I was the only Israeli in the room. Around me, I identified Vice President Walter Mondale, National Security Adviser Brzezinski, Secretary of State Vance, Secretary of Defense Brown, but where was Israeli Ambassador Simcha Dinitz?

Accidentally or not, he had been left outside. Could that be the custom around here? I did not know how to proceed. I wanted Dinitz with me so that he could provide Jerusalem with a reliable report on the substance of the conversation. I was afraid that my unaccompanied admission into the oval office would be misconstrued by my cabinet colleagues at home. I could already visualize the leaks on the subject and the ensuing hullaballoo. Could I request the president to invite the ambassador to join us?

"Defense minister"—Carter commenced the proceedings—"I want to stress, here and now, the United States' commitment to Israel's security."

There was no time to pose the question. Dinitz remained outside.

Carter's Georgian accent made it hard for me to distinguish his words at first. Observing my difficulty, the president raised his voice and slowed down his delivery. His voice was very vigorous, but despite the warmth of his words, he exuded a certain chilliness—an expression of the current strain in U.S.-Israeli relations.

Carter went on to speak of the snags bedeviling the peace talks. "It is of tremendous importance to exploit the momentum that has been created so as to promote the peace process," he said. His expression was resolute; his tone carried more than a hint of military command. The look in his eyes was not to my liking.

I had expected to feel a certain closeness to Carter. Both of us were former career officers—he had served in submarines, I in the air—and I'd hoped we would find some common ground.

"Did you know," he said as though imparting a confidence, "that

President Sadat once proposed that I come to Jerusalem, together with Tito of Yugoslavia, Callaghan from Britain, and Schmidt from West Germany, to hold a peace conference?"

I had heard of this idea of Sadat's a number of times; he had proposed it before deciding to come to Jerusalem alone.

"I rejected the proposal at the time," Carter related. "I told the Egyptian president that the idea was no good, that if any one of those invited refused to take part, the conference would fail."

I wondered why he was going to the trouble of recounting all this for me. Perhaps it was his way of telling me that in his eyes matters of prestige are not as important as practical deeds.

"And then," Carter went on, "President Sadat decided to go to Jerusalem."

There was a brief silence.

"He did not tell me about it beforehand," Carter said. "But he certainly considered my views and assumptions about what Israel wants," he added.

I sank into an armchair. The president, probably sensing my tension, tried to assuage it with his smiles. At his side sat the vice president, Fritz Mondale. All the others had left the oval office— they were probably waiting outside.

"I certainly don't discount Sadat's step," I said in response to the president's words. "But its dramatic and unexpected nature has overshadowed the far-reaching proposals put forward by Prime Minister Begin." The expression on Carter's face indicated that he did not share that opinion. Repeating what I had said on various occasions since my arrival in the United States, I explained the enormity of Begin's response, which was a greater departure from the policies of previous governments, from his party's election manifesto, and from his own personal and political beliefs. "Mr. President," I said. "As a politician, you must be aware of how dangerous it is to deviate from your election manifesto."

Carter said that the United States aspired toward a comprehensive settlement but believed it feasible to achieve a peace treaty with Egypt alone. He brought up the recent visit of Foreign Minister Moshe Dayan to the United States. "Dayan doubts whether Sadat would make peace without Hussein," he said. "But I believe it's possible even if Jordan doesn't come in."

I had one president in my family and have met two in my political career. Sadat was the first. Now, sitting next to the second, I was very curious about what was going on in his mind. Here was the man charged with the safety—and survival—of the Western world. I wanted to get inside his head, but his words sounded as though they had been programmed by a computer. He did not utter a single superfluous syllable. *That's the way an engineer thinks,* I reminded myself. *In squares and rectangles.*

Carter said that the United States had not decided, and did not intend to decide, where the border would run in Judea and Samaria. "However," he added, "it is essential to find a formula that will permit Sadat to show Jordan, the Palestinians, and the Arab world that the problem can be solved.

"Begin's plan for the West Bank—with certain modifications— can be taken as an interim arrangement," the president proposed.

That came as a surprise. In recent weeks, the administration had almost totally rejected Begin's plan, bringing relations between Jerusalem and Washington to a rift of unprecedented magnitude.

However, Carter did not permit me to entertain any delusions. "After five years, we will reexamine the arrangement, possibly by means of a plebiscite among West Bank inhabitants," he said.

"What will be up for decision by plebiscite?" I asked.

I could foresee the president's reply, as he must have foreseen that there was no hope of his proposal being adopted. Carter suggested that the plebiscite should give West Bank inhabitants the chance to decide whether they wanted a link with Jordan or with Israel or a continuation of their self-governing status under the autonomy plan.

"What happens if the inhabitants opt for a link with Jordan?" I broke in. Carter's proposal seemed too crude a booby trap to fall for. The president of the United States was aiming for a Palestinian entity or national home, affiliated with Jordan but not necessarily part of the Hashemite kingdom. This would be the embryo of a Palestinian state, which Israel had rejected hands down.

"Even in that case, an Israeli military presence will be maintained," Carter promised.

I knew that Israeli military bases on the Jordan River would be a festering wound that the citizens of a Palestinian state would not tolerate.

"We cannot agree to anything of the sort," I said. Carter looked both disappointed and angry. All in all, I was reiterating the published views of the Israeli government—while he may have expected me to differ. If so, he had erred in his assessment; he must now regard me as unyielding, no less than my colleagues.

"Whatever happens"—the president tried to reassure me—"an independent Palestinian state will not be one of the options." Even that failed to hearten me.

I tried my luck. "I propose that we consider the problems of the

West Bank and the Gaza Strip in terms of coexistence, not of restoration of territory."

Carter shook his head. Vice President Mondale did likewise. "To whom do we restore Gaza?" I demanded. "Not even the Egyptians want it!"

I told the president and vice president of the close economic ties between Israel and Judea, Samaria, and Gaza. "On Muslim holidays, all construction work in Israel comes to a standstill," I said with a smile, "because all the construction workers are from the West Bank and Gaza."

The two men remained poker-faced.

Three cups of coffee were set on the table. Carter and Mondale each took one; the third one waited for me. Usually, in such a situation, I resist drinking coffee lest in the middle of making a point I spill the coffee and stain my suit. On previous occasions—when meeting President Sadat, for example—I had left the coffee on the table. This time, however, I thought that Carter and Mondale had noticed my indecision. Picking up the cup, I took a sip of coffee, taking advantage of the momentary lull to look around.

The office of the president of the United States is flooded with the light that pours in through its numerous windows. It overlooks a splendid view, colorful and restful—the rose garden and a huge stretch of green lawn. The American flag, paintings on the walls, deep carpets, couches and armchairs, a huge desk—all these are appropriately imposing props for a president.

Carter went on to express his admiration for Sadat. "When I first met him," he recollected, "I proposed a peace plan with full normalization, including diplomatic and commercial relations. Sadat said he could not make that kind of peace. By our second meeting, he had changed his mind completely. He accepted all the components of peace—just the kind of peace the Israelis want." The hint was plain. Carter expected us to undergo a similarly far-reaching change of outlook.

"We are surrounded by a hundred million Arabs." I repeated the well-worn tale. "We need a sense of security after thirty years of war . . ."

I spent the last few minutes telling the president and vice president about the personal relationship that had developed between the Egyptian minister of war and myself, about our Zahava station in Cairo—things that still stirred my imagination. They did not seem particularly impressed.

I understood that the time had come to take my leave.

At the door, the president grasped my hand firmly. "I shall pursue peace aggressively," he promised.

Outside, snow mingled with driving rain to create an icy sleet. The sky was a dismal gray.

"How was it?" demanded the journalists who had waited outside for our meeting to end.

"The atmosphere in U.S.-Israeli relations," I said, "is like today's weather in Washington. But I can begin to see the first strip of blue sky."

I returned to New York where I intended to spend the Sabbath. My timetable was less crowded now. The Israeli consulate was to hold a large reception in my honor Saturday night. The prime minister would arrive in another day or two, and the dizzying round of talks and contacts would be renewed. But in the meantime, I could relax. My wife went off to see friends. My military aide, Ilan, took the opportunity to scour the stores of New York and do some shopping for his family.

I went up to my room, on the ninth floor of the Regency Hotel. Having called Begin to report on my talk with Carter, I got ready to rest.

It was morning in New York; in Tel Aviv, it was early evening. I put my head on the pillow.

The telephone rang.

On the line was my friend David Kolitz, speaking from his home in Herzlia Pituach, a garden suburb near the Mediterranean coast beside the main Tel Aviv-Haifa highway.

"Ezer!" David cried in agitation. "There's shooting going on around here . . ."

21

RETRIBUTION FOR THE BLOOD OF A SMALL CHILD

Peace was under fire.

I had never imagined that the terrorists would put away their arms. The day President Sadat had notified the Egyptian parliament of his intention of going to Jerusalem, the gallery was occupied by a guest of honor: PLO leader Yasir Arafat. Arafat had joined the thunderous applause that followed Sadat's statement. Like many others, he probably thought it was mere lip service.

By the time the PLO chairman had realized the truth, it was too late to persuade Sadat not to act out his intention. Balked, Arafat declared himself Sadat's enemy. Our defense experts predicted that the PLO leader would send in terrorists on increasingly intensive attacks against Israel in a bid to spark off a conflagration that would send Egypt's quest for peace up in flames. We had made a great effort to forestall any terrorist sorties, but the fish had found a hole in the net.

The news from Tel Aviv came through in bits and pieces. The first reports were vague and imprecise: the terrorists had landed from a boat . . . one dead . . . two perhaps . . . a bus seized . . .

The extent of the attack was still unclear. There was nothing to give me any idea of the tragedy that lay in store.

As the hands of the clock advanced, reports of the terrorist attack began to come through. The telephone rang constantly.

Long years of military experience have taught me to be careful about the first reports emanating from the scene of any action:

excitement, incomplete information, rumors, and hitches in communications often combine to paint an inaccurate picture that can be very harmful to decision making. I still did not know what was happening, but I had a powerful longing to be in Israel.

I could already see myself in "the pit"—the high-command bunker—taking charge of affairs. My suite in the Regency Hotel bore little resemblance to our GHQ war room. The comfortable armchairs, the wide beds, the fruit bowl on the table, the windows facing out onto the New York City skyline—all these were in glaring contrast to the overcrowded rooms down in the bowels of the earth where neon lights shine day and night and the air is thick with cigarette smoke, while red arrows are moved around on the wall maps in response to the incessant stream of reports emitted by crackling radios. . . .

Thousands of miles away from all that, I could not even enjoy the wonders of electronic technology that make it possible to sit in the high-command post, remote from the battlefield, and listen in on operations in progress, practically treading on the heels of each soldier. This degree of involvement often tempts one to nag the field commanders with demands for information and for participation in operational decisions. To fight the temptation, one must learn to listen in, follow events, visualize what is going on—and keep quiet. That takes restraint.

I needed even more restraint now, stranded as I was far away in New York. There was nothing I could do. Knowing that Chief of Staff Motta Gur and other senior officers had their hands full directing the action against the terrorists, I forced myself to refrain from bothering them.

Anyway, it was a small-scale terrorist attack. So I believed—or was that what I wanted to believe? It was noon in New York; in Israel, darkness had fallen.

I had time to assess the situation. How would this event affect the peace process? Would the goal of the terrorists—to end or at least disrupt the negotiations—be achieved? If the terrorists had inflicted no more than one or two Israeli fatalities, that would not disrupt the existing timetable: in another day or two, Begin would come to the United States for his scheduled meeting with Carter—which Dayan and I were also to attend. But what would happen if the number of casualties were larger? I knew the answer: a reprisal raid would be unavoidable. Israel knows no other way.

Thirty years of war and terrorist action have created a kind of fixed "exchange rate" for vengeance and retribution—a balance of debits and credits in the blood bank. The success or failure of an operation or a war, the compelling necessity to hit back or the feasibility of exercising restraint—all these depend on the number of coffins on either side of the border. As a soldier, I never came to terms with the idea that our actions should be subject to this kind of yardstick—just as I never came to terms with war's painful toll. War is no football game, and its outcome cannot be gauged in terms of a numerical "score."

"It seems that there are seven dead" came the report.

According to the conventional tariff of revenge, seven fatalities heightened the likelihood of a reprisal action. I knew that the balance was tilting toward an action of that nature. Where? When? I had no clear idea as yet—just as the telephone reports still had not given me a clear picture of the tragedy and its scale.

How strange, I thought. Here I was, on a peace mission in New York— listening to battle reports from Tel Aviv. As far as today's victims were concerned, my efforts had come too late. What could be done to ensure there would be no more victims?

I wondered what was being planned in "the pit" at this moment. Reprisal raids—like wars or any other form of combat—demand the peak of our military effort. There is no justification for failure. For decades the people of Israel have been paying in sweat and blood to make sure that when the moment came, their military machine would function effectively. As defense minister, I had insisted on perfection. Now, far from the scene, I was full of questions: would the correct objective be chosen? The right commanders? The timing? The best available forces? Were the intelligence reports accurate? Did the operational plan guarantee success?

By this time, our GHQ command post would be a teeming hive of activity: intelligence reports being collated, operational maps pinned up, plans in preparation, forces redeployed. I wished I were there. Since becoming defense minister, I had spent many tense nights down there during operational sorties—most of them against the terrorists in Lebanon.

"The pit" is one of the most carefully guarded and exclusive places in Israel: relatively few people enjoy the privilege of being admitted into its secret recesses. Down there, elaborate signals installations keep close track of developments. On the eve of any of our operations, the atmosphere in "the pit" was always extraordinary. It was characterized by a heavy silence—broken only by the voice of Deputy Chief of Staff General Yekutiel (Kooti) Adam. A superb combat commander, familiar with every topographical feature on the enemy side no less than on our own, Kooti would translate the terse messages emitted by the crackling radios, leading the occupants of "the pit" on an imagined sortie across the border along with our assault troops. "They're walking . . . they're crawling now . . . now they're storming the objective!"

But I was not in "the pit." I was in my New York hotel suite, and the somber reports kept pouring in from Tel Aviv. It was a painful chronicle. Two weeks before, our military intelligence had alerted me to disturbing news: on the base of Damour, near Lebanon's Mediterranean coast, terrorists were training for a special sea-based operation. We had launched a raid to destroy the Damour base, but to avoid harming civilians it had been limited in scale. Our naval commandos had landed and encountered the base's sentries; after destroying two commando boats, they withdrew. To avert civilian casualties, they had refrained from penetrating farther inland. But that must have been precisely where the terrorists were quartered.

It was not the first time that concern for the safety of innocent civilians had restricted the dimensions of our cross-border operations. Our sorties into Lebanon almost always ran into great difficulties on this score. The terrorists mingled with the civilian population, which sheltered their activities—at times, the terrorist positions were no more than a few paces from a hospital or school, a church or mosque.

At first, I was not as concerned about harming the Lebanese population, in view of its cooperation with the terrorists. If civilians were hurt—even unintentionally—I hoped that would goad the Lebanese into casting the PLO groups out from their midst. I had in mind the example of the Jordanian border in the late 1960s: when terrorist incursions from east of the Jordan River had multiplied, our bombs and shells had reduced the Jordan valley—formerly a veritable paradise—into a desolate wilderness. Tens of thousands of villagers had fled to Amman, ultimately forcing King Hussein to take action against the terrorists. He did so effectively: no Israeli has ever killed terrorists in numbers to rival those felled by the Jordanian king. That showdown occurred in September 1970—the month named "Black September" by embittered Palestinians and perpetuated by the terrorist organization of that name.

Though directed against the terrorists, our massive actions in Lebanon—shellings and aerial bombings—aroused world opinion against us. Foreign television commentators, who never showed much interest in thousands of children dying of starvation in Cambodia, drew tears from the eyes of millions of viewers by filming a Palestinian child grubbing in the rubble of his home. Accusing Israel of "a massacre of the Palestinians," they linked those operations with the peace negotiations, alleging that the reprisals were an attempt to annihilate the Palestinian people and deny it the self-determination it was fighting for.

Every morning, my desk was swamped with cables from our embassies abroad, describing the effect of the bombing raids on Israel's international standing. In view of our eagerness to convince world opinion of Israel's genuine desire for peace, I was compelled—albeit reluctantly—to recommend that bombing raids be kept to a minimum, particularly in densely populated areas.

"We'll pay dearly for it!" GHQ colleagues commented angrily, but I signed very few authorizations for further bombing attacks.

Another report from Tel Aviv: "There are fifteen dead . . ."

Re'uma returned from the visit with her friends. Ilan entered with large shopping bags, trophies of his successful forays to Macy's and Alexander's. When I told him the latest news, he almost unthinkingly headed for his room and began to pack.

I called the prime minister's Jerusalem home. Menachem Begin came on the line, our dispute of a few days ago overshadowed by the emergency.

"I am returning immediately," I told him. Begin said he would notify me within a few minutes whether or not I should come home.

"I am returning immediately," I repeated.

I could not understand why the prime minister had to delay his answer. Who could he be consulting on such a matter at this time? A few moments later I was informed that Begin had agreed to my decision to leave for Israel immediately; in his version to the public, "the prime minister had instructed the minister of defense to return home without delay."

Gradually, as the reports piled up, I learned the magnitude of the disaster. It appeared that the terrorists had come in from the sea. On reaching land, they had encountered an American photographer, Gail Rubin—a niece of Senator Abraham Ribicoff. She was taking pictures of birds in flight at the nature reserve near Kibbutz Ma'agan Micha'el, close to the highway from Haifa to Tel Aviv. The terrorists, who had lost their bearings, asked her where they were. Gail Rubin told them, and then they killed her.

From the beach they had headed for the main highway where they'd ambushed a bus taking vacationers on an outing. Turning the bus toward Tel Aviv, they sped down the road, blasting away at passing cars. Then they hijacked a second bus whose passengers they squeezed into the first.

Crowded with captives—men, women, and children—the bus was on its way toward Tel Aviv when our security forces managed to halt its journey of death. After a gun battle, the bus had exploded into flames with over thirty men, women, and children dying among its charred remnants.

Israel was shocked and appalled by the calamity. The terrorist attack on the coastal road, with its large number of fatalities, sparked off a wave of fury in the people—in addition to their widespread frustration over the raiders' success in penetrating into the very heart of the country. There was an understandable passion for revenge—a desire to "show 'em."

My first instinctive reaction was a natural sorrow over the blood that had been shed. But I also considered the peace process: the attack had again poisoned relations between Israel and the Arab world—to the delight of fanatics on both sides of the border. The horrifying story of the Jewish mother whose baby daughter the terrorists had hurled into the flames was sufficient to resurrect the wall of enmity that had begun to be torn down. However, a large-scale reaction on our part was liable to revive Egypt's dormant feelings of Arab solidarity. It looked like a perfect trap.

Even before the attack, the peace process had hovered between breakthrough and breakdown. Now Arafat and his emissaries had succeeded in reviving the old hostility between Jerusalem and Cairo. I was furious.

While still in New York, I was notified that the ministerial committee for defense was meeting at the prime minister's home. It was important that the discussion break out of the routine framework: beyond retaliation, the committee had to think about resuming the peace process.

"Tell them that!" I instructed my young military aide-de-camp, Aryeh Shor, who had remained behind in Israel.

As soon as the defense committee concluded its meeting, Motta Gur called me. The chief of staff described the situation—as far as was possible over an open telephone line. I got the rest in code: the prime minister and the cabinet had agreed on a large-scale operation.

I flew home.

Terrorism is not a purely Israeli problem. It is the fatal ailment of twentieth-century civilization, a modern mode of assailing the liberal democracies. Today's terrorism encompasses the whole world. It makes use of the innovations of advanced technology, of international communications, of the freedom of travel from one country to another, of money transferred from one bank to another, of links with like-minded colleagues beyond the frontiers. Terrorism has spread like an epidemic—largely because the governments, parliaments, and media have for many years refused to tackle it with the seriousness it deserves. Many people saw it as nothing more than a nuisance that the world must get used to living with.

Terrorism will not bring about the collapse of Israel—or that of other countries. The greatest danger lies in its philosophical justification of violence—an updated version of the Leninist and Trotskyite doctrines. Morally, this outlook justifies murder—not merely as a means to an end but also as an end itself. A world that comes to terms with such a philosophy will soon find itself in chaos. The world order will be totally disrupted, together with the accepted code of international behavior. This is already evident in the situation of the American hostages in Iran. That episode ought to have been met by collective sanctions on the part of the free world to prevent Iran from breaking away from the recognized standards of international practice.

The war against terrorism is a long and wearisome battle between the free world and those totalitarian states that finance terrorism and provide its adherents with sanctuary and shelter, training camps and bases, with money, weapons, and diplomatic assistance. Should terrorists prevail, it would be a victory for states like the Soviet Union, Libya, Iraq, Cuba, and Algeria—encouraging them to launch even more brazen onslaughts.

Many free world governments fell into the error of a policy of moderation and conciliation toward terrorism, thereby indirectly fostering its growth in recent years. Entering into negotiations with the terrorists, they inevitably give in to some of their demands: ransom payments or liberation of terrorist colleagues facing trial or already convicted. By granting the terrorists status—by giving them prerogatives and benefits and, above all, by awarding them legitimization through negotiating with them—those governments have sapped society's willingness to defend itself.

In its Middle Eastern version, terrorism appears in its most intensive and violent form. The Palestinian terrorist organizations have declared their goal: to overcome the state of Israel, erasing it from the map and bringing back Palestinians living outside the country to replace its present Jewish population.

Terrorism is one of the techniques the Arabs adopted to combat the Jewish presence in Palestine—long before the creation of Israel. Since the emergence of the state, it has become a feature of pan-Arab strategy. Arab terrorism has always used the same tactics: indiscriminate slaughter of unarmed men, of women and children. The only thing that has changed in the course of the years is the methods and the weapons. On the whole, the Arabs used these tactics whenever they were afraid or unable to confront the Jews directly.

Palestinian terrorism against Israel began as far back as the early 1950s. Its political organization—the PLO and the Fatah terrorist organization—both predate the Six-Day War, in which Israel gained control of the territories she now occupies. Furthermore, some people contend that the terrorist raids before the 1967 war—along with the Syrians' attempts to divert the tributaries of the Jordan River to prevent water reaching Israel—began the escalation that culminated in that war.

My colleague, the former head of military intelligence, General Aharon Yariv, once pointed out that the Palestinian terrorist organizations are the only ones of their kind in the world to enjoy such luxurious conditions, with their facilities handed to them on a silver platter: the Arab states give them full backing and assistance, allowing them complete freedom of action and providing them with anything they need.

General Yariv claims that the PLO's combatants are not "underground fighters" in the classic sense of the term. They operate in the open, wear uniforms, carry arms, and have arsenals of weapons and ammunition. Within the Arab host states, they have almost total autonomy. They have bases, training camps, recruiting offices, command headquarters, newspapers and radio stations. They have the use of privileged diplomatic mail for conveying instructions, information, money—even weapons. They benefit from identity papers and passports, including diplomatic documents, on their travels.

Egypt and Syria have always kept the activities of the Palestinians under control. But Jordan took a long time before plucking up the courage to confront the terrorist organizations; she came close to paying for that hesitation with her regime and her independence. Lebanon has not even tried to face up to the Palestinians. For several years, there has been no effective government in Beirut; in Lebanon's towns and villages—as the Bible would put it—"each man does that which is right in his own eyes."

Lebanon's role as host of the Palestinian command headquarters and training camps placed us in a dilemma. We have always declared that we would hold sovereign states that sheltered the terrorists responsible for their "guests." We took repeated action against such states to induce their governments to block terrorism. Lebanon, however, has no government: in the prevailing anarchy, there is no one to clamp down on the terrorists. It then becomes necessary to hit the terrorists themselves.

In Lebanon, the terrorists are located within the refugee camps or in small bases in the countryside, which are very hard to pinpoint. There is little point in expending great effort to knock out an isolated rocket launcher in the shrubbery in some gulch. Why prescribe aspirin when surgery is required?

Consequently, when the ministerial committee decided to "go big" in response to the terrorist attacks on the coastal road, the decision had my full approval.

On my arrival at Ben-Gurion Airport, I found my loyal driver, Avi Makiss, who had brought along my army boots and field gear. I hurried to the war room of the Northern Command where the atmosphere was as on the eve of battle: senior commanders—bleary-eyed from lack of sleep—pored over maps; radios crackled, combat rations were gobbled down hastily. I was given a rundown of the operational plans by the chief of staff and the head of the Northern Command, Avigdor (Yanush) Bengal.

My first meeting with Yanush had taken place under totally different circumstances: he was lying in a hospital bed, his thin, lanky body covered with burns. It was all he could do to mumble a few words—which I couldn't make out. A few hours before, on a tour along the Syrian border, Yanush, in the company of several other officers, had driven over a mine; he was badly injured.

That was in 1966, just two days after I had become head of the GHQ's staff branch. On getting word of Bengal's injury, I set out directly for the hospital.

I had never met Yanush before. I had not even heard of him. My sphere in the air force was a long way away from the armored brigades—literally the distance from heaven to earth.

Then Yanush and I became friends. He later commanded an armored battalion on the Suez Canal front during the War of Attrition, and I followed his progress there. One time, he and I came under Egyptian fire together: nothing can equal that kind of experience for forging a friendship. About that time, Yanush told me that he intended to resign from the army as soon as quiet was restored: he wanted to study medicine. But that was not to be, and he extended his military service. Yanush was one of that select band of officers commanding the Israeli forces that blocked the deluge of Syrian steel on the first day of the Yom Kippur War.

Yanush always dressed sloppily. Other officers had commented to me about his long and unkempt hair, so in the course of a conversation with him, I asked him to set a personal example by improving his appearance. Without saying a word, he raised his hand to his head, thrusting his hair aside to reveal his naked skull. The hair tumbling over his ear was there to conceal the scars of his injury. I never troubled him again on that subject.

Now, at Northern Command headquarters, Yanush and Motta Gur outlined our attack on the terrorist bases in southern Lebanon. The thrust would be launched all along the sixty-mile-long border, and penetration would be to a depth of six miles into Lebanon. As far as possible, the intention was to avoid clashing with the Syrian army, to refrain from harming the civilian population, and to operate in a manner that would keep our own casualties to a minimum. The goal was to create a security zone in southern Lebanon in collaboration with the Christian forces there. The operational plan looked good to me: after discussing a number of modifications, I gave it my approval.

"Okay," I said, "we're on our way!"

Even while plunging into these preparations for battle, I did not forget for a single moment that the overall circumstances were quite unlike those of the past thirty years: although still in its infancy, the peace process with Egypt was a new factor to be taken into account. I was concerned about the possibility of our partners to the peace process—Egypt and the United States—reacting unfavorably to our operation inside Lebanon.

"The Americans will disapprove out of guilt," I said. "They didn't lift a finger to prevent the massacre of the Christians in the Lebanese civil war. Israel—the state of the Jews!—was the only country in the world to save the Christians from annihilation."

More worrying than the possible displeasure of Washington was the fate of the nine Israelis manning our Zahava station in Cairo while our operation was in progress inside Lebanon. The Israeli military action would further exacerbate existing tensions between us and the Arab states—and the Egyptians would not be able to overlook the angry reactions from Beirut, Baghdad, Damascus, and Riyadh. I held consultations about whether to recall our people from Cairo. In view of the shaky state of relations with Egypt, I knew that they would not again return if they left now. After some debate, I decided to preserve the last remaining link. I took a risk: Zahava would stay in Egypt.

On a chilly winter's night, thousands of our troops set out to launch "Operation Stone of Wisdom"—printed out by a computer, the code name did not seem appropriate either to the operation or to the circumstances that had necessitated it. In his final briefing to our forces, then deputy to Motta Gur, Rafful Eitan, quoted our national poet, Chaim Nachman Bialik: "Retribution for the blood of a small child has never been devised, not even by Satan." The horrors of the burned-out bus were still fresh in everyone's memory.

A few minutes after the first Israeli tank crossed the border into southern Lebanon, the telephone rang in the office of Eliezer Rimon, the head of our delegation in Cairo. The late hour notwithstanding, Rimon was instructed by headquarters in Tel Aviv to contact the head of Egyptian intelligence, General Shaukat, with an important message. It was not easy: the Egyptian soldier on duty was afraid to call up his general at such an unusual hour. Finally, he was persuaded by Rimon's urgency.

"A short time ago," Rimon notified Shaukat, "our forces began a limited operation along the Lebanese border to dislodge the terrorist bases from the area. I hope this limited operation will not disrupt talks between our two countries." This was the substance of the message—the first of its kind—conveyed to Egypt's chief of military intelligence after its text had been agreed upon between Begin, Dayan, and myself.

When operations are in progress, I cannot be content with dry written reports on official forms. I need to be at the scene of the action.

War has its own sounds and smells: the thunderclaps of artillery and the chatter of machine guns; the acrid fumes of explosives and the stench of corpses. The first hours after battle also have their own uniqueness: the silence, the wind whistling through the shutters of abandoned houses, the smell of the dust clogging your nostrils.

That first tour provided me with some unusual sights. There are no joyful wars, but the battle I saw in southern Lebanon brought joy to a party that was not involved in the fighting: the Christian minority population in south Lebanon. For two years, the burden of slogging it out against the Palestinian terrorists had fallen upon the Christians, bringing them to almost total exhaustion. At various times in the past the Palestinians had come close to beating them down; the Christians would then have been wiped out. Our army had provided the Christian militia with extensive aid; indeed, the Christians would have liked our troops to do the whole job for them. For a long time, we had refrained from doing so. Now, as the Israeli forces went into action, the militiamen were left with nothing to do. They dashed back and forth in their antiquated vehicles, brandishing their machine guns and having their photographs taken with their fingers raised in the "V" sign. Every time an Israeli cannon fired, its roar was sweet music to Christian ears.

The setting of this battlefield was striking. Most of our wars have been fought in the Sinai's yellow dunes and endless sands. Southern Lebanon was a total contrast: its air clear and fresh, the countryside green with rich vegetation and trees, blue water in the irrigation reservoirs. But there were black scars, too—the craters where our bombs and shells had landed. Seeing those black holes in the green landscape highlighted the devastation of war.

In the township of al-Him time seemed to have stopped. The township—a strategic position overlooking extensive areas of land and lying at the end of the "Arafat trail" from Syria into Lebanon—used to have fourteen thousand inhabitants, Shi'ite Muslims. When I arrived, the only ones left were two old women who had not fled with all the others for the simple reason that they were unable to walk. A week before our attack, al-Him's population had consisted of one hundred terrorists. The place looked as though no one had lived there for a generation. The township was devastated; scarcely a single house remained undamaged.

I was told that the Christian militiamen had driven into the township from Merj' Uyun to load up their cars with loot: iron bars, ovens, tables. There were hundreds of houses in al-Him, and the militiamen did not miss a single one. Very little was left to plunder. A Samuel Waters safe lay in the main street; it was too heavy to take away, but the resourceful militiamen had cracked it open to find any money inside. In a grocery store in the center of the township, dozens of empty Pepsi bottles stood on a partially demolished counter. Outside, water was gushing out of a cracked main pipe; there was no one to repair it.

North of al-Him, the fighting was still at its height. From nearby came the thunder of detonation, as one of our tanks fired its 105-mm. cannon at some invisible target. Dodging the tanks, I paced about among the soldiers, taking in their glances and comments. Suddenly, I caught sight of a familiar face.

"Sandy!" I yelled. "What are you doing here, son?"

Sandy is the son of Paul Kedar—a man who had been my comrade-in-arms for many years. Paul had enlisted in the RAF during World War II. He'd briefly joined the Irgun underground to fight the British and then gone on to serve in the Israeli air force.

This young soldier was named for his mother's brother, Sandy Jacobs, a pilot in our air force who had fallen in active service. Jacobs had been a good friend of mine, a fine man and a fine pilot; we had flown together as combat pilots during the 1948 War of Independence.

Young Sandy was a tank crewman. His grandfather, Ben-Zion, had fought against the Turks in the ranks of the Jewish Legion of the British army during World War I. His father Paul had fought in World War II and then in our wars. And now it was Sandy's turn.

He looked to me like a little boy astray in a place he had no business being. "Sonny boy—go home!" I wanted to say. But the command I gave him was a different one: "Get behind the tank and write a letter for me to take to your father and mother!"

Sandy—Alexander—did as he was told. Crouching behind the Centurion tank, he wrote a note to his parents. Every now and then, the thunder of exploding shells disrupted his scribbling.

The first phase of the operation—clearing the six-mile zone along our border—was completed successfully. We paid a price in casualties, but we destroyed the terrorists' bases; a large amount of arms and military equipment fell into our hands. Our forces occupied convenient positions well beyond our border settlements, which now lay far behind the front lines. The Syrian units stationed in Lebanon did not intervene; they did not even alter their deployment. Taking advantage of our success, the Christian militias seized control of additional areas around their three enclaves, providing a continuous link among them for the first time in years.

As the operation's first phase came to an end, I realized that the situation could not be left as it now stood. We had to decide whether to press on—and if so, in what direction. One possibility open to us was a withdrawal back into Israeli territory: that would categorize the operation as nothing more than a large-scale raid. Or we could advance further, to the Litani River, clearing the terrorists from the area to the south of the river. Motta Gur suggested that we try to reach some understanding with the Syrians, who were the only stable element in the vicinity.

The various proposals were submitted for consideration by the ministerial committee on defense, chaired by the prime minister. During the meeting, one of the committee members, who was extremely restless, remarked to me: "When I see the operations and hear the reports from our forces, I suddenly feel like an old horse

OPERATION LITANI,
MARCH 1978
Right: With Yanush Bengal
ARMY SPOKESMAN'S OFFICE
Center: In South Lebanon
ARMY SPOKESMAN'S OFFICE
Bottom: Visiting wounded
soldier ARMY SPOKESMAN'S OFFICE

Left: Sadat, Ezer and Gamasy
in Salzburg, July 1978
ARMY SPOKESMAN'S OFFICE
Lower left: Re'uma Weizman
visiting Jehan Sadat and her
granddaughter in Cairo
MINISTRY OF DEFENSE PUBLISHING HOUSE
Below: Re'uma, center, at home
at a reception for Egyptian
women ARMY SPOKESMAN'S OFFICE
Overleaf: At Camp David,
Sept. 1978 ISRAELI GOV'T PRESS OFFICE

CAMP DAVID
Left: Begin and Ezer
Below: Ezer, Kamel, Sadat
Right, top: Ezer, left, Sadat,
Carter, Begin, guide,
Dayan at Gettysburg UPI
Right, bottom: Aliza Begin,
left, Carter, Begin, Rosalynn
Carter at Friday night dinner

Above: Conferring with Carter
OFFICIAL PHOTOGRAPH, THE WHITE HOUSE, WASHINGTON
Right, top: Israelis meeting after
Sadat's threat to leave. From left: Ezer,
Dinitz, Dayan, Tamir, Barak,
Rosenne, Begin, Kadishai, Patim, Poran
Right, bottom: In Sadat's cabin
about to toast the final agreement

Top: With Ali at peace treaty
signing, March 1979 SHALOM BAR TAL
Bottom: Meeting with
Secretary of State Vance UPI
Right: Outside the Egyptian
embassy in Teheran
WIDE WORLD PHOTOS

נעשה בוושינגטון, די.סי. ביום זה כ"ז באדר לשנת תשל"ט, 26 במרץ 1979,
בשלושה עותקים בשפות העברית, הערבית והאנגלית וכל נוסח אמין במידה שווה .
במקרה של הבדלי פרשנות, יכריע הנוסח האנגלי .

حررت فى واشنطن دى . س . فى ٢٦ مارس ١٩٧٩م ، ٢٧ ربيع الاول ١٣٩٩هـ
من ثلاث نسخ باللغــــات العبريـة والعربيـة والانجليزية وتعتبر جمعها متساويـــة
الحجيـة ، وفى حالة الخلاف حول التفسير فيكون النص الانجليزى هو الذى يعتد به .

DONE at Washington, D.C. this 26th day of March, 1979, in
triplicate in the Hebrew, Arabic, and English languages, each
text being equally authentic. In case of any divergence of
interpretation, the English text shall prevail.

בשם ממשלת הרפובליקה הערבית   בשם ממשלת ישראל :
של מצרים :

عن حكومـة   عن حكومـة
جمهورية مصر العربيـــة :   اسرائيـــــل :

For the Government of the   For the Government
Arab Republic of Egypt: of Israel:

קועד על-ידי :

شهد التوقيـع :

Witnessed by:

גימי קארטר, נשיא
ארצות הברית של אמריקה

جيمى كارتر ، رئيس
الولايات المتحدة الامريكيـة

Jimmy Carter, President
of the United States of America

Left: Last page
of the actual document
Above: Signing the peace
treaty, March 26, 1979
WIDE WORLD PHOTOS

Left: Ezer and Begin
SHALOM BAR TAL
Below: Israeli settlers
protesting eviction. The
Hebrew says: Begin
= traitor.   SHALOM BAR TAL
Right: Re'uma and
Sha'ul at a surprise
party for Ezer   "24 PLUS"

harnessed to a wagon, its nostrils widening when it hears the call of battle." Need I name the speaker? Arik Sharon, of course.

No decision had yet been reached on how to complete the operation when a report reached me from Northern Command headquarters: the township of Tibnin had surrendered, its inhabitants hoisting white flags. Tibnin lies outside the six-mile zone marked out for our operation, beyond which we had not planned to advance. Tibnin's example was soon followed by numerous other villages north of our operational area. Even so, we might not have pushed on were it not for the intervention of the United Nations. When we learned that the Security Council was deliberating whether to send a UN force to southern Lebanon, it was suggested that we advance to the Litani, ensuring that the UN units would take control of the whole area between the river and our border, while the terrorists would have to pull back their forces north of the river. Both the prime minister and I approved of this proposal.

"Push on toward the Litani without delay!" The chief of staff sent the order from the prime minister's home in Jerusalem to the General Staff and the headquarters of Northern Command. We decided to complete our occupation of the area by the time the Security Council had convened to make a decision.

"I propose," said Motta, "that we change the name of the operation." From that moment on, it was referred to as "Operation Litani."

I have never believed that "eating sharpens the appetite." Nevertheless, I was now eager to chalk up additional successes. Since our forces were approaching the Litani, I contemplated the possibility of bringing the whole operation to a close with an imposing final chord, which would signal the complete downfall of the terrorists.

"What about Tyre?" I demanded.

Situated on the Mediterranean shore, Tyre is southern Lebanon's most important population center—though few of its native citizens now remained in the large, white town; those who'd left had been replaced by terrorists.

"If I get the planes and artillery, I'm prepared to take Tyre," said Yanush. "It's a key town. I expect the terrorists will resist and the inhabitants will flee."

We were standing on the top of a high hill, with Tyre below us. It looked deserted and shattered after months of battering by artillery and airplanes. A long snake of black asphalt caught my attention.

"That's the Beirut road!" I recalled.

Memories of my youth came flooding back to me. That was the

route we used to take for our weekends in Beirut. When had I last been to the Lebanese capital? When I was seventeen!

Motta Gur advised against our getting embroiled in capturing Tyre. We had learned from experience that combat in built-up areas is always difficult, with many casualties. It was pointed out that the Syrian army—inactive until now—would feel compelled to respond to our occupation of the city.

I dropped the idea.

My involvement in Lebanon did not prevent me from keeping a close watch on Israel's quieter border. I gave orders to step up our vigilance and keep a sharp eye on Egyptian reactions: military activity, official statements, and media comments. I was curious to see how the Egyptians would respond. From our point of view, the operation in Lebanon was a test of Egyptian intentions. Would the Egyptians react strongly or remain silent?

After our message was conveyed by way of Zahava, the first Egyptian response was chilly, although it could have been worse: "We do not welcome your stay in Lebanon. Whatever you have done so far, it is important that you pull out quickly. A rapid withdrawal will further peace."

This lukewarm Egyptian response to Operation Litani inspired me with an idea that belonged to the realm of fantasy. Nevertheless, I suggested that the head of our military intelligence, Shlomo Gazit, brief Egyptian War Minister Gamasy and provide him with up-to-date assessments on the situation in Lebanon. Our offer was accepted—a pleasant surprise.

"Thank you for your briefings," Gamasy replied to one of our messages. "We, too, are prepared to answer your questions—if we are asked. By the way," he added, "what is the make of the Zodiac boat used by the coastal road terrorists?"

The talks and discussions about the stationing of UN units in southern Lebanon led me to meet the head of the UN force in the Middle East—Finnish General Enzio Siilasvuo, an affable man who saw his job as providing good services without any pretense of being the world's policeman. We helped him a great deal.

The other person I met was UN Secretary General Dr. Kurt Waldheim—one of the most unpleasant men I have ever had the doubtful pleasure of encountering. He was hostile and chilly; he'd learned nothing and understood less.

Operation Litani brought our forces great achievements—as well as considerable criticism. Planning and execution were marked by mistakes—some stemming from our failure to foresee the extension of the arena beyond the six-mile zone near the border. We should have blocked the terrorists' escape route. Too many of them got away by the skin of their teeth—even though several hundred of their fighters were killed. There was too much firing into civilian population centers—even though these were precisely the places where the terrorists were sheltered; in one case, three of our paratroopers were killed while a white flag was hoisted in front of them.

The operation's objective was correct. However, in retrospect, there are several things I would have done differently.

Southern Lebanon is no longer what it was before Operation Litani. Admittedly, the terrorists have moved back into the region south of the river, but in much smaller numbers. With their bases demolished, they are no longer capable of building up an independent strategic foothold like the one they held in the past.

The Christians have tightened their control of the area around them. Their enclaves—formerly separated—have been unified into a single continuous entity, occupying extensive areas along the Israeli border and thus forming a "security cordon." Our heightened cooperation with the Christian militia has given our forces greater freedom of movement and action in southern Lebanon, where they can protect the Israeli border. In preventing terrorist excursions into Israel, our troops are now assisted by the Christian militias, which operate in southern Lebanon in a manner that reminds me of the Westerns I used to watch in my youth: there is no government, no taxes, no economic development plans.

But there is a sheriff.

His name is Saad Haddad. I always saw him more as a television star than a soldier, having first become acquainted with him by way of the small screen. During the years of fighting in southern Lebanon, he was the sole authoritative spokesman for the Christian forces; he made almost nightly appearances on our television news, threatening to dethrone Israeli telecaster Chaim Yavin from his position at the top of the viewers' popularity poll.

It was Haddad's English that drew my attention. He used the simplest words to express the most elemental and powerful desires: human freedom and dignity.

Haddad is a Catholic from the township of Merj 'Uyun, near the Israeli border. He came back to southern Lebanon as an army officer after attending training courses in France and the United

States—though he retained little affection for his hosts in either country: "I don't like them," he told me once. "The only thing that interests them is the price of gas."

As a child, he had collected clothes for the Palestinian refugees of the 1948 war. During his military service, he stood out as a courageous officer, taking part in clashes with our forces; on one occasion, he fired at one of our troop carriers.

Now Haddad has succeeded in uniting thousands of Christians and Shi'ite Muslims under his command—while his former colleagues in the Lebanese army denounce him as traitor, quisling, careerist.

"I'm a simple man," he says.

His home in Merj 'Uyun looks out on beautiful scenery, but he can see nothing of it from within: the windows are blocked up with sandbags, giving the house the appearance of a war room. His family—his wife Therese and his five daughters—live on the ground floor and in the shelter.

"I believe in our victory," he used to tell me at difficult moments. "If not—this will be my burial place."

Maintaining the tradition established by previous defense ministers—Moshe Dayan and Shimon Peres—I did my utmost to assist the Lebanese Christian minority. Nevertheless, I differ with many Israelis in my belief that our future depends on links with the Muslim world whose hundreds of millions of believers surround us on all sides. It would be an error for Israel to rely overmuch on ties with other Middle East minorities just because we, too, are a minority in the region, with supposed interests in common. Our exceptional attitude toward the Lebanese Christians is for humanitarian reasons; being a minority ourselves, we cannot bear to see the pain and suffering of another minority. As a Jew and as a member of the human race, I found it hard to hear half a million Lebanese Christians begging for help against the threat of annihilation hanging over them while the Christian world—including the Vatican—remained silent.

The Lebanese Christian leaders of all ages—from thirty to eighty—present their case with friendship and with eloquence. They have always seen Israel as all powerful. Not infrequently, I was regretfully obliged to disappoint them.

They have paid a high price for their willingness to defend life and dignity against forces vastly superior to their own: the Syrian army, the Palestinian terrorist organizations, and the Lebanese Muslims. I always bore in mind that aside from its token participation in the 1948 war, their country has never entered the battle-field against Israel.

It has often been stated that Lebanon will be the second Arab state to make peace with Israel. However, to bring that about, another Arab country would have to be first.

A few weeks before, it had seemed that Egypt was willing to take the plunge. Now, after the snags bedeviling the peace talks and the tension created by Operation Litani, did anything remain of that willingness?

22

"THE BLOOD BANK OF THE ARAB WORLD"

Paradoxically enough, it was a warlike move on the part of Israel that convinced me of Egypt's genuine commitment to the peace process. Our sortie into Lebanon—the largest operation our forces had undertaken since the end of the Yom Kippur War—may not have evoked Egyptian applause, but neither did it prompt our neighbors to inundate us with curses and imprecations, as had been the case in the past. For what may have been the first time, an Israeli military operation found Cairo close-mouthed.

We could have simply allowed it to pass as self-understood, but I thought it only right to let the Egyptians know that the change in their policies and behavior had been noted. When a long message was sent from my office to the Egyptian war minister, clarifying the situation in our Lebanese operation, I added a couple of lines: "We are following your views and utterances regarding the crisis which has occurred," I wrote. "We are gratified by the restraint of those utterances."

Not all my cabinet colleagues saw it my way. One or two found Sadat's behavior quite normal and everyday, as if that was how he should always have acted. In the course of private conversations with several of them, I sketched out how the Lebanon operation had exacerbated Sadat's predicament in the Arab world, but I still could not persuade them to appreciate Egypt's forbearance.

To me, recent events were an important test for future relations between Egypt and Israel.

"After all"—I pointed out during our deliberations—"one of the most important questions about any agreement is its potential for bearing up and remaining effective under the pressure of incidents in other sectors."

"Big deal!" one minister commented scornfully in English.

My growing inclination to see the positive side of our peace contacts turned some of the ministers against me, making me the target for the complaints or wisecracks they thought up whenever some nonsense was mouthed in Cairo. Some ministers related to me as if I were the Egyptian ambassador to Jerusalem, the ombudsman, and the healer of every ailment afflicting the peace talks—all rolled into one.

"I wonder if you know what Sadat meant when he said. . . ?" Questions in this note of malicious glee were directed at me whenever the Egyptian president adopted a harsher tone or stepped up his attacks and charges.

I did my utmost to understand the Egyptian views—with the counsel of Orientalists as well as heads of our military intelligence—but even the greatest experts proved incapable of answering all my queries. There were times I, too, occasionally found Egyptian behavior bizarre, to put it mildly. On one occasion, I tried to send a personal present to the proprietor of an Egyptian souvenir store who had shown great courtesy to my wife Re'uma. But the Egyptians refused to transmit the small gift on the absurd pretext that Egyptian citizens are not permitted to accept presents from abroad. Another time, the Egyptians withheld permission for an Israeli military rabbi to come to Cairo to prepare the Passover Seder meal for the small Israeli delegation of Zahava. They also refused to let us send matzos and wine to Zahava and to the small Jewish communities of Cairo and Alexandria. On the eve of Passover, we were forced to use a teleprinter to transmit the text of the Passover Haggadah from Tel Aviv to Cairo so that our delegation celebrating the festival in one of the rooms of the Tahara Palace could relate how the Lord of Hosts of Israel had multiplied afflictions upon the Egyptian pharaoh and his armies.

I attributed this surly behavior to a desire on the part of the Egyptians—Sadat himself, perhaps—to demonstrate their displeasure over the deadlock in the peace talks. However, when it was proposed that we kick up a fuss about the way the Egyptians were behaving, I rejected the idea outright.

"There are mines under the road to peace," I said. "If we step on them, they'll blow up. But we can also dismantle them."

I could hardly blame the members of the cabinet. On the whole, they had very little say in matters connected with the peace talks— through no fault of their own. Frequently briefed after the act or very shortly before it took place, they were denied any opportunity to modify or delay decisions adopted by the prime minister and the foreign minister and quite often by me as defense minister.

At the end of March 1978—early spring in Israel—peace looked threatened. Cairo, Jerusalem, and Washington vied with one another in making every conceivable blunder. I knew little of the considerations and assessments guiding the other two capitals, but personal factors seemed to color national considerations in the decision-making process in Jerusalem. I was one of the participants in that process—one side of the triangle completed by Begin and Dayan.

Dayan's enthusiastic allegiance to the Begin cabinet convinced me that my former brother-in-law harbored plans that he was resolved to put into effect at almost any price. His resilience and determination in the face of the demonstrations directed against him by the bereaved families of Yom Kippur War victims, as well as by the former Labor party colleagues he had abandoned, made me feel sure that he was firmly committed to extricating the state of Israel from the tribulations resulting from the 1973 war.

I was not wrong. Sometime later, I learned that while Begin had been forming his cabinet and holding talks with Dayan before the latter's acceptance of the foreign affairs portfolio, Dayan was already submitting his proposals for a peace agreement with Egypt. Even before I knew this, I was not surprised when I heard rumors about Dayan's ideas for a peace settlement. In 1971, while Dayan had served as defense minister in the cabinet of Golda Meir, he'd emerged as the driving force behind the proposal for a large-scale interim agreement with Egypt. He had proposed then that Israel allow the Egyptians to reopen the Suez Canal for navigation and restore life to normal in the Canal cities as a first step toward an overall settlement. His initiative was rejected by Golda Meir. Less than two years later, Egyptian troops crossed the 200-yard-wide Suez Canal, subjecting the state of Israel—and Dayan personally—to the most painful and terrible setback either had ever suffered.

On joining Begin's cabinet, Dayan intended to resume where he had left off in 1971. In his view, everyone wanted a settlement: Sadat knew another war would bring him no benefit, and he was utterly disillusioned with the Russians. Carter was apprehensive about a further oil embargo as well as increases in fuel prices; he was in favor of a comprehensive settlement and of a homeland for the Palestinians. As for Israel—the answer was obvious.

Almost from the first moment, Begin kept his door open to Dayan far more than to any of the other ministers. I was not particularly impressed by the friendship that sprang up between the two men. I told my confidants that it would be short-lived. Even before joining the cabinet, Dayan had succeeded in twisting Begin's arm. Dayan had made his membership conditional upon the prime minister's willingness not to extend Israeli sovereignty to Judea and Samaria—even though this was Begin's lifelong dream. The prime minister does not enjoy having his arm twisted. However, when someone does succeed in doing so, Begin does not yell at the top of his voice. He remains silent—and stores everything in his memory. Begin consented to foot the bill for Dayan's entry ticket into the cabinet, but he would grab the first available opportunity to settle accounts with the foreign minister and show him who was cock of the roost.

The opportunity was not long in coming. In the fall of 1977, when Dayan—acting on behalf of the Israeli government—had consented to the inclusion of a clause in the working paper he'd worked out with the U.S. administration stating that "anonymous Palestinian representatives will take part in negotiations on their future," Begin hit the ceiling. He had been hospitalized at the time with a heart attack and had known nothing of Dayan's move. For the second time within a few months, Dayan had drawn him into making a far-reaching political concession.

"I do not intend to be confronted with any more *faits accomplis!*" the prime minister had thundered from his bed in Tel Aviv's Ichilov Hospital to Dayan in Washington. From that day, Begin put a ban on any agreement being concluded without his approval. The prime minister would be the only one to pronounce the yeas and nays.

Dayan has his own modes of operation, which have characterized his career for many years. It is his habit to send out feelers and test the ground while avoiding any head-on confrontations. He has adopted Mao Tse-tung's maxim: "When the enemy attacks—retreat; when he rests—regroup; when he forms up for defense—rest; and when he tires—attack!" It was this approach that led him to back down from a confrontation with Golda Meir over his proposal for an interim agreement in 1971.

My own style is quite different: I always laid my cards face up on the cabinet table. I said it all, loudly and not always in the most elegant language. Some of my cabinet colleagues did not like my style. They retain a weakness for the hints and nuances so characteristic of political life. I could never get used to it. "I am no politician!" I would concede.

As the peace process went downhill in the winter of 1978, my expressions grew more and more peppery. Cabinet colleagues naturally hastened to quote them, not always accurately, to the media, with the principle purpose of showing me up as reckless and irresponsible toward Israel's security and future. The atmosphere at cabinet meetings grew progressively murkier, but I did not let it get to me.

I used to quote the Arabic saying: "The dogs bark, but the caravan proceeds on its way."

However, the caravan was at a standstill: the talks, the discussions, the contacts. Peace had run aground. "Our next visit to Cairo will be on the turrets of Arik Sharon's tanks," I predicted with doleful exaggeration. In the wake of Sadat's courageous mission to Jerusalem, the idea of another war was a nightmare.

As could be expected, the American capital turned its most surly face upon Menachem Begin and Moshe Dayan when the two men came to the White House for their meeting with President Carter at the end of March 1978. The colorful reception laid on for them on the White House lawn, with the strains of the Israeli national anthem filling their ears, could not drown out the discordant notes coming from the administration and the president. My brief sojourn in Washington had taught me that the melodies of the White House political ensemble could have some very jarring overtones. The Egyptian president had reached an understanding with the president of the United States; Begin, having begun his career as prime minister with the proud declaration that there was no further need for strategic coordination with the White House, now found himself confronting an inevitable coalition: Carter and Sadat. Carter had changed the tone as well as the substance of his statements. Not content with his role of honest broker, he now tried to influence the course of the negotiations, proffering solutions comparable with those of Sadat in their inflexibility.

Begin was shaken when he left the White House for Israel. After having placed Carter on an almost equal footing with his own teacher and mentor, Jabotinsky, after having boasted of Carter's praises for his peace plan—a somber Begin now described his talks with the U.S. president as "the hardest of my life." Carter and Begin had vied with one another in threatening to employ what each one viewed as his own secret weapon: Congress, the Senate, the American Jewish community.

My own attitude toward American Jewry has always been ambivalent. On the one hand, the world's largest Jewish community enjoys my admiration and respect. On the other, I am sorry that this cargo of human resources was unloaded on the wrong shore.

When waves of Jewish emigrants fled eastern Europe at the end of the nineteenth and beginning of the twentieth century, no more than a tiny trickle reached the Promised Land. Over 90 percent of the emigrants decided to try their luck in the United States—a land whose banner was emblazoned with the principles of freedom and equality that offered newcomers, after centuries of enslavement, discrimination, and persecution, the opportunity of using their talents and energies.

The manner in which the Jews have integrated into American society is one of the great success stories. The United States welcomed them as Jews. While the Jewish communities in Europe were forced to take the route of assimilation to be accepted by the society about them, American Jews did not have to abandon their religion, their origins, or their people. It is gratifying that most of the five or six million American Jews identify with Zionism and the state of Israel. In good days and bad, Israel largely depends on the economic, political, and moral fortitude of U.S. Jewry.

The American electoral system gives the larger states in presidential contests a great deal of clout. With the Jews concentrated in the more populous states—New York, Pennsylvania, Illinois, Michigan, and Texas—the "Jewish vote" was long believed to be an important key to political power. Many Israeli cabinets thought they could use the "Jewish vote" to put pressure on American politicians and officials. There was a measure of truth to this: many American official decisions were influenced by the activities of the Israeli lobby in Washington or by the political activism of Jewish organizations acting on signals from Jerusalem.

I have never undervalued the Jewish vote; but we must not overrate its importance—particularly since American Jews are not at Israel's unconditional beck and call. I believe that American Jews would be prepared to do battle if they felt Israel's existence imperiled. They would fight to prevent any harm to vital Israeli interests—as they perceive and define "vital Israeli interests." But I do not believe Israel will succeed in enlisting the political power of American Jews for the achievement of objectives they themselves do not fully share. One of my main disagreements with the prime minister was over my warning that U.S. Jews would reject any attempt to make use of them as a means of forcing their administration to consent to a settlement program that had no clear military purpose. I saw no point in placing them in such a dilemma over their support for Israel. Begin, of course, thought otherwise. Sometimes he seemed to see American Jews as an integral part of the state of Israel.

In the event of a conflict between American national interests and Israeli national interests, I do not believe that American Jews will automatically rally behind Israel. On the contrary: apart from a situation where—heaven forbid—Israel's existence is genuinely endangered, U.S. Jews will support whatever they perceive as the national interest of their own country.

I found backing for this assessment in the arguments over the three-way deal on planes when the Carter administration had proposed to supply planes to Israel, Saudi Arabia, and Egypt as a single package. The Israeli government decided to recruit American Jews for a campaign against this linkage of plane deliveries to Israel and to the Arabs. The Israeli lobby in Washington set to work to try and foil the deal, but it functioned hesitantly and with reluctance. The Carter administration contended—with considerable justice—that plane deliveries to all three countries were part of a regional defense plan and of U.S. global strategy. In attempting to block arms supplies to Saudi Arabia, the Jews were widely perceived as supporting petty Israeli interests over global American interests. I was not surprised that the Israeli lobby failed in its campaign.

The 1980 presidential elections delivered a further blow to the belief in the power of American Jewry. From an Israeli viewpoint, Jimmy Carter had been a good president. He was the prime mover in the conclusion of the Camp David agreements and in the Israeli-Egyptian peace treaty that resulted. He granted Israel lavish economic and military aid. There was no reason why American Jews should not have supported him, as they had supported other Democratic candidates like Humphrey, Johnson, and Kennedy— and Carter himself in 1976. But that was not how it worked out. Only 54 percent of Jewish voters opted for Carter—a relatively low proportion of Jewish backing for a Democratic candidate.

If I do harbor any concerns, they are over the future development of the Jewish community in the United States. I am worried by statistical data indicating that the rate of intermarriage is very high and that the Jews are an ethnic minority in the United States whose numbers are dwindling from year to year.

It is difficult to predict the relationship between Israel and U.S. Jewry in the years to come. American Jews have been—and will be—the warmest and most faithful friends Israel has anywhere in the world. I know they will do everything possible to guarantee Israel's existence, security, and integrity. They have proved that by years of Zionist activity, generous donations, and political backing. However, we in Israel must not overestimate their ability to help us; nor can we expect them to do anything to harm their standing within the United States, the country they view as their native land.

President Sadat's success in casting his spell over Carter and on American public opinion affected the Jewish community, too. For perhaps the first time, many American Jewish leaders began to see Sadat and his country as the aggrieved party in the Middle East conflict. In view of Sadat's success in capturing position after position and in undermining Israel's strongholds, I urged my colleagues in the cabinet—and their leader—to reconsider their actions.

However, no one listened. Clinging to every clause and subclause of his program, Begin refused to give any consideration to our difficult international predicament. As far as Israel's prime minister was concerned, Carter had praised the Israeli plan, and if the American president now changed his mind, that was his own problem.

The Egyptian leader was losing patience over the snail's pace at which talks were progressing. I shared his belief that, as in battle, swiftness in promoting the peace negotiations would bring benefits: seeing the achievements, the other Arab states would follow in Sadat's footsteps.

"Ezer!" Sadat once said to me in an almost pleading tone. "If we go about it in the right way, the Arab world will follow. Egypt is still the leader of the Arab world, but if we don't move quickly toward peace, we shall lose that position, too."

The outcry from the other Arab countries, the PLO's activities, the resurgence of Egypt's domestic opposition, Israel's rejection of almost every proposal he put forward—all these made Sadat's position increasingly difficult. He grew embittered and withdrawn, neglecting his custom of occasional outings to meet the common people of Egypt. The number of bodyguards around him grew. People who had met him recently told me he was changed. The spark had gone out of him.

Like Sadat, I, too, watched the last flickering hopes of peace dying away while I flung myself into supervising our operations in Lebanon.

A coded cable transmitted by our Zahava station in Cairo rekindled the flame. My colleagues at GHQ and in the Defense Ministry saw no prospect of the peace talks being renewed as long as our forces were engaged in active operations in Lebanon, but the top-secret cable confounded all our predictions: the Egyptian president was asking me to come and meet him on March 30, 1978.

I was overjoyed. If the talks resumed, there was still some hope for peace. I brought the unexpected invitation to the notice of the prime minister. On the other end of the line, Begin was angry and offended after having been subjected to an abusive campaign by Egypt's officially inspired press.

Begin sighed that there was nothing to be done. Sadat didn't like him, he liked Weizman better, Begin said.

If it were possible, I think the prime minister would have vetoed my journey to Egypt. However, neither he nor his government could afford to do any such thing. Instead, he summoned the ministers for a consultation.

Such ministerial conclaves were of very little value: they had the atmosphere of a debating club. While Begin gave each person a chance to have his say, it was obvious that a decision had already been reached by the prime minister—alone or in consultation with Dayan. I went along with this masquerade of democracy, playing my role so as not to provide a pretext for anyone to foil the impending peace talks. In many cases, these deliberations were a complete waste of time.

At the time of Sadat's coded cable to me, Cairo was packed with Arab foreign ministers gathering for an Arab League conference. An invitation to Israel's defense minister, while Israeli forces were stationed on Lebanese soil, was an open challenge to the Arab world.

Again, Sadat was seizing the initiative: he dictated the moves, laid out the course, and took us by surprise.

"Gentlemen!" I addressed the ministerial consultation. "The situation is rather delicate, and the Egyptians have requested that there be no prior announcement of the meeting."

The ministers nodded their comprehension. I hoped peace was important enough to keep them—just this once—from leaking the news to the media.

"What am I to tell the Egyptians?" I went on.

"Tell them 'Shalom,' " quipped Finance Minister Simcha Ehrlich. Our political predicament had robbed me of any desire to laugh. Such a long time had elapsed without any direct contacts between us and the Egyptians that I thought we would have to start all over again.

"The defense minister should say there is no party in Israel that will consent to dismantle the settlements," said Begin, setting the intransigent note that was to dominate the discussion. " 'What you Egyptians want is total withdrawal and the establishment of a Palestinian state'—tell them. 'Both are unacceptable. Are you prepared to adopt any other terms?' "

I reminded myself that Begin's strident tone was the natural outcome of the pressures to which he was being subjected—American, Egyptian, European, as well as domestic Israeli. Tension was high: the atmosphere seemed explosive. It was important to defuse the bomb.

"Shall I propose a meeting between you and Sadat?" I asked Begin.

Begin bridled. "At this stage? No!" he thundered. He went on to justify his negative reply by saying he thought the proposal would be refused, putting him to shame.

I sensed that he did not trust me to present the meeting in a proper manner. In the atmosphere of suspicion he was creating about me, I could be of little use to Begin. What could I tell him? That I represented him better than he imagined? That my last meeting with the Egyptian president had ended with Sadat's saying: "Help Begin. I know you are loyal to him"?

I repeated my proposal. This time, Begin gave in. To my relief, I was empowered to sound out Sadat as to whether he would welcome a visit to Egypt by the Israeli prime minister.

From the very first moment, Trade and Industry Minister Yigal Hurwitz had shown no trust in Sadat. "Ezer has been invited to Cairo," he explained, "because they imagine him to be closest to them. He should tell Sadat to find a formula which doesn't take us back to the 1967 borders. . . . After the prime minister's visit to the United States, and with Carter taking sides with Egypt, Sadat's mood is sky high, and his eyes are in the clouds. His self-confidence will grow unless someone restores him to sanity."

Fortunately, few of the other ministers shared Hurwitz's oversimplified, unsophisticated view, which saw the world exclusively in black and white. However, there was an unarticulated measure of mistrust—possibly mingled with envy—toward me. Some ministers complained that my reports on my conversations in Egypt were incomplete. Others accused me of attributing political significance to meaningless remarks.

Moshe Dayan, as is his wont, launched into his onslaught in a roundabout manner. "In my view," he said, "Ezer should not consent to private talks à deux. I, for example, always take someone else along." It was an elegant way of telling me that doubt was being cast upon my word. I got the hint. If Dayan was voicing more than his own private opinion, I was under heavy suspicion. What did they imagine I was telling Sadat when we met together?

"They're trying to catch me red-handed," I remarked to myself and my immediate neighbors at the cabinet table. I was suspected of selling out to the Egyptians, of disregarding cabinet decisions. I would have to do something to dispel their misgivings.

Looking around the cabinet room, my eye fell upon the man seated at my right. "I propose"—I blurted out as the idea hit me—"that Aharon Barak join me for tomorrow's meeting with Sadat."

Silence fell upon the room.

Law professor and attorney general, Aharon Barak was the cabinet's legal adviser. He is a man of extensive learning and considerable independence, decisive, energetic, and firm on matters of principle. I was pleased to see his political influence grow from day to day, so much so that some people called him—jokingly but with a degree of justice—"the director general of the state."

I have a great deal of respect for Barak: he is wise, clear of thought and word, knowledgeable, and sharp-witted. His somewhat sloppy appearance—hair unkempt, tie awry, his pants not matching his jacket—give him the look of an absent-minded professor. I loved the ink stains on his fingertips: while listening to cabinet deliberations, he was in the habit of doodling on scraps of paper, emitting occasional sighs, which I interpreted as his way of asking himself what on earth he was doing here. We had inherited Barak from the previous regime, and I fancied that the present cabinet and the atmosphere characterizing its meetings were not to his liking.

Aharon! I thought. *He'll be my state's witness!*

"It is agreed that Professor Barak shall accompany the defense minister," the prime minister said with unconcealed gratification.

It was a short flight from Cairo International Airport to Sadat's home near the city, and I was in good spirits. The television teams awaiting my arrival at the airport and outside Sadat's house were a favorable sign of his determination to proceed with the peace process in spite of the awkward position he and his country were in from our operations in Lebanon. He was inviting me to see him even though the Egyptian press was critical of him.

"Weizman's hands are smeared with blood," they wrote.

Regardless of such sentiments, Sadat shook my hand warmly. In a way I felt I was back home.

"I welcome the defense minister, and I rejoice at his arrival," said Sadat. "You ought to know there was opposition to your coming here. King Khalid of Saudi Arabia was against it. My own Foreign Ministry was also against it. But I wanted to see you."

I had come to comprehend Sadat's growing difficulties on all fronts. Within the Arab world, he had to contend with the broadly based Refusal Front, which had succeeded in winning over the moderate states whose support was so vital for his policy, such as Saudi Arabia and even Morocco, which had hosted the first direct contacts between Egypt and Israel. On the domestic front, the opposition within his own country was growing more vociferous. I had heard of several attempts by students to hold rallies against Sadat at various places in Cairo. The left-wing National Unity party had sharply denounced the peace initiative. "It will divide Egypt from the Arab world," its leaders warned.

Opposition of a more threatening nature—from Sadat's point of view no less than ours—came from the Egyptian Foreign Ministry. I first became aware of it at the Ismailia conference when Sadat was to some extent in the thrall of the "Palestinian group" headed by Boutros Ghali and Osama el-Baz, as well as a number of jurists. These men handled Egypt's contacts with the Arab world—more than Sadat—and they served as his lightning conductors. The talks showed up the Foreign Ministry heads in their inflexibility: they saw no prospect of peace without a solution of the Palestinian problem. The hard-hitting line followed by the "Palestinian group" in the Egyptian Foreign Ministry had led us to a renewed appraisal of the situation, in which Sadat was no longer seen as all powerful.

"We have to reach some decisions," I told Sadat. "Unfortunately, there is at present a misunderstanding between you and my prime minister. You must understand that we, too, have our problems. Without harming your high standing in the Arab countries, we have to find a way of enabling you to be the first to conclude a peace treaty with Israel."

Whether or not Sadat would agree to sign a separate peace treaty with Israel was one of the central bones of contention in our deliberations and assessments. Statements he made on various occasions had given us to understand that he would not consent to a separate peace agreement. However, without his ever putting it in so many words, he had impressed me as being prepared to resume the peace process even if he were left on his own, without the other Arab states coming to the negotiation table. With such enormous significance being attached to every single word and with the whole Arab world listening in intently, I sought every possible way of avoiding the use of the phrase "separate agreement." "Why don't we call it a 'first agreement'?" Chief of Staff Motta Gur had proposed before I'd left. I bought the idea.

"The Sinai is going to be under Egyptian sovereignty," I reminded Sadat. "Some people criticize us for being overhasty on this point. I think we can reach agreement over the Sinai, but Israel will not be able to forfeit a presence in the West Bank and Gaza. On the Golan Heights, we have no claims to sovereignty, but we shall argue for our presence up there, too. As for Judea and Samaria—Jordan has no right to sovereignty there, but we haven't exercised our own claim to sovereignty, either. Therefore, let us seek a solution. I presume it won't be acceptable to every Israeli and to every Arab; it won't let the Jordanians into the West Bank. Both you and the Americans have said there won't be a Palestinian state. We can talk about a federation, or something similar, with Jordan. We don't want to rule over the Arabs of the West Bank. We don't want to take their land. Why should the problem of Judea and Samaria constitute an obstacle to a peace treaty between Israel and Egypt?"

When angered, Sadat is in the habit of flinging his head backward, saying a loud: "No! No! No!" That is what he did now. "Even if we resolve the problem of the Sinai, without solving the Palestinian problem, there is no peace!" he warned. "I understand your concern over the West Bank, and I know Israel has a security problem there, that it's a matter of life and death for her. But without solving the Palestinian problem, there will be no peace. A separate agreement with Egypt will not bring peace."

Whenever the Egyptian president referred to the Palestinian problem, I waited to see whether he would use that phrase almost every Israeli dreads: a Palestinian state. But he did not use it. In fact, I have never heard him express outright support for the establishment of a Palestinian state. In the circles surrounding the Egyptian president as well as in Egyptian public opinion at large, I have frequently sensed an aversion for the Palestinians, particularly for the Palestine Liberation Organization, whose leaders Sadat called "cabaret warriors."

"We don't want them!" I was once told by an Egyptian politician of the first rank. "We're sick of them! Take them off our hands!"

Years of war have given the Israelis a stereotyped portrait of "the typical Arab"; seen from the Israeli point of view, all Arabs resemble one another. The sand curtain thrust aside by Sadat's peace initiative revealed a different set of notions: the Egyptians do not always view themselves as thoroughgoing Arabs. They feel a link to their pharaonic ancestors, who were not Arabs. Egypt boasts of five thousand years of history, beginning thirty-five hundred years before the birth of Islam.

Nasser tended to highlight the Arab characteristics of his people and their allegiance to the Arab world of which he regarded himself the leader. Sadat is more modest. Under his rule, greater emphasis is placed on Egyptian national characteristics. It was Sadat who restored the name Egypt; under Nasser, the country was known as the United Arab Republic.

Resentments against the Palestinians stem from an additional source: the Egyptians view them as the root cause of all their country's troubles, particularly its economic malaise. It was on behalf of the Palestinians that the Egyptians plunged into a series of wars for which they paid a terrible price: more than a hundred thousand dead and wounded.

"We are sick of being the blood bank of the Arab world," an Egyptian politician told me as he cursed the PLO leaders for the life of luxury they lead. The Egyptians view themselves as having been betrayed by the "ingrates" of the PLO.

"I understand that the Palestinian problem is important," I ventured tentatively, looking hard at Sadat. "But a first agreement could promote peace. You have to decide whether you're going for the whole game or only part of it. If the Palestinian problem has to be solved, then the autonomy plan we've proposed may solve it. Our proposal guarantees them self-rule. They can find some link to Jordan; if Jordan consents to a separate peace with us, that would greatly encourage Israeli willingness on the subject. You must understand our insecurity. The average Israeli doesn't feel safe. An agreement with Egypt will contribute to his sense of well-being."

"A separate peace would harm us all," Sadat retorted. "The Soviets will say: 'Sadat wanted a separate peace, leaving the rest of the Arab states to their fate. He has a secret agreement with the United States and Israel.' That will serve no one, neither me nor you."

My most serious differences with my cabinet colleagues—principally with Moshe Dayan—hinged on the extent that Sadat considered himself bound to a solution of the Palestinian problem. In our deliberations, I reiterated that the faster we understood Sadat's problems and responded to his demands—while the Arab world's pressure upon him was still relatively mild—the less would be required to satisfy him. At Ismailia, all he had wanted on the Palestinian issue was a general declaration of principles, which were scarcely binding upon anyone.

"He wants a fig leaf," I repeated over and over again. "If we don't give it to him now, the Palestinian problem will become a branch, and then it will grow into a tree. . . ."

The other ministers may have enjoyed my botanical imagery,

but they did not heed my advice. Moshe Dayan contended that
Sadat would want something far more concrete.

"He'll be satisfied with the autonomy scheme we've proposed!" I
assured my fellow ministers. "But it's got to be proper autonomy!"
By the restrictions and qualifications they had imposed, Begin and
the others had reduced the autonomy plan to a caricature of
genuine self-rule.

"What is the solution, then?" I now asked the Egyptian president.

"In Ismailia," Sadat recalled, "I thought we were setting out
together on the road toward peace and friendship in the region.
But I am disappointed in Begin. I can't say a thing to him without
him going to the newspapers and telling them everything. We have
a long way to go before we can convince the Arab world. We also
have a long way to go with the Jewish people. Try to win the hearts
of the Arab people: no Arab, from any country, will give you
friendship like Egypt. You will find it very hard with the Syrians,
with the Ba'ath party above all. The test for both of us is the
Palestinian problem. I must tell my people that I have induced the
Israelis to withdraw from the West Bank. I have excluded the PLO
from my lexicon. By their own behavior, they have excluded themselves from the negotiations. But I can say this only to you—not to
Begin because the next day Begin would announce: 'Sadat has
excluded the PLO!' I have to be able to tell the Arabs: 'The Arabs of
the West Bank and Gaza will be able to shape their future, and the
Israelis will leave.' I don't care whether Hussein comes in or not.
The West Bank and Gaza should be demilitarized. Any solution
must guarantee your security. We shall try to find a suitable formula."

"From your point of view—who is to take charge of Judea,
Samaria, and Gaza? Who will rule there?"

"If Jordan enters into the negotiations—Jordan, the representatives of the local population, and you."

"From that, I understand there won't be a Palestinian state."

"Right! But if I say so to Begin, he will proclaim it from the
rooftops the following day. But I can tell *you:* No state! And a small
number of military strong points for Israel."

"There will be no sovereignty over Judea and Samaria," I said.
"Neither Israeli nor Jordanian. And there won't be an independent
state, either. We have settlements there. They've got to stay; we
have close links with the soil. My own mother was born in a farm-
ing community, in Rishon Le-Zion. My family has had its roots in
Israel for a hundred years. The healthy Jew is one who lives on the
soil. No Israeli government could uproot a settler from his land. It

must be possible for Jews to continue to live in Judea and Samaria: we'll need our army there."

"We must revert to the pre-1967 situation," Sadat replied, "with the West Bank linked to Jordan and Gaza to Egypt. In both cases, you will have an active role in protecting your security. The Palestinian state can wait."

We were seated in a splendid garden beneath a giant sycamore tree. I had heard a lot about this sycamore, referred to as "the tree of decision." Sadat had made some of his most crucial decisions while reclining in its shade. A large lawn stretched as far as the eye could see; alongside it stood an old colonial-style building. The presidential residence at Kanatar al-Hiriya stands at the edge of the ancient Nile dam known as "the barrage." Silence reigned all about us, in sharp contrast to Cairo's uproar. Aharon Barak sat at my side. Also with us were Vice President Hosni Mubarak and War Minister Gamasy; they did not join in the conversation without the president's permission—which he rarely granted.

"I want to free Israel of the responsibility," Sadat said with great decisiveness. "You must leave the occupied lands, just as long as each party reaches an agreement with you on the security problem. If you tell me: 'We have settlements,' I will reply; 'We can discuss them!' I won't consent to your army defending them. Join me in the administration. You must announce that you will withdraw as soon as the security problem is settled."

"There can be no discussion of total withdrawal from the West Bank!" I said.

Sadat did not give up. "It's enough if you say you are willing to withdraw," he said.

"Who will be the central administration in Judea and Samaria?" I wanted to know.

"There will be no Palestinian state! On the West Bank, you can talk with King Hussein. A legislative council and an executive council will be elected. Jordan and Israel will be represented on those councils. In Gaza, it will be Egypt and Israel."

"Suppose we find the suitable terms for a declaration," I said. "Will Hussein come along?"

"If he doesn't, I will share the responsibility with you. If the Arab world is angry with me, I will take it on myself. I will share responsibility for the West Bank because I want peace."

"The council will enact laws," Aharon Barak broke in. "Suppose it passes a law banning Jewish settlement?"

"Israel and Egypt will have the power of veto over any law. If an Arab is willing to sell his land to you, I have no objections. But you must proclaim your willingness to withdraw. As to the question of sovereignty—that will remain open. It won't be mine, and it won't be yours."

"And the daily life of the Arabs in Judea and Samaria—will it be the way it is now?"

"I agree to freedom of movement—of people and merchandise—between the West Bank and Gaza and Israel," Sadat replied. "If the Arabs want to work in Israel—let them! The problem is how it will look to the world. It must be seen that you have withdrawn. After your declaration of a full withdrawal, I promise that we shall solve everything."

"Your proposal resembles ours," I pointed out. "What's wrong with ours?"

"Your proposal implies a continuation of the occupation. It makes the occupation official."

"But we have specifically declared that the military administration will be revoked."

"No one will believe you!" Sadat said scornfully. "But when I come along together with you and say that this will be the arrangement, everyone in the Arab world will believe you. You must proclaim your withdrawal. If Hussein doesn't come to negotiate—you don't withdraw! When you do withdraw, it will be to military strong points."

Sadat always takes his time in conversation. He never seems pressed—and he has the knack of letting a guest feel that he, too, has all the time in the world. All the same, I felt that the hour had come to conclude. I asked Sadat how he foresaw the resumption of political contact. It was my intention to put out cautious feelers about a meeting between him and Begin.

But Sadat must have guessed what I had in mind. "We cannot conduct any contacts aside from your visit. Begin offends me. If it weren't for you, we would receive no one. When Begin says the settlements will remain and the Israeli army will defend them—that's terrible!"

"Begin did not intend to offend you. He is a courteous man with good manners—"

"You can't say that!" the president shot back.

"Mr. President, you ought to explain your ideas to Begin. He feels left out. There has to be an understanding between the two of you."

Sadat was not convinced.

"For the solution of our problem," he said, "it is not enough to use the ordinary politics of the ordinary parties. We don't have a normal problem. Its solution calls for a great man, and there has to be trust and confidence."

I tried my luck for the last time. "In my view," I remarked, "it would be desirable for Dayan to come here."

"Not yet. He doesn't keep secrets."

Sadat was not being entirely candid. My previous conversations with him had already convinced me that he is not interested in talking with Dayan. I tried to guess why. Perhaps the Egyptian president sees Dayan as the symbol of the past and of those Egyptian setbacks and defeats he wants to erase.

Summarizing my conversation with Sadat put me into a better mood. Like us, the Egyptian president was not interested in a Palestinian state; he was willing to leave our West Bank settlements in place; he would substitute for Hussein should the king refuse to take part in negotiations. I was gratified to have had Aharon Barak listening in on our conversation; without his testimony, no one in Israel would believe me.

An upholstered helicopter flew us back from the presidential residence to the Tahara Palace in Cairo's Heliopolis quarter. Approaching Almaza Airport, near Cairo, I saw in the distance the Egyptian air force base of Inshas.

In one of my encounters with Egyptian air force pilots, one of them—a senior officer—had stared at me as if he wanted to say something. I'd given him a reassuring look, and finally he plucked up the courage to address me.

"Sir," he said in a quiet tone. "In the 1967 war, I shot down an Israeli plane."

Since beginning my visits to Egypt, I have experienced this several times: the abrupt switch from talk of peace to the bitter memories of the war. All the same, I have yet to get used to it.

"I was on standby at our base in Inshas when your planes came over. I took off in my Mig-21 and attacked one of your Mirages. I saw the plane go up in flames, but the pilot managed to operate his ejector seat, and he parachuted down. I followed his descent. I was afraid that if he came down in a country area, the peasants would harm him. I immediately landed at my air base and got into a car to race to the place where he had come down. I got there—"

His face took on a mournful expression—or was it just my imagination? "I got there too late," he concluded sadly. "The villagers had killed the pilot."

I thought he had finished his story. I was struck by the peculiarity of it: an Egyptian air force pilot telling the Israeli minister of defense about the death in combat of an Israeli pilot—

"I know the name of the Israeli pilot," he added unexpectedly. "It was Ya'ir Neuman."

There was a choking sensation in my throat. I knew Ya'ir: a

lighthearted man with sharp wits, he had served as a pilot during the period in which I had commanded the air force. Ya'ir had achieved renown as one of only two Orthodox pilots in the air force. Because of this unique combination—combat pilot and religious observance—he had been interviewed frequently by the media. Before going out on a sortie, he was in the habit of reciting the "prayer for a journey." On the first day of the 1967 war, Neuman had taken part in two sorties; he was killed during the third. For a couple of months, he was posted as missing until his remains were finally discovered and given a Jewish burial. Five months later, his wife give birth to a son who was named for the father he would never see.

That evening's conversation at the Tahara Palace was a blend of business and idle chatter. Mustafa Khalil—secretary of the ruling party—sighed about Sadat's intention of dragging him into politics. Boutros Ghali complained of Egypt's isolation within the Arab world—without drawing too much sympathy from me. Israel has suffered from isolation for some thirty years, with Egypt setting the tone for the ostracism.

"Two million Egyptians are employed outside our borders," Ghali said. "They send home a lot of money. What will happen if they are expelled from the countries where they are working?"

"A friend of mine went on a pilgrimage to Mecca," Khalil broke in. "When she was about to return to Cairo, she phoned a travel agent. As soon as they heard her Egyptian accent, they slammed down the receiver."

I smiled, remarking that Egypt should be able to withstand these kinds of tribulations.

Professor Barak and War Minister Gamasy conducted a fruitful exchange. They withdrew for a long conversation, in the course of which Gamasy proposed secret talks between our two countries— to be held in Egypt, Israel, or anywhere else. If the sides so desired, the Americans could be brought in, he said. The aim of the talks would be to work out the details of the arrangements for the West Bank and Gaza and of the bilateral relations between Israel and Egypt. At the conclusion of the talks, two documents would be initialed—in secret.

The document detailing the arrangements in the West Bank and Gaza would include a declaration of intent. From an Egyptian viewpoint, there would have to be an Israeli proclamation of willingness to withdraw from the West Bank and Gaza—other than those points our forces would continue to occupy for security reasons such as our settlements along the Jordan River, or on the tops of the mountain ridges. Sadat would then announce that Israel and Egypt had agreed on a declaration of intent and go on to invite the confrontation states to enter into negotiations on a bilateral basis. He would wait a few weeks. After that, he would sign a peace agreement with Israel with regard to the Sinai. If Jordan came into the picture, Hussein would handle Judea, Samaria, and Gaza. If Hussein refused to take part in the negotiations, Sadat would enter in his place and sign an agreement to cover the West Bank and Gaza.

Under the agreement, the existing settlements would remain. Settlement would be permitted to continue on private land purchased by Jews. A solution would also be sought for state lands, which would be made available for Jews to buy. The Israeli army would be stationed in agreed-upon bases, such as those along the Jordan, in the settlements and at other points. Should there be any PLO activity in the West Bank or Gaza, the Israeli army would have a free hand to take care of the terrorists. The settlements in the Sinai could remain—under Egyptian sovereignty. The inhabitants would become Egyptian citizens and could not enjoy the protection of the Israeli army. Gamasy presumed that the settlers would leave within a short period of time.

I had good cause to feel satisfied. In my report to the cabinet, I intended to point out that considerable progress had been achieved.

On the morning of March 31, I was all set for my return to Israel when I got an urgent phone call. General Gamasy was on the line.

A short time later, we returned to the presidential residence near the "barrage." President Sadat was extraordinarily tense and on edge. His words were clipped and incisive.

"After Carter's meeting with Begin," he began, "Carter asked me if I insist on a Palestinian state. I gave it a great deal of thought, and my thoughts led me to make the far-reaching proposal I put forward yesterday. After meeting with you, I had a meeting last night with Palestinian representatives from Gaza. They did not accept my ideas. They want self-determination. At this point, Palestinian support is important to us. In view of their opposition, I cannot say that my plan of yesterday is still in force."

This sharp turnabout on the part of Sadat was most distressing. The Egyptian president was vindicating the critics who accuse him of being changeable and of reneging on undertakings he has already committed himself to. I could already see the rejoicing in Israel and the jubilant expression on the face of Yigal Hurwitz, who was so violently opposed to the peace process. I wanted to say something, but the president frowned, as though refusing to listen.

"We have a problem," he said. "I know my limitations, and I will not propose anything I can't carry out. But when I make an offer—I stick to it. Now, in view of the opposition of the Palestinians, I don't know if I can stick to it. Therefore, I return to the position existing before yesterday: Begin must display flexibility. I don't demand a Palestinian state—only a link with Jordan. A link with Jordan implies that there is no Palestinian state. That was my view before the peace initiative. That is my view now. There will be a plebiscite—"

"A plebiscite is unacceptable to us," I broke in, trying to salvage the situation. "Let us go back to our talk yesterday and my proposal that we conclude a peace treaty with Egypt as the first stage. You are a courageous man. You expelled the Russians, you launched the peace initiative, and you should have the courage to bring it to a conclusion."

Our brief exchange ended without any results. We were back to where we had been two or three days before.

As we took our leave of one another, Sadat asked me to convey his regards to Dayan, Yadin, and President Katzir, but the look in his eyes struck me as a warning signal.

At Cairo Airport, I made efforts to be cordial toward my hosts. Noticing the scarred hands of General Hassan al-Kattab, the Egyptian army spokesman, I asked him where he got his wounds.

"In 1956, between Qantara and Port Said," he answered. "I was a captain in the infantry, serving as deputy battalion commander. A plane picked out our unit and dropped napalm bombs on us. I was badly burned. After that, we were strafed, and I got a 30-mm. bullet in my shoulder. I was seriously wounded, and my convalescence took a long time. My wound put an end to my service in the infantry."

It was stupid of me to have asked him. His expression indicated that he must have suffered terribly.

"I'm sorry," I said.

"You have no cause to be sorry," the general replied. "It was a British plane."

"Thank God!" I said to myself.

Our leavetaking was more doleful than usual. Gamasy noticed my mood. "The president said: 'No more war!' " he reminded me. "We'll carry on working on it."

His words gave me no comfort. "I wouldn't like to fight you again." I shook his hand, fearing that this might be our last meeting.

At the military airfield near Tel Aviv, the chief of staff and other army generals were waiting to hear my report on the course of the talks. Throughout my conversation with them, I could not get that strange look in Sadat's eyes out of my mind. I didn't like that look. I called the chief of staff over to a corner of the room.

"Motta," I said. "You have to prepare the army for war."

23

CROCODILES IN THE IRRIGATION PIPES

If the road to hell is paved with good intentions, the same is true of the road to peace. In the summer of 1978, good intentions were an inadequate prop for the peace process as it sagged toward imminent collapse under the weight of events no one had predicted.

A rising tide of Islamic fanaticism had engulfed parts of the Arab world, reaching its most extreme and alarming form in Iran. This Islamic wave also threatened to wash away the foundations of the Israeli-Egyptian peace process, justifying Sadat's belief that peace talks must be concluded quickly before new difficulties had time to emerge. I was particularly concerned about the peace talks because the Islamic fundamentalism that made Khomeini the ruler of Iran also sent out ripples toward Egypt, particularly to that country's younger generation. In 1977, I had seen many young Egyptian women in jeans; by 1979, I was to see relatively large numbers with veils over their faces.

Sadat and his policies encountered sharp opposition from young Egyptians, who had adopted the popular American slogan of the sixties: "Don't trust anyone over thirty!" In addition to objecting to peace talks with Israel, they also criticized Egypt's links with the United States as well as economic development and secular modernism.

My assumption that the Islamic wave would soon peter out like any other fashion ran contrary to the unanimous opinion of experts, who see the Islamic movement still growing, with a long way to go before it peaks. But history has witnessed quite a number of such manifestations, and I am convinced that the Islamic tide will reach its high-water mark and ultimately ebb away.

The turbulence shaking the Arab world left Jerusalem staid and unruffled. I cannot recall the cabinet ever discussing the effect of those events on the peace process.

The process itself was well and truly aground. It sometimes seemed as if the prime minister and some of my cabinet colleagues were panic-stricken at their own daring. Having taken one step of great—perhaps excessive—courage in giving up the Sinai peninsula, they seemed intent on scrambling back off the limb on which they felt themselves marooned. After showing no hesitation in agreeing to restore the entire peninsula to Egyptian sovereignty, they now began to demand rebates and discounts in the form of the Rafah settlements and the airfields.

Israel's decision to return the Sinai to Egyptian sovereignty effectively sealed the fate of the Rafah settlements. Having consulted no one before agreeing to cede the whole peninsula, Begin and Dayan now sent me to try and save the settlements. Some ministers continued to foster the settlers' delusions that they could have their cake and eat it, too. I sensed that the battle was hopeless right from the outset. All the same, I resolved to grapple with the Egyptians to the best of my ability—while not neglecting to tell the truth to my fellow Jews.

"The government's proposals are far-reaching," I told representatives of the Rafah settlers when they came to see me. "They will be hard on you. If I were in your place, I'd be worried. . . ."

One of the representatives got the hint. "But Israel has never given up a settlement." He tried to salvage the situation: "One hundred and twenty children have been born in Moshav Sadot!"

"True," I conceded. "But neither has Israel ever been on the verge of signing a peace treaty. If there is peace, the one hundred and twenty children born in Sadot will never have to go to war."

The anguished expressions of the Rafah settlers hovered like ghosts over the cabinet's deliberations, which were likewise disrupted by the frenzied cries of thousands of "Peace Now" demonstrators.

I looked on in astonishment at this switch of roles among the different sections of the Zionist movement. Organizations that had formerly shown nothing but contempt for agricultural settlement

were suddenly displaying an enthusiastic eagerness for all settlement projects. At the same time, the young followers of "Peace
Now"—largely drawn from the movements that had always been
at the forefront of Zionist settlement—were now marching in noisy
demonstrations.

The members of "Peace Now," many of them reservists belonging to elite combat units, were just the type of young men into
whose eyes I wanted to be able to look with a clear conscience
should I ever have to order them to go to war. Under their slogan:
"Peace is better than a Greater Israel!" they attracted tens of
thousands of Israelis to their rallies and demonstrations.

I do not like demonstrations—whether "for" or "against." I consider them valueless. Neither did I like the eagerness with which
"Peace Now" advocated that we give up our bargaining counters.
Forfeiting an asset like the Sinai peninsula is no cause for dancing
in the streets—particularly when such domestic pressures immediately take on external political significance. The sound and
fury of "Peace Now" actions had not the slightest impact on government decisions. To the best of my recollection, not a single
decision adopted by the cabinet in recent years was influenced by
the cries of protest uttered by the demonstrators or by their youthful naïveté—however much that trait of theirs may have charmed
me.

What those thousands of demonstrators failed to achieve was
almost brought about by one man: Finance Minister Simcha
Ehrlich nearly brought down the government. Ehrlich, too, meant
well, but his good intentions almost pushed us over the brink into
disaster. The sweeping economic liberalization he had advocated
and put into effect soon turned out to be a misconception that
propelled our economy into a spiral of soaring inflation. This
accelerated devaluation of our currency threatened to unravel the
fine threads that held together the fabric of our society. The economy plunged into anarchy.

"And I promised"—I recalled our election campaign—"I promised to bring inflation *down!*"

At each successive cabinet meeting, Ehrlich assured us that it
was only a matter of days before he had inflation licked.

"By the time he licks inflation," I predicted gloomily, "he'll have
licked the government!"

Begin was repeatedly alerted to the gravity of the economic

situation and its probable effects. He was warned that the government would fall and that he would lose the next election if inflation hit 100 percent. He was told that the constant price rises would overshadow everything—including a peace treaty with Egypt. Unlike the price of milk and cheese, peace is not on display on the counters of every Israeli grocery or supermarket.

But Begin did not lift a finger. He has never showed any particular interest in economics. "What can I do?" the prime minister would ask. Begin's confidants explained that his heart was too soft to permit him to offend his friend, Simcha Ehrlich.

"Good God!" I thundered. "And what about the people of Israel and *its* heart?"

The heart was Begin's weak spot. After nearly thirty years of unrelenting efforts to win the post of prime minister, his heart let him down just as he tasted the fruits of success. His functioning in office was hampered by successive heart attacks, which forced his ministers to acquire detailed expertise on cardiology and pharmaceutics. Some of these medications apparently had the effect of reducing the prime minister to a listless mood. His vitality dwindled, while his alertness plummeted to near zero. His spirits were low.

Under these bleak circumstances—his personal health deteriorating along with the economic and political situation—Begin tried to fight off the attacks launched against his government and against himself. Each morning brought a fresh onslaught, fiercer and more damaging than its predecessor.

Many of the attacks were aimed at Begin in person. He was subjected to the worst forms of abuse and depicted as an obstacle to peace.

"He's got to be replaced!" senior Washington officials declared openly, following up their declarations with deeds that—aside from trying to force Israel into going along with the political demands from Washington and Cairo—seemed overtly aimed at intervening in Israel's domestic affairs by shunting its prime minister out of office.

Some observers attributed these American pressures to the sagging popularity of President Carter, whose own domestic standing was at rock bottom.

"Our feeling over here is that the United States is trying to twist our arms," I told Dick Weitz, counselor to the American embassy in Tel Aviv. "If your president needs an achievement, he'd better not try and get one at our expense."

The attacks coming from Cairo could not be interpreted other than as attempts to bring about Begin's removal or to address the Israeli people over the head of its prime minister and government. Sadat openly cultivated his contacts with opposition leader Shimon Peres—hardly a subtle hint.

But however much I cared about the personal destinies of Begin or Sadat, I was far more concerned about the peace process being stymied by personal squabbles.

"You might as well know," I once told Sadat in a remonstrative tone, "that Begin is your only negotiating partner. He's the only man capable of delivering the goods."

The main issue at this stage was the fate of the West Bank. In cabinet deliberations, I told my colleagues that our own foot dragging was to blame for the question now being brought up with such vehemence. Having shaken themselves out of their initial state of shock brought on by Sadat's peace initiative, the Arab states were accusing him of selling out Arab interests as the down payment he was making for the sand dunes of the Sinai. This left Sadat with no choice: despite having been prepared previously to settle for a general declaration of principles, he now raised his price.

Whether or not we found a solution for the impasse would decide if we achieved peace—or achieved nothing. Secretary of State Cyrus Vance and his advisers concluded that Begin and Sadat were incapable at this time of reaching agreement on the fate of the Palestinians. So as not to hinder progress toward an Israeli-Egyptian agreement, an undertaking had to be extracted from Begin, binding him to reach a decision on the issue at a later date.

The initiative adopted by U.S. Secretary of State Vance—acting with the knowledge and approval of President Carter—consisted of two questions directed at the Israeli government.

Would we be willing to settle the final status of the West Bank and Gaza Strip at the end of the five-year interim period?

If so—what mechanism did Israel propose for this purpose?

The Americans put forward their own proposal for the wording of the Israeli answer: "Israel is prepared to make a final decision on the permanent status of the West Bank and Gaza Strip in five years' time by means of negotiations between representatives of Israel, Egypt, Jordan, and the Palestinians residing in the area. The outcome of the negotiations will be approved by the people residing in the area."

The United States wanted to bind Israel to a solution that would leave the final say to the local Palestinian population. The Americans wanted to allow the Palestinians to hold a plebiscite—an idea Begin had rejected during his talks with Carter when he'd told the U.S. president that it would lead to the emergence of a Palestinian state.

As I have already mentioned, I was not overjoyed at the extent of American involvement in the peace process. "Carter is acting on Sadat's behalf!" I told the cabinet. "So why do we have to give our reply to the secretary of state? This very day, I'll call up the Egyptian war minister and tell him our views directly." The Egyptians were our only partners, and I saw no reason to bring the United States into the resumed negotiations.

My proposal was rejected.

Under the circumstances, I saw no choice other than an affirmative answer to the first question. "Israel is prepared to determine the final status of the West Bank and Gaza Strip in five years' time." I stressed that such a status—whatever it turned out to be—would be determined by all the parties engaged in the peace process and that Israel—like all the others—had to reserve her right of veto.

In a cabinet whose head and at least some of whose ministers attributed almost mystical significance to words, it was to be expected that the American questionnaire would be handled as though Moses the Lawgiver had brought it down from Mount Sinai, together with the stone tablets bearing the Ten Commandments. The discussions were relentless and uncompromising. The ministers realized that Israel's reply to the questionnaire was liable to settle the fate of Judea, Samaria, and the Gaza district. I told my cabinet colleagues that from the moment it had been decided to grant administrative autonomy to the Palestinian population of these regions, there had been almost no prospect left of bringing them under Israeli sovereignty after the end of the five-year period. My views were shared by a number of ministers, but they were afraid to express them aloud, preferring to leave Begin's dreams intact for the time being.

My arguments with my cabinet colleagues were very fierce; on top of everything else, these disagreements showed up the deplorable relations between ministers, as they dragged on for weeks in a savage lack of restraint.

The peace talks would end in failure if we started digging in our heels over matters of formulation. I was familiar with the views of most of the ministers, many of whom supported my approach. But not a word was to be heard from the two leading figures in the cabinet; Begin and Dayan held their tongues. Having picked up hints that Dayan, like me, was ready to go along with the term "final status," I hoped it would be possible for me to join forces with him on this point.

I went to see Dayan at his home. Our talk was brief; he did not want to tell me his proposals for Israel's answer.

Before I took my leave of him, Dayan said: "I'm not sure Begin understands what is in the balance."

I adhered to my view that we must not miss this opportunity by blocking the road to negotiations with Egypt. With regard to Judea and Samaria, our answers ought to be direct and candid, not cloudy or confused. But my opinion ran counter to that of Begin and Dayan, who favored evasive tactics and a reply that failed to answer the questions.

At this time, my relations with my former brother-in-law hit an unprecedented low. "He's leading us down the garden path!" I complained.

I could not help asking myself what had happened.

Only a few months before, my relations with Dayan had been excellent. During the morning hours of May 23, 1977—a few days after the Likud's election victory—Dayan had summoned me to his home in Tzahala, near Tel Aviv. A few hours earlier, in the middle of the night, Begin had been rushed to the hospital; it was suspected that he had undergone yet another heart attack.

Dayan was frank. He confirmed what I already knew: that Begin had offered him the foreign affairs portfolio. After sketching out the political situation liable to arise should Begin prove incapable of serving as prime minister, he suddenly said: "I propose that you become prime minister; I am prepared to serve under you as foreign minister."

His proposal was very flattering. A few hours later, it transpired that the whole thing had been a false alarm: Begin's heart was unaffected, and he was permitted to return home. I have often wondered whether Dayan regrets his haste in summoning me that morning.

The arguments about our reply to the American questionnaire went on for many weeks. Like Dayan, Begin refused to express any opinion, leaving the ministers guessing. During our deliberations, the prime minister seemed indifferent to what was going on around him, taking no part in the cabinet discussions or even maintaining order among those who did. He presided over the meetings, withdrawn within himself, his glassy eyes focused on some remote spot. Rumor had it that his medication was getting the better of him.

The relatively extensive support for my position from other ministers encouraged me to stick to my guns and demand cabinet approval for my draft replies to the American questions. However, even as my supporters multiplied, it came to my ears that Begin was extremely depressed and liable to tender his resignation. I decided to take action and asked to come and see him at his Jerusalem residence.

I found Begin most despondent. Being subjected to such enormous pressures, he was glum and pessimistic and close to collapse. He dropped hints about a possible resignation.

"Don't you dare resign over our answers to the Americans!" I almost shouted at him. "Don't be down. Go out and meet the people. The people are waiting for you! I took you on a tour of our aircraft industry; you saw what our people do. Did you see what we invent and manufacture? You really enjoyed that! Now tell Arik Sharon to take you to see our wonderful farms, and Hurwitz will take you on a tour of industry. Sir, the people will replenish your strength!"

I tried to fire him with my own optimism, and my words seemed to have some impact. When we went on to discuss our replies to the Americans, I got the impression that the prime minister would accept a wording closely resembling mine. In the sentence "The permanent status will be discussed . . ." he proposed the term "a different status."

His modification struck me as evasive, but all the same, it was a step forward, and from Begin's point of view a great concession.

Our leave-taking was emotional. "You said great things today," Begin mumbled. "Wonderful things . . ."

The day of our next cabinet meeting, I chanced to enter the prime minister's office a few minutes before the ministers were due to convene. Suddenly, Begin's aide, Yechiel Kadishai, said to me: "The prime minister invites you to step inside."

I was astonished. "Just like that? Accidentally? If I hadn't passed by before the cabinet meeting, he wouldn't have called me in!"

I found Begin in his office. He appeared more robust than when I'd last seen him two days earlier. He showed me a sheet of paper with writing on it, and he said: "I am going to bring the cabinet a proposal referring to the nature of future relations, including the status of these areas and of their inhabitants." I made out Begin's illegible script on the paper. I was not enraptured with the wording he proposed, but I felt that his reference to the areas themselves—Judea, Samaria, and Gaza—rather than to their inhabitants alone—was the most I could accomplish without entering into a confrontation with him.

A few minutes later, when the prime minister presented his proposal to the cabinet, I was astonished to realize that on the way from his office to the cabinet room, the words "including the status of these areas" had been deleted from Begin's proposal, leaving only, "the character of future relations with the inhabitants." Understanding that Begin's assurances had been nothing more than a ruse to bypass my vigilance, I lost my temper.

"What is all this?" I demanded. "I have fought in every one of our wars. To fight and win, you need passion and faith! For peace, too, you need passion and faith, no less than for war. Without such passion, peace can't be attained. On the eve of the Six-Day War, the late Levi Eshkol lacked the fortitude to give the order to go to war. Today, Begin lacks the fortitude to give the order to make peace. Eshkol was the prisoner of his fears. Begin is the prisoner of Greater Israel."

Some of the other ministers had been equally astonished, but they had kept quiet, reluctant to anger Begin. One of my colleagues slipped me a note: "I am finally convinced there is no prospect of achieving peace. Consequently, either there'll be an interim agreement or war. The people of Israel will have to hold out another twenty years till there arises a political constellation capable of grappling with the future of our nation."

"There's no choice," I said that day. "I'm going to prepare the army for war."

That evening, I was at home in Ramat Hasharon. News poured from the radio and television; journalists called incessantly. Egypt was seething with fury. Inside Israel, I was pilloried mercilessly. Zahava in Cairo transmitted an unfriendly message from the head of Egyptian intelligence: "You have left the Palestinians nothing to hope for," it read. "We are extremely disappointed in Israel's replies to the United States."

Knesset members demanded a debate on my remark about getting the army ready for war. Members of Herut demanded my expulsion from the movement. Admittedly, this was not the first time I had let my tongue run away with me. As I once said: "My tongue is as sharp as a sword, and my temperament is as fiery as a furnace stoked up to a million degrees." All the same, I saw no reason to withdraw what I had said. I felt I had been cheated.

When our Knesset faction convened to discuss my harsh statements, it was like facing a field tribunal. The atmosphere was tense. Some of our Knesset members were out for my blood. "I am in favor of 'Israel on both banks of the Jordan!' " fumed one of my accusers, Dov Shilanski. "I haven't given up that ideal. I want to know what your ideology is!"

Shilanski's invoking the old slogan did not please me at all. The late seventies—on the threshold of a peace agreement with Egypt—hardly seemed the appropriate time for ideas that had proved ineffective and anachronistic. I had hoped, that having assumed power, the Herut movement would adapt to the new circumstances and become somewhat more pragmatic. My own ideas ran totally counter to those of Shilanski: "I believe in a Greater Israel," I said. "But I am also alert to developments and to current possibilities. There are certain things you can and should dream of—and there are others which belong to the realm of reality."

Geula Cohen was aflame with her own fiery beliefs. I respect her more as a fighter than as a politician. She may have been the first to notice that Begin was retreating from Herut's published principles. "The trouble with you, Ezer Weizman, is that you took the prime minister's peace plan seriously, and you ran ahead with it. For Begin, it was the last word—but for you, it was the beginning of the road, and you raced on."

My views and hers were like east and west; nothing could be further apart. There was no way we could remain under the same political roof, and, in fact, she would subsequently leave Herut to found a new party over her opposition to the government's peace policy.

All this time, while disagreements with Egypt and the United States persisted and the cabinet continued its deliberations, I made efforts to renew direct contacts with Gamasy and Sadat. The door to peace was locked—and the key was to be found in Cairo.

One day a message arrived from Colonel Rimon, rota commander of Zahava in Cairo: "Gamasy is prepared to meet Weizman tomorrow, July 13, in Salzburg, preferably before midday. When I asked if that was the only time the meeting could take place, he replied that he thought so because the president would return to Egypt afterward."

Whenever I had visited Cairo, it was never certain ahead of time whether or not I would be seeing Sadat. General Tamir, then in charge of our contacts with Cairo, had developed an indirect tactical approach to the question. In the course of the preliminary talks that preceded such a visit, he was in the habit of inquiring whether to prepare winter or summer clothing. If told to bring warmer clothes, he understood that the meetings were to be held in Alexandria or Cairo, but lighter suits indicated that we were to go south, to Aswan, for a meeting with Sadat. This time, however, such ruses were unnecessary. It was evident that the scheduled meeting with Gamasy was nothing more than a cover; the message from Cairo said so in almost as many words.

As on previous occasions, the invitation to meet with Sadat came without any forewarning. In a few days' time, the foreign ministers of Israel, Egypt, and the United States were scheduled to hold a conference in London where it was hoped they would achieve a breakthrough. I could not figure out what reason Sadat could have for inviting me to a meeting before the foreign ministers convened in London.

He probably knows what he's up to, I reassured myself.

I flew to Salzburg in an Israeli-manufactured Westwind plane. The flight would have been nothing out of the ordinary had the plane not been piloted by two old friends: Danny Shapira and Nachum Yahalom. Shapira, a childhood friend and a graduate of the air force's first-ever pilots' course, had taken an active part in every war we fought since. Two of his sons are following in his footsteps. Like Shapira, Yahalom, too, was an air force veteran.

It was a strange turn of events to have these two men with me on this entirely new form of combat sortie without shooting or casualties.

We arrived in Salzburg to be greeted by European sunshine and hundreds of policemen and security agents, with a corresponding number of vehicles and dogs. These official precautions for our safety were a further—if indirect—boost to my faith in the peace process: Egypt, with which my country was still officially at war, managed to guarantee my safety when I was there with a far smaller number of police and security agents.

The Austrian city of Salzburg highlighted the difference between Europe and the Middle East—between the thunder of battle and the gentle murmurs of peace. Salzburg is a sleepy city, peaceful and indifferent to the storms raging in the distance. Its medieval churches and Baroque buildings create a charmed, fairy-tale atmosphere. Contrasting with the frenetic tempo of the Middle East, Salzburg lives in slow motion; it feels as if little has changed since the time Mozart lived there, writing his wonderful music.

On a hilltop in the center of the town stands a mansion that has been converted into a luxury hotel. The Foschel castle was one of

Sadat's favorite vacation spots, for good reason. It is a truly spectacular sight.

My meeting with Sadat was scheduled for the afternoon, and I intended to take a rest in the meantime. But no sooner had we arrived at the hotel than the telephone rang.

On the line was Fuad Timor, the Egyptian head of protocol. "Why wait till later?" he said. "Come over now." Right or wrong, this gesture also struck me as a good omen.

On my arrival at the picturesque castle, I was welcomed by General Gamasy, looking somewhat strained.

Gamasy led me to Sadat's suite. The Egyptian president gave me his usual warm welcome. He said nothing to Gamasy, but his expression left little room for misunderstanding, and the war minister took the hint. A soldier through and through, he snapped to attention and made his departure, closing the door behind him.

"Well, Ezer, we meet again."

I glanced about me. My previous meetings with Sadat had all been in Egypt where I got used to holding our talks in enormous, high-ceilinged conference chambers or on endless expanses of lawn in the fresh air. Now, for the first time, we were meeting in a tiny room, so small we were almost touching one another. Sadat sat close to me, just as in our first meeting in Jerusalem. He looked well.

"When we finish our talk," Sadat promised, "I'll introduce you to my wife."

My previous encounters with Sadat during my visits to Egypt had always been formal affairs, with police guards and motorcycle escorts and helicopter trips ending with members of the presidential staff ushering me into official offices. Whatever I knew about the Egyptian president's private life came from newspaper accounts. If he now intended to introduce me to his wife, I attributed the gesture to the friendly relationship we had established. Sadat's voice took on a note of pride: "Jehan," he said, "has just completed her master's course in Arabic poetry and literature at Cairo University." Sadat's pleasure at his wife's achievements was evident in his expression. His mood was so ebullient that even the faltering peace process failed to mar it.

"I asked to see you before our delegation left for England." The president went on to the main topic. "I'm afraid the London talks will fail. That's why it is important now, before the conference convenes, to prepare for contact afterwards."

This opening gambit by the Egyptian president was tremendously encouraging. In spite of the extraordinary difficulties,

Sadat was resolved to maintain contact even if the forthcoming conference were not successful. I was profoundly impressed by his determination to keep up the peace talks. "I want you to be the one to hear what I have to say and convey my words to your government. This way, I will be able to relieve my conscience."

The Egyptian president expressed the view that negotiations had been dragging on too long—a view with which I heartily concurred. "There is the pressure of the timetable," he said. "I face two decisive dates: in October, the mandate of the UN peacekeeping force runs out, and we have to decide whether or not to extend it. And November marks the first anniversary of my visit to Jerusalem."

That was worrying. He was quite capable of abrogating the mandate of the UN force, leading to a deterioration of the situation in the Sinai.

"And if there is no change by October," he added suddenly, "I'll resign."

This stunning announcement was uttered in a calm, steady tone, as though to stress that his decision was final.

I did not say a word, but I swallowed hard. Sadat loves springing surprises. I was afraid he might carry out his threat. I also considered the possibility that it might be yet another ruse, a further way of pressuring us.

"You'll be making a mistake if you resign." I tried to argue with him. "The Egyptian people need you, the whole region needs you. You mustn't do it; it would harm the peace process—"

Sadat grinned, as though pleased with himself for having pulled my leg. "But I know the Egyptian people won't allow me to resign," he added swiftly.

I heaved a sigh of relief.

"Anyway," Sadat pressed on, "I hear that you are also threatening to resign."

"That's right," I conceded.

"In that case, it's my turn to be worried!"

He fell silent briefly before going on to say: "You Israelis must do something for me. No, not for me—for Egypt. When I came to Jerusalem in 1977, if you had only made some gesture in response—if you had only withdrawn to the El Arish-Ras Mohammed line! I was expecting you to do something like that. But you were silent! You thought you were smart and wise. What ever became of Israel's smartness and wisdom?"

"I don't know whether a unilateral gesture is feasible at the moment," I replied, "but I will tell my prime minister what you say."

However, it now became evident that this had been no more than the appetizer. "I propose," Sadat went on, "that Israel declare that she is immediately restoring El Arish and Jabal Musa [Mount Sinai] to Egypt. Even before the peace treaty is signed, we shall make them into Egyptian-administered enclaves. We don't need any road—we'll fly in by air."

Sadat's words confirmed the position I had held all along: that he was expecting some openhanded gesture on our part—even if it were only a token act—in response to his gesture in coming to Jerusalem. Had he been permitted to dazzle the Arab world with some immediate gain, that would have tempered the opposition to his step. At the time, Agriculture Minister Arik Sharon had come forward with the proposal that we hand over El Arish to Sadat as a mark of appreciation for his great step. But the proposal had been rejected.

When I had told Begin that we should meet Sadat halfway, as his situation in the Arab world was very difficult, Begin's response was: "My situation is also difficult!"

"At the end of the feast of Ramadan," Sadat promised, "I shall go to St. Catherine's monastery, accompanied by a clergyman." Since St. Catherine's lay in the Israeli-occupied part of the Sinai, this was Sadat's way of stressing his firm resolve. "I hope," Sadat added, grinning from ear to ear, "you won't fire at us."

"What will you do at St. Catherine's?"

"I'll build a mosque, a synagogue, and a church," Sadat said.

The idea of building three places of worship at St. Catherine's was not new. Sadat had brought it up on various occasions in the past; each time, Israel's response was negative, if not downright derisive. I'd never joined in the sneering. I knew that in Sadat's religious beliefs there is a genuine element of universalism. In speaking of Islam, he stresses those of its principles common to all the monotheistic faiths.

Such a unified view accords with the philosophy of Islam, which regards itself as the continuation of Judaism and Christianity. Islam is the most recent form, but it remains intimately connected with the older religions. The Muslims view Moses and Jesus as prophets who preceded Muhammad.

On top of that, however, Islam also displays some unfavorable traits in its attitude toward the Jews. Islamic countries placed Jews in the status of vassals—hardly an ideal role. The Koran and Islamic tradition in general feature negative stereotypes of the Jewish people.

The peace process had forced Sadat to comb through his people's traditions for some way of presenting Israeli society in a favorable light. This was particularly difficult in view of the anti-Zionist ideology prevailing in Egypt for decades. His solution was to focus on the age-old link between the religions—a link symbolized by Mount Sinai.

"What will you do in El Arish?" I asked.

"We'll make it into a center for the peace talks," he said firmly. "We'll invite the other Arab leaders, too—Assad from Syria and Khalid from Saudi Arabia." His ideas seemed completely fantastic to me. Under the present circumstances, there was not the faintest likelihood of the Arab leaders' coming to El Arish. I thought he was putting me on. But, a moment later, I remembered that only a few months ago I would have been equally incredulous at the idea of Sadat's coming to Jerusalem.

I shared Sadat's desire to extend the peace talks. Right from the onset of our contacts with Egypt, I had been hoping to see additional Arab states joining in. I pictured the leaders of the Middle East reclining in the shade of the date palms of El Arish, convening in an enormous marquee instead of shuttling back and forth between Cairo, Washington, and Jerusalem.

"A fine idea," I complimented him. "I shall convey it to our prime minister." Without hesitating, I went on: "It is most important that you meet Begin again."

Relations between Sadat and Begin were totally ruptured, each man resentful of the other. The rift was complete and apparently final.

In recent weeks, Sadat had been trying to outflank Begin. I felt it was up to me to rebuke Sadat for initiating contacts with opposition leader Shimon Peres—and infuriating Begin. "Mr. President!" I said. "You must understand Israel's political system. Begin is prime minister, Dayan is foreign minister, and Peres is leader of the opposition. He was minister of defense, but he is no longer a member of the cabinet. If you take any interest in developments inside Israel, you also know that the polls predict a Likud victory in the forthcoming elections." (So they did, at the time.)

Fixing my gaze on Sadat, I went on: "I should tell you that people in Israel suspect you of trying to split our leadership and divide it from the ordinary people. The mood in Israel is not good. People in the street say that Sadat is laying a trap for us. That he wants everything. There are growing misgivings about the degree of your candor and about your intentions." My last words were uttered with a note of disappointment, underlaid with an implied threat.

"I understand," Sadat replied, "but that's not why I did it. I have no such intentions." Raising his voice to stress his words, he proclaimed: "I'll be willing to meet Begin only when we sign the peace treaty. I'm sorry if the prime minister feels embittered toward me. That's not the way I feel toward him."

He grew pensive for a moment or two. "Do you know what?" he went on. "I want to maintain direct contact with Begin—by way of you. You'll be our messenger."

"You should meet other Israeli leaders," I said, hastening to seize the opportunity. "You should get to know Israel's official leadership."

"Carter advised me to meet Dayan," Sadat revealed. "I refused."

"Why?"

"Because he would have taken advantage of our meeting to stage a big show," Sadat ventured dourly. "Everything would have come out in public."

"You ought to know what sort of things we are worried about," I insisted. "Next time, I'll bring along our agriculture minister, Arik Sharon."

"If you do," Sadat retorted, "I'll put him in prison!" He roared with laughter—but he did not reject the proposal outright. "That could be considered."

The window looked out on the glorious Austrian landscape: green and blue and white. Every now and then, I heard the barking of German shepherd dogs on guard around the hotel.

"I like this place," Sadat remarked.

The room and its surroundings exuded a Germanic atmosphere. I could not overlook Sadat's persistent affection for everything connected with Germany and the German way of life.

Our conversation was interrupted two or three times—but only by Sadat's personal valet, who follows him everywhere. I knew the man well and felt as if by now he was my old acquaintance. On his part, the valet soon became familiar with my favorite drinks. Whenever the aroma of mint tea filled the room, I was reminded that while our meeting might be held in the land of strudel and Mozartkugel—we had come from the Middle East, and that was where we would return.

Once again, the president stressed the urgency of an immediate conclusion of the peace agreement. Once again, he listed his demands. The agreement must include an undertaking for an overall withdrawal from the Sinai, the West Bank, and Gaza. When the peace treaty was signed, the military government would be revoked. Sadat agreed that we would not begin our withdrawal before security arrangements were concluded for the areas to be evacuated.

"But," he stressed, "the discussions must not go on for long."

"What happens if there is disagreement?" I demanded.

Sadat said nothing.

"It's not just a question of our defense from Jordan," I pointed out. "It's the whole of our eastern front."

"I fully understand that," Sadat said. "Security arrangements will have to include Israeli military footholds in the West Bank and Gaza Strip."

"What about internal security?" I demanded.

"We can set up a joint police force," Sadat replied.

"Would Hussein consent to such a proposal?" I asked, expecting a negative answer.

"Yes!" Sadat said surprisingly. "I think he would. I, too, will provide policemen for the joint force. Hussein needs Saudi help; he depends on it. I maintain close contact with Hussein on this matter. My deputy, Hosni Mubarak, went to see him to discuss the plan."

"What's Hosni like?" I asked, changing the subject. "I scarcely know him." I wanted to shift the conversation to a personal plane.

"Hosni? He's excellent!" Sadat exclaimed. "I left him at home to look after things."

The conversation reverted to Jordan.

"I'm more optimistic than I was about Jordan taking part in the peace talks," Sadat said. "Hussein will come along, but I think Assad will refuse." He shrugged. "Other Arab states now support my initiative—more than in the past. Assad is stuck in Lebanon, and he can't get out. When he moved his troops into Lebanon, I warned him he was digging his own grave." Sadat made no secret of his dislike for the Syrian president, twisting his features into a gesture of contempt whenever he mentioned Assad's name.

Sadat's concern about Hussein was, to my mind, excessive. I have never had any particular affection for the Jordanian king. "You're too worried about Hussein," I said. "He has made three great mistakes in the course of his lifetime: the first was in attacking us in 1967 in spite of our warnings to him to stay out; the second was in not joining the attack on us in 1973; and the third was when he didn't come to meet you in Jerusalem."

Having given my evaluation of Hussein's record, I returned to more immediate concerns. "What happens if Hussein doesn't come to the peace talks?" I demanded.

"Then I will take responsibility for the West Bank and Gaza!" Sadat announced. "Don't worry, my policemen will use their guns! But we will have to hold elections. I want you to withdraw your veto on a plebiscite."

"Mr. President! That is out of the question!" I pronounced. "If there is a plebiscite, the inhabitants will want a Palestinian state—and the PLO will take control. You must understand that the West Bank is the central issue."

Sadat waved his hand in disdain. "The PLO is finished," he said in a harsh tone. "Arafat will lose his job," he added. "Abu Ayad will replace him." Apparently aware how much I wanted to hear him say that, he repeated firmly: "Ezer, you've got nothing to worry about—there won't be any Palestinian state."

The cordial mood made it possible for me to raise some of the issues I had already discussed with Sadat during our previous encounters. I told him that the greatest contribution to our security would be an appropriate political solution for Judea, Samaria, and Gaza. "When you talk about security," I said, "every general will come up with a different solution. The question is: how do we live together?"

Sadat nodded.

"We must find a way to live together," I said, referring to Begin's autonomy proposals, which I perceived as a feasible foundation for coexistence.

"What will become of our settlements in the West Bank?" I then asked.

"We shall have to consider them separately," said Sadat. "The problem of Jerusalem will also be discussed in the same framework."

I was taken aback. "What has Jerusalem got to do with the settlements?" I demanded.

"I agree with your view that Jerusalem must not be repartitioned," Sadat said earnestly. "But the city will have to be administered in a different way—not as it is today."

Sadat must have noticed my reaction to that proposal, but he went on: "There will have to be two municipalities, one Arab and the other Jewish, and over them a joint council for both peoples. Our holy places will require some special arrangement. What we need there is Arab and Muslim control. That has to find its clear expression—by means of a flag, for example."

Mentally, I noted that the Egyptian president's demands were increasing with every passing day under the impact of his isolation within the Arab world, the pressure from the other Arab countries, and their charges that he was abandoning Arab and Muslim interests. He spoke courteously and affably, but that made his words no more palatable. I could imagine Begin's face when I returned to Jerusalem and reported on Sadat's new demands. There was no prospect of meeting them.

"Do you think Hussein will agree that Jerusalem not be repartitioned?" I asked.

"We shall have to discuss that."

Sadat's reply angered me. "You ought to remember that we have
built up and expanded the city since 1967."

"Yes, yes," Sadat mumbled. "You Israelis—you are great foxes."

His comment was rather offensive, and I decided to pay him
back in his own coin. "Up to seven months ago, you wanted to
throw us into the sea!" I reminded him. "So what did we do? We
built up our country. Do you remember during your visit to Jerusalem how I showed you the city from the window of your suite in
the King David Hotel?"

Sadat nodded eagerly; each minute of those great hours in Jerusalem must have been etched in his mind.

"Do you remember my asking you if it would be possible to
repartition the city?"

Sadat remembered perfectly. I had made it plain that this was a
point on which his prospects of extracting concessions from Begin
were zero.

Our conversation turned to the Israeli settlements and airfields
in the Sinai. I proposed that the Gaza Strip be extended south-
wards as far as the Israeli-built town of Yamit with the aim of
including it in the peace settlement. I said that we would not be
able to give up the flourishing Israeli settlements in the Rafah
approaches. "Whatever goes for Gaza," I suggested, "will go for
the Israeli settlements as well." Sadat did not respond to my proposal.

"Israel will have to hold on to at least one of the airfields we
have in the Sinai," I added. "The military threat against us comes
from the east—from Syria, Iraq, Jordan, and even Saudi Arabia,
and we'll need protection."

"You are an experienced soldier," the president broke in. "Are
you really afraid of the Saudi threat? That is no threat for you!" He
growled, with obvious disdain for Saudi military might.

I remained silent, faithful to the biblical precept "Let the
stranger praise ye, and not thine own mouth."

"As for the military airfields," Sadat said, "I am ready to let you
retain them for two years. After that, we will convert them into
civilian fields. And I won't station a division in the Sinai, as
Gamasy wants—perhaps only a brigade."

That was not acceptable. We could not manage without at least
some of the Sinai airfields.

I did share his view that the presence of a UN force in the Sinai was unnecessary. Sadat said he was prepared to consider any kind of outside military presence in the peninsula, but he made no secret of his preference for the Americans.

"Carter is my friend," he said. "He has never let me down to this day, and I feel an obligation toward him. I want Carter to take the credit for peace."

"In the last resort," I told him, "the credit will come back to you!"

"We need the Americans," Sadat emphasized. "Without the United States, we will not be able to reconstruct our country. We need them—and so do you. They will foot the bill for the peace agreement."

Our conversation that went on a long time—two hours, possibly more—included extensive disagreement. All the same, Sadat created a relaxed, unstrained atmosphere around him. I felt not the slightest inclination to get up and leave him.

The door was opened, and Sadat's valet came in bearing a large champagne glass filled with ice cream. Both of us looked at him in astonishment as the valet set the glass down on the table before me. Sadat shook his head in bewilderment; the valet bent down and whispered something in his ear. Then the Egyptian president smiled broadly. "It's for you, Ezer. A small offering from my wife."

I grinned back at him. Although I am no great addict of ice cream, I picked up the glass—fearing, as usual, that I was about to stain my elegant suit.

An unusual aroma filled the room: a blend of the strawberry flavor of the ice cream and of the Erinmore tobacco Sadat was smoking. His valet was always at hand to refill the pipe, and the Egyptian president puffed at it incessantly.

After the break, Sadat sketched out the dangers of Soviet subversion, pointing out that the Russians had managed to get a foot through the door in the Horn of Africa, South Yemen, and Afghanistan. He described the extent of Soviet aid to Libyan ruler Muammar el-Qaddafi. "The Russians and Libyans want to mount a revolution inside Egypt," he said. He leaned toward me as though about to share a confidence. "Not long ago, we foiled a plot involving Egyptian officers who got 750,000 dollars from Libya."

A mischievous glint lit up Sadat's eyes. "Poor Qaddafi, he didn't know that the men who got the money were agents of my intelligence service," he said proudly.

Three hours had passed—without the telephone ringing once. Aside from the valet, no one had ventured to enter the room to interrupt our tête-à-tête.

Speaking in the manner I so enjoyed, Sadat now went on to talk of the future and the excellent relations that were in store for our two peoples. "Egypt will sell oil to Israel, receiving in turn scientific advice. Together, we will lay a large pipeline from the Nile to irrigate the Sinai and the Negev."

The idea of channeling Nile water to the Negev sounded as though it came from a science-fiction fantasy. I am not even sure it is physically feasible. I recalled that my deputy, Tzippori, had come up with such an idea during an early phase of the peace talks; it had been scornfully dismissed. All the same, I thought, there are times when reality soars far beyond the wildest fantasy.

Then I recalled the difficulties we faced, and the people we had to deal with—the Israeli opponents of the peace talks. "Heaven forbid!" I groaned. "They'll probably accuse Sadat of wanting to use the water pipe to flood the Negev with crocodiles!"

The talk of oil had reminded Sadat of his country's economic difficulties. "Consider the change in Egypt's status within the Arab world," he said. "Before oil became of such vital importance in the world economy, Egypt was the richest of the Arab states. Now—she is the poorest."

The 1973 Yom Kippur War had brought the world its first experience of the oil weapon. But the Israeli army had already given some thought to a contingency of this nature. As far back as 1970, our General Staff had drawn up an assessment of the political and strategic implications of the enormous reserves of oil at the disposal of the Arab states.

The use of various natural resources for political or strategic purposes is not new, and the Arabs were not the first to use this weapon. For lengthy periods during the sixteenth and seventeenth centuries, a country's might was gauged by the amounts of gold and silver it possessed. In modern times, the United States has used its economic power as a political weapon: when it launched the Marshall Plan to prevent a Communist takeover of Western Europe; when it refused to assist Egypt in constructing the Aswan Dam; and when the Americans imposed an embargo on the export of wheat and sophisticated technological products to the Soviet Union.

At present, oil is a most vital commodity—far more than wheat, for example. Wheat can be replaced by substitutes. There is not yet a substitute for oil. Attempts are underway to develop oil substitutes, but it is unrealistic to expect the Western world to be able to substantially reduce its dependency on oil before the year 2000.

It is widely believed that most of the world's oil reserves are in the Middle East and North Africa. That is incorrect. These regions have reserves totalling a hundred billion tons of oil, but there are four hundred billion tons in the rest of the world, including the Soviet Union, which recently reported the discovery of a rich new oil field. However, in the oil fields in the Middle East and North Africa the precious mineral can be extracted by relatively simple and cheap techniques, whereas extraction in other regions calls for much more expensive and highly developed methods.

If no breakthrough can be expected soon in the development of oil substitutes, Israel—like other countries—must brace herself for a future that is far from rosy. Oil will continue to be vital to the world economy and will remain largely under Arab control.

From this point of view, Israel is in a perilous situation. Like all the other countries that did not have the good fortune to find oil within their borders, Israel must ensure external sources of supplies while at the same time seeking alternate sources such as solar or nuclear power. The principal problem Israel faces is the danger of her oil supplies being cut off. The Arabs wield decisive influence in OPEC, and they may try to impose a further oil embargo upon us—even though a considerable portion of our supplies comes from non-OPEC sources. Israel's oil supplies come in by sea: in times of war, attempts may be made to cut off these routes—as has already occurred in the past. Another possibility is that the Arabs would impose an embargo on those states aiding or supporting Israel, as they did in the winter of 1973–1974 when they unleashed the oil crisis on the West.

It is annoying to find so many people in the West—in Western Europe particularly—who see the oil problem so simplistically: let the Arabs have whatever they want from Israel—and they will provide us with oil! Or, expressed in different terms: if pressure is not brought to bear upon Israel—there will be no Arab oil! Aside from being oversimplified, this view is also incorrect. The Arabs do not enjoy untrammeled freedom to use the oil weapon—this is particularly true of the more conservative Arab countries that control most of the oil reserves. In the oil emirates of the Persian Gulf as well as in Saudi Arabia under the current regime, national security depends on the security and stability of the West. An oil embargo may be counterproductive and boomerang on the rulers of these states, who must preserve the stability of their regimes by leaning upon Western power.

There is another factor that deters the Arabs: depriving the world of oil or demanding unreasonable prices for it could become a *casus belli*. At present, the idea of a military occupation of the oil fields is confined to the lunatic fringe in the West. It is still cheaper to buy oil than to go to war over it. However, if the economy of the Western world faces collapse because of oil, it is extremely likely that war would break out. Since the Arabs understand this point very well, the possibility of using the oil weapon in the Arab-Israeli conflict is limited.

Anyone who believes that oil supplies can be guaranteed by means of pressures on Israel is fooling himself. Existing data indicate that the Arab-Israeli conflict is marginal in the considerations of the OPEC countries. Proof of this can be found in the Iran-Iraq war.

Economic considerations have the greatest impact on the oil-exporting countries. The countries are torn between their eagerness to sell oil in large amounts, and quickly, to be able to construct an industrial infrastructure for their economies as a potential substitute for oil in maintaining national income—and their desire to hoard the oil in the bowels of the earth, much as one protects one's money in the vaults of a bank.

Be that as it may, Israel cannot rely on miracles or prayers or the tender mercies of others. We are storing oil in our subterranean reservoirs, in whose construction Israel is one of the world's most advanced countries. As a result, we have enough oil to carry us through a prolonged period in case of emergency. Israel is also surveying her own territory, seeking supplies of oil and gas—so far, without any luck. That is why we are buying up overseas concessions for oil extraction as well as acquiring oil tankers.

"Mr. President," I said at the end of our conversation. "You must have heard of the outcry in Israel over my comments on the answers to the American questionnaire."

Sadat replied that he had.

"I am plunging into this peace process because I have faith in it—and in you," I declared in all sincerity. "Can you imagine what it was like for me to go on television and say I trust you? I was deluged with letters and telephone calls—for and against. It's less than a year since you were saying you'd throw us into the sea . . ."

The conclusion was obvious, and I saw no need to go on.

"Now," said the president, rising from his armchair, "come with me."

Standing up, I straightened out my suit, crumpled after my prolonged spell in the chair. My muscles ached from hours of immobility.

"I am going to introduce you to my wife," Sadat said.

On the threshold, he tugged at my sleeve. "Don't forget," he said. "Congratulate her on her master's degree."

Grinning broadly, I gave the required promise. Sadat led me into his bedroom: it was empty. "Don't forget!" he cautioned me once again.

Jehan Sadat entered by another door. She is an imposing and attractive woman. She inquired about me and my family, asked me my impressions of Cairo.

I answered all her questions.

"And your wife's?" she asked.

I told her that Re'uma's impressions resembled my own and talked of the experiences of my son, Sha'ul.

The conversation tripped along, and Sadat listened intently, scarcely commenting.

"I hear that you have just completed your master's course at the university," I said. Sadat smiled from ear to ear, gratified and delighted. "Permit me to congratulate you—and express my admiration and astonishment. How does a grandmother manage to get so much done?"

The compliment found its mark. "I am also going to become an assistant lecturer at the university," she related proudly.

We took our leave of one another.

"Gentlemen!" I addressed the dozens of journalists lying in wait outside the hotel. "It isn't a trick or an ambush, as some of you may believe. Peace is on its way! There are still a number of things which need doing—but peace is on its way!"

War Minister Gamasy's version of the meeting was less optimistic: "There is a rapid deterioration in the situation in the Middle East," he told them. "It is vital that something be done quickly; otherwise, a situation will arise that can no longer be rectified. There is no choice: every formulation and every position must be scrutinized."

As the evening drew on, Karl Kahana proposed that we get together with the Egyptian war minister for dinner. Kahana, an old friend, is a wealthy Austrian Jew; being an intimate of the Egyptian president, he viewed himself as a partner in the peace process. I accepted his invitation—on one condition: that it also include the pilots of the Westwind, Danny Shapira and Nachum Yahalom. I wanted to get their impressions of the Egyptian war minister. After all—I might be wrong.

We dined at a luxurious restaurant on top of the hill, looking out on the lights of Salzburg. It was one of those meals in which the menu is not the most important thing. "The president is looking well," I said, even before we poured the first toast. "Better than ever."

Gamasy did not share my view. "I get the impression that he doesn't feel well—and that he's not calm or relaxed."

Gamasy's views on the political outlook strongly resembled those of Sadat: the London conference's prospects of success were extremely dim.

"Shall we go to London and join the foreign ministers?" he suggested playfully.

"That's fine," I fired back. "I'll keep an eye on your foreign minister, Kamel, and you look after Dayan."

"Your job will be easier than mine," Gamasy smiled.

"Before the end of the month, we will have to meet at Alexandria," he added, "to rectify everything that goes wrong in London!"

I did not reject the idea. Various remarks of his had led me to understand that the Egyptian army was more open to Israel's proposals than the Egyptian Foreign Ministry.

"It's easier to get on with generals," he said. However, Gamasy also showed signs of concern that the prolonged deadlock in the negotiations might have an unfavorable effect on the army, too. "Some officers are losing patience," he said. "You ought to know that certain officers are demanding that we harden our positions, and those demands are on the rise."

His description was disturbing. In a country like Egypt, dissatisfaction among the officer corps could spread like wildfire. In view of this, I tried to learn the Egyptian army's views about the mandate of the UN peacekeeping force, due to run out in October 1978, and expressed my own misgivings about what lay in store after the mandate ran out if there were no progress in negotiations.

"I hope that we don't get into a situation in which you expel the UN forces and send five divisions into the Sinai," I said. "That could place all of us in an unpleasant situation." The warning in the last sentence was plain: Gamasy could not have forgotten the events of 1967.

"Don't worry," he said. "Before we send in our army, I'll call you up on the phone."

Our conversation turned to other matters. "Why do you need such a large army if we are heading toward peace?" I demanded.

"I have proposed in the past," Gamasy retorted, "and I propose now: a mutual reduction of our armies—immediately! Why do *you* need such a big army, with so many tanks and airplanes?" The ball was back in my court.

"We are also threatened by other Arab states," I reminded him, "from Iraq and Syria to Jordan and Saudi Arabia. All of them are acquiring lots of arms—particularly Iraq."

"You have nothing to fear," Gamasy reassured me, showing off his expertise. "The Iraqi threat is not so great, however many arms they get. At most, they could move one brigade to the Syrian frontier—within seventy-two hours."

"Our experts think differently," I replied. "Otherwise, why would Saudi Arabia need so many F-15s? They don't need the planes to protect their oil fields. They need them to use against us. That has to be taken into account in our planning for any future offensive against us. We told the Americans as much."

"General Weizman!" There was a note of ridicule in Gamasy's voice. "You are a serious general. Are you really worried by the Saudis?"

Our conversation over dinner covered many topics, both political and private. When we pursued personal matters, I recalled that Gamasy's wife was suffering from a severe kidney disorder.

"How is she?" I asked him.

"She is not too well," he replied. "She is in the hospital undergoing treatment."

"We have excellent doctors in Israel," I blurted out. "Our medicine is out of the ordinary. I know a doctor at the Tel Hashomer hospital who is an expert on her disease. Why not bring her to us for treatment?"

Instantly, I realized I had made a mistake.

"We have excellent doctors in Egypt," Gamasy retorted stiffly.

I had spent months warning colleagues to avoid any appearance of arrogance in their contacts with the Egyptians; I told them to consider Egyptian sensitivities by refraining from referring to our superiority in any sphere. And now, here I was, falling into precisely that trap! I had no one to blame but myself—even though I'd had the best of intentions.

On my return to Israel, I notified the prime minister of Sadat's requests for a gesture involving El Arish and St. Catherine's. I recommended that we respond positively, possibly demanding a *quid pro quo* in the form of Egyptian permission for Israeli-bound supercargoes to go through the Suez Canal in Israeli ships. I warned my cabinet colleagues to keep the matter confidential; should word of Sadat's request leak out, it would put him in an intolerable position within the Arab world.

Two days later, the story of Sadat's request had been leaked to the press. I was furious. Hitherto, very little had reached the papers about my conversations with Sadat, and the Egyptian president had expressed his appreciation of the point on various occasions. In my view, this leak had been a deliberate attempt to harm me as well as to foil Sadat's requests and sabotage the peace process.

Less than two hours after an Israeli morning paper had published the story, a cable from Cairo was laid on my desk: "I must notify you that our president is most astonished that you did not adhere to what was agreed. Gamasy."

My fury grew. I knew there was no point in trying to pinpoint those who had leaked the report.

"To Gamasy." I wrote an urgent cable to Cairo. "I apologize for what has happened. You will probably understand that such things happen at times, and they cannot always be prevented in the Israeli political system. We must not permit this to affect the spirit of trust we have built up between us, and which must be retained in our relations. Convey my message to the president, with all my respect. Weizman."

When the matter was discussed, I urged my cabinet colleagues to respond favorably to Sadat's requests. I explained the difficulty of his predicament in the Arab world, recalling that a similar idea for a unilateral Israeli gesture had been put forward at the time of the Egyptian president's visit to Jerusalem. I pointed out that responding to Sadat's requests would highlight our generosity, resulting in a more sympathetic image of us in world opinion.

However, the atmosphere prevailing in Israeli-Egyptian relations left no prospect for acceptance of my demand. The prime minister took advantage of our Zahava station in Cairo to say as much to the Egyptian president, in Begin's own terms.

"Dear President," Begin wrote. "My friend and colleague, Weizman, has conveyed a message from Salzburg. You proposed that we take a unilateral step by transferring El Arish and the Mount of Moses [Mount Sinai] to Egyptian sovereign territory. You will certainly agree, Mr. President, that no state takes unilateral steps. However, contacts on a bilateral basis are feasible. I propose a meeting between our representatives in Jerusalem, Cairo, Alexandria, or Haifa."

This public rejection of Sadat's requests was a painful personal affront to the Egyptian president—a stinging slap in the face. I was profoundly regretful but found few of my cabinet colleagues to share my sentiments. Several ministers even relished Begin's act of retaliation against Cairo. They perceived it as a display of "backbone," to which I responded: "Only those whose spines are bent talk all day long of 'backbone'!"

Cairo did not swallow the insult. Zahava transmitted a message that contained a very broad hint: "The parliament has brought up the question of the presence of the military delegation. The problem is going to be kept quiet for the time being, but not for long. The president has instructed me to set up contact with you and ask your opinion. Gamasy." What could be plainer?

It did not take long for the process to reach fruition. "Regret to inform you," read the message from Cairo, "that the National Security Council has decided today that there is no need to keep the Israeli military group in Egypt. We have made arrangements to send the group back home tomorrow, July 27, in an Egyptian civilian Boeing-737 to Lod. Hearty wishes. General Gamasy."

The tenuous thread linking Cairo and Jerusalem, spanning the chasm of thirty years of war, had been severed.

"Never mind," I said, my tone of voice belying my words. "We'll be back for the opening of the Israeli embassy in Cairo."

Some of my hearers turned their heads away; they did not want me to see the grins on their faces.

24

THE LONE WOLF FALTERS

From week to week, from one cabinet meeting to the next, my cabinet colleagues grew more mistrustful of me. I felt that I was operating in a vacuum. My failure to convince the other ministers of the importance of the process in which we were engaged caused me enormous frustration. I was often made to feel like a soldier abandoned on the battlefield left to fight on alone.

"Some people here want to carry on living in a fortress state and in a ghetto atmosphere!" I said angrily. "In battle, if you're hesitant, you're likely to find yourself dangling from the barbed wire. . . ."

Judging by the opinions they professed, many of the ministers ought to have supported my positions—but that was not the way they behaved in practice. Almost all of them bowed to Begin's views; only a few occasionally attempted to resist.

All of us had learned to live in a world of contradictions the likes of which no previous Israeli cabinet had ever experienced. The prime minister had lost almost all control over his cabinet, generally showing little interest in the work of the various ministries and certainly making no attempt to coordinate between them, as his post demands. However, whenever it came to some issue connected with his fundamental political beliefs, Begin succeeded in imposing his will, even on ministers belonging to other parties whose views diverged widely from his. In cabinet meetings, the prime minister presented his position in a manner that implied that its rejection was tantamount to a vote of no confidence in him.

"We must look after Menachem," his confidants declared in agitation to the ministers. "He's liable to resign!" The ministers—only too well aware that the prime minister's resignation involved the resignation of the whole cabinet—realized what was required of them if they wished to hold on to their jobs.

In my own work as defense minister, I found a strange contradiction characterizing my relations with the prime minister. On the one hand, I enjoyed a freedom of action far exceeding that of any of my predecessors, but I also found myself wishing Begin would display more than the statutory minimum of interest in my sphere of responsibility.

I offered to take the prime minister on tours of army units—to no avail.

But for all his indifference to the development of the defense establishment, Begin enthused over the chief of staff's decision forbidding soldiers to wear their berets under their shoulder straps and ordering them to put their headgear back on their heads. He spent longer talking this over with me than he did when he came to inquire why the air force needed F-16s.

Begin's principal cabinet support should have come from the ministers of his own party, but to the extent that he was intimate with anyone, it was with the ministers belonging to the National Religious party and the Democratic Movement. While he exercised great influence upon his party colleagues—the Herut veterans who had marched shoulder to shoulder with him for decades—he despised those few Herut leaders who had reached the cabinet. At the same time, he cultivated the senior officials bequeathed to him by the previous Labor regime. Those who once worked for Ben-Gurion and Golda now worked for him.

"That's his revenge against those who kept him away from power for thirty years," his confidants grumbled.

In time, some of the Herut members employed in the prime minister's office left their jobs. Some bore their distress in silence; others told their close friends of the prime minister's mode of operation. On the whole, such stories were received in disbelief. "Out of the question!" the Herut old guard proclaimed.

The men Begin chose to fill the cabinet slots allotted to Herut included Dayan, Sharon, and myself—none of us a product of his own ideological hothouse. There were times during the peace process when I suspected him of using us as his "fall guys": we would do the dirty work of flagrantly contradicting Herut principles, while he would stand out as the guardian of ideological purity.

Begin's physical feebleness, his habit of never leaving his office, his anachronistic political thought, and his "lone wolf" mode of operation and decision making—all these made me wonder whether he had always been like this or whether he had changed upon entering the prime minister's office in Jerusalem. *I am the man who sold Begin to the electorate,* I thought. *Did I mislead the buyers?*

The replies from Begin's confidants were divided. Some said he was that kind of man and had always worked in this manner but that before he became prime minister, only a few insiders had known it—and, anyway, they claimed, it did the country no harm. Others said he had been badly affected by his heart ailment. The truth probably lies somewhere in between.

At any rate, I was profoundly disappointed in him. His one-dimensional outlook left no room for the kind of flexibility that was so urgently needed. He perceived everything in the black-and-white terms of "us" and "them." In domestic policies, "us" meant Herut and the Likud; anyone else was "the enemy of our movement." Begin saw foreign relations in the same way: "us"—Israel—against "them"—the gentiles. The only questions he allowed himself were rhetorical.

In cabinet discussions on the peace process, Begin emanated depression. "Cabinet meetings resemble a funeral procession," I remarked. "Only in this case, it's the dead who are listening to the eulogies." The feeling was that we were on the losing end: we were losing the sympathy of world opinion, we were forfeiting our close relations with the United States, and we were giving up the Sinai and the settlements, the airfields, and the oil fields—everything.

"But we are winning peace with Egypt!" I cried, in an attempt to put their conclusions in perspective.

The prime minister and at least some of my colleagues were not impressed by this argument. The advantages that would accrue to Israel from a peace treaty with Egypt were so obvious as to require no further justification: an end to the bloodletting on the battlefields, recognition of Israel as an integral part of the Middle East, a chance to change the whole way of life of our citizens, wide-open opportunities for our economy. Who could ask for more?

Egypt's gains from the peace treaty with Israel would have to be weighed against her isolation within the Arab world. The fact remains that Egypt would be getting back the Sinai without a single shot being fired, allowing the Egyptians to straighten up and regain their self-respect so that they could turn to their basic problems.

There were additional advantages for Egypt in removing herself from the cycle of wars against Israel. The wars had sapped Egypt's strength and blocked the country's progress. I share the view of the Orientalist scholar Professor Shimon Shamir who holds that if Egypt had continued to divert its meager resources to the conflict with Israel, it could have led to a national catastrophe. The burden of war is heavy enough for Israel to carry, but our society has a per capita national product of twenty-five hundred dollars annually, leaving us a certain amount of "fat." But in Egypt, where the comparative figure is three hundred, many citizens live at subsistence level; any further burden would snatch the last crusts of bread from their mouths.

Peace would allow Egypt to develop its national economy. The Americans and Europeans, or any other foreign investors, will not put a penny into Egypt if war is liable to break out at any moment. Areas such as the Suez Canal Zone would be devastated in the event of a new eruption of violence; only peace could make it possible to develop them. With the region about to enter the nuclear age, the threat of physical destruction provides the final logical rationale for Sadat's choice of the road of peace. Furthermore, peace with Israel would improve Egypt's relations with the United States, possibly up to the level of strategic cooperation, allowing the Egyptian army to receive more up-to-date weapons systems; it would also lead to diplomatic coordination and economic collaboration between Egypt and the United States.

My relations with the prime minister, bad enough before, grew even worse on my return from Austria. Some of the ministers treated my report on my talks with Sadat like the account of a tourist back from the Mozart festival. My impression that they had an aversion to peace was confirmed by the triviality of their gripes. Foreign Minister Dayan asked why I had not brought back precise minutes of my conversations in Salzburg.

"Sadat always chooses the time and place for these talks—and the participants," I defended myself. "There's nothing I can do about that."

It was no use.

This attitude on the part of the cabinet and its outright rejection of Sadat's requests made me furious. Time was against the peace process, and that awareness fueled my impatience.

At the entrance to the cabinet room, I noticed a Government Information Center poster welcoming peace. I yanked the poster down, growling: "I'm not sure the government wants peace."

I attached little importance to the gesture, but an aide to one of the senior ministers had witnessed it. Within hours, the story was making headlines on radio, television, and in the press. Instead of focussing on peace, everyone talked about the poster and my stormy temperament.

By this time, I had come to terms with Dayan's view that we needed an American tow truck to get the stalled peace talks moving again. But American involvement had brought little progress so far. Secretary of State Vance and his assistant, Alfred Atherton, who shuttled between Jerusalem, Cairo, and Washington, had barely managed to alter Israeli positions.

American efforts to promote the peace process brought Vice President Mondale to Jerusalem, after which he was to go on to Cairo.

"Here, in this room," I told him in his suite at the King David Hotel, "I had my first meeting with President Sadat." I described that encounter, looking back with longing at those heady moments and the enthusiasm that had since been frittered away in months of fruitless talks.

Mondale has great personal charm; tall and elegant, his cheerful expression usually produces an atmosphere of relaxed confidence. But now he was worried.

"I'm troubled by the time factor," Mondale said, "and about Egyptian public reactions to Sadat's policies." He described with concern events inside Egypt. I shared his anxiety: our own sources had brought to my attention the growing strength of the Egyptian opposition, which had mounted a number of demonstrations against Sadat's regime.

"Sadat will try to keep up his peace initiative for some time longer," Mondale predicted. "But if there is no progress, he may give it up, and that could lead us into very difficult times." His words were clearly a warning to Israel—which I resolved to ignore.

I did not share Mondale's view that Sadat was likely to drop his peace initiative. "He has gone far beyond the point of no return," I said. It was difficult to imagine the other Arab leaders welcoming him back into the fold. But everything is possible in the Middle East, I reminded myself.

From the window of Mondale's suite, Jerusalem basked in the midday sun. But the vice president looked downcast and worried, as did the rest of his party.

"We can't push too far." I tried to explain the slowness of our progress. I told Mondale of the dangers still lying in wait for Israel. "If the Egyptians reach our international border in the south while the eastern front continues to be threatening, we'll be in a difficult situation. God knows I don't want to meet Gamasy on the battlefield again, but I can't say that such an eventuality is out of the question."

Mondale seemed well briefed on Israel's security problems; I could tell him little he did not already know. Ignoring my remark about the possibility of a future war, he returned to the peace talks. "What can you do to meet Sadat halfway?" he asked.

"If he tries to twist our arm, the whole thing will break down," I warned. "He's got to be convinced that he must show the Arab world that it's possible to live with Israel and provide an example for the other Arab states."

I took the opportunity to launch an oblique attack on the U.S. positions. "I hear that Sadat is in the habit of saying: 'It's easier to reach Israel with an American passport than on top of a Russian tank!' As long as he knows that the United States insists that we withdraw to the 1967 borders, why should he make any concessions? He will become more flexible only if he knows that this isn't your view."

"What do you want us to do?" Mondale demanded.

"You Americans attach too much importance to the issue of the settlements," I said. "I suggest that Sadat terminate the state of belligerency with us and devote himself to Egypt's economic problems." I reminded him of the gravity of those problems.

Mondale confirmed my account of the difficulties of life in Cairo. "An expert told me that their telephone system alone needs an investment of twenty billion dollars."

I went on to speak of a new strategic alignment in the Middle East, advocating an alliance of Morocco, Egypt, Saudi Arabia, Israel, Iran, and Turkey—under the sponsorship of the United States and the West. Mondale appeared to agree with me.

Still smarting from the humiliating attitude of my cabinet colleagues, I urged Mondale to convince Sadat he should meet with Begin, Dayan, Yadin, and Sharon. "It's no good having one single Israeli as the sole link between the two countries," I said. If Mondale succeeded, I hoped such meetings would reduce the pressure on me from the other ministers. Mondale promised to convey my proposals to Sadat.

The visit of the U.S. vice president made little difference—for better or worse. The summer of 1978 saw the peace train jammed. Nor could I draw much hope from the next scheduled event, the London conference of foreign ministers, which seemed doomed from the outset.

Inside Israel, there were growing demands for Begin to resign if he failed to restore momentum to the peace talks. Irritated by these attacks, the prime minister flew off the handle. Standing in the Knesset's cafeteria, in the presence of countless visitors, he flung an obscene expression at opposition leader Shimon Peres. Well known for his courtly manner, Begin's use of strong language indicated the great tension he was under.

That was the atmosphere when Dayan set off in mid-July 1978. For security reasons, the London conference had been shifted to Leeds Castle, some thirty miles from the British capital. In effect, Sadat and Gamasy had guaranteed that the conference would come to naught long before the foreign ministers of Egypt, Israel, and the United States reached England. I found it strange to see these men set off for a pointless meeting, but on second thought, I welcomed the conference. As long as the sides carried on talking and arguing, efforts would continue, and there were prospects of attaining peace.

A few days later, when Dayan returned from Leeds Castle, the papers reported on a far-reaching change in the foreign minister's views. His suspicions of the Egyptians had melted away, and he now began to believe in the possibility of peace.

What brought about the change?

Dayan said nothing on this point. But when I asked him, he talked about the harsh exchanges between the delegations when the conference ran into its foreseeable deadlock. Faced by strenuous Egyptian demands, Dayan addressed Ibrahim Kamel and Boutros Ghali: "If that's your position on all these issues, if you are so demanding and extreme—wouldn't Israel be justified in withdrawing the offer of a total evacuation of the Sinai?"

It worked. Dayan had given the Egyptians the choice: either they showed greater flexibility or Israel would go back on her offer. The Egyptians—and the Americans no less—were alarmed at the prospect of the peace efforts completely breaking down. No one dared to contemplate the idea of starting the whole process from the beginning again.

After putting forward the most intransigent demands, the Egyptians showed themselves most eager to keep up the contacts—convincing Dayan of their sincere desire for peace. "The Egyptians really do want to make peace with us," Dayan told the press. "In my talks with them, I heard them say over and over again how much they want peace. I got the impression that they are ready for peace with Israel even though the terms proposed by Cairo are still far from our views."

At long last, the foreign minister was speaking optimistically; like me, he had returned from his encounter with the Egyptian representatives "in a good mood." Dayan's new identification with the more enthusiastic proponents of the peace process strengthened my position within the cabinet as well as with the public at large. All the same, I could not help wondering why I had received such scathing treatment when I came back from my meeting with Sadat in Austria. After all, I had said only that the Egyptian president honestly desired to make peace with Israel.

I expected that Dayan—like me—would now encounter a solid wall of resistance from ministers skeptical about Sadat's sincerity. However, I knew that he and I would be able to lean on one another. Many people would doubtless be astounded by the sight of the Dayan-Weizman duo united in the campaign for peace with Sadat.

"It must be said that a man in Weizman's position needs strong nerves and a profound faith in the correctness of his course to persist in it in spite of his growing isolation within the cabinet"— that was how one paper perceived the situation. But there was now some consolation in the fact that Dayan had come over to my side.

After many months, my words in the government and the Knesset began to fall on willing ears. The attitude toward me was changing. Hundreds of letters piled up on my desk expressing sympathy for my peace efforts. At the same time, the prime minister's standing in the polls took a sharp plunge, from eighty percent support after Sadat's visit to Jerusalem to fifty percent in the summer of 1978.

In view of the recurrent crises and deadlock, it became evident that summer of 1978 that something had to be done—some exceptional, dramatic effort. The only apparent way was a meeting between Begin and Sadat, who had refused to see one another since December 1977.

Organizing such a meeting was a "mission impossible." But Jimmy Carter took it upon himself to set it up.

25

OF SQUIRRELS AND PRESIDENTS

It had been ten months since Sadat had arrived in Israel. There had been hours of splendor and despair, days of conversation in Jerusalem, Cairo, and Washington—as well as Rabat, Salzburg, and London. Presidents and prime ministers, ministers of defense and foreign affairs had figured in the drama. Finally, at the moment when it seemed that all the effort had proved fruitless, Jimmy Carter did what no other leader had been able to do.

In the crisp fall of September 1978, all the participants—Israelis, Egyptians, and Americans—flew to Camp David for a meeting of eleven days that would influence world history.

Camp David lies in the hills of Maryland, seventy miles from Washington, D.C. First built as a presidential retreat during World War II, its original name was "Shangri-la." President Franklin D. Roosevelt frequently withdrew to this shady camp, situated within a forest and enclosed by barbed wire. Truman and Kennedy rarely went there; on the other hand, Eisenhower and Nixon came often, and it was "Ike" who changed its name to "Camp David," after his grandson. There he had hosted Soviet leader Nikita Khrushchev for a meeting of reconciliation, giving rise to the term "spirit of Camp David."

It was the White House that came up with the idea of bringing together the presidents of Egypt and the United States and the

Israeli prime minister for a summit conference at Camp David. The idea had made me rather apprehensive, although the historical precedent should have been encouraging: in 1905, President Theodore Roosevelt had summoned the representatives of Russia and Japan to the U.S. naval base at Portsmouth, New Hampshire, to put an end to the war then raging between the two countries. Isolating the two delegations from the outside world, Roosevelt had induced them to reach a peace agreement; his efforts earned him a Nobel peace prize.

The successes of the past notwithstanding, I was concerned: in the event of failure of the conference—so dramatic and conducted at so high a level—the peace process would come to an abrupt and final end. What else would be left to try?

I was not alone in my apprehension. While Israel made its preparations for the conference, there were predictions that the Egyptians were liable to cause it to break down so that Israel would be left bearing all the blame while Sadat might—with some admitted difficulty—start working his way back into the affections of the Arab world.

"If the conference does not succeed," I warned my colleagues, "it will lead to a severe rift with the United States—and even with the American Jewish community." I was appalled at the prospect, which would further erode Israel's already precarious position. Failure seemed so certain that it was even suggested we waste no time in preparing a propaganda organization to explain the breakdown!

During the preparatory discussions, Moshe Dayan said that the main issue at Camp David would be the future of the West Bank; he proposed that our autonomy plan be constructed in a manner that would leave room for the Jordanians to come in at some time in the near or distant future.

Once again, Dayan and I differed. "Jordanian participation would make it impossible for Begin," I said. The prime minister would never consent to Hussein's demands over the West Bank— and that deadlock would demolish any prospects of a settlement with Egypt. I proposed that we convince the Americans to keep Hussein out of the negotiations—for a time, at least. "If we leave the issue of the West Bank open for discussion, there is a chance of an agreement with the Egyptians," I argued.

When Begin and Sadat arrived in Washington, their sensitivity about parity in honor shown them verged on the ridiculous: I watched Israeli and Egyptian officials count the number of salvos fired off in honor of each leader and how many seconds the welcoming embrace was held; comparisons were also made about the warmth of the terms used in each of the welcoming addresses. The Americans made herculean efforts to preserve equality, aware that a couple of inches off one of the red carpets could be fatal to peace.

As we flew from Washington's Andrews Air Force Base to Camp David, I looked out at the landscape, astonished at the abundance of water. Having grown accustomed to the yellow sand dunes of the Sinai, my eyes were dazzled by the bright green of this landscape. The views unfolding below us tied into the peace we were about to discuss: I imagined water from the Nile turning the desert into a flowering garden. My dreams soared sky-high.

Camp David is not exactly a nature lover's dream. It has a somewhat claustrophobic feeling. The tall trees make the light gloomy, and one has to lift one's eyes to find a patch of blue sky. Only the squirrels leaping back and forth between the treetops and the cabin roofs lend a mischievous note to the scene.

I would have preferred that the peace talks be held in the Sinai, in the shade of the date palms of El Arish—and without any American mediators. However, as we made our way from the helicopter pad to the camp itself, I remarked: "It's better to have Camp David with peace—than El Arish without it." I was consciously parodying Dayan's famous slogan about Sharm el Sheik, and the barb found its mark.

As we followed Jimmy and Rosalynn Carter to the camp, we looked like a bunch of boy scouts on an outing, with everyone trying to huddle up as close as possible to the instructor in an attempt to get into the snapshot. Walking a few paces behind, I laughed to myself as I watched various officials—Israelis as well as Americans—trying to elbow their way into full view of the television cameras, near Carter and Begin, in a bid to ensure their place in the history books. The bodyguards shoved them aside, gently but firmly—but the elbowing was resumed. Some people just had to make it into the albums.

Walking along behind the president, the prime minister, and our foreign minister, my position in the procession defined my status here at Camp David. It was a conference of national leaders: Carter, Begin, Sadat; they would decide the fate of the peace process. My contribution looked more modest here in the shade of the great trees, and I would have to behave accordingly.

Looking back, I had no regrets about what I had accomplished. My talks with Sadat and the other Egyptian leaders had laid the groundwork for continuing the contacts; they may have made it possible for this summit to be held. *I kept the embers glowing*, I told myself. I saw myself in the role of the soldier who flings himself at the barbed wire, allowing his comrades-in-arms to make the breakthrough to the objective.

Many hours and days of talks lay behind us, weeks and months of contacts and exchanges spanning the period since Sadat's mission to Jerusalem. Nevertheless, I knew that the real bargaining—tough and merciless—was about to begin. There was no more room now for vague, imprecise answers. Our arrival at Camp David marked the moment of truth.

The damp, musty scent of the trees and the rustling of their leaves reminded me of my youth in Haifa thirty or forty years earlier. I recalled the woods of Mount Carmel, with rope ladders lashed to the tree trunks and campfires flickering in the clearings. As we were guided around the camp, with its wooden cabins and the marines hurrying about their tasks, I was reminded of my days as a new recruit in the RAF. Any moment, we could be called to sign for four blankets and a mess tin!

Bicycles had been placed at our disposal—yet another reminder of the bygone days of my youth; it was nearly forty years since I had last ridden a bicycle. I tried to imagine Begin and Sadat cycling along the paths, and the thought tickled my fancy. I laughed aloud, though no one could get me to say why.

I found a sad reflection of the state of Israeli-Egyptian relations in Camp David's telephone network. Immediately after my arrival, I tried to call up one of my Egyptian friends—only to learn that contact could only be made by way of the American delegation. Although only a hundred yards separated us, there was no direct link between the Israeli and Egyptian delegations.

Damn it all! I thought. *From Tel Aviv, I can make a direct call to the office of the Egyptian war minister in Cairo!*

The rupture in personal relations was given more concrete expression by Sadat, who withdrew to his cabin and stayed holed up there. Begin likewise dug himself in.

"The first step is always the hardest," I said. "But does it have to be this hard?"

The situation was awkward and embarrassing. Begin's aides tried to break the impasse. On the first day, they saw the Egyptian president leave his cabin dressed in a blue training outfit as he set off for his daily walk, a long-standing custom.

"You ought to go out to meet him," the Israeli officials urged Begin.

The two leaders met on one of the woody paths where they exchanged polite greetings. Of the two, Begin had taken the worse mauling from the unrestrained attacks of the Egyptian press. Being well acquainted with Begin's character, I foresaw that it would call for an enormous effort on his part to patch up his relations with Sadat.

I jumped on to my bicycle and headed for Begin's cabin to see how he was managing. Halfway along the wooded path, I saw Sadat walking along in his track suit, with his foreign minister, Kamel, making vain attempts to keep up.

Our paths crossed, and I leaped from the bicycle.

"I'm glad to see you again!" I cried, embracing him.

"Me, too!" he replied.

It was strange to see the Egyptian president perspiring with the physical effort. I had always seen him as the incarnation of masculine elegance: brushed and combed, carefully dressed in the most expensive of fashions, giving off the aroma of after-shave lotion. His sweaty track suit changed my view of him, making him less glamorous and more human.

"Come and see me!" Sadat called over his shoulder before vanishing into the shadowy gloom.

These chance meetings—of Sadat and Begin, Sadat and me—did little to reduce the tension. Neither did the informal atmosphere. Right from the outset, the Americans made an enormous effort to make their guests feel at home. Around the clock, waiters stood ready to serve sandwiches and drinks. One cabin offered almost incessant movie showings; the Americans must have known of Begin's fondness for films. The guests were requested to dispense with ties, but this was too much for Begin. "When you go to see the president," he proclaimed, "you should always be properly dressed." He would never let himself be seen in less than formal garb. Carter walked around in jeans or running shorts, Sadat in his track suit, Dayan in a marine tunic; there were facilities for playing billiards, chess, and tennis; there were movies; one could drive about in an electric buggy. But these playground devices, to the background music of crickets and toads, still failed to loosen the atmosphere.

What I saw that evening when I strode into the large dining hall shared by all three delegations told the whole story: on the lower level sat the Egyptians, in a somber mood; a table on the upper level was occupied by the Israelis, who stared into their plates as though they were alone in the world. At both tables, conversations were in progress very, very quietly.

For nearly thirty years, Egyptians had been ignoring Israelis, and vice versa. At international conferences, delegations from the two countries had avoided any direct contact; frequently, they even refused to meet under the same roof. All that had changed, with Israelis visiting Egypt, Egyptians visiting Israel, handshakes, talks, discussions. But here, in Camp David, we were back to the old, familiar picture: each side was ignoring the other. The same Egyptians with whom I had recently held long conversations in Cairo now stared everywhere—at the ceiling or down at the floor—to avoid meeting my eyes.

I refused to tolerate this state of affairs. With rapid strides, I crossed the twenty yards dividing the two delegations.

"*Ahalan!*" I greeted them.

"*Ahalan wa'sahalan!*"

We shook hands. I remained seated at the Egyptian table for a minute or two before returning to the Israeli table. I had relieved my own personal unease, but that was not enough. The atmosphere remained oppressive and tense.

The first surprise of the conference came from Rosalynn Carter. She proposed the text of an identical prayer for the success of the conference to be used by followers of all three faiths.

Dayan did not take the proposal very seriously. With more than a hint of savagery in his grin, he told Begin: "You will have to take off your hat for the Christians and your shoes for the Muslims—and then you'll end up putting on a yarmulke for the Jews." I, too, saw little point in the prayer.

Begin's response was totally different. Whipping out a pen, he studied the text, making minor corrections and modifications—as usual, attaching supreme importance to wording.

The way things look, I thought to myself, *we really need prayers.*

I was convinced that Carter and his aides would try to speed matters up, to exert pressure on Begin and Sadat. How long could the president of the United States afford to remain in the gilded cage of Camp David?

Carter made it plain that an agreement must be reached before the conference concluded. "There isn't much hope for resumption of talks if this conference ends in failure," he said. The president was risking his own personal and political prestige. His popularity ratings were at a low point, and the failure of the conference would demolish him completely. Yet he told Begin: "The achievement of making peace between Israel and Egypt is even more important to me than my political prospects." As an Israeli, I felt the greatest admiration for this step of Carter's; he would sacrifice himself for his devotion to peace.

Late that evening, Begin returned from his first meeting with

Carter at Aspen Lodge, Carter's cabin. We awaited him on the veranda of his own cabin. In addition to his almost mystical regard for words, Begin also has an inclination to overblown interpretations. When Begin makes his reports, one has to sort the substance from the packaging.

Carter had told Begin that Sadat wanted Israel to accept the principle of nonacquisition of territory by force. This had been the Egyptian president's aim right from the start, resting upon the assumption that our consent to such a principle would automatically entail our withdrawal from all the occupied territories. For that reason, there was no chance of Israel's consenting to his demand.

"There are such things as defensive wars," Begin had replied to Carter. "If such a principle is accepted, the whole map of Europe would have to be changed." The arguments on this point had begun right at the outset of Sadat's peace initiative, to be resumed at Ismailia—and a conclusion had still not been reached. There was no chance of budging Begin on this point.

"It won't be long before we're on our way home," I whispered to Abrasha Tamir.

That first talk between Begin and Carter had touched on almost every point of dissension: the future of the West Bank, the Palestinian problem, the Israeli settlements in the Rafah approaches, the new settlements on the West Bank, American bases in the Sinai, Sadat's demand for an Israeli gesture over El Arish and St. Catherine's. Carter's views strongly resembled Sadat's. But Begin was not showing any particular sign of concern.

"Sadat is impulsive," Carter had warned Begin. "If there is no progress in the negotiations, he is liable to launch military action."

On the veranda of Begin's Laurel Lodge, it was after midnight. For the first time, Begin was following the proper procedure of consulting his colleagues. These nocturnal consultations were to become part of our regular routine throughout the conference. It reminded me of the hallowed Israeli custom of Friday-night get-togethers in which social groups met to bemoan the state of the nation.

"We have a tough nut to crack," Begin concluded the first consultation. "His name is Anwar Sadat."

If not for the fateful issues being discussed, Camp David would have resembled a high-spirited vacation camp. Carter's blonde secretary rode her bicycle in denim shorts. The head of the White House staff, Hamilton Jordan, tried his luck with one of the secretaries. Presidential adviser Zbigniew Brzezinski invited me to a game of chess; I soon regretted my rash acceptance as he tore me to pieces. Leaving me, Brzezinski went off in search of other victims; later on, he hit upon Begin. When the score between the two men was two to one in Begin's favor, several Israelis bumped into Hamilton Jordan.

"I hear that Begin's playing chess with Zbig," said Jordan.

"Begin's leading two to one," the prime minister's military aide reported proudly.

"Do me a favor and make sure Begin wins," Jordan begged. "Otherwise, nobody will be able to get a word out of Zbig."

When Begin won the tournament, the other Israelis hastened to notify Jordan; relieved, he congratulated the Israeli prime minister.

That night, I could not fall asleep. The atmosphere of doubt and uncertainty was getting to me. Like the other participants, I wondered how the peace process could be salvaged. Dayan proposed that we start off by summarizing the points already agreed upon, leaving the controversial issues for the end of the conference on the assumption that everyone would be more conciliatory by then. I did not buy the idea. We would have to make an enormous effort or we would soon be packing our bags.

The next day, tension rose with the approach of midday, the time set for the first joint meeting between Carter, Begin, and Sadat. I was very apprehensive. When Begin summoned us to his cabin for a further consultation, the tension was evident in his expression.

Dayan proposed that the meeting between the three leaders be channeled toward the issue of the Sinai. He believed that an agreement on the peninsula would reduce Egyptian eagerness to foil the conference. I held that it was vital to tackle the knottiest issue: Judea and Samaria. "That is where the peace talks stand or fall."

Dayan disagreed.

"There's a considerable measure of agreement on the Sinai, apart from the settlements"—I stuck to my guns—"we should start with the toughest problem."

The consultation ended inconclusively. "Our aim," said Begin, "is to reach an understanding with the United States and an agreement with Egypt."

"How do we do that?" I demanded.

Begin gazed at me, sighing. "Yes, indeed, there is a chasm between us and the Egyptians."

Before lunch, I was surprised by a call from Egyptian Deputy

Prime Minister Tohamy, inviting me to meet President Sadat. Notifying Begin, I headed for the Egyptian president's cabin.

"The president is praying," I was informed on arrival.

I waited. When Sadat came to meet me, he was calm and relaxed. He ordered tea with honey; I asked for coffee with cardamom. It was strange here, in this American environment, to be drinking coffee prepared in the Middle Eastern style; at any event, it was a great improvement on American coffee, whose taste I find intolerable.

"After the publicity about our Salzburg meeting," I said hastily, "I sent you a cable of apology in consultation with the prime minister. I hope you got our apology?"

"I did," he replied. "And when I addressed our students in Alexandria, I told them openly that when I sit down with Ezer Weizman, there are no limits to the subjects we discuss. When I talk with you, I feel at ease, and I am prepared to discuss any subject."

"Before you came into the room," I confided, "I told Tohamy that it would be a good thing if you were to meet with Dayan here in this informal atmosphere." Sadat's refusal to meet Dayan had created further unnecessary tension.

Dayan had been equally reluctant to meet Sadat. During a cabinet meeting shortly before our departure for Camp David, he had sent me a note: "Ezer: there is one thing I request. Under no circumstances should you propose that I meet Sadat, whatever the forum."

"President Carter made the same proposal," Sadat replied to my suggestion, "but I refused. But when you request it, Ezer, I won't refuse. I have no objection to meeting him." His unexpected willingness was a gesture of good will on his part. (Needless to say, I did not have Dayan's permission to make the suggestion; I prudently refrained from telling our foreign minister of Sadat's consent.)

I went on to the main topic. "If we don't make some concrete achievement here in Camp David," I warned, "the situation will be very grave." My remark was an attempt to elicit Sadat's own appraisal.

"I shall do my best," the Egyptian president promised. "I don't think Camp David should conclude with a declaration of principles. Instead, we should seek a framework for future discussions. We must make certain the peace process is maintained—that it never stops. No one will be able to blame me if it does. I have come with all the possible alternatives, and I shall submit them in writing."

Sadat's words were encouraging in spite of their threatening undertone. I did not like his "whip and carrot" techniques—as he must have guessed from my expression.

"Tohamy just asked me if our hearts are as open as the hearts of the Egyptians," I said, trying to steer the conversation in a more positive direction. "I answered: 'Yes.'"

"I hope so," Sadat replied. "I must say, our meeting at Salzburg was twisted by the press in such a way that I asked myself if it was wise of me to meet with Weizman. I choose my friends carefully. But that is over," he concluded. His voice was stern, and I interpreted his remarks as a rebuke.

"How is my friend Gamasy?" I asked. It was more than mere politeness; recently, I had observed that Gamasy's standing with Sadat had fallen. The last time I had seen him, in Austria, he had not looked well; Sadat's refusal to leave him in the room during our conversation had struck me as significant.

"He is very well," Sadat replied, evidently reluctant to say anything more.

"I must repeat a question I already asked you once in Cairo: do you want an agreement which will embrace the Sinai and the West Bank and Gaza as well?"

Sadat scowled. "Ezer," he said. "Don't force me into the arms of the Soviets. If I only insist on the Sinai, the Soviets will gain control of the whole region. I look forward to peace. Here at Camp David, we shall sign only a framework agreement, not the peace treaty itself; that can be signed later. I am willing to let Hussein join the negotiations, but I'll continue to negotiate even if he doesn't. I will be frank with you. I am fully entitled to conclude a separate agreement with you, particularly after the attacks on me from various Arab leaders. But we have a traditional saying that a father cannot neglect any of his children. If Jordan doesn't come to the negotiation table, then I will be prepared to continue the talks and take the responsibility."

This was an encouraging sign of things to come. Even if he remained alone, he would not sabotage the conference.

I considered it important to improve relations between Sadat and Begin. "I hope you find Prime Minister Begin in the right mood for discussion," I said. "The past months have been very difficult for us because of the attacks on him in the Egyptian media. You must understand our prime minister: there have been attacks on his dignity, and our people are like yours; we cherish the honor of our leaders, just like that of our forefathers."

"Protecting honor is very important to us," Sadat agreed. "For example, I did not smoke in my father's presence even when I had been elected president."

Our conversation turned to other matters. "You must understand the profound concern for security which exists among our people and its leaders," I said.

"Ever since the October war," Sadat replied instantly, "we have no more complexes on the subject of wars. That was why I defied the world and the Arab states that attacked me when I went to Jerusalem. We must find a way of proving that we are capable of being more than just good friends. Our two peoples and our faiths have a lot in common."

"We will have a lot in common in the future"—I continued his line of thought—"particularly in the fields of economics, health, and social matters."

I went on to a very topical subject. "I understand that Iran is in a difficult position."

"And it causes me much pain," Sadat said. "The shah is a good friend of mine. I think he made three serious mistakes: he unified the parties; he did not do enough to fight corruption; and he was in constant conflict with the Iranian religious leaders. That is a difficult situation."

"It's also difficult for Saudi Arabia," I commented.

"But such a thing couldn't happen in Saudi Arabia because there the regime is tribal."

"What is Qaddafi's situation?" I inquired. The Libyan leader was the leading instigator of the attacks on Sadat.

"He's gone crazy again." Sadat brought me up to date. "He's allowed the workers to take control of the factories, the stores, and private cars. The man is mad!

"The situation in Africa is very tense." Sadat resumed his survey of regional politics. "President Giscard d'Estaing did a sensible thing when he sent planes to Chad; that changed the course of events there. In a way Giscard acted more wisely than our host here at Camp David. . . ." he concluded obliquely.

Before taking my leave, I told him: "I'm ready to come here whenever you think it's appropriate." I realized that Sadat remained determined to continue the peace process even though his patience was fraying, but I was concerned over the fact that his entourage at Camp David was largely comprised of his "ideological" aides: Deputy Prime Minister Tohamy, the Foreign Ministry group—Boutros Ghali, Osama el-Baz, and others—who had always adopted hard-line positions throughout the negotiations. Their ideological convictions did not permit them to accommodate new ways of thinking. I was also perturbed by the large number of jurists in the Egyptian delegation—as in the Israeli and American groups. "There are lawyers who find a solution to every problem," I observed, "and there are those who find a problem for every solution." Camp David teemed with the second kind.

The three leaders were scheduled to meet on the veranda of Carter's cabin. The president's secretary had requested that Begin come along ten minutes ahead of time; apparently, Carter wanted to talk to him without the presence of Sadat. It later transpired that Sadat had come to Camp David with a written exposition, which Carter had already seen; he was afraid it might lead to a rupture in the conference.

When all three leaders were assembled, the atmosphere was cordial—even though each one knew what lay in store. As Begin later related, Carter launched the meeting with a few brief words.

Begin, anticipating the approaching storm, said: "We must turn a new page. Negotiations require a lot of patience."

"That's true," Sadat conceded. "We won't sign a peace treaty here. There is no point in a declaration of principles or in a separate agreement: we should talk about the substance of an overall agreement. We must not turn Camp David into a television war, like the Geneva Conference, where everyone was competing as if they were amateur singers seeking success so that they could go professional. We shall prepare a framework agreement, and our aides will deal with the details later. I think that will need three months' work."

Sadat took out copies of an eleven-page booklet. "I shall now read out the Egyptian view of the framework for an overall agreement."

When Begin briefed us afterward on the Egyptian demands, I was filled with despair. The prime minister had read aloud what Sadat had proposed:

> Creation of a just and abiding peace on the basis of "non-acquisition of territory by war" requires Israel to withdraw to the international boundaries and the armistice lines in the Sinai, the Golan, the West Bank and Jerusalem, with minor modifications that will not reflect the outcome of the occupation; removal of Israeli settlements from the occupied territories; abrogation of the military government in the West Bank and the Gaza Strip, with its powers reverting to "the Arab side."
>
> At the end of a period not to exceed five years (from signa-

ture of the framework agreement), Jordan will supervise administration of the West Bank (Egypt will do likewise in Gaza)—"with the collaboration of the elected representatives of the Palestinian people, who will directly conduct the administration of the West Bank and Gaza Strip."

Six months prior to the termination of the interim period, the Palestinian people will exercise its fundamental right to self-determination and be allowed to constitute a national entity. Egypt and Jordan will recommend that this entity be linked to Jordan, in accordance with the wishes of the inhabitants.

The Palestinian refugees will be entitled to exercise their right to either return to their former places of residence or receive compensation, in accordance with UN resolutions.

In Jerusalem, a committee will be set up on the basis of parity between Palestinians and Israelis; it will handle all municipal matters, as well as guaranteeing free access to the Holy Places.

The framework agreement proposes further that in order to guarantee the security, territorial integrity, and political independence of each state, the following measures be adopted:

Creation of a demilitarized zone; a thinning-out area; creation of early-warning stations on a basis of mutuality; supervision of arms purchases by the sides; all sides to sign a treaty for the nonproliferation of nuclear arms and undertake not to manufacture or purchase such arms; the principle of the freedom of innocent passage be applied to the Strait of Tiran.

Israel will undertake to pay full compensation for all the damage caused by the operations of her armed forces and for exploitation of the natural resources of the occupied territories.

When Begin finished, there was a moment's silence as the members of the Israeli delegation tried to digest what they had just heard.

"The Egyptians have fired off their first round," I murmured to Abrasha Tamir, who was seated beside me.

Like me, Abrasha was an enthusiastic proponent of the peace process. He had frequently defended the Egyptians to our political leaders as well as to ordinary citizens. Now Abrasha was as shaken as I.

"We're going to have to start all over again," I whispered to him.

This was what I had feared all along. There was too much drama. The communications media were massed outside the camp's fence, the U.S. president desperately needed some achievement to rebuild his political standing, Egypt was exploiting her newfound international stature—all these were intolerable psychological pressures. Various members of our delegation predicted that the Egyptians would leak the text of their proposals to the press, placing Israel in a difficult predicament in international opinion. Publication of the document would make it impossible for Sadat to withdraw his demands—particularly with the eyes of the Arab world directed at him in the hope of his imminent downfall.

The militant mood of the consultation was reinforced by Begin, who claimed that the Egyptian document was designed to force Israel to break up the conference and incur international condemnation. "We won't play the Egyptian game," Begin declared; the other members of the delegation seconded his view.

Begin had some support from Carter. The prime minister related that when Sadat had finished reading out the Egyptian text, the U.S. president requested Begin not to respond immediately—probably with the aim of forestalling the sharp reaction that was liable to imperil the continuation of the conference. Carter had then invited Sadat to join him on a stroll, perhaps to soften him up somewhat; but Sadat did not accept the invitation. When Carter made a similar offer to Begin, the prime minister had joined the president for a walk through the woods.

"The document is extremist," Carter then said to Begin. "It seems designed to make an impression on the Arab world." The U.S. president did not promise to try and temper Sadat's positions, but he must have known that there was no prospect that the present demands would be accepted by Israel. In effect, Sadat was saying: all or nothing. At the end of the first day of talks, the balance seemed to be tilting toward nothing.

Talking to us, Begin reached into his lexicon for the harshest characterizations he knew. His tone was exceptionally strong. "If I'm wrong about the Egyptian document," he thundered, "I'm a flower pot!" That was the first time I had ever heard Begin use Israeli Sabra slang, which, being totally out of keeping with his usual mode of expression, brought weak smiles to the lips of his listeners.

My own words were no less fierce. "This document is crazy," I said. For the first time in months, I found myself agreeing with Begin and the others. All the same, our points of departure were not identical: the prime minister believed this was the beginning of the end, whereas I held that it was no more than the end of the beginning. Like the rest of the participants in the consultation, I raised my voice, making it carry far beyond Begin's veranda; since we assumed that the Americans were listening in on our confidential discussions, it would be just as well to highlight the unanimity of our opposition to Sadat's proposals.

All the same, I had to question my assumptions: Maybe I was wrong, after all? Maybe the whole Egyptian effort until now was nothing more than a gigantic strategic deception? In my mind I reviewed all the meetings I had held with them—their words, their declarations, their hints and remarks, the expressions on their faces. I tried to recall moments when they had aroused my suspicions. In the course of the peace talks, there had been at least two occasions when I thought war was about to erupt. Should I now phone home to tell the chief of staff to prepare the army? I was torn by uncertainty.

"If Sadat is so eager to make peace, why did he bring such a document to Camp David?" My question was directed at myself, no less than at my colleagues.

"If we had submitted a similar document," speculated Meir Rosenne, apparently reading my thoughts, "Sadat would have packed his bags and gone home without delay." Rosenne, an excellent jurist, had been involved in the peace talks right from the outset. Even earlier, during the talks on the disengagement agreements after the Yom Kippur War, he had displayed outstanding expertise and exceptional bargaining powers on legal matters. He is the kind of jurist who would say nothing that could not be thoroughly supported by precedent.

Sadat's demands to be compensated for damages his country had suffered in the various wars was the last straw for Begin. "What chutzpah! What impertinence!" Begin growled. "That's the way to address a defeated nation required to pay for its aggression. We won't be addressed in such a way!"

"Chutzpah," Dayan said, "is an understatement."

This new Egyptian demand—never even mentioned previously —struck me as bizarre. Why were they suddenly coming up with it? What would happen if we presented demands for Jewish property left behind in the various Arab countries? I tried to understand Sadat, to put myself in his shoes: why was he making such a demand?

I looked for the answer in the realm of Egyptian-U.S. and Israeli-U.S. relations. Perhaps Sadat had made his demands so far-reaching in the hope that the ultimate American proposals would be closer to his own positions: there could be no other explanation.

Nothing came of various well-intentioned attempts to arrange a meeting between Begin and Sadat. After months without any direct personal contact, the two leaders were now at loggerheads, and it was worth reconsidering before leading the two ravenous lions into the same den.

"Gentlemen," I said, trying to sum up the intractability of the situation, "the relations between Sadat and Begin seem to be marked by inorganic chemistry." No one smiled; it was the wrong moment for wisecracking.

The most vivid reflection of the crisis atmosphere looming over the conference was provided by the dining room the following morning. The Israeli representatives were not even stopping at the American table, to say nothing of the cold shoulder they gave the Egyptians. Each delegation sat alone, its members hunched over their yogurt and cheese, withdrawn and remote, or conversing with each other in whispers.

In retaliation against Sadat's proposals, the Israeli delegation spent the night drawing up an impromptu document aimed as a double-edged sword against Carter and Sadat. It would be made plain to the other two leaders that publication of the Egyptian document would automatically entail publication of the Israeli proposals—whereupon the international reaction would get completely out of hand. Begin, like other members of our delegation, attached great importance to winning over public opinion to our side should the conference end in failure. There was talk of preparations for mass rallies and media appearances in Washington if the summit broke up.

The document that was prepared that night detailed Israel's demands. The only innovation in the Israeli position was a counterdemand for war damages from the Arab states. Although it was important to present our views on salient points like the Rafah settlements and the airfields, the counterdemand for damages struck me as ridiculous and puerile. "We don't have to go aping them," I said.

I was puzzled by the behavior of the Americans. Like us, they thought that Sadat's proposals went far beyond the limits of rationality, and they therefore ought to have urged him to moderate them. But they did not lift a finger. I began to suspect them of playing a Machiavellian game, allowing the two sides to go to extremes so that the Americans could later emerge as mediators and conciliators coming to the rescue of the peace talks.

The riddle was solved for me by President Carter in person: "The Egyptian plan is unacceptable to us," he said, "but we have to go on." On second thought, this approach struck me as logical. Seeing Sadat as impulsive and liable to kick over the traces if angered, the Americans ignored his proposals and went straight to the second phase, which turned out to be extremely awkward for us—to put it mildly.

At that morning's meeting, the American team, headed by the president, demanded an immediate freeze on new settlements in Judea, Samaria, and the Gaza Strip since it viewed the settlement program as the greatest pitfall on the road to peace. In the wake of Sadat's proposals, this demand had even less prospect of acceptance by the Israeli delegation. Breathing fire, Begin rejected it immediately. At the same time, he flung out a remark that thoroughly alarmed the Americans. "Perhaps Sadat should be requested to withdraw his proposals?" The Americans seemed panic-stricken at the mere thought, convinced that returning the document to Sadat would signal the end of the conference.

Begin returned from his second meeting with Presidents Carter and Sadat in a belligerent mood. His encounter with Sadat and the active participation of Carter had combined to send his blood pressure soaring. From an Israeli viewpoint, the picture was now clearer—and gloomier: Sadat, with Carter's backing, was interested in the establishment of a Palestinian state linked to Jordan. On the issue of the Rafah settlements, Begin insisted that they remain in place, stressing that this was the general consensus in Israel on this point, "with the exception of the Communist members of the Knesset."

The second meeting between Begin and Sadat—like their encounter at Ismailia in 1977—was exacerbated by verbal misunderstandings. Angered by Sadat's demand for war damages, Begin had remarked that such a demand is presented to a "defeated nation." Sadat, thinking the term was being applied to Egypt, hit the roof: "A defeated nation? We were—but after October 1973, we are defeated no longer!" Even after Carter intervened to clear up the misunderstanding, Sadat remained angry and fuming. The honor he had succeeded in regaining for the Egyptian army in October 1973 was dear to his heart.

"Sadat sounded very provocative," Begin told our delegation.

Another meeting between the two leaders later on the same day did nothing to improve matters. Each side was adamant, and there was no progress.

The only practical proposal came from Carter. "If the Rafah settlements are the sole and final obstacle to peace," he advised Begin, "I suggest you bring the issue of their evacuation to the Knesset."

Begin apparently dismissed the proposal outright. "There will be an absolute majority against evacuation," he assured Carter.

My own assessment differed; I knew we would have to make some painful decisions if the settlements were the last remaining obstacle to a peace agreement.

"We offer you peace, and you want territory!" an angry Sadat had said to Begin. "If you don't consent to dismantle the settlements, there will be no peace!"

"We will not consent to dismantle them!" Begin had retorted.

The three direct meetings Sadat and Begin held at Camp David—with the active participation of President Carter—were totally fruitless. They did nothing for the peace negotiations, serving the two leaders more as opportunities for a mutual settling of accounts. All the other participants at the conference soon realized that further meetings between Sadat and Begin were a sure recipe for failure. Consequently, the White House team eagerly leaped at the suggestion of a member of the Israeli delegation that there be no further direct meetings between the two leaders; any contacts would be conducted in the future by their aides and ministers.

Sadat's demands, along with the American call for a freeze on any further settlements, overshadowed the discussions that went on over the weekend.

I was not charmed by the idea of leaving Camp David empty-handed because of the settlements issue. Given the current political situation, there was not the slightest prospect of convincing Western opinion of the wisdom of forfeiting peace in favor of the settlements. I proposed that we freeze the number of settlements at their present number, in return for an agreement that they be allowed to remain; we would also proclaim that the establishment of settlements in Judea, Samaria, and Gaza was our right.

"It's no tragedy if we don't set up another settlement in the Jordan valley," I said. "But it is liable to be a tragedy if we leave Camp David with nothing."

In the militant mood prevailing in the Israeli delegation, there was no prospect of getting my view across. "What shall we tell our young people?" demanded Begin with his usual pathos. "It would be madness, particularly for a government which claims sovereignty over the whole land of Israel. What kind of freeze can be imposed on the land of Israel?"

This outright rejection of the American proposals angered Carter and his men, who had hoped for a breakthrough before the end of the week. The change in the American attitude soon made itself evident: demonstrating their irritation, they spoke in increasingly harsh terms. "You Israelis!" said Dr. William Quandt, a member of the U.S. delegation. "You always accept our proposals—but it's always six months too late, and you pay dearly for it." There was more than a grain of truth in his complaint.

The Americans decided to soften the warlike mood by a social evening for all three delegations, with a drill display by a marine detachment. At the same time, the hundreds of journalists waiting outside were permitted a glimpse at the conference site. Until then, in a rare exception to what usually occurs at such conferences, nothing of the proceedings at Camp David had leaked out. Even the most prominent journalists—Walter Cronkite, Barbara Walters, and others—were groping in the dark, trying to draw up their political evaluations on the strength of nothing more than their visual observations. During the marine display, Carter stood on the platform, his face showing no trace of his famous horsy grin. Begin and Sadat did not exchange a single word. There was no way of concealing the truth from the inquisitive eyes of the journalists. The conference was evidently bogged down.

The social evening was more of a success. In a bid to captivate the palates of their Middle Eastern guests, the marine cooks had barbecued shashlik and kabob on glowing embers. I still found the sight amazing: a Filipino cook in an American camp making eastern delicacies for Egyptian and Israeli guests. This gastronomical exercise on the part of our hosts sent the aroma of scorching meat wafting through the trees, bringing memories of home. The question of when we would have to return home was always on my mind.

As the week drew to a close, Rosalynn Carter's prayer had proved ineffective.

Rosalynn did not seem to play any active role. She could often be seen strolling with her young daughter Amy, who ran about obviously feeling very much at home in spite of the constant surveillance by a bodyguard. Life must be hard for a ten-year-old with an armed guard always in attendance. But Amy's ringing laughter brought pleasant associations: in a few weeks, I was going to become a grandfather for the first time. My daughter Michal was nearing the end of her pregnancy.

That weekend, the mood at Camp David was despondent. The Egyptian peace plan had delivered a body blow to the prospects of peace, and the American demand for a freeze on new settlements and evacuation of the existing ones in the Sinai seemed likely to provide the final knockout. It all reminded me of the World War II films about submarines: here we were, in the enclosed, claustrophobic atmosphere of Camp David, with Captain Jimmy Carter at the periscope as we watched the tantalizingly slow descent of the depth charges, holding our collective breaths and wondering whether or not they were going to hit their target, whether or not they would go off. True, the "charges" at Camp David were typed out on sheets of paper, but they were nonetheless destructive for that.

All this time, Sadat remained withdrawn inside his cabin. Even members of the Egyptian delegation gave it a wide berth; rarely did I see any of them in the vicinity of the president's lodge. I noticed that Foreign Minister Kamel was even more on edge than usual; at joint meetings, he rarely opened his mouth.

On Saturday, I went to Sadat's cabin, accompanied by General Tamir. Our conversation began with the usual greetings and small talk as we sipped coffee.

Sadat looked somewhat distracted. I wondered whether his impatience would induce him to order the Egyptian delegation to head back to Cairo. Sadat could never bring himself to devote time or attention to what he perceived as trivial and minor details. "I think bi-i-ig!" he would declare.

"Mr. President," I told him. "We must make progress!"

"Definitely!" Sadat replied. "We must!"

"I get the impression that a lot of things aren't moving for psychological reasons, not practical ones."

"Of course," Sadat agreed. "I'm sure it's ninety percent a psychological problem."

"Before Camp David, I hoped you would hold direct and open conversations with Begin, and the two of you would reach agreement, or at least an understanding, on the principal points of dissension." My regret that this had not transpired was obvious.

"The official side is the principal difficulty," Sadat explained. "Peace does not depend only upon the peace treaty. It depends on the relationship which unfolds. Things happen that are not necessarily on the official plane."

On this point, at least, I fully shared Sadat's approach. "I suggest you talk with Dayan," I said, bringing up a familiar issue.

"Yes, of course," Sadat promised. "I want to invite him in."

"Mr. President!" I addressed him boldly, sending out feelers to gauge whether he intended to break off the talks. "You can't stop what you began last year. You can't go backwards!"

"I won't go backwards," he replied. "It is impossible to go backwards. I shall continue with my initiative."

His reply cheered me. "There are still a number of key problems"—I pushed on—"and I would like to know how you imagine their solution. There is no argument about the Sinai being your country. But a lot of things have happened in the course of thirty years. You must understand the mentality of our people. On the one hand, they never believed that an Arab leader—certainly not the leader of the largest and strongest Arab nation—would come to Jerusalem. But the Israelis are still convinced that any error is liable to bring a disaster upon them. That is why the time factor is so decisive for us. And that is why Israeli control is so vital. So if we have decided to advance toward an agreement, let's use our understanding and patience to bridge the disagreements. Allow me to present a few of them: the Sinai—we must find a way to solve this without undermining your sovereignty so that we don't need the UN to supervise demilitarization and the thinning out of forces."

"You know my opinion," Sadat broke in. "I'm ready to go ahead without the UN. Supervision can be by means of a joint committee."

I had deliberately chosen to start with the points of agreement. But I now turned to the most difficult problem of all: the Sinai settlements. "Do you remember my proposal that the Yamit area be attached to the Gaza Strip so that whatever the status of Gaza, it would apply to Yamit as well? I want to stress again that a solution must be found for these settlements because our people are unanimously opposed to evacuating them."

"Ezer, I make no restrictions," Sadat said, his expression growing severe. "I've thought about it, but I won't give the Rafah approaches to the Gaza Strip. I told Carter that I cannot agree that after a peace agreement there will remain on Egyptian soil settlements protected by an Israeli force. How can I show my face before the other Arab states if that is the price I pay for peace? I refuse to have settlements with Israeli protection! I will not be able to receive my people's consent, and I cannot consent, either, because whoever succeeds me will blame me for my consent. This will cause problems between us in the future. Begin offended me when he presented a peace plan that said that your settlements will remain in the Sinai with an Israeli defense force."

"And the airfields?" I tried my luck.

"They have to be evacuated within two years!" Sadat reiterated. His reply dashed the hopes I still clung to.

"I suggest Gamasy and I find a solution that could take place over a longer period of time." I tried to save what I could. "And a permanent solution for the Etzion airfield. As I told you, the time-table depends on how long it takes for us to build new bases."

"I am prepared to build them for you in six months," Sadat fired back. "I have done it in less. You saw the Janklis airfield."

"How about the phases of withdrawal?" I demanded.

"I told Begin I was prepared for withdrawal by phases, with the first phase going to the El Arish-Ras Mohammed line. I told him other things he did not understand before. Full recognition? Yes! International waterway in the Tiran Strait? Yes!"

That he did not mention diplomatic relations was a bad sign. Previously, this point had been one of the more convincing features in favor of a new relationship between our two countries. During earlier conversations, Sadat had given me his personal assurance of it.

"We also agreed on diplomatic and commercial relations," I reminded him immediately.

"That is my sovereign prerogative," Sadat stressed. "And I must choose the appropriate time. I know I spoke to you about it, and I meant it, and I can tell you that I want it. But Begin said in the Knesset: 'I will not give anything without getting something in return.' I will behave the same way."

"What about open borders?"

"Yes, that will be part of our peaceful relations."

"You must meet Begin halfway on all these points I've mentioned," I said. "Here at Camp David, we need more than a partial success. What do you want to achieve here?"

"I want to reach agreement on a framework," Sadat said slowly. "Afterwards, our advisers will sit down and work out the details of the framework. There will be no time pressure; we'll be able to maintain direct contacts and continue to hold consultations until we find solutions."

I went back to one of the principal obstacles. "Judea and Samaria have never been under anyone's sovereignty," I pointed out. "And we have more rights there than Jordan does."

Sadat's expression was sober. "I told Carter that neither you nor Hussein have sovereignty over the West Bank. The area belongs to its population."

"We said Israeli forces would remain in Judea, Samaria, and Gaza," I reminded him.

"I tell you—yes. I still think so. In the interim period, they will be in the places assigned to them, and afterward when the Palestinians decide on their future, it will be necessary once again to make arrangements for your military deployment. I also recommend a link with Jordan."

"Do you expect Hussein to join the negotiations?" I asked him yet again.

"I believe he will," Sadat affirmed. "If he doesn't, I'll go it alone! I'm prepared to go with everything I have, including deployment of Egyptian forces."

"That will do for this morning," I said, rising to my feet. "I will report to my prime minister. Don't forget how important it is for you to meet with Dayan!" I reminded him.

My conversation with Sadat showed that he was not prepared to make any overwhelming concessions—but neither did he want the talks to break down. The failure of the Camp David conference would be a personal setback for him. Israel would be left holding on to the airfields, the Rafah settlements, and the oil wells, but Sadat would have to put on sackcloth and ashes if he wanted to be taken in again by the Arab world. According to what I knew of him, in such an event, he would prefer to resign. I concluded, therefore, that his "lunatic" document was far from being his last word. He may have climbed too far up on his high horse, in which case he would need an American ladder to help him down. This state of affairs might make it possible to resolve the outstanding points of disagreement, whose number was diminishing from hour to hour.

"Our hope is not yet lost!" I hummed the refrain from our national anthem.

The American team, headed by Carter, Vance, and Brzezinski, now went about steadying the ladder for Sadat's descent. The second week at Camp David was marked by American efforts to flush Israelis and Egyptians out of the defense positions each side had clung to. Carter was most active in the effort.

I was full of admiration for the American president. The world's busiest man, whose every minute and second were measured frugally, dropped all his current engagements, dedicating himself day and night to the cause of peace in the Middle East. He earned my respect with his bulldoglike persistence and his ability to deal with the tiniest details. He attended numerous discussions, listening in and making notes in his neat engineer's handwriting on a yellow letter pad. He led his talks with great authority, alternately growing angry or flashing his teeth in a brilliant smile as the need arose. His swift and clear grasp was a great advantage; he could understand immediately what was being discussed.

In addition, Carter's team functioned with admirable efficiency. It held its internal deliberations and prepared position papers and reports, composing dozens of drafts for every proposal and setting out answers to every conceivable query. The team, orchestrated by Secretary of State Vance, was marked by a high degree of unanimity. Balanced and to the point, Vance chaired meetings with a quiet determination that left no doubt who was the boss. He overshadowed National Security Adviser Brzezinski, who kept a low profile, possibly aware that he was suspect in Israeli eyes.

Begin remembered every remark of Brzezinski's that was less than complimentary to Israel. Begin attaches great weight to the past in the way he relates to people—as I can testify from my own experience. He may have viewed Brzezinski as the descendant of those Polish feudal lords who made life so miserable for his own parents and grandparents in Brest-Litovsk.

The American attempts to break the deadlock produced a document meant as a compromise between the extreme position presented by Sadat and Begin's views. Begin had been very worried about what the American proposal would be, fearing that if the conference ended in failure, the American and Egyptian proposals would be published—while Israel would be caught empty-handed merely because no official Israeli proposal had been submitted. Begin was always king when it came to documents, and he could not afford to be left behind by Carter and Sadat. He'd given orders for the preparation of an Israeli proposal. However, almost all the members of our delegation agreed that its presentation at this point would only cause the others to dig in even further; consequently, the Israeli proposal would be kept in reserve, to be brought out only if the American and Egyptian documents were published.

The American proposal was seventeen pages of high explosive. In an attempt to manipulate the discussion, the Americans circumvented controversial issues like the fate of the Sinai settlements and airfields; at the same time, they added a whole series of worrisome conditions relating to Judea, Samaria, and the Gaza Strip. The blood drained from Begin's face as his eyes flickered slowly down the various sections of the American paper. His face twisted into a scowl of slowly rising anger. Any one of the American proposals provided an adequate pretext for us to order our flight home with El Al!

Within three years, according to this document, talks would commence on the final status of Judea, Samaria, and the Gaza Strip—including the question of borders and of Palestinian participation; there would be a self-governing authority—and not a council; the self-governing body would not draw its authority from the Israeli military government; Jordan would enjoy a special status; further settlements would not be established, and the existing ones would be frozen; and a plebiscite would be held to determine the final status of the West Bank and the Gaza Strip.

"Gentlemen," Begin said, "the Americans have simply copied the Egyptian plan." His expression was grim. I was worried over his quiet tone. He was swallowing his anger, and I feared the valves of his heart might burst. I hoped his personal physician was in attendance; at all events, I knew the camp's medical unit was on constant alert—hardly surprising when two of the conference's leading figures, Begin and Sadat, suffered from heart ailments.

"Looks like we're going home, Abrasha!" I voiced my disappointment to General Tamir.

It was Menachem Begin's night. Seated at the head of the Israeli delegation, he faced Carter and the others: his voice raised to eliminate any doubts or misunderstandings, he rejected or amended considerable portions of the American proposal.

In the course of the discussion, Carter said he intended to bring up the issue of the national rights of the Palestinians, including their right to self-determination.

"Out of the question!" Begin replied. He was afraid that such a discussion might open up the possibility in the distant future of a Palestinian state.

When the American president proposed a freeze on new settlements, the Israelis rejected it immediately.

Then Carter went on to suggest that Israeli units remain in the West Bank over and beyond the five-year period. At long last, the Israeli delegation found one point on which it could agree with Carter.

But Carter also declared that Sadat would not make concessions with regard to Israeli settlements and airfields in the Sinai, and therefore Israel should evacuate them.

"We do not dismantle settlements," Begin said with great emphasis. "We don't plough them up or demolish them."

The discussion went on far into the night, with increasing intensity. In the course of the talk, both sides of the Israeli-American confrontation were raising their voices, but Carter maintained firm control, refusing to allow either side to interrupt the other. It was a crucial role he played, one that should not be underestimated.

When we reached the clause about the "nonacquisition of territory by force," Begin's reaction was extremely fierce. "There is no such situation in our case. The territories we occupy were conquered in a defensive war. You should know, Mr. President"—Begin pointed at Carter—"that in all the wars, we were the victims of Arab aggression."

Begin vigorously objected to a sentence in the preamble that stressed that "occupation of territory by force is unacceptable." It sounded innocent enough, but Begin smelled a trap, foreseeing that it might be used later to dislodge Israel from the Golan Heights.

"We will not accept that," the prime minister told Carter.

"Mr. Prime Minister," Carter replied, "that is not only the view of Sadat, it is also the American view—and you will have to accept it." By now it was around three o'clock in the morning. Carter compressed his lips, no longer capable of concealing his fury. He crumpled up the papers lying on the table before him and flung down his pencil, his blue eyes alight with rage.

"You will have to accept it!" He seemed to be repeating the words to himself.

"Mr. President," Begin said tersely. "No threats, please."

Mentally, I applauded his retort.

The unequal facedown between Carter and Begin had begun almost from the moment the Israeli prime minister had assumed office. The American president had been working for a total Israeli withdrawal to the June 4, 1967, borders—with a few minor changes—in exchange for an overall and complete peace agreement. He'd sought a political solution for the Palestinians, and officials of his administration had held contacts with the PLO in a bid to bring it into the negotiations.

The verbal confrontations between the president of the world's greatest superpower and the prime minister of puny Israel had often been brutal, reaching a peak during Begin's visit to the White House in March 1978. While Begin referred to Carter as "a great friend" and defined their talks as "good," White House briefings stigmatized Israel's prime minister as an obstacle to peace. Top administration officials indicated that they wanted him replaced. Indeed, it was rumored in Israel that the Americans had gone beyond mere talk, though I have no proof of it.

Begin was totally opposed to a withdrawal to the 1967 borders, and doubly so to any solution liable to lead to the establishment of a Palestinian state. He'd rejected with abhorrence any reference to Palestinian "rights of self-determination" or recognition of their "legitimate rights."

Now, at Camp David, there were so many Israeli amendments to the American proposal that it was changed beyond recognition.

After lunch the following day, exhausted from the night-long discussion, I headed for my cabin to catch a nap. Undressing, I lay down on my bed in my shorts. Outside, the weather had changed: it was chilly and drizzly—an appropriate reflection of the climate of the conference. I imagined that Carter must have been furious over the Israeli replies to his proposal; they must have shown him plainly that there was no change in Israel's position: no evacuation of the Sinai settlements, no withdrawal from the West Bank, no consent to the Security Council resolution about "nonacquisition of territory by force."

My rest was disrupted by strides approaching my cabin. Assuming that it was one of the security guards, I closed my eyes again when suddenly I heard a voice say: "Mr. Weizman!" I looked up. Jimmy Carter's figure was filling the doorway. It must have been a charming scene: the president of the United States facing an Israeli minister in a state of almost total nudity.

"I'm sorry!" I blurted out, leaping toward the chair where I had laid my pants.

"That's okay, Mr. Weizman." Carter tried to reassure me. Seeing my embarrassment, his mouth broadened into its famous smile. "I would like to talk to you."

What does one say to the president of the United States under such circumstances? Should I say: "Mr. President, please wait outside!"? Or ask him to sit down? Ignore him? I doubted that protocol had covered this one.

Carter's blue eyes focused somewhere in the middle distance—and I flung myself into the first available shirt.

As Carter strode along the path at my side, his expression was grim. I realized that something extraordinary was afoot, and my guess was confirmed when Carter told me he had met with Sadat, who totally rejected the Israeli proposals and was threatening to leave for home. "Sadat can't accept Israel's demands for the maintenance of the Sinai settlements," the president said. "He also rejects the idea of leaving them there under UN protection and of the Ofira airfield at the tip of the Sinai being operated under UN supervision."

We had now reached Carter's cabin—and the crucial point in the talks. Evidently, someone was going to have to give way. As things stood, with Egypt and the United States joining forces, there was little doubt who that "someone" was going to be.

The eighth day of the Camp David conference was not unlike its predecessors; in some ways, it was worse. A mood of dejection prevailed in all three delegations. Clearly, talks would not be allowed to drag on endlessly; at the same time, any firm conclusion seemed a long, long way away.

"However great my concern over the peace process," I said to my confidants, convinced that the conference was doomed, "I am even more concerned over our future relations with the United States." In my view, Sadat had succeeded completely in winning Carter over to his side; in the event of a breakdown, our position would deteriorate progressively. Israel had managed to survive thirty years without a single day of peace—but I doubted whether we would be able to survive without the political, military, and economic support of the United States. "This is going to end with us clearing out of here," I said. "But Sadat will remain—and that's the worst thing of all."

The American role at the conference was incomplete. In the first phase, when the sides were putting forward ideas, the Americans had served as mediators. In the second phase, they put forward their own proposals for the sides to accept or reject; they then received Egyptian comments and amendments to convey to Israel, and vice versa. That was where the American delegation had left off—at the wrong time and place.

Much more than that would be needed to convince Begin and Sadat to make painful concessions. Only Jimmy Carter had the power to bang their heads together and force them to reach agreement. Indeed, Carter proceeded to come up with a new idea, which ultimately facilitated the breakthrough. Resolving to focus on the Sinai, he decided to aim for two agreements: one dealing with peace between Israel and Egypt, the second dealing with an overall settlement for the Middle East conflict.

I was invited to see Carter, who wanted to know everything and anything on the Sinai. General Tamir and I gave him a thorough introduction to the peninsula and the military problems associated with it. Carter's grasp of the material was remarkable: within hours, he had produced the draft of an agreement on the Sinai, including a delineation of a demilitarized zone and specified dates for each phase of the withdrawal. He presented the plan to Sadat; astonishingly enough, the Egyptian president accepted it almost in entirety, making no more than a few minor modifications.

Unlike Sadat, Begin was still in a belligerent mood. When the Israeli delegation assembled at his Laurel Lodge for consultation, he could barely conceal his anger: speaking of the American draft of the preamble, with its reference to the nonacquisition of territory by force, he said: "If I sign it—may my right hand lose its cunning! I won't sign!"

I had the clear impression that his words were directed at Dayan and me as much as at the Americans. He must have sensed that the foreign minister and I were in favor of meeting the Americans and Egyptians halfway. "Are there any among us who are faint of heart?" he asked ominously.

The temperature rose. When the Americans resubmitted the previous day's proposal with some amendments, it remained nearer to the Egyptian position than to our own. Most of the clauses we had angrily deleted on the previous day had been restored in no more than a slightly different wording. "What is the point of discussing things when the clauses we remove are put straight back in?" Begin demanded indignantly.

"Mr. Prime Minister," said Vance, momentarily losing patience. "You are not alone here. There's also the other side to be considered."

Developments followed one another in rapid succession. Dayan let it be known that he was leaving for Israel within the day; the delegation's legal adviser, Meir Rosenne, advised Begin to concede the reference to nonacquisition of territory by force since it appeared in the preamble, which in any case had no binding validity; Carter proposed that a jurist from each of the delegations come to discuss the wording until a solution was found. Then, to top it all off, Begin met with Carter for what he later described as "the most serious conversation of my lifetime," in the course of which he proclaimed that he was sensitive to Egyptian views but was "even more sensitive to Jewish blood."

Carter held a marathon round of talks with the two jurists— Aharon Barak for Israel and Osama el-Baz for Egypt—producing a series of drafts, some of which were rejected by Begin because of their references to "the legitimate rights of the Palestinian people" and "the possibility of permitting the Palestinians to take part in deciding on their future."

There were other proposals that proved to be obstacles to agreement: hoisting an Arab flag over Jerusalem's Temple Mount; a freeze on new settlements while negotiations were in progress; and—of course—the return of the Sinai airfields and settlements.

On his part, Sadat rejected Carter's proposal that the sentence about nonacquisition of territory by force be deleted.

It was the eighth day of the conference, and we seemed to be stuck more or less where we'd been at its opening session.

"It's a pity I came," I exclaimed, deeply disappointed.

There were hints from the Egyptian delegation that Sadat was planning to leave Camp David.

Begin prepared the text of what purported to be a joint communiqué, which would concede that the conference had failed.

"It's my impression that everything is collapsing," a dejected Sadat told me over the phone.

That afternoon, I had a further meeting with Sadat, who had already been briefed by Osama el-Baz. "My mood is not good," the Egyptian president said. "I won't be able to get this across in the Arab world."

I made one more effort to soften him up with regard to our Sinai settlements. He frowned. "I won't give up a single inch of my land!"

There was nothing else to be done. The Egyptian president was correct in his behavior toward me, he even made a show of friendship, but he did not hide his anger and perplexity.

When the Israeli delegation assembled, I phrased our dilemma bluntly, without mincing words. "We don't have any other choice. We have to choose between a peace agreement and the Israeli settlements in the Sinai."

Previously, Dayan and I had been invited for a talk with Carter, who had made it plain that Israel could no longer evade the harsh choice: settlements or peace.

Moshe Dayan shared my views. Earlier that day, he'd finally had his first private meeting with Sadat, from which he returned convinced that the Egyptian president was immovable on this point. Dayan had gone with the hope of achieving some kind of partial agreement if an overall agreement proved unattainable.

"Out of the question!" Sadat had declared—which Dayan promptly reported to Begin and the rest of our delegation. "This is the end of the road," our foreign minister concluded. The consultation ended with Begin's deciding to invite Vance for a final talk.

Dayan, looking extremely downcast, headed for his cabin. Knowing Dayan well, I sensed that he had reached an inner decision.

A few moments later, I knocked at the door. When I walked in, I found him squatting on the floor. He was packing his suitcase.

"Moshe," I urged. "Don't be hasty. I still have faith."

It was General Tamir who came up with the best proposal that day. He suggested contacting Agriculture Minister Arik Sharon and briefing him on the situation at the conference; Sharon should then be persuaded to call Begin and urge him to consent to evacuation of the settlements. Sharon had been the moving spirit behind the settlement program; as head of our Southern Command, he had sponsored the establishment of the Rafah settlements, which were the apple of his eye. I found it hard to believe that Arik would allow himself to be convinced even though Tamir and he were close friends.

"We've got nothing to lose." I shrugged. "Call him!"

A few hours later, a deeply moved Begin was telling the Israeli delegation that Arik Sharon had phoned him; to his surprise, Sharon was in favor of evacuating the settlements if they were the last remaining obstacle to a peace agreement. "I see no military objection to their evacuation," Sharon had told the prime minister. Sharon's intervention was bound to have some influence on Begin's eventual decision, and I could guess that his telephone conversation with Begin on an open line must have caused rejoicing in the American camp.

Despite Sharon's call, the morning meeting of the Israeli delegation was marked by a mood of failure and frustration. Sadat was still insisting on a freeze on new settlements in the West Bank in addition to the removal of the existing ones in Rafah and the handing over of our airfields. On these points, Carter had given his consistent backing to the Egyptian president.

When it came to my turn to speak, I went straight to the point. "Evacuation of the settlements is essential if we want peace."

"I heard you!" Begin barked at me angrily. He appeared to be firm in his opposition to dismantling the settlements.

While our deliberations were at their height, a message was brought in: "President Carter requests that Dayan and Barak come and see him for a further talk."

With all the misunderstandings, frustrations, and sometimes personal animosity among us, there was one solid personality on the Israeli team—the legal adviser to the Israeli cabinet, Aharon Barak, who was first introduced to the Egyptian-Israeli problems and possibilities when he'd joined me on my March 1978 visit to Egypt. Besides giving constructive advice and finding the wording to solve intricate problems, his greatest contribution was his relationship with President Carter, who had full confidence in him.

I went along with Dayan and Barak. Carter greeted us with a gloomy expression and went straight to the point: "You must agree to evacuate the Sinai settlements to achieve a peace treaty."

We listened attentively. We were not empowered to diverge from the official policy of our delegation, but Dayan tried to signal the change in his own personal view: "Such a thing cannot be agreed upon here," he told Carter. "It can't be done without the consent of the whole cabinet and of the Knesset."

Carter and his aides noticed the shift in the Israeli position as expressed by Dayan; they were already aware that I held similar views. What remained was to convince Begin to get into line with his colleagues.

Meanwhile, the hands of the clock were moving inexorably forward. Clearly, the summit would have to be concluded within a day or two. Word came to us from the direction of Aspen Lodge that President Carter intended to appear before Congress at the beginning of the next week. The hint could hardly have been broader.

I reached my own decision to concede the Sinai airfields—whose military importance I rated above that of the Rafah settlements—after realizing that there was no prospect of successfully concluding the conference without such a concession on our part.

"Could you build us substitute airfields?" I asked U.S. Defense Secretary Harold Brown. My intention was to tie his hands and place the Americans under an obligation to us in the event that the new airfields were not ready on time. Otherwise, a delay would prevent us from evacuating the existing airfields on the date agreed upon—constituting an infringement of the peace agreement. A further reason for harnessing the Americans to a solution of the airfields problem was our reluctance to further burden our inflation-ridden economy with the enormous expenditure involved in constructing and equipping new airfields inside Israel.

Brown must have been expecting such a question. His reply was in the affirmative—and the die was cast as far as I was concerned. My air force experience left me in no doubt that we were giving up a military asset of the first order, but we were up against the wall.

And no one more so than Israel's prime minister.

Menachem Begin faced the dilemma of his lifetime. He was in

growing disagreement with the leading members of his own delegation. He was under enormous pressure from the Americans. Equally urgent was his own desire to go down in history as the man who had brought peace to Israel. But all these constraints, which favored his making necessary concessions, were in conflict with the ingrained philosophy he had followed throughout his life.

For many long and nerve-racking hours, it appeared that Begin's ideology would outweigh the dictates of immediate reality. Israel's prime minister refused to make the concessions everyone demanded of him—particularly because Sadat refused to budge on issues, such as his insistence that the final communiqué agree to the "nonacquisition of territory by force."

Carter now launched his desperate onslaught. Summoning President Sadat for a private talk, the U.S. president pulled out all the stops. Without regard for his own dignity, Carter explained that the present impasse was endangering his political prospects. Finally, Sadat gave way and agreed to give up mention of the "nonacquisition" principle, resting content with a reference to Resolution 242 and the Aswan formula on the Palestinian issue.

Now it was time for Carter to turn his guns on Begin once more. It seemed a hopeless undertaking, with the Israeli prime minister deeply entrenched in his positions. Begin had vowed that he would not dismantle the Sinai settlements. He would surely not go back on his word.

With the conference apparently headed for a final rupture, Carter and Begin held their last private meeting.

It was the breakthrough. Informed by President Carter of Sadat's concession and under unprecedented pressure, Begin reversed the whole course of events with a dramatic declaration. "If what is holding up peace are the Sinai settlements," he told the president of the United States, "I shall submit the matter to the decision of the Knesset and honor whatever the Knesset decides. I shall even recommend that on this important and sensitive issue, party discipline shall not be enforced in the voting. That is all I can do. Nothing more."

In the course of that talk, Begin understood that he had to decide—then and there—whether he preferred the airfields or peace. In choosing the latter, he surrendered the former. He also agreed to include in the framework agreement a term never previously accepted by Israel, "recognition of the legitimate rights of the Palestinian people," although his consent did not include recognition of the Palestinians' rights to establish an independent state within the boundaries of the land of Israel.

Begin, who had only recently explained the danger involved in using terms like "legitimate rights," now denied to us that what he had agreed to jeopardized Israel.

"What is the ultimate importance of the term 'legitimate rights'?" he asked, promptly answering his own question: "The origin of the word is in the Latin *lex*, denoting 'law.' With the development of language, this turned into the English word 'legitimate.' What is the meaning of 'legitimate right'? If it is a right—that means it is legitimate. Can a right be illegitimate?"

By such verbal acrobatics Begin managed to come to terms with reality.

Sunday morning—the last day of the summit conference—found us exhausted and battered, but satisfied. There was a sense of historic achievement, of "All's well that ends well."

Then it suddenly transpired that Carter had promised Sadat a letter in which the United States would declare that it viewed east Jerusalem as occupied territory, just like the rest of the territory Israel had been holding since 1967.

"If that's the case," Begin said grimly, "we can pack our bags and go home without another word."

If the talks were to fail at the very moment when success was finally possible, no issue was better chosen than Jerusalem. Every Jew the world over would justify Israel's obduracy.

The problem was resolved by a letter stating that the U.S. position on Jerusalem remained as defined by the American delegation to the UN General Assembly in June 1967 when the United States had called for international supervision of the holy places while refusing to recognize Israel's annexation of east Jerusalem.

I was walking along one of the paths when a bicycle veered toward me, driven by Bill Quandt.

"There's agreement!" he whooped. "There's agreement!" and pedaled off furiously down the path.

However, a few secondary issues remained to be resolved. It emerged that the agreement also required Israel to demilitarize a zone along our borders, albeit a small one.

All the same, it was hard for Israel to concede this point. We wanted to enlarge the force we would be permitted to station within this zone. I went to talk with Sadat to see if I could win his consent.

"How many battalions do you want?" Sadat demanded.

"Three battalions of our border guard," I replied.

"All right, Ezer," Sadat said grandly. "For you—four battalions. Ever since the October war, I have no more complexes."

The Camp David Conference did not produce a complete peace agreement. Instead, there were two framework agreements that the two sides were required to complete within three months. The agreements laid down lines for future developments; however, it was evident right from the outset that many issues had been left open—deliberately.

One agreement provided the framework for an Israeli-Egyptian peace treaty. It was the easier and simpler of the two. Israel gave up the whole of the Sinai, including the settlements and airfields. The United States lent its assistance by a verbal undertaking to construct two airfields inside Israel to replace those we were abandoning in the Sinai, promising to complete them before the time came for our withdrawal.

The United States was abandoning its umpire role. It would continue to supervise; however, unlike the previous arrangements, neither side could remove the UN observers without the consent of the other and without the unanimous agreement of the Security Council. With the exception of combat planes and antiaircraft missiles, the Sinai would not be demilitarized as Israel had once desired; however, a wide buffer zone would be created between the two armies.

The second agreement was a framework for an overall Middle East peace settlement. While it dealt with peace between Israel and all the Arab states, including Egypt, it was mainly directed at the West Bank and the Gaza Strip. In it, Egypt recognized Israel's need for security guarantees with regard to those areas, while Israel undertook to grant full autonomy to their inhabitants.

In the framework of this agreement, Israel consented to the inclusion of terms and concepts she had never previously accepted: negotiations to include Palestinian representatives, not restricted to the inhabitants of those areas; solution of the Palestinian problem "in all its aspects." The agreement specified that a solution must acknowledge the legitimate rights of the Palestinian people and their just demands. Both sides agreed that autonomy would apply for no more than a five-year interim period. However, Israel reserved a veto over a number of central points of particular sensitivity as well as the right to demand full sovereignty in the future.

In this second agreement—even more than in the first—most of the issues were left open to later negotiations. The two sides parted well aware that they could scarcely hope to reach agreement on some points, such as the status of Jerusalem, Israeli settlement in the occupied territories, and the argument over "abrogation" or "withdrawal" of the Israeli military government.

Some of my colleagues were still dubious about the agreement, and I tried to reassure them. "An agreement," I said, "is like a Jewish marriage contract. You don't look at it, you put it away in the closet. If things go wrong with the marriage, you get it out and study it—but by then, it's too late, and heaven help you if you need it!"

Israel and Egypt attended the Camp David Conference because they were unable to refuse the invitation from the president of the United States. In view of the minimal goals set by the sides—concluding the conference without suffering any harm in their vital interests—the conference's success in working out a framework agreement came as a surprise. The success evidently stemmed from the desire to reach agreement, which outweighed the desire of each side to protect its own private interests, and from the role played by the United States in the deliberations.

The greatest achievement of the Camp David Conference lay in reaching an agreement, with all the implications of that achievement: breaking the psychological barrier between the Israeli people and the Arab world; eliminating the taboo imposed on Israel thirty years ago by restoring the Arab-Israeli conflict to the conventional terms of international disputes. At the same time, the road to the stabilization of a permanent peace in the region is still long.

Study of the two framework agreements reveals clear distinctions: while the bilateral agreement with Egypt is clear, the framework agreement about the future of Judea and Samaria and Gaza is marked by its deliberately vague formulations. While there is no conditional link between the two agreements, the mere fact of their simultaneous signing constitutes a kind of conditional link. It would be naive to imagine that progress could be made in implementing Israeli-Egyptian peace without some progress in Judea, Samaria, and Gaza. President Sadat continues to point out that he has not signed a separate agreement or relinquished a single Arab national objective with regard to Israel.

In the immediate future, the key to any further progress is in the hands of King Hussein, whose commitment to the peace process

376 THE BATTLE FOR PEACE

would affect the outcome of the negotiations and particularly developments in the occupied territories as the agreements go into effect during the interim period and subsequently. On the other hand, without Hussein's commitment, it is doubtful whether Israel can implement the autonomy plan unaided. Hussein seems to be in no hurry to give an affirmative answer; if he does, he will probably attempt to squeeze out the maximum number of concessions—in advance.

The dangers facing the first agreement hinge on Sadat. In the whole Camp David mosaic, Sadat constitutes the key link whose fracture would lead to the disintegration of the entire chain. However, Sadat does not seem overly vulnerable. There is no prospect of popular unrest, revolution, or coup attempts against Sadat in consequence of the agreements. The Egyptian army and its commanders seem likely to remain loyal.

Two risks do remain: an assassination attempt and Sadat's state of health.

Inter-Arab pressures against him are probably not going to threaten the Camp David accord. Sadat's most important backing comes from the Saudis. Even if they are not overjoyed with the agreements, they will probably not enter into an overt confrontation with him. On the other hand, Syria's interests draw her in the opposite direction, although her room for maneuver in trying to foil the agreements is not great. Syria was greatly surprised by the agreements, having long believed that Sadat's initiative was doomed to failure. Syria could choose the military option against Israel, but such a move would not likely undermine the Israeli-Egyptian agreement. On the contrary, there is the danger that Israel would see herself as being at greater liberty than she is now in her actions against Syria. In view of this, the Syrians may be expected to undertake anti-Egyptian moves while trying to draw Hussein to their side.

With all that, I do not rule out the possibility of Syria joining in the political process, particularly if Jordan decides to take part in the negotiations.

The agreement has placed the PLO in a dilemma. On the one hand, they naturally want to foil this development; on the other, they're afraid of being left out in the cold. The result will probably be increased terrorist action—against Israel, against individual candidates for membership of the autonomy council, against Egypt, and perhaps even against Sadat in person. A less likely possibility is that they'll go for a daring political gambit, with a

PLO initiative toward a direct understanding between Israel and the PLO.

In any event, the Israeli-Egyptian agreement is difficult for the Arab world to swallow—because of the very fact of Sadat's signing an agreement with Israel and putting an end to the boycott against us.

Outside Camp David, a storm was raging.

I looked at Begin. "I suggest we go and pay a visit to Sadat," I said. The prime minister thought it over for a moment or two. Then he phoned Sadat's lodge. The Egyptian president answered. Begin congratulated him on the agreement, adding that he would like to come and visit.

"With the greatest of pleasure," Sadat replied.

When Begin entered Sadat's lodge, he shook the Egyptian president's hand with great warmth. It was their first meeting since their joint outing to Gettysburg, ten days previously, at the early stages of the conference.

Later, Sadat paid a return visit to Begin's cabin.

I filled up glasses with wine for everyone, including Sadat— forgetting in my excitement that as a devout Muslim, he does not drink alcohol.

"I'm not a heathen like you!" he rebuked me. "I drink fruit juice!"

Standing there, holding our glasses of wine or fruit juice, we drank to one another's health. *"L'chaim!"*

Later, we all flew by helicopter to Washington for the closing celebration. When the ceremony ended at the White House, it was late at night in Washington—early morning in Israel. I dialed the familiar Israeli number. My wife answered.

"Re'uma," I said, "it's peace."

26

MARCH 26, 1979

When she came to Washington, Re'uma brought along a bottle of Janklis wine—one of the bottles I had received as a gift a year before from Egyptian War Minister Gamasy.

"General," I had said at the time. "We will open the bottle the day we sign the peace treaty between Israel and Egypt." As I'd said the words in December 1977, at the Janklis estate near Alexandria, peace had seemed a distant dream, a concept for writers to toy with, a word to inspire poets. Cairo was still a distant planet. A conversation with an Egyptian was still defined by Israeli law as contact with a foreign agent, punishable by a long term of imprisonment.

Now, standing on the White House's northern lawn, I exchanged a hearty handshake with Kamal Hassan Ali, Egypt's defense minister. In view of the impending peace agreement with Israel, the Egyptians had changed the title: they no longer had a minister of war.

On March 26, 1979, the weather in Washington was springlike, auguring a new beginning. We had traveled the long and painful road to peace.

No sooner had the Camp David Conference ended, late in September 1978, than it became evident that the problems remaining between the two countries far exceeded the "2 percent" airily dismissed at the time. The desire on the part of all three participants—Israel, Egypt, and the United States—to bring the conference to a successful conclusion had resulted in a number of important issues being swept under the carpet. But they had reemerged in all their complexity at the Blair House Conference held in Washington in October 1978 to complete the wording of the Israeli-Egyptian peace treaty. The cabinet had delegated Moshe Dayan and me to represent Israel in the negotiations. Dashing my hopes that they would be very brief with few snags, the talks had dragged on for nearly two hundred days.

My direct partner in the negotiations was no longer General Gamasy, who had been replaced—apparently because of deteriorating relations between him and other government members. The inner changes I had undergone since the launching of the peace initiative were clearly illustrated by the regret I felt on hearing of his removal. In the course of our contacts, I had found a common language with Gamasy; my only consolation over Gamasy's dismissal came from recalling something he'd said on one of the occasions when peace talks were in danger of breaking down: "Whatever happens," he had assured me, "we will always remain friends."

Throughout the talks, it had been repeatedly stressed that "peace is made between nations, not between leaders." This slogan was put to the test before the ink had dried on the Camp David accords. At the most critical moment in the flight of the peace plane, as it prepared for its landing—the second pilot was being replaced. I knew next to nothing about Kamal Hassan Ali. Our intelligence files could not produce more than an unclear portrait of the man. Anyway, experience had taught me that intelligence reports are no substitute for personal acquaintance.

"General Ali," I told him over the phone, "I am coming to say hello."

It was just after our arrival in Washington for the resumption of the peace talks. General Ali had already arrived in the U.S. capital. I could have waited for some official event to shake hands with him, but I preferred to launch a direct assault, without delaying.

I found him intelligent and affable, open-minded and warm, with an enchanting sense of humor. We hit it off as though we had known each other from the first grade.

The following morning, the telephone rang in my suite at the Madison Hotel. "Kamal speaking," said the voice at the other end. "Can I come over?" He had been interviewed by a television crew, with whom he'd discussed the wars of the past and hopes of a peaceful future.

"Ezer"—he addressed me by my first name—"do you know I

have a souvenir of your air force?" Uncovering his belly, he pointed to the scar.

During the five weeks' stay at the Madison Hotel in Washington, the Egyptian and Israeli delegations grew close to each other: General Tamir with General Labib Shar'ab, General Ali and myself, the legal and technical advisers of both teams. We compared notes, discussed the future, and analyzed the past. Many battle stories—some tragic and some unusual—came up.

I was introduced to a young Egyptian air force colonel who told me that I was the first Israeli he had ever met. I smiled and he added: "I wish I could meet the Israeli fighter pilot who saved my life."

When I expressed my interest, he told me that on the last day of the Yom Kippur War he was, as a major, leading a formation of Mig-17s west to the Suez Canal when he got into a hot dog-fight with Israeli Mirage fighters. He was badly shot up, his engine damaged and smoking, his controls stuck, and at an altitude of seven thousand feet he found himself alone with a heavily damaged plane. He therefore decided to eject, but discovered that the canopy over his cockpit, damaged by a bullet, had jammed. He was completely trapped in a damaged aircraft flying westward, and as he put it, the only thing left for him was to pray to Allah.

Suddenly, a lone Israeli Mirage noticed him, apparently drawn by the smoke, circled once around him, took a shot at him and hit him. But it was a lucky hit, for it released the canopy and blew it away. He immediately ejected and came safely down by parachute on Egyptian soil.

He concluded: "Now, Mr. Minister, I would like to meet this pilot who saved my life!"

Talks went on day and night, for weeks and endless weeks. New hitches arose, new crises and difficulties. Scarcely a week passed without some fresh disagreement. Both sides demanded changes and modifications in the existing texts. The points of dissension included the target date for self-rule in Judea, Samaria, and Gaza; guaranteeing the primacy of the Israeli-Egyptian peace treaty over any other international obligations by either side; elimination of any linkage between the Israeli-Egyptian treaty and the new administrative arrangements in the West Bank and Gaza; Egypt's demands to define the interim phases for the withdrawal of our forces from the Sinai; and Israel's rights to the oil fields we had discovered in the peninsula.

As I had foreseen, there were fewer disagreements on the military side, which came within my province as defense minister. But there was an enormous amount of work, involving thousands of details—including lines sketched with scientific precision on the maps of the terrain. Carefully drawn up, word by word, clause by clause, the military agreement covered everything: demilitarized zones and thinning-out zones, supervision, patrols, types of armament, reconnaissance flights and early-warning stations, numbers of troops and vehicles. Nothing could be overlooked.

However, demands from both sides for changes in the existing agreements and endless haggling again marred the atmosphere. In Jerusalem, poisonous barbs were directed at Moshe Dayan and at me. While we spent weeks in Washington engaged in talks, we lost the confidence of our cabinet colleagues. In effect, we had to report back on every detail of our talks and request prior permission before agreeing to any point, however trivial. In keeping with the mood prevailing in Israel as a result of having to give up settlements and airfields, it was almost natural that the cabinet usually began its grilling with the venomous question: "Well, what have you sold today?"

Cyrus Vance arrived in the Middle East for further talks. Dayan, Vance, and Egyptian prime minister Mustafa Khalil met in Brussels. A second Camp David Conference was held. Begin went to Washington where his talks with Carter were again harsh and unfriendly.

I suddenly found myself involved in matters—economic aid, oil—in which I had never previously taken any interest and dealing with individuals with whom I found it hard to establish a common language because they did not share my military background.

On one occasion, I was despatched in all haste to Washington to prevent cuts in the $3.3 billion aid package promised to Israel after the conclusion of the peace agreement. The administration now approved no more than $2.8 billion.

Through the mediation of my lawyer friend, Leon Charney, I arrived at the Arlington, Virginia, home of Robert Lipshutz, an outspoken friend of Israel. After downing a couple of glasses of Jack Daniel's, I proceeded to vent my fury—at Lipshutz, at President Carter, at the Camp David accords. When my rage reached its peak, I slammed the door behind me, leaving Lipshutz and Charney, I hoped, understanding.

The following morning, President Carter called me. He promised to make up the controversial half billion dollars.

*   *   *

As far as I know, no American president has ever helped Israel as much as Jimmy Carter. I cannot claim that Israel has responded with appropriate gratitude. On one visit to the White House, I was introduced to his mother, Miss Lillian, and I noticed that she wore a Jewish medallion.

"Where did you get that?" I asked, intrigued.

"From a Jewish rabbi in Miami," she replied.

Her son the president added: "You see, the American Jewish community treats my mother far better than me."

When the peace talks were again in a state of crisis, Carter came to the Middle East. In the course of his visits to Egypt and Israel, he subjected both countries to rigorous pressure, even going so far as to threaten them. There did not seem to be any other way of achieving progress. At the conclusion of his nerve-racking tour and its marathon round of talks, the message went out from Cairo and Jerusalem: a peace agreement had been reached.

In Washington, D.C., on March 26, 1979, the chill of winter had receded before the pale sun. It was not the setting I had imagined for the signing of the peace treaty. In a dream I had once seen the ceremony being held on board an Israeli ship steaming through Egypt's Suez Canal, signaling the end of war and the dawning of a new era. . . .

The circumstances were not what I would have ideally chosen, but once I could not even have dreamed this was possible. The imperfect reality was far more important than any unrealized vision. I looked around. Carter, Begin, and Sadat were seated on the platform. In a ceremony lasting less than five minutes, the three leaders affixed their signatures to the hope that thirty years of bloodshed and suffering were at an end. The band began to play; the audience got up from its wooden seats.

Later, I held on to the hand of my son Sha'ul when Sadat enveloped him in a warm embrace.

Re'uma opened the bottle of Janklis wine.

EPILOGUE

On Wednesday, May 28, 1980, I took down the pictures from the wall of my Defense Ministry office. Two of them were the familiar pictures that had followed me from job to job, from one task to another: the color snapshot of a World War II Spitfire; and a rare historical photograph of a meeting between David Ben-Gurion and Menachem Begin, with me sitting between the two leaders. The third was a more recent addition dating from 1977. It showed President Sadat's Boeing coming in to land in Israel, escorted by four of our Kfir fighter planes. With the pictures under my arm, I planted a kiss on the cheek of Sarale, the tea girl. Then I left.

I followed the path out of the building toward the parking lot, as I had done thousands of times in the past three years. But, unlike those routine departures, on this day there was a ceremonial parade awaiting me: drums and pipes, banners and streamers, soldiers presenting arms.

The defense establishment was bidding me farewell.

The letter I had sent to Prime Minister Begin stating my decision could have come as no surprise. It had been common knowledge in recent months that our disagreements were on the rise—above all, over peace with Egypt. Alarmed by the peace treaty they had just concluded, Begin and his supporters had eroded their achievement by provocative settlement programs and unnecessary land confiscations, trumpeting verbal challenges to the world as they withdrew into their mental ghetto.

Menachem Begin led Israel to its first-ever peace treaty. I disagreed with his way of going about it, but his achievement cannot be belittled: it was he who piloted our ship into the haven of peace. The Jewish people will always be indebted to him for that.

However, no sooner had the treaty been signed than Begin gave up promoting the peace process. Instead of forging ahead, leading Israel into a new era, he withdrew into his pipe dreams. At the same time, he began to treat this peace we had struggled for as something banal, almost despicable. I was increasingly dissatisfied with Begin's retreat from decisions he himself had authorized. Finally, I no longer found it possible to serve in the cabinet he headed. "Mr. Prime Minister," I wrote as required by law, "I hereby tender my resignation as defense minister, and as a member of the Israeli cabinet."

Now I walked past the ranks of soldiers—men and women— while press photographers jostled forward for close-ups. They tried to coax one final smile out of me; I am not sure they succeeded. It was a difficult moment: seeing the tearful secretaries; the tense faces of senior officials; clusters of humanity hanging out of every window in the great office building—Defense Ministry employees whose devoted labors I had supervised over the past three years.

Applause from the crowd I'd passed tempted me to turn my head for a final glance back. Resisting the urge, I strode on to the parking lot, where my long-time driver Avi was awaiting me.

At home, Re'uma and Sha'ul welcomed me with a cup of hot tea. They had listened to the radio broadcast of the farewell parade; they'd heard the fanfares and the silence that followed. My daughter Michal phoned, convinced I needed cheering up. A number of friends did the same. But the stream of calls was already dwindling.

Picking up a book, I slumped into my favorite armchair—a relic of my parents' home. I was in no hurry to go anywhere. Suddenly, I had all the time in the world. It was a peculiar sensation, as if I were an old-age pensioner.

People offer me their comments on my resignation. "Weizman— that was a stupid thing to do!" they say. I ought to have bowed my head a little or kept my mouth shut a little or waited a little . . . If I had heeded their advice, they assure me, I would have gone even higher.

"Weizman," they say, "you blew it!"

Maybe.

But if political realities in the state of Israel in 1980 are such that silence is the golden key to a top government office, I prefer to spend my time at home. Power is only a means, not an aim, and I am not prepared to buy it at bargain-basement prices. Those who censure me for resigning usually gauge the matter with their own private yardsticks. I cannot blame them. On the contrary, I fully understand their point of view. In our achievement-oriented society, what counts is what you are, not who you are.

I see things differently. Nevertheless, it occasionally crosses my mind to wonder: was I right in resigning? I gave up a life's dream; was that a mistake?

This painful self-interrogation is conducted in the clear memory of a night of glorious splendor: May 17, 1977. That night my hopes had burned with a white heat; 583,361 citizens of Israel had given their votes to the Likud, elevating it to power after thirty years of opposition. Our supporters—as well as many of those who voted for other parties—had hoped that we would lead our country well; that we would create a society that was just and righteous; that we would make Israel into a spiritual and cultural lodestar for Jewish communities all over the world; that its economy would flourish and its society become something of which they could be proud.

As for us: the victorious Likud and its leader Menachem Begin had vowed to "do well by the people."

Three years later, what remained of all this? The bright flares of hope had spluttered away, leaving no more than flickering embers and a plunge into darkness. Israel now held the world record in annual inflation rate—overtaking Argentina and Turkey. Our foreign balance of payments had deteriorated. The economic crisis had undermined the basic values of our society. There was no respect for work—just as there was no faith in our currency. By 1980, the state of Israel found it hard to look in the mirror. The reflection was less than attractive. Pursuing policies that turned friends into enemies, we had isolated ourselves internationally and even alienated Jewish communities whose support had until now been unswerving.

I was a member of that government. I'd shared the credit for its successes; I had to bear the blame for its failures. With the latter outweighing the former and the growing conviction that my continued membership in the cabinet was benefiting no one, I considered resignation.

My colleagues in the Likud advised me not to get so excited. Things aren't so bad, they reassured me. Election promises are no banker's draft; there is no cast-iron rule saying they must be honored at all costs. Anyway, the voters won't even remember. . . .

I gave our electorate more credit. I wanted to be able to look our supporters straight in the eye, always. When I felt I could no longer do that, there was no alternative but to resign.

The Likud government's performance was poor in many fields. All the same, it might have been forgiven—it might have earned eternal honor—had it made the most of the historic opportunity that came its way within a few months of taking office. True, we were taken unawares: Sadat's willingness to come to terms with Israel, to terminate the state of belligerency and conclude a peace treaty—all this took Israel by surprise. Sadat's peace offensive of 1977 was almost as unexpected as the Yom Kippur onslaught he had unleashed four years before, or as our own stunning air strike had been for the Egyptians in the morning hours of June 5, 1967.

It seems strange to compare a peace offensive to a battle launched with tanks and planes, with bombs and shells. But in a way, war and peace are alike. Both are means of attaining political ends. Of the two, war is the brutish way of going about it—a testimony to the failure of human intelligence. When human beings can't get through to each other's minds, they kill each other's bodies. Thirty years of military service and its bloodshed taught me the stupidity of that choice.

It is equally stupid to miss the alternative when it is offered. When Sadat came along in 1977 and said: "No more war!" the challenge was to hurl ourselves at peace as we'd hurled ourselves into war in 1967. Had we not been resolute and determined in 1967, we would have won no more than a half-baked victory.

Unfortunately, we may be headed for a half-baked peace because we do not seem to be able to find the courage and determination to storm peace the way we stormed the Egyptian defenses in the Six-Day War. I apologize to my Egyptian friends for the analogy— but, just as we swooped down on their airfields on that June morning, just as we blew their airplanes sky-high, so we must now fling ourselves at the Egyptian people and earn their good will and understanding with the same determination, the same unflinching devotion with which our pilots pressed home their attack regardless of the cost.

This is precisely what Israel's leadership has failed to do. The past two years have seen Israel backing off from the consequences of peace. For thirty years, we lived in a beleaguered society, growing accustomed to dwelling in the shadow of the wall of hostility enclosing us. Unfortunately, when the wall was torn down, the light was too bright for some eyes. Many of my former colleagues, blinking in the sun of peace, hastily fumbled for their dark glasses. Instead of conducting the battle for peace with open-eyed zest, they are now groping their way backward into their familiar—and unlit—dugouts.

Worst of all, their hesitation and uncertainty have affected the people of Israel, making it harder to tackle what lies ahead with confidence. One challenge is to try to understand the problem of those with whom we want to live peacefully. Here again, peace resembles war: a key to success in battle is the ability to read the mind of the enemy commander—to follow his thought patterns and comprehend his difficulties. But it seems that few people in power in Israel are attempting to read the minds of our partners in peace, as we did so successfully when they were our adversaries at war. We have to understand that Sadat is part of the Arab world and must consequently set an Arab price—as well as an Egyptian price—for peace. He cannot be expected to lower that price beyond reason.

Many Israelis used to believe that the only guarantee of our security was to hold on to every dune in the Sinai desert. Now we are learning to do without. If we need a security guarantee, it is not exclusively in the form of real estate—whether it is the yellow sands of the Sinai or the black hills of the Golan Heights, our best and most reliable insurance policy is our armed might.

This thought was uppermost in my mind as I—assisted by my colleagues of the General Staff—helped draw up the military codicil to the peace treaty. In all the security arrangements we worked out, we treated the Egyptian army as an enemy, paying the strictest attention to every detail out of concern for Israel's security.

I am accused of being too rash and naive about Sadat. "But can you *trust* him?" I am asked over and over again. The answer is simple: as in the world of business, if there is someone you don't trust from the beginning, don't deal with him! On the other hand, complete and unreserved trust is no less foolish. That is why the business world has lawyers, insurance companies, and bonds as safeguards. Similarly, in relations between states—particularly between neighbors who have spent decades in mutual slaughter—guarantees of a different kind are called for. Our guarantee is our army—just as Sadat counts on the Egyptian army when he is simi-larly asked: "Can you trust the Israelis?"

With our army backing us, we can afford to be bold and daring in plunging into peace. I cannot understand official hesitations in carrying out our promises. I sometimes get the feeling that Begin regrets his signature on the autonomy plan—his own invention! It goes without saying that we must protect our own security interests on our eastern border—just as we did in the Sinai. We told the Egyptians they could have the peninsula as long as it did not constitute a military threat against us. We have to tell the Palestinians the same: they can have their own authorities and run their own affairs as they think fit—just as long as they do not threaten us. We cannot permit them to create an army and station it half a mile from our border settlements. We cannot afford to let them conduct an independent foreign policy that would allow them to enter into military alliances, because we might wake up one morning and find an Iraqi, or a Syrian—or a Soviet! army on our threshold.

Barring these restrictions—which are vital guarantees of our security—there is no reason why they should not live their own lives and conduct their own affairs, for better or worse. They can make one another happy or miserable, rich or poor; they can live in love and harmony or slaughter one another three times a week. That is their problem—not ours. Ours is to protect ourselves.

Speaking for myself, there is nothing I would like more than to see Judea and Samaria incorporated into the state of Israel. These landscapes are a part of me; they are my homeland in the simple, everyday meaning of the word "home." But the clock cannot be turned back. We must deal with realities, including the reality of living in a world in which no one enjoys complete independence. I wish we did not have to go running to Washington every time we need a few dollars or a couple of rifles or an F-16 interceptor. I wish we could live our own lives, within our own language and culture, cultivating our own civilization.

But such isolation is no longer feasible. We live in a world with far more independent nations than before—the UN numbers over 150 members—yet we are all bound by a far greater interdependence. This double prospect is made possible for us by our peace treaty with Egypt. We would no longer need to make our living by selling our electronic gadgetry and our agricultural know-how to Argentina or Mexico when there are forty-two million Egyptians on our doorstep. By doing business with Egypt, we would lessen our dependence on countries with whom we have little in common and at the same time join forces to be part of a region that we need as much as it needs us.

It is not a one-sided process. We have a lot to offer the Egyptians—but we must be careful never to imply that we have all the answers. We cannot come to the Egyptians only as teachers; there is much to learn from them: their tolerance, their warmth, their hospitality and humor.

Together with our Egyptian neighbors—and the other Arab peoples of the Middle East—we can turn this region into a flourishing garden. Our nations can be the wonder and envy of the world, and the fight toward that objective promises to be no less exciting—and no less arduous or demanding—than the bloody confrontations of war.

In peace, no less than in war—we must be prepared to take risks. I have yet to meet the commander who can predict the outcome of an engagement. A good general is not one who launches a plan and then sits back and waits but one who can rectify foul-ups and, equally, leap at unforeseen opportunities.

That is why hawks make good commanders and why I still call myself a hawk. When people say to me: "Weizman, whatever happened to you? Have you turned into a dove?" they do not understand what a hawk really is. A dove bills and coos, fluttering about in hesitation and uncertainty, while a hawk swoops down, seizes the initiative, and takes advantage of changing situations to serve his cause.

Doves and hawks are like different types of airplanes. A dove is a slow machine, a hawk a fast one. A slow-flying plane has no choice: it flies at low speeds because it lacks the ability to go any faster. But a hawk has the choice: it can fly at top speed or slow down. With its greater flexibility, it is the hawk that can maneuver better in an unknown situation.

These lines are being written at my home in Caesarea on the Mediterranean coast. The surroundings are a fascinating blend of old and new, of what was and what will be. It is a place to hunt for antiquities—and a development town for new immigrants. Its past is glorious: an old Phoenician city, it was built up and expanded under Herod and the Romans, who made it into the largest city in Palestine.

Here the most beautiful hour of day is sunset, when the fiery ball plunges into the waves while the birds wheel and turn, seeking a resting place for the night. The peace fills me with a spirit of tranquillity.

Every day brings dusk and dawn: so it has always been, and so it shall be.

In the morning, with the sun's return, I look out at my favorite sights: before me, the ancient Roman aqueduct; to my right, the colorful houses of the Arab villages of Jissar al Zarka; to my left, the neat functional buildings of Kibbutz S'dot Yam.

There it is, the future of my country: opposite the relics of an empire vanished and gone, S'dot Yam and Jissar al Zarka alive in the morning sun.

INDEX

Israel and its ~~~X-D~~~ ~~~~orders

LEBANON

Kuneitra
SYRIA

Haifa

Tiberias

Mediterranean

Sea

Nablus

Tel-Aviv

Jericho

Jerusalem

Gaza

Dead
Hebron
Sea

Beersheba

El-Arish

Abu Awugeila

Bir el Hasana

Bir Gifgafa

Gidi Pass

Bir eth Themada

Suez

S i n a i

Mitla Pass

Ras es Sudar

Eilat

Nuweiba

Abu Rudeis

St. Catherine's
Monastery

Dahab

SAUDI

ARABIA

Et-Tur

Snapir

M e d i t e r r a n e a n

I S R A E L

J O R D A N

Suez Canal

E G Y P T

G u l f   o f   S u e z

G u l f   o f   E i l a t

S t r a i t   o f   T i r a n

Area occupied
in Six-Day War

Cease fire line 1967

Armistice line 1949

| 0 | 10 | 20 | 30 miles |
| 0 | 20 | 40 km | |

© **carta**, JERUSALEM